Love Hina

By
Ken Akamatsu

Volume 9

TOKYOPOP®
Los Angeles • Tokyo

Translator - Nan Rymer
English Adaption - Adam Arnold
Retouch and Lettering - Tomas Montalvo-Lagos
Cover Layout - Anna Kernbaum

Senior Editors - Luis Reyes & Mark Paniccia
Managing Editor - Jill Freshney
Production Coordinator - Antonio DePietro
Production Manager - Jennifer Miller
Art Director - Matthew Alford
Editorial Director - Jeremy Ross
VP of Production & Manufacturing - Ron Klamert
President & C.O.O. - John Parker
Publisher - Stuart Levy

Email: editor@TOKYOPOP.com
Come visit us online at www.TOKYOPOP.com

A ⊙ TOKYOPOP® Manga
TOKYOPOP® is an imprint of Mixx Entertainment, Inc.
5900 Wilshire Blvd. Suite 2000, Los Angeles, CA 90036

ISBN: 1-59182-103-7

First TOKYOPOP® printing: February 2003

10 9 8 7 6 5 4 3 2
Printed in the USA

Love Hina

The Story Thus Far...

Fifteen years ago, Keitaro Urashima made a promise to a girl that the two of them would go to Tokyo University together. For fifteen years, Keitaro Urashima had slaved away at the books, stumbling through academia until the day he could take the entrance exam for Tokyo University. For fifteen years, Keitaro Urashima had been driven by that promise, a drive that had outstripped even his memory of the girl's name. And here he is, fifteen years later, having failed the entrance exam three times already, having readied himself so thoroughly to fail again, having discovered that the girl to whom he made that fateful promise is the girl that has recently studied with him, helping beat his fear of tests, at last the saga has ended, the impossible has become reality. Keitaro Urashima, after fifteen years, has passed the entrance exam. This is one boy that won't live another year as a ronin. He is going to Tokyo U. But he almost screwed that up. Convinced he had failed, Keitaro left the exam hall and ran straight to the solace only a tropical isle in the Pacific can offer. Luckily enough, Naru and the gang trekked out there to retrieve him in time to register for school. And while there, Keitaro was turned on to archeology. But perhaps we should back up a bit?

This chapter in Keitaro Urashima's life began a year ago when he inherited from his globe-trotting grandmother the Hinata House, an all-girls dormitory whose clientele is none too pleased that their new, live-in landlord is a man or as close to a man as poor Keitaro can be. The lanky loser incessantly (and accidentally) crashes their sessions in the hot springs, walks in on them changing, and pokes his nose pretty much everywhere that it can get broken, if not by the hot-headed Naru — the mystery girl from fifteen years ago — then by one of the other Hinata inmates — Kitsune, a late-teen alcoholic with a diesel libido; Motoko, a swordsman who struggles with a feminine identity; Shinobu, a pre-teen princess with a colossal crush on Keitaro; Su, a foreign girl with a big appetite; Sarah, an orphaned ward resentful of being left there by her archeologist guardian; Mutsumi, an accident-prone lily also studying for her exams; and Haruka, Keitaro's aunt and de facto matriarch of the Hinita House.

Now, he's back, he's bookish, and he's finally going to tell Naru that he loves her. If he can only get the girl alone. But he has to start thinking about his future, and how much will she figure into his grand life scheme.

CONTENTS

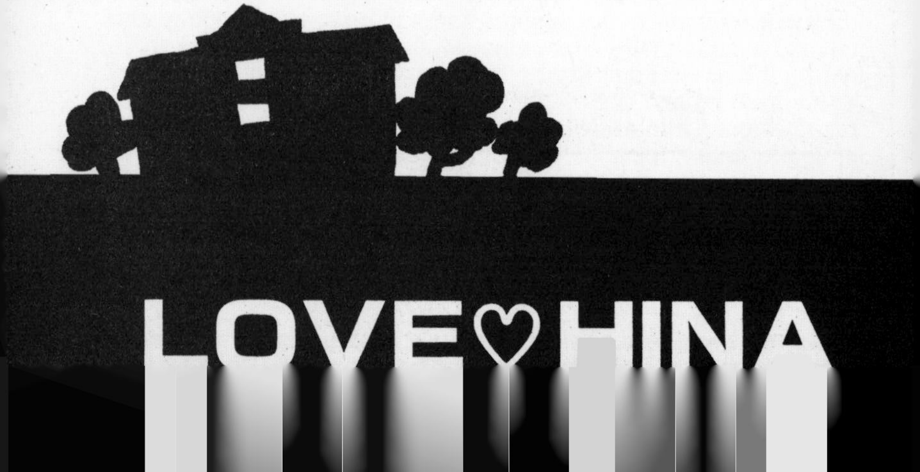

LOVE♡HINA

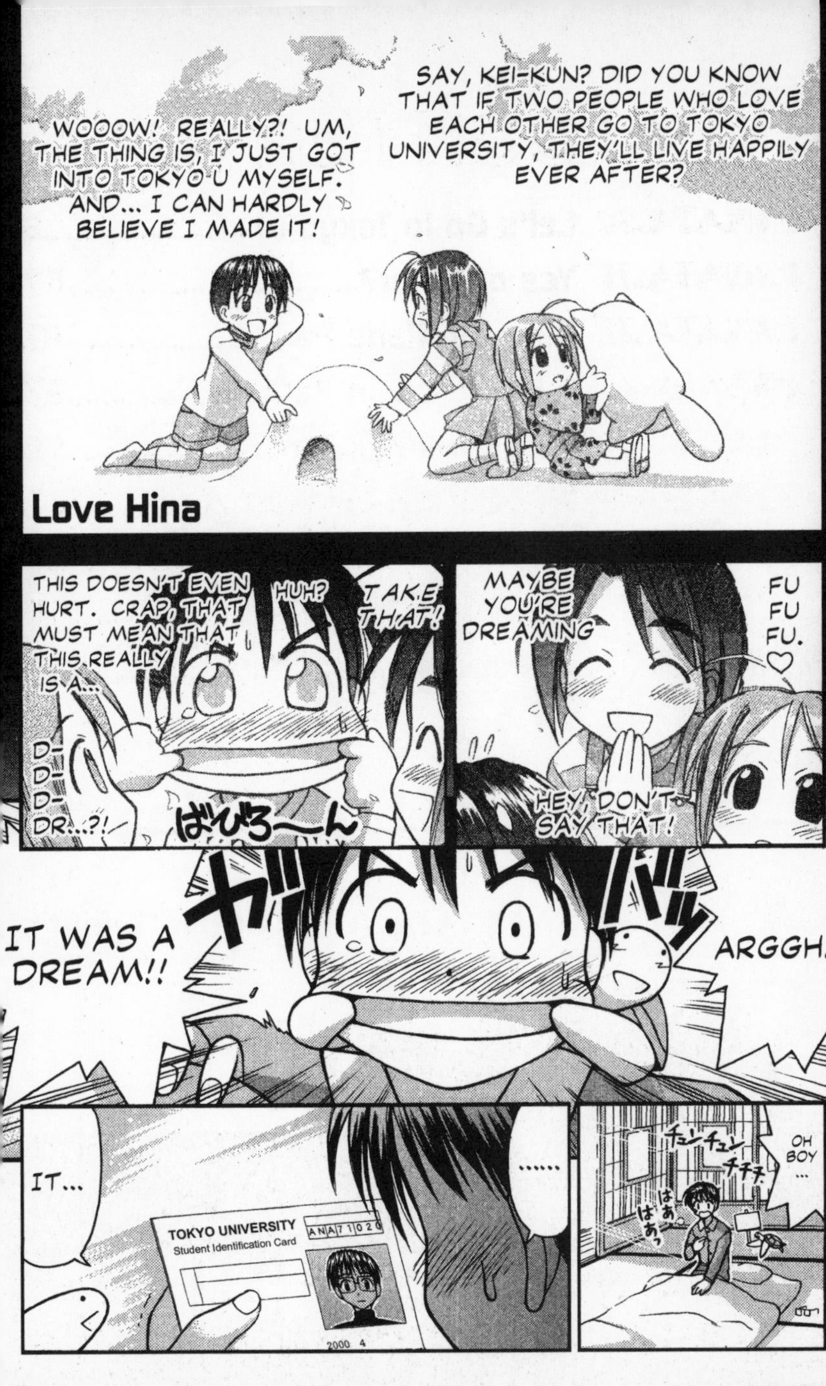
SAY, KEI-KUN? DID YOU KNOW THAT IF TWO PEOPLE WHO LOVE EACH OTHER GO TO TOKYO UNIVERSITY, THEY'LL LIVE HAPPILY EVER AFTER?
WOOOW! REALLY?! UM, THE THING IS, I JUST GOT INTO TOKYO U MYSELF. AND... I CAN HARDLY BELIEVE I MADE IT!
Love Hina
MAYBE YOU'RE DREAMING
FU FU FU. ♥
HEY, DON'T SAY THAT!
TAKE THAT!
HUH?
THIS DOESN'T EVEN HURT. CRAP, THAT MUST MEAN THAT THIS REALLY IS A...
D-D-D-DR...?!
ばびろ〜ん
ARGGH!!
ガバッ
IT WAS A DREAM!!
OH BOY ...
チュンチュン
チチチ
はぁ はぁっ
......
IT...
TOKYO UNIVERSITY
Student Identification Card
ANA71020
2000 4

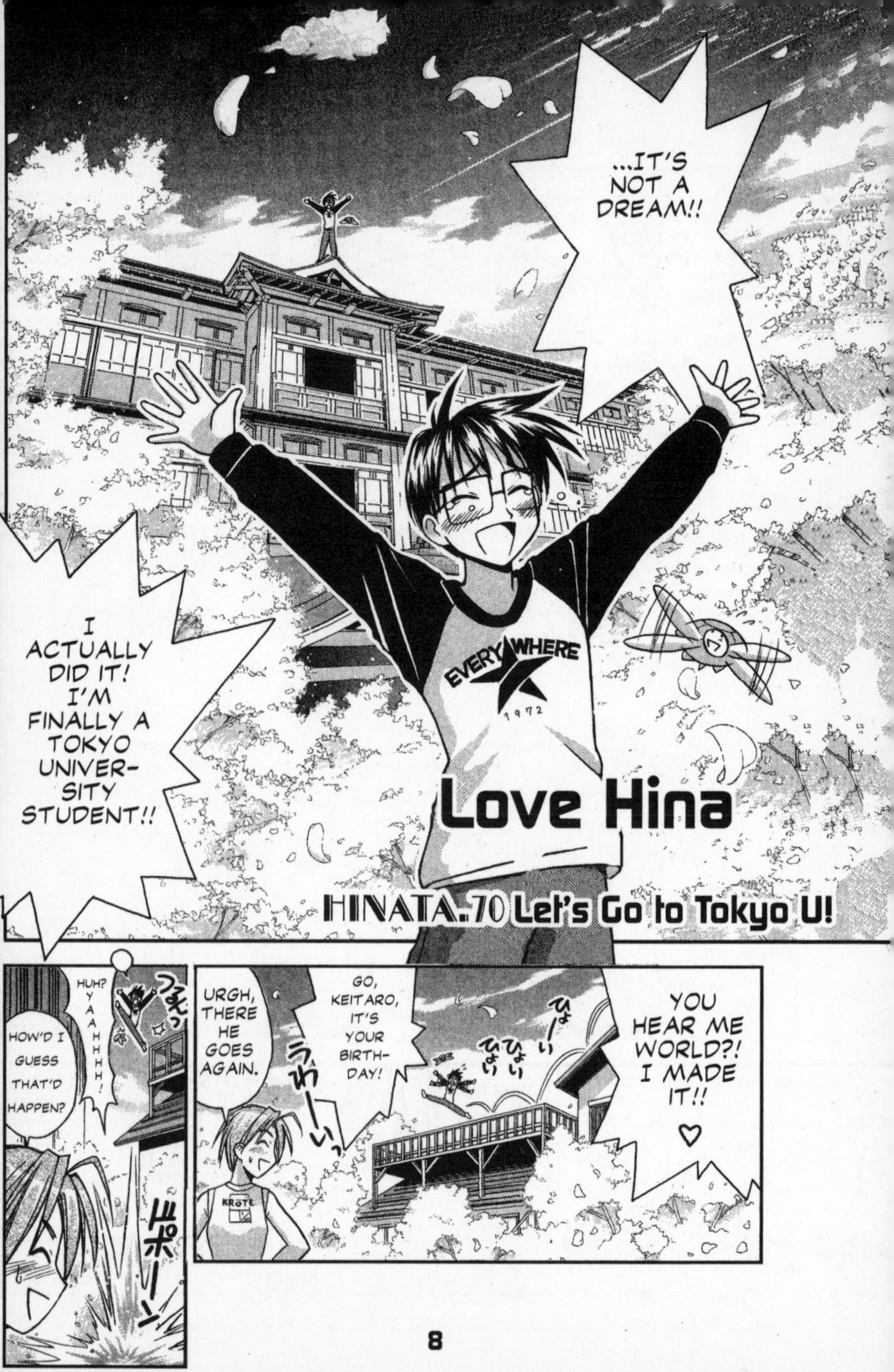
...IT'S NOT A DREAM!!
I ACTUALLY DID IT! I'M FINALLY A TOKYO UNIVERSITY STUDENT!!
EVERYWHERE 1972
Love Hina
HINATA.70 Let's Go to Tokyo U!
YOU HEAR ME WORLD?! I MADE IT!! ♡
ひょーい ひょい ひょい
GO, KEITARO, IT'S YOUR BIRTHDAY!
URGH, THERE HE GOES AGAIN.
うわーいっ
KRÖTE
HUH? YAAAHHHH!
HOW'D I GUESS THAT'D HAPPEN?
スポーン

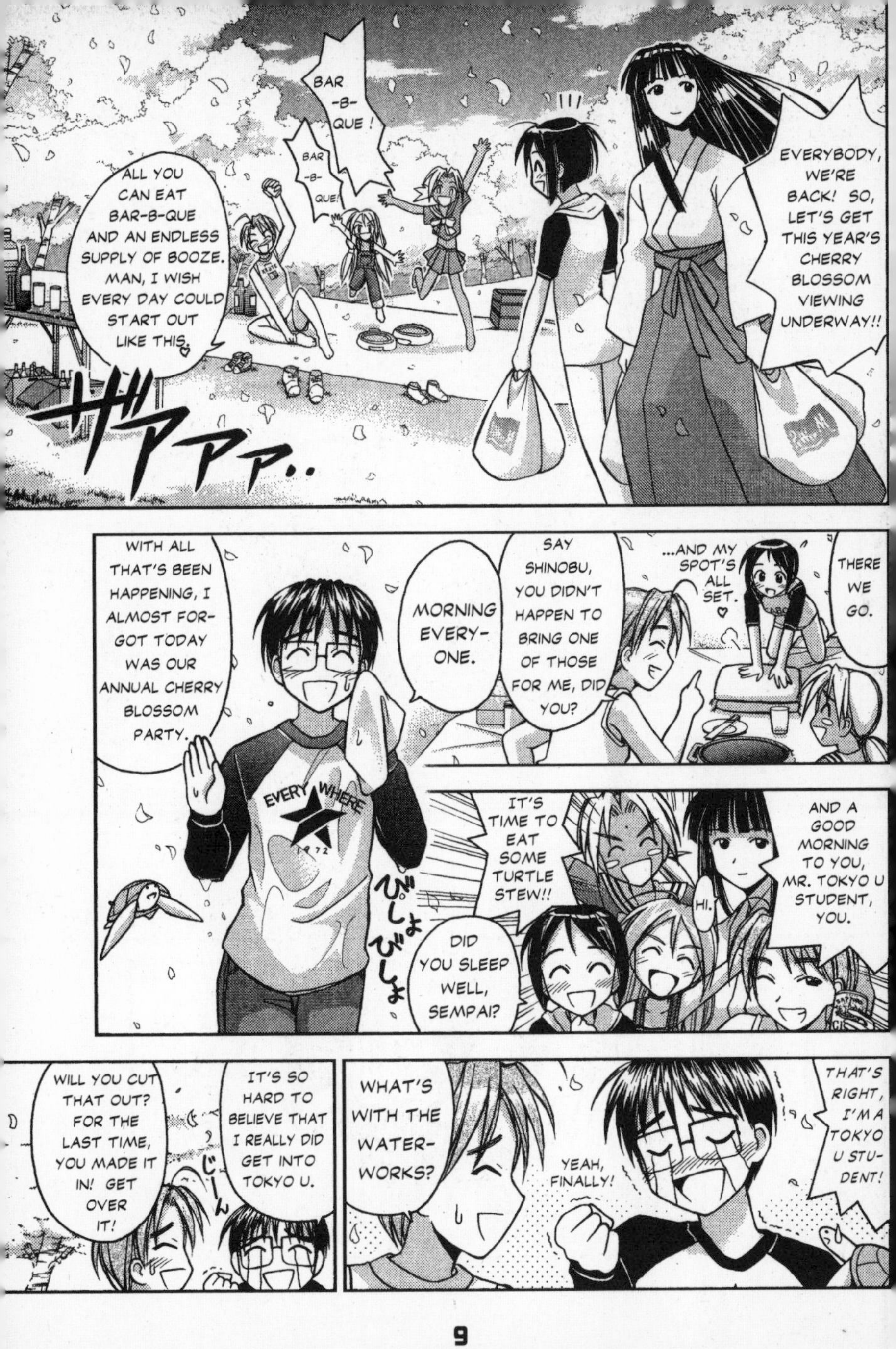
EVERYBODY, WE'RE BACK! SO, LET'S GET THIS YEAR'S CHERRY BLOSSOM VIEWING UNDERWAY!!
BAR -B- QUE!
BAR -B- QUE!
ALL YOU CAN EAT BAR-B-QUE AND AN ENDLESS SUPPLY OF BOOZE. MAN, I WISH EVERY DAY COULD START OUT LIKE THIS.♡
ザアァ..
THERE WE GO.
...AND MY SPOT'S ALL SET.♡
SAY SHINOBU, YOU DIDN'T HAPPEN TO BRING ONE OF THOSE FOR ME, DID YOU?
AND A GOOD MORNING TO YOU, MR. TOKYO U STUDENT, YOU.
HI.
IT'S TIME TO EAT SOME TURTLE STEW!!
DID YOU SLEEP WELL, SEMPAI?
MORNING EVERY-ONE.
WITH ALL THAT'S BEEN HAPPENING, I ALMOST FOR-GOT TODAY WAS OUR ANNUAL CHERRY BLOSSOM PARTY.
びしょびしょ
THAT'S RIGHT, I'M A TOKYO U STU-DENT!
YEAH, FINALLY!
WHAT'S WITH THE WATER-WORKS?
IT'S SO HARD TO BELIEVE THAT I REALLY DID GET INTO TOKYO U.
じーん
WILL YOU CUT THAT OUT? FOR THE LAST TIME, YOU MADE IT IN! GET OVER IT!

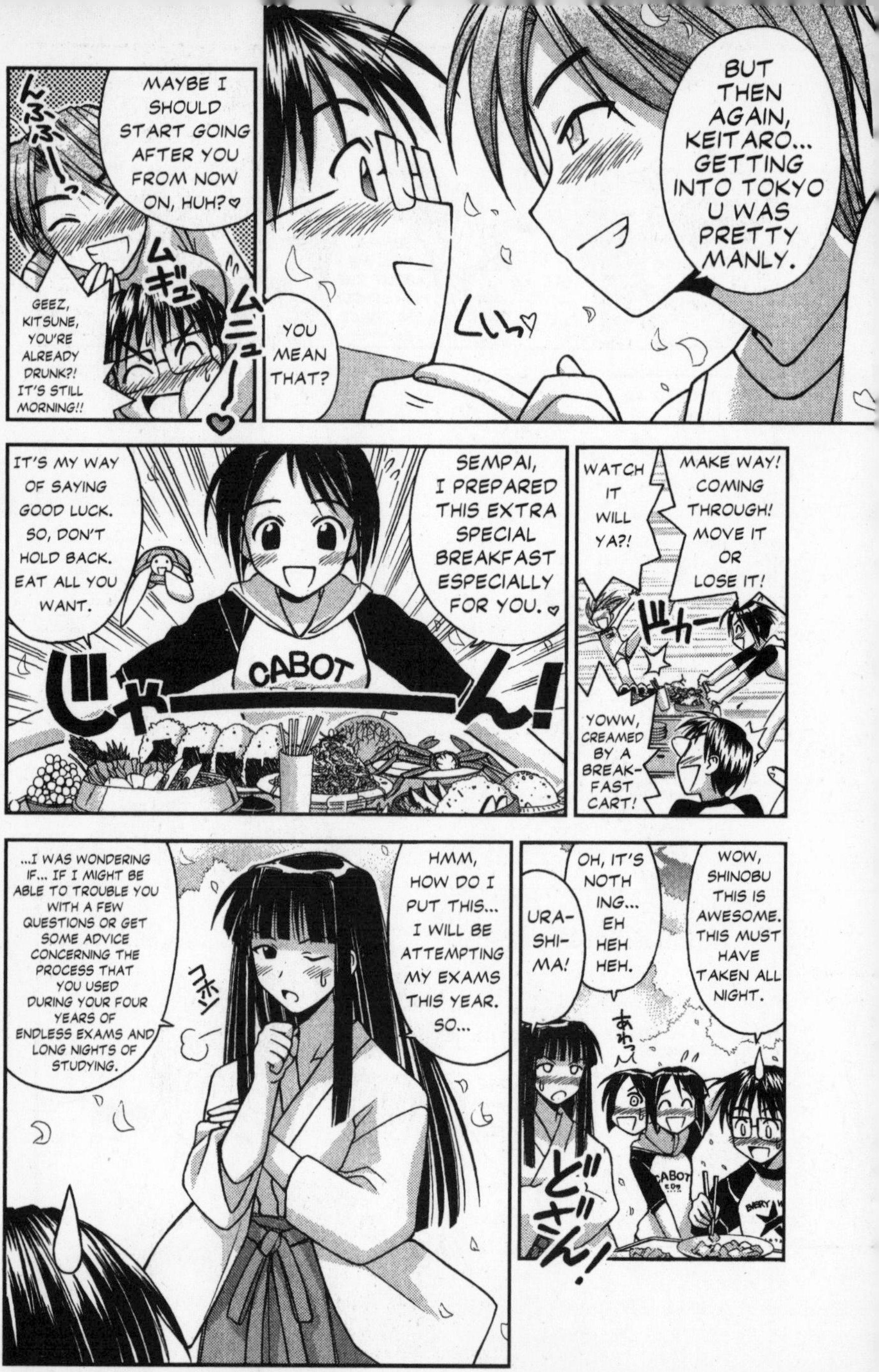
BUT THEN AGAIN, KEITARO... GETTING INTO TOKYO U WAS PRETTY MANLY.
YOU MEAN THAT?
MAYBE I SHOULD START GOING AFTER YOU FROM NOW ON, HUH?♡
GEEZ, KITSUNE, YOU'RE ALREADY DRUNK?! IT'S STILL MORNING!!
MAKE WAY! COMING THROUGH! MOVE IT OR LOSE IT!
WATCH IT WILL YA?!
YOWW, CREAMED BY A BREAK-FAST CART!
SEMPAI, I PREPARED THIS EXTRA SPECIAL BREAKFAST ESPECIALLY FOR YOU.♡
IT'S MY WAY OF SAYING GOOD LUCK. SO, DON'T HOLD BACK. EAT ALL YOU WANT.
CABOT
WOW, SHINOBU THIS IS AWESOME. THIS MUST HAVE TAKEN ALL NIGHT.
OH, IT'S NOTH ING... EH HEH HEH.
URA-SHI-MA!
HMM, HOW DO I PUT THIS... I WILL BE ATTEMPTING MY EXAMS THIS YEAR. SO...
...I WAS WONDERING IF... IF I MIGHT BE ABLE TO TROUBLE YOU WITH A FEW QUESTIONS OR GET SOME ADVICE CONCERNING THE PROCESS THAT YOU USED DURING YOUR FOUR YEARS OF ENDLESS EXAMS AND LONG NIGHTS OF STUDYING.

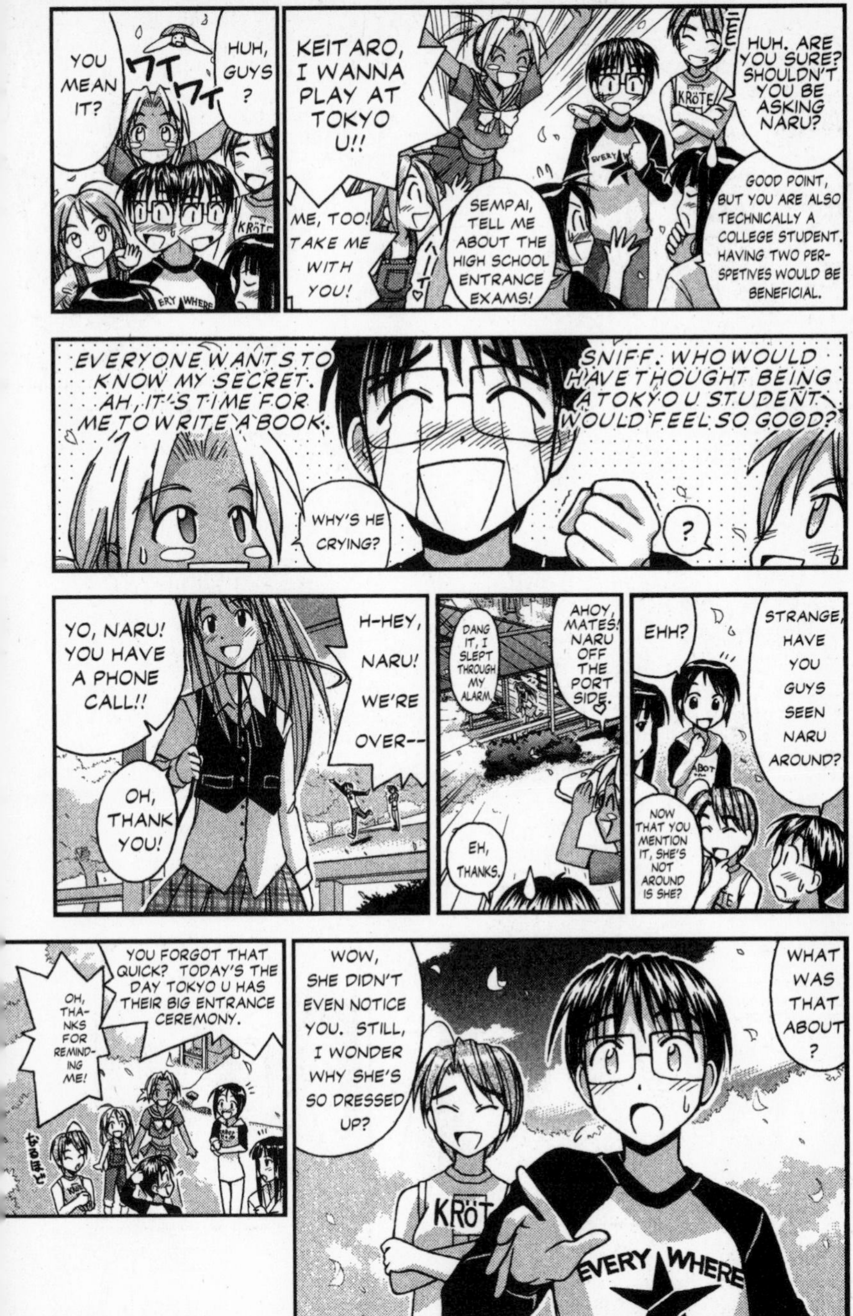
HUH. ARE YOU SURE? SHOULDN'T YOU BE ASKING NARU?
GOOD POINT, BUT YOU ARE ALSO TECHNICALLY A COLLEGE STUDENT. HAVING TWO PERSPETIVES WOULD BE BENEFICIAL.
KEITARO, I WANNA PLAY AT TOKYO U!!
SEMPAI, TELL ME ABOUT THE HIGH SCHOOL ENTRANCE EXAMS!
ME, TOO! TAKE ME WITH YOU!
HUH, GUYS?
ワイワイ
YOU MEAN IT?
SNIFF. WHO WOULD HAVE THOUGHT BEING A TOKYO U STUDENT WOULD FEEL SO GOOD?
EVERYONE WANTS TO KNOW MY SECRET. AH, IT'S TIME FOR ME TO WRITE A BOOK.
?
WHY'S HE CRYING?
STRANGE, HAVE YOU GUYS SEEN NARU AROUND?
EHH?
NOW THAT YOU MENTION IT, SHE'S NOT AROUND IS SHE?
AHOY, MATES! NARU OFF THE PORT SIDE.
DANG IT, I SLEPT THROUGH MY ALARM.
EH, THANKS.
H-HEY, NARU! WE'RE OVER--
YO, NARU! YOU HAVE A PHONE CALL!!
OH, THANK YOU!
WHAT WAS THAT ABOUT?
WOW, SHE DIDN'T EVEN NOTICE YOU. STILL, I WONDER WHY SHE'S SO DRESSED UP?
YOU FORGOT THAT QUICK? TODAY'S THE DAY TOKYO U HAS THEIR BIG ENTRANCE CEREMONY.
OH, THANKS FOR REMINDING ME!
なるほど

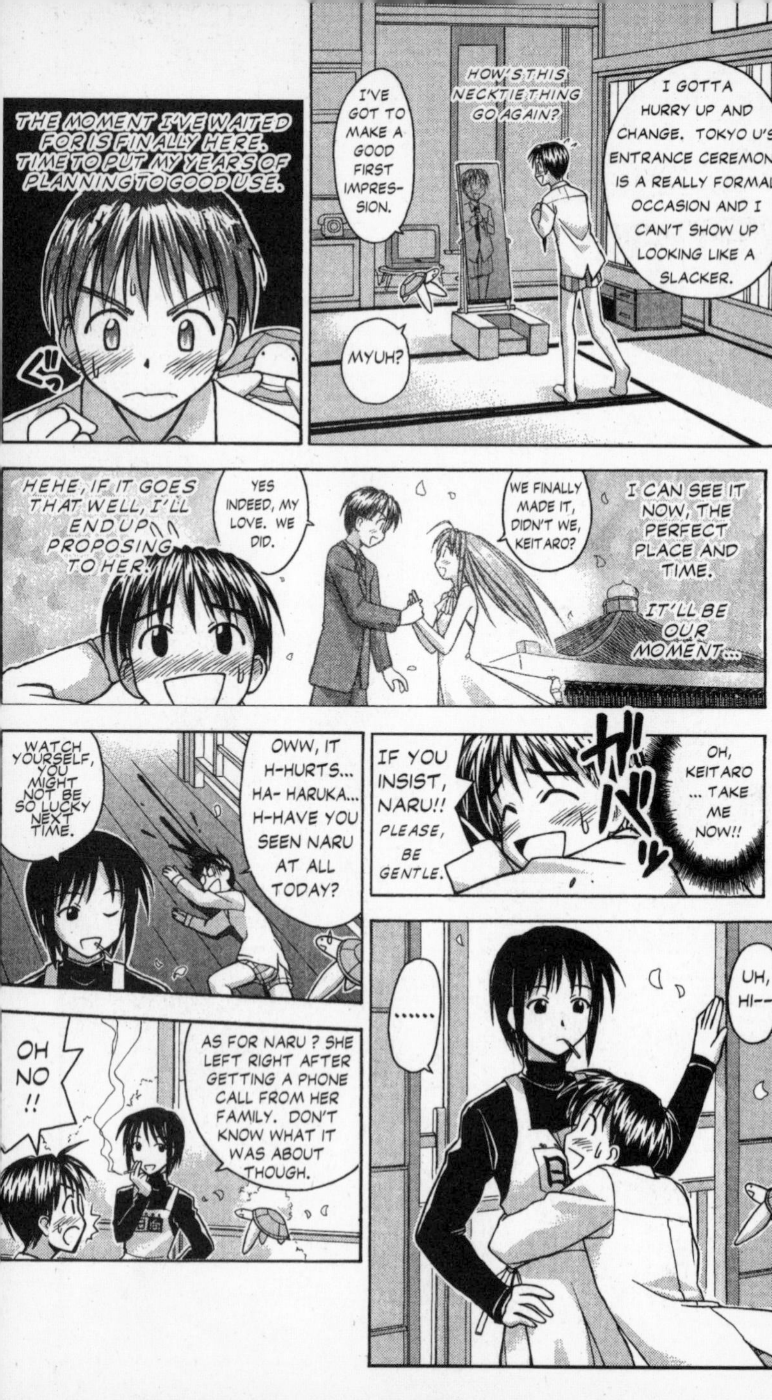
I GOTTA HURRY UP AND CHANGE. TOKYO U'S ENTRANCE CEREMONY IS A REALLY FORMAL OCCASION AND I CAN'T SHOW UP LOOKING LIKE A SLACKER.
HOW'S THIS NECKTIE THING GO AGAIN?
I'VE GOT TO MAKE A GOOD FIRST IMPRES-SION.
MYUH?
THE MOMENT I'VE WAITED FOR IS FINALLY HERE. TIME TO PUT MY YEARS OF PLANNING TO GOOD USE.
I CAN SEE IT NOW, THE PERFECT PLACE AND TIME.
IT'LL BE OUR MOMENT...
WE FINALLY MADE IT, DIDN'T WE, KEITARO?
YES INDEED, MY LOVE. WE DID.
HEHE, IF IT GOES THAT WELL, I'LL END UP PROPOSING TO HER.
OH, KEITARO ... TAKE ME NOW!!
ガバッ
IF YOU INSIST, NARU!! PLEASE, BE GENTLE.
UH, HI--
......
OWW, IT H-HURTS... HA- HARUKA... H-HAVE YOU SEEN NARU AT ALL TODAY?
WATCH YOURSELF, YOU MIGHT NOT BE SO LUCKY NEXT TIME.
AS FOR NARU ? SHE LEFT RIGHT AFTER GETTING A PHONE CALL FROM HER FAMILY. DON'T KNOW WHAT IT WAS ABOUT THOUGH.
OH NO !!

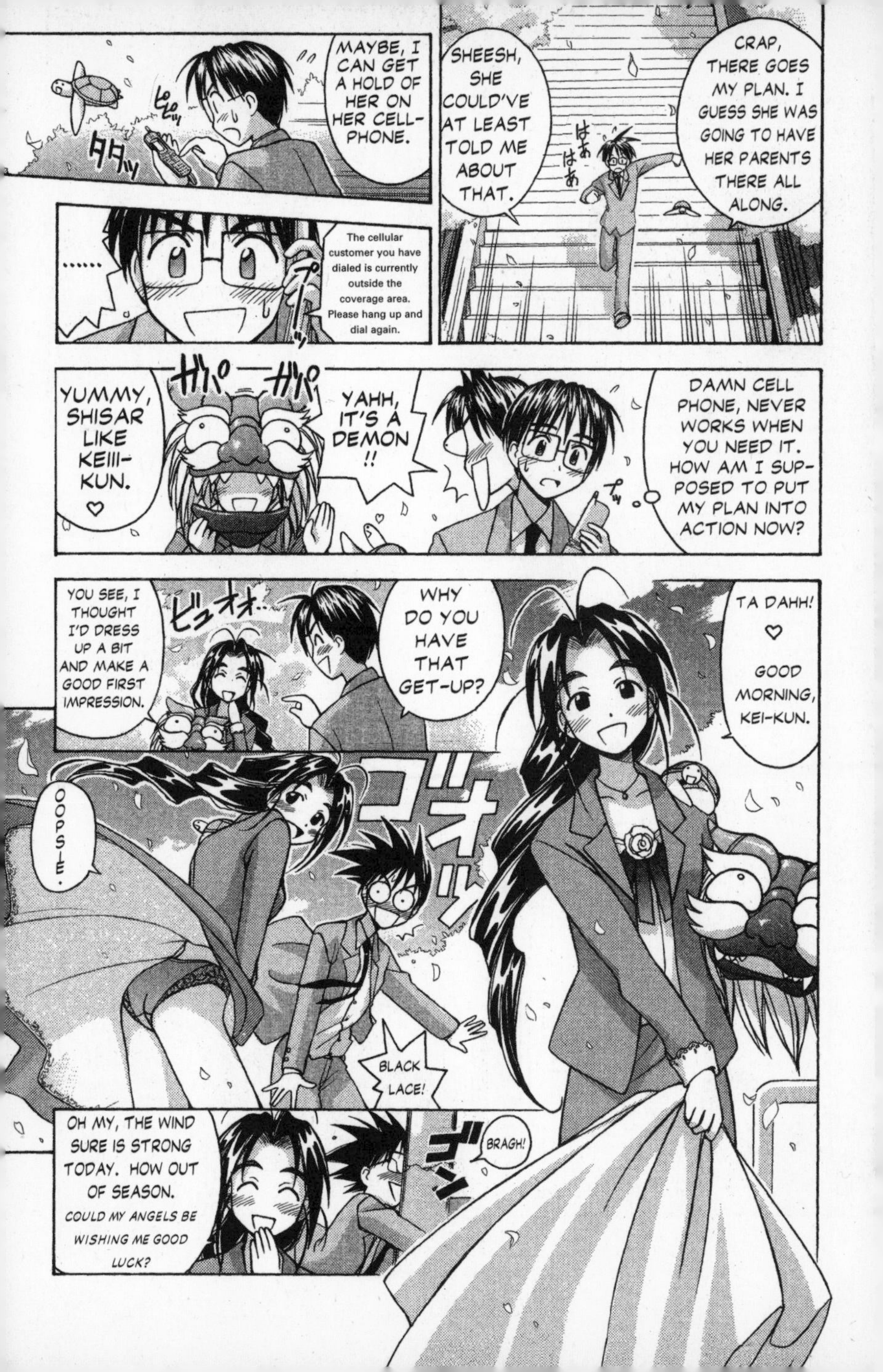
CRAP, THERE GOES MY PLAN. I GUESS SHE WAS GOING TO HAVE HER PARENTS THERE ALL ALONG.
はぁ はぁ
SHEESH, SHE COULD'VE AT LEAST TOLD ME ABOUT THAT.
MAYBE, I CAN GET A HOLD OF HER ON HER CELL-PHONE.
ピピッ
タタッ
The cellular customer you have dialed is currently outside the coverage area. Please hang up and dial again.
......
DAMN CELL PHONE, NEVER WORKS WHEN YOU NEED IT. HOW AM I SUPPOSED TO PUT MY PLAN INTO ACTION NOW?
YAHH, IT'S A DEMON !!
ガパ ガパ
YUMMY, SHISAR LIKE KEIIII-KUN. ♡
TA DAHH! ♡ GOOD MORNING, KEI-KUN.
WHY DO YOU HAVE THAT GET-UP?
ビュオオ…
YOU SEE, I THOUGHT I'D DRESS UP A BIT AND MAKE A GOOD FIRST IMPRESSION.
ゴオッ
OOPSIE.
BLACK LACE!
BRAGH!
ゴン
OH MY, THE WIND SURE IS STRONG TODAY. HOW OUT OF SEASON.
COULD MY ANGELS BE WISHING ME GOOD LUCK?

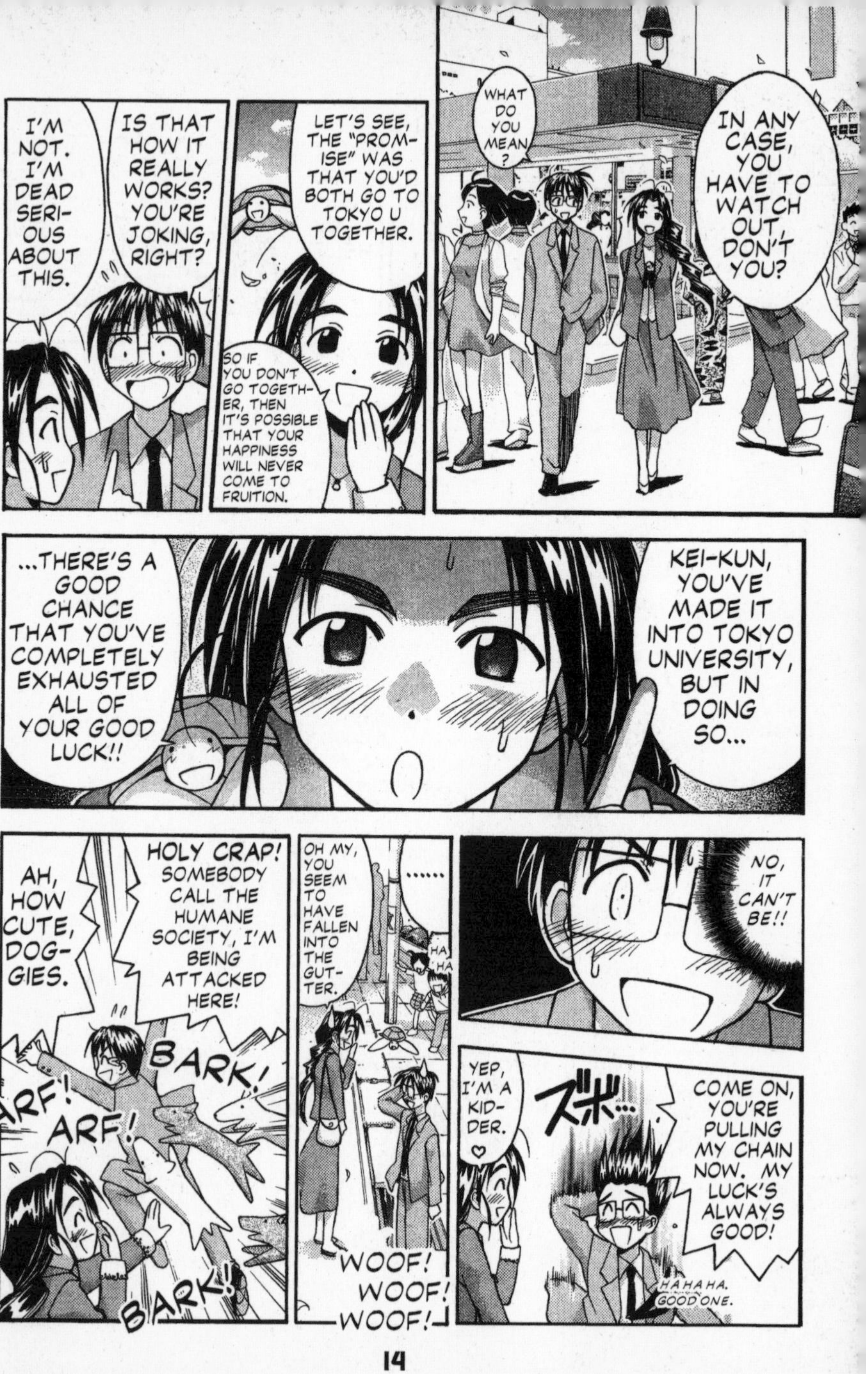
IN ANY CASE, YOU HAVE TO WATCH OUT, DON'T YOU?
WHAT DO YOU MEAN?
LET'S SEE, THE "PROMISE" WAS THAT YOU'D BOTH GO TO TOKYO U TOGETHER.
SO IF YOU DON'T GO TOGETHER, THEN IT'S POSSIBLE THAT YOUR HAPPINESS WILL NEVER COME TO FRUITION.
IS THAT HOW IT REALLY WORKS? YOU'RE JOKING, RIGHT?
I'M NOT. I'M DEAD SERIOUS ABOUT THIS.
KEI-KUN, YOU'VE MADE IT INTO TOKYO UNIVERSITY, BUT IN DOING SO...
...THERE'S A GOOD CHANCE THAT YOU'VE COMPLETELY EXHAUSTED ALL OF YOUR GOOD LUCK!!
NO, IT CAN'T BE!!
COME ON, YOU'RE PULLING MY CHAIN NOW. MY LUCK'S ALWAYS GOOD!
HAHAHA. GOOD ONE.
ズボ...
YEP, I'M A KIDDER.
......
OH MY, YOU SEEM TO HAVE FALLEN INTO THE GUTTER.
HA HA
WOOF! WOOF! WOOF!
HOLY CRAP! SOMEBODY CALL THE HUMANE SOCIETY, I'M BEING ATTACKED HERE!
AH, HOW CUTE, DOGGIES.
BARK!
ARF! ARF!
BARK!

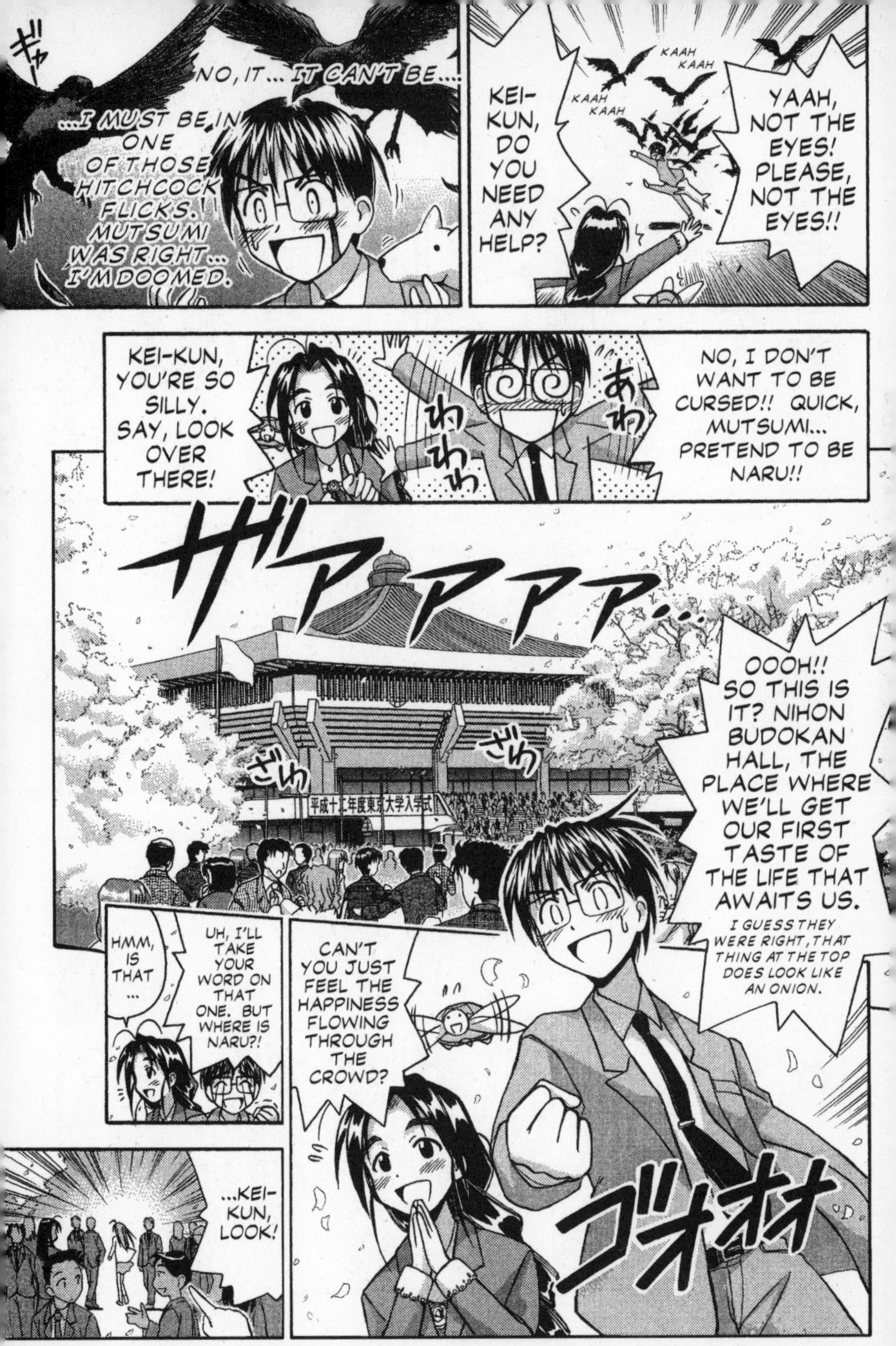

YAAH, NOT THE EYES! PLEASE, NOT THE EYES!!
KAAH KAAH
KAAH KAAH
KEI-KUN, DO YOU NEED ANY HELP?
ギャー
NO, IT... IT CAN'T BE...
...I MUST BE IN ONE OF THOSE HITCHCOCK FLICKS. MUTSUMI WAS RIGHT... I'M DOOMED.
NO, I DON'T WANT TO BE CURSED!! QUICK, MUTSUMI... PRETEND TO BE NARU!!
あわ
わわわ
KEI-KUN, YOU'RE SO SILLY. SAY, LOOK OVER THERE!
ザアアア...
OOOH!! SO THIS IS IT? NIHON BUDOKAN HALL, THE PLACE WHERE WE'LL GET OUR FIRST TASTE OF THE LIFE THAT AWAITS US.
I GUESS THEY WERE RIGHT, THAT THING AT THE TOP DOES LOOK LIKE AN ONION.
ざわ
ざわ
平成十二年度東京大学入学式
CAN'T YOU JUST FEEL THE HAPPINESS FLOWING THROUGH THE CROWD?
ゴオオオ
UH, I'LL TAKE YOUR WORD ON THAT ONE. BUT WHERE IS NARU?!
HMM, IS THAT ...
...KEI-KUN, LOOK!

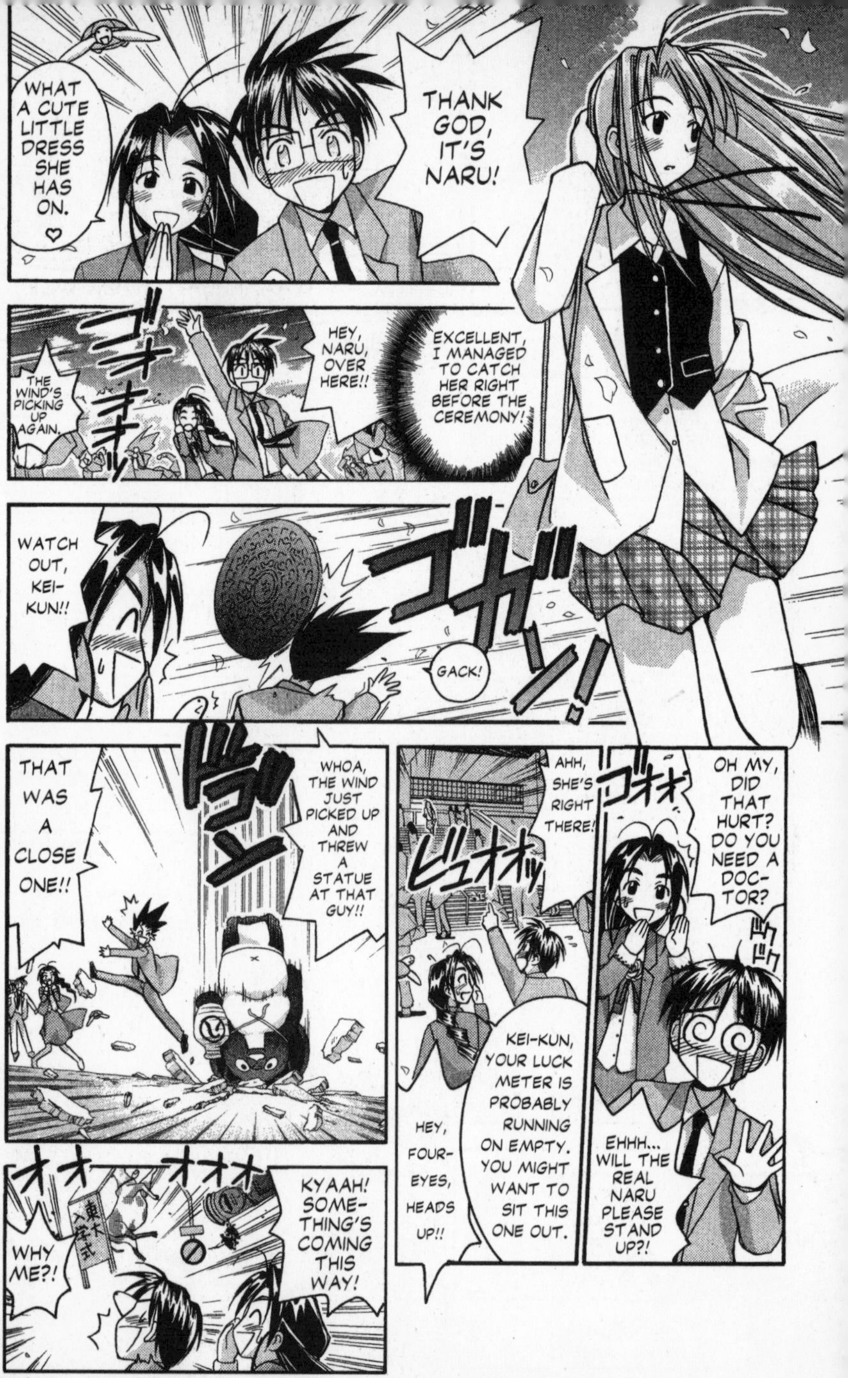
THANK GOD, IT'S NARU!
WHAT A CUTE LITTLE DRESS SHE HAS ON. ♡
EXCELLENT, I MANAGED TO CATCH HER RIGHT BEFORE THE CEREMONY!
HEY, NARU, OVER HERE!!
THE WIND'S PICKING UP AGAIN.
GACK!
WATCH OUT, KEI-KUN!!
OH MY, DID THAT HURT? DO YOU NEED A DOCTOR?
EHHH... WILL THE REAL NARU PLEASE STAND UP?!
AHH, SHE'S RIGHT THERE!
KEI-KUN, YOUR LUCK METER IS PROBABLY RUNNING ON EMPTY. YOU MIGHT WANT TO SIT THIS ONE OUT.
HEY, FOUR-EYES, HEADS UP!!
WHOA, THE WIND JUST PICKED UP AND THREW A STATUE AT THAT GUY!!
THAT WAS A CLOSE ONE!!
KYAAH! SOMETHING'S COMING THIS WAY!
東大入学式
WHY ME?!

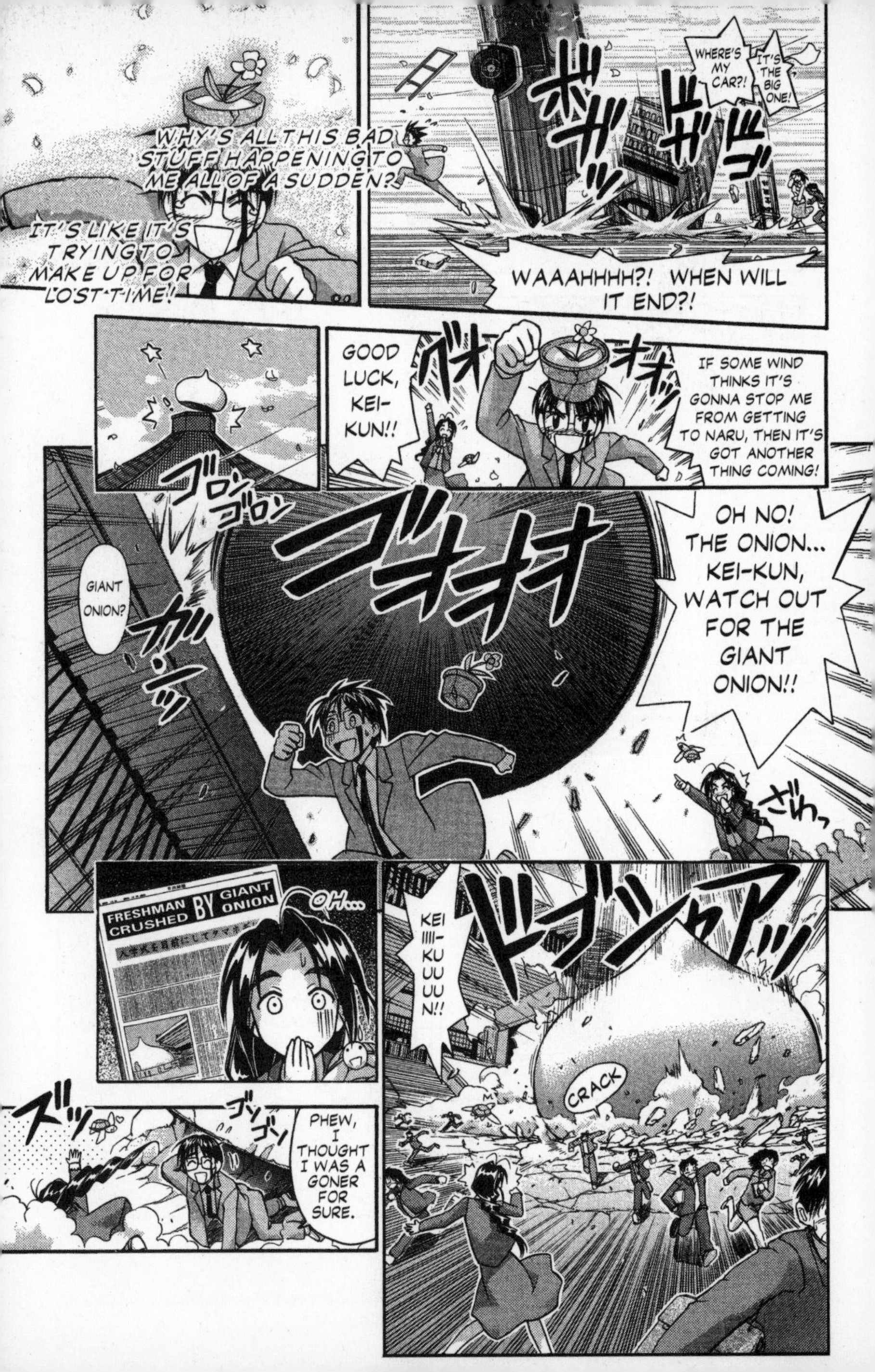
WHERE'S MY CAR?!
IT'S THE BIG ONE!
WAAAHHHH?! WHEN WILL IT END?!
WHY'S ALL THIS BAD STUFF HAPPENING TO ME ALL OF A SUDDEN?!
IT'S LIKE IT'S TRYING TO MAKE UP FOR LOST TIME!
IF SOME WIND THINKS IT'S GONNA STOP ME FROM GETTING TO NARU, THEN IT'S GOT ANOTHER THING COMING!
GOOD LUCK, KEI-KUN!!
OH NO! THE ONION... KEI-KUN, WATCH OUT FOR THE GIANT ONION!!
GIANT ONION?
KEI IIIII-KU UU UUN!!
CRACK
FRESHMAN CRUSHED BY GIANT ONION
OH...
PHEW, I THOUGHT I WAS A GONER FOR SURE.

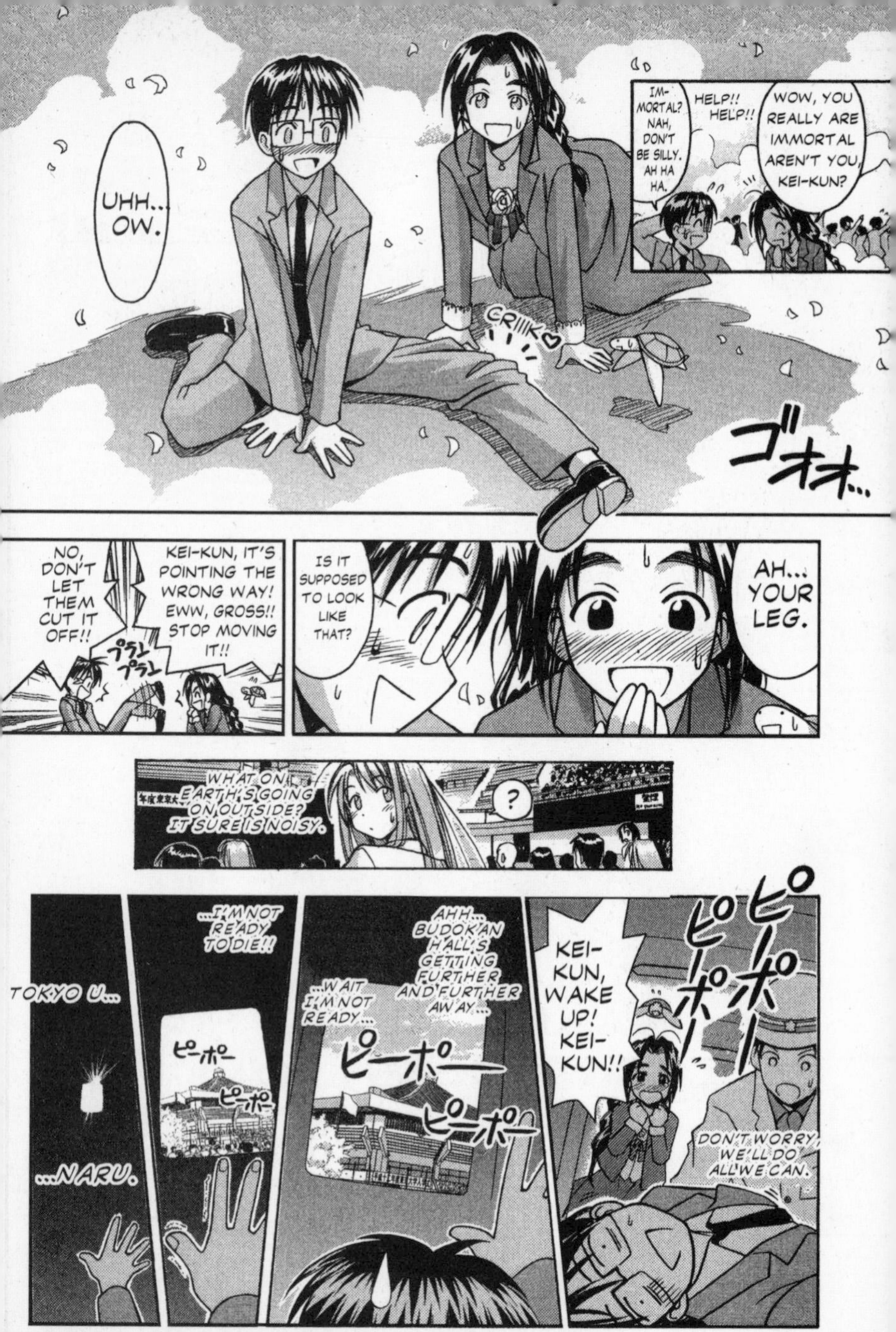
WOW, YOU REALLY ARE IMMORTAL AREN'T YOU, KEI-KUN?
HELP!! HELP!!
IM-MORTAL? NAH, DON'T BE SILLY. AH HA HA.
CRIIK♡
ゴオオ…
UHH... OW.
AH... YOUR LEG.
IS IT SUPPOSED TO LOOK LIKE THAT?
KEI-KUN, IT'S POINTING THE WRONG WAY! EWW, GROSS!! STOP MOVING IT!!
NO, DON'T LET THEM CUT IT OFF!!
プラン プラン
WHAT ON EARTH'S GOING ON OUTSIDE? IT SURE IS NOISY.
?
ピーポー ピーポー
KEI-KUN, WAKE UP! KEI-KUN!!
DON'T WORRY, WE'LL DO ALL WE CAN.
AHH... BUDOKAN HALL'S GETTING FURTHER AND FURTHER AWAY...
...WAIT I'M NOT READY...
ピーポー
ピーポー
...I'M NOT READY TO DIE!!
ピーポー
ピーポ
TOKYO U...
...NARU.

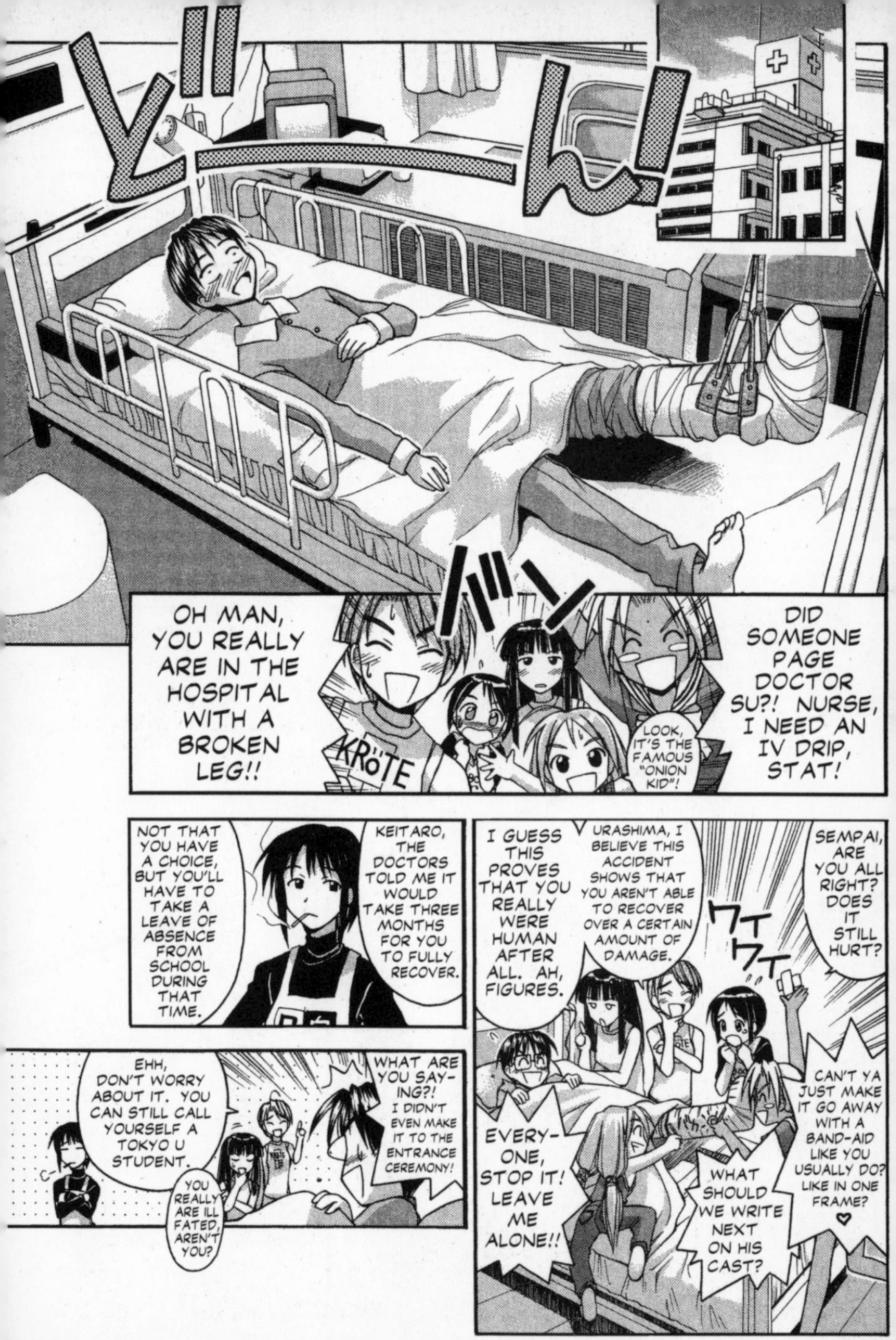

ど———ん!
DID SOMEONE PAGE DOCTOR SU?! NURSE, I NEED AN IV DRIP, STAT!
バン
LOOK, IT'S THE FAMOUS "ONION KID"!
OH MAN, YOU REALLY ARE IN THE HOSPITAL WITH A BROKEN LEG!!
KRöTE
SEMPAI, ARE YOU ALL RIGHT? DOES IT STILL HURT?
ワイワイ
URASHIMA, I BELIEVE THIS ACCIDENT SHOWS THAT YOU AREN'T ABLE TO RECOVER OVER A CERTAIN AMOUNT OF DAMAGE.
I GUESS THIS PROVES THAT YOU REALLY WERE HUMAN AFTER ALL. AH, FIGURES.
CAN'T YA JUST MAKE IT GO AWAY WITH A BAND-AID LIKE YOU USUALLY DO? LIKE IN ONE FRAME? ♥
WHAT SHOULD WE WRITE NEXT ON HIS CAST?
EVERY-ONE, STOP IT! LEAVE ME ALONE!!
KEITARO, THE DOCTORS TOLD ME IT WOULD TAKE THREE MONTHS FOR YOU TO FULLY RECOVER.
NOT THAT YOU HAVE A CHOICE, BUT YOU'LL HAVE TO TAKE A LEAVE OF ABSENCE FROM SCHOOL DURING THAT TIME.
WHAT ARE YOU SAY-ING?! I DIDN'T EVEN MAKE IT TO THE ENTRANCE CEREMONY!
EHH, DON'T WORRY ABOUT IT. YOU CAN STILL CALL YOURSELF A TOKYO U STUDENT.
YOU REALLY ARE ILL FATED, AREN'T YOU?

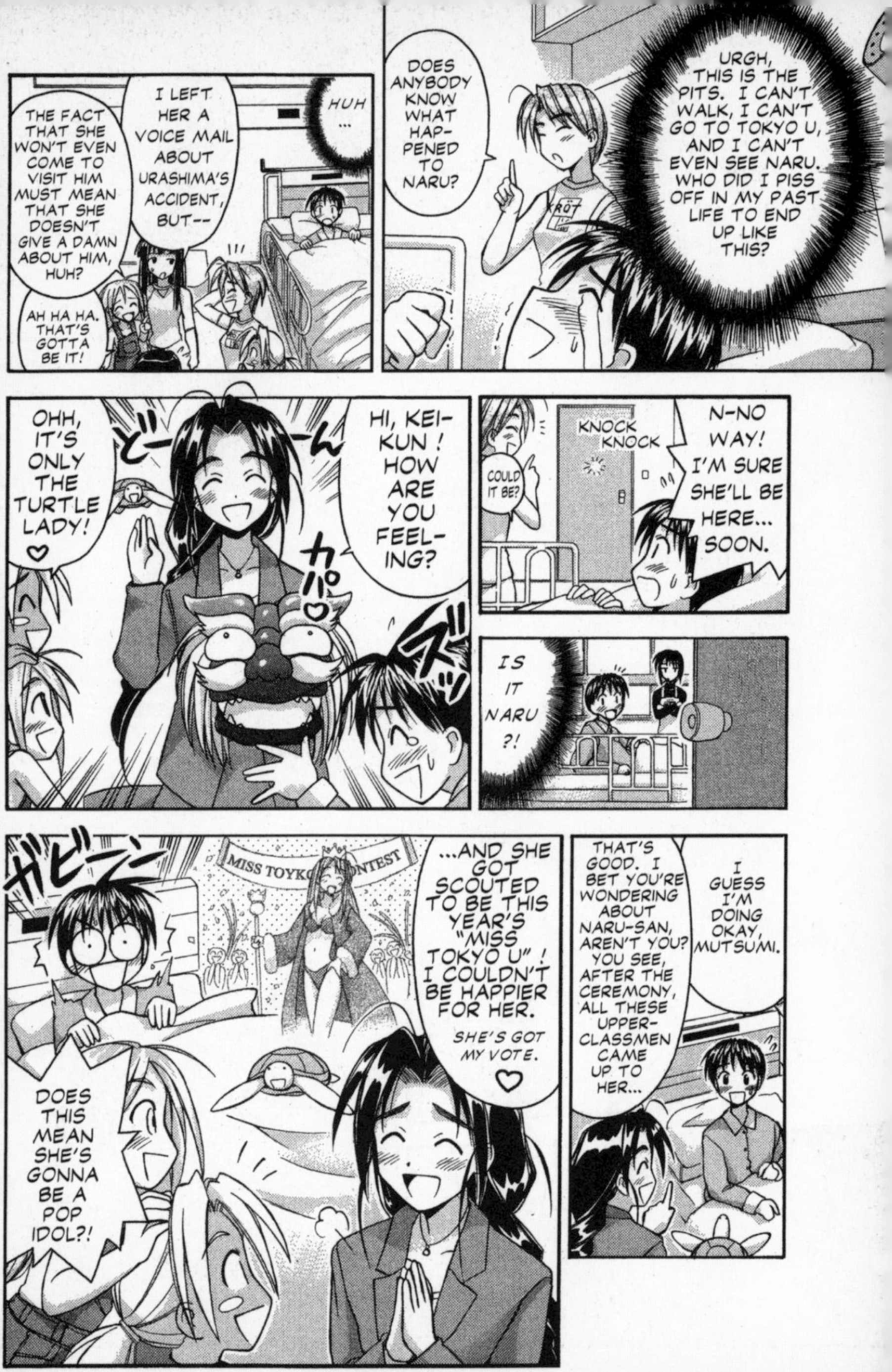
URGH, THIS IS THE PITS. I CAN'T WALK, I CAN'T GO TO TOKYO U, AND I CAN'T EVEN SEE NARU. WHO DID I PISS OFF IN MY PAST LIFE TO END UP LIKE THIS?
DOES ANYBODY KNOW WHAT HAP-PENED TO NARU?
HUH ...
I LEFT HER A VOICE MAIL ABOUT URASHIMA'S ACCIDENT, BUT--
THE FACT THAT SHE WON'T EVEN COME TO VISIT HIM MUST MEAN THAT SHE DOESN'T GIVE A DAMN ABOUT HIM, HUH?
AH HA HA. THAT'S GOTTA BE IT!
N-NO WAY! I'M SURE SHE'LL BE HERE... SOON.
KNOCK KNOCK
COULD IT BE?
IS IT NARU ?!
HI, KEI-KUN! HOW ARE YOU FEEL-ING?
OHH, IT'S ONLY THE TURTLE LADY! ♡
I GUESS I'M DOING OKAY, MUTSUMI.
THAT'S GOOD. I BET YOU'RE WONDERING ABOUT NARU-SAN, AREN'T YOU? YOU SEE, AFTER THE CEREMONY, ALL THESE UPPER-CLASSMEN CAME UP TO HER...
...AND SHE GOT SCOUTED TO BE THIS YEAR'S "MISS TOKYO U"! I COULDN'T BE HAPPIER FOR HER.
SHE'S GOT MY VOTE. ♡
DOES THIS MEAN SHE'S GONNA BE A POP IDOL?!

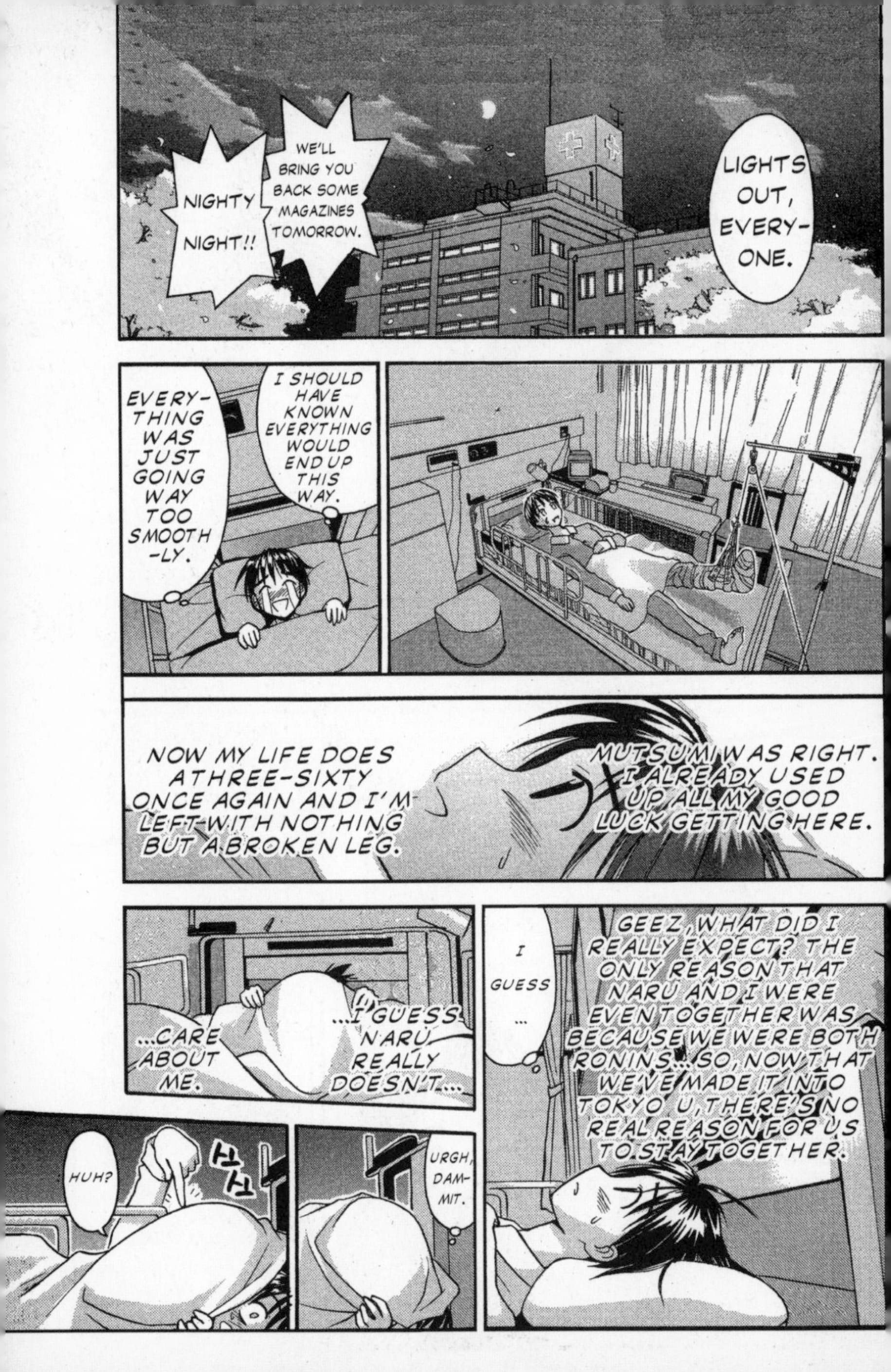
LIGHTS OUT, EVERY-ONE.
WE'LL BRING YOU BACK SOME MAGAZINES TOMORROW.
NIGHTY NIGHT!!
I SHOULD HAVE KNOWN EVERYTHING WOULD END UP THIS WAY.
EVERY-THING WAS JUST GOING WAY TOO SMOOTH-LY.
MUTSUMI WAS RIGHT. I ALREADY USED UP ALL MY GOOD LUCK GETTING HERE.
NOW MY LIFE DOES A THREE-SIXTY ONCE AGAIN AND I'M LEFT WITH NOTHING BUT A BROKEN LEG.
GEEZ, WHAT DID I REALLY EXPECT? THE ONLY REASON THAT NARU AND I WERE EVEN TOGETHER WAS BECAUSE WE WERE BOTH RONINS... SO, NOW THAT WE'VE MADE IT INTO TOKYO U, THERE'S NO REAL REASON FOR US TO STAY TOGETHER.
I GUESS ...
...I GUESS NARU REALLY DOESN'T...
...CARE ABOUT ME.
URGH, DAM-MIT.
HUH?

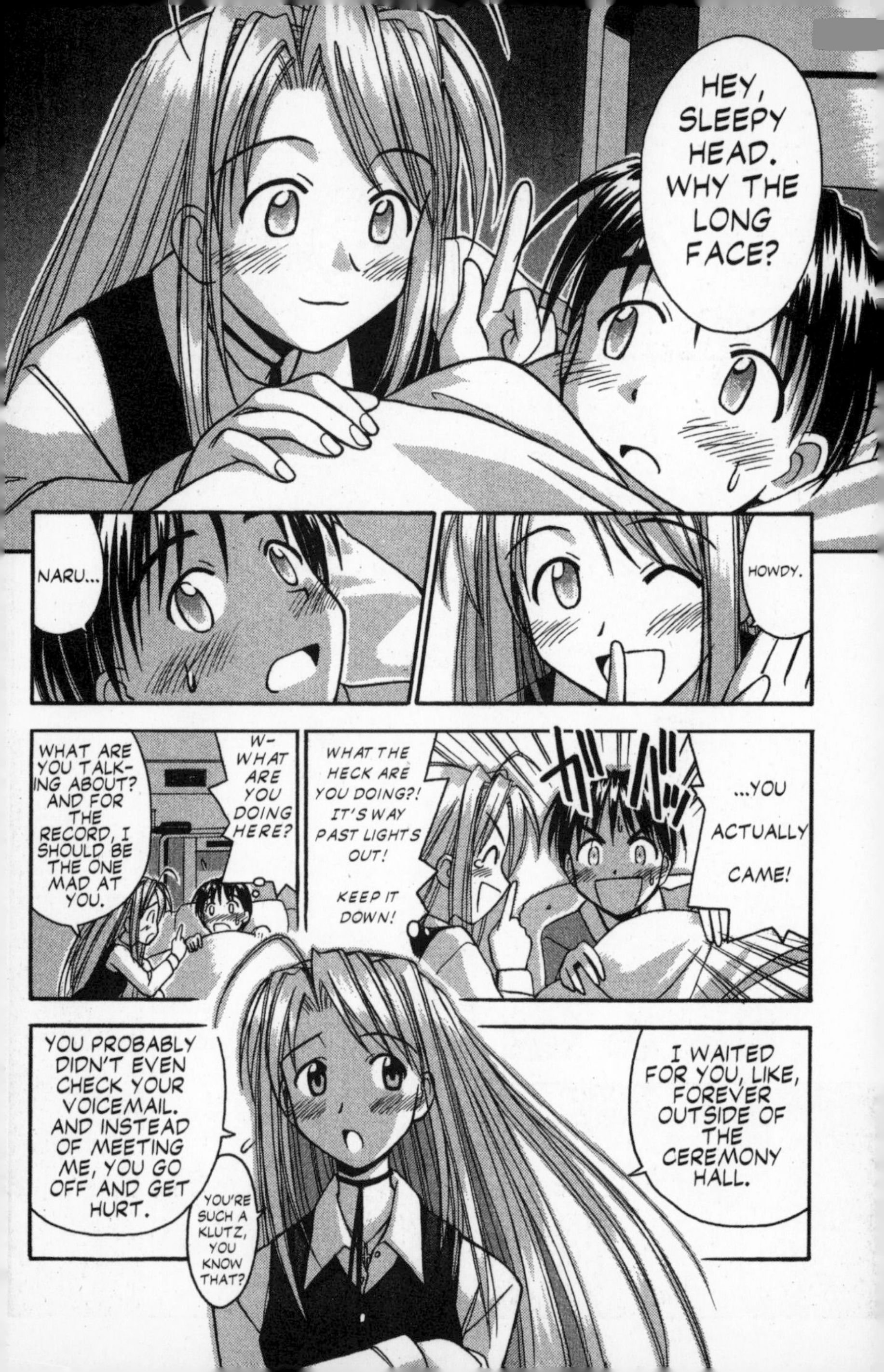
HEY, SLEEPY HEAD. WHY THE LONG FACE?
HOWDY.
NARU...
...YOU ACTUALLY CAME!
WHAT THE HECK ARE YOU DOING?! IT'S WAY PAST LIGHTS OUT!
KEEP IT DOWN!
W-WHAT ARE YOU DOING HERE?
WHAT ARE YOU TALKING ABOUT? AND FOR THE RECORD, I SHOULD BE THE ONE MAD AT YOU.
I WAITED FOR YOU, LIKE, FOREVER OUTSIDE OF THE CEREMONY HALL.
YOU PROBABLY DIDN'T EVEN CHECK YOUR VOICEMAIL. AND INSTEAD OF MEETING ME, YOU GO OFF AND GET HURT.
YOU'RE SUCH A KLUTZ, YOU KNOW THAT?

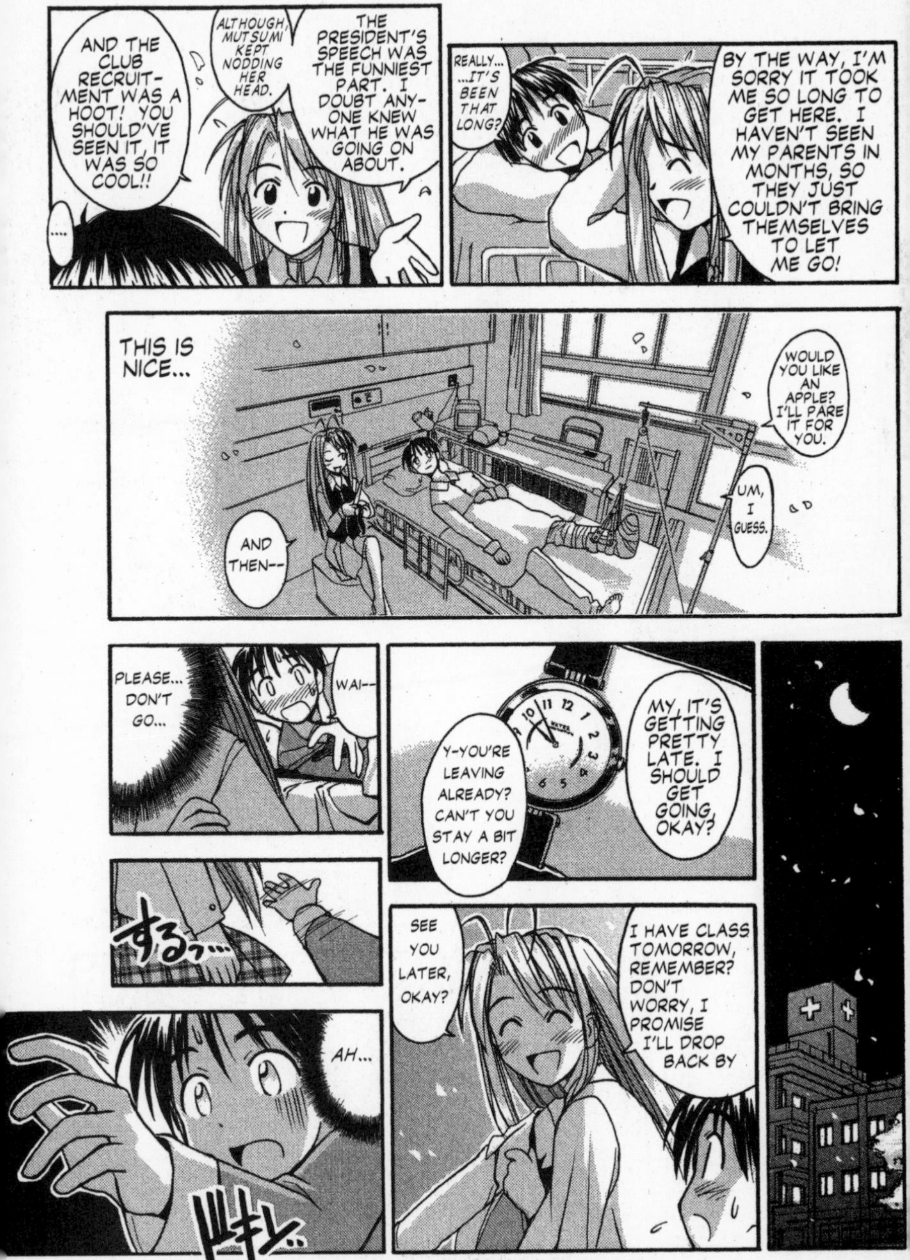
BY THE WAY, I'M SORRY IT TOOK ME SO LONG TO GET HERE. I HAVEN'T SEEN MY PARENTS IN MONTHS, SO THEY JUST COULDN'T BRING THEMSELVES TO LET ME GO!
REALLY... ...IT'S BEEN THAT LONG?
THE PRESIDENT'S SPEECH WAS THE FUNNIEST PART. I DOUBT ANY-ONE KNEW WHAT HE WAS GOING ON ABOUT.
ALTHOUGH, MUTSUMI KEPT NODDING HER HEAD.
AND THE CLUB RECRUIT-MENT WAS A HOOT! YOU SHOULD'VE SEEN IT, IT WAS SO COOL!!
....
WOULD YOU LIKE AN APPLE? I'LL PARE IT FOR YOU.
UM, I GUESS.
THIS IS NICE...
AND THEN--
MY, IT'S GETTING PRETTY LATE. I SHOULD GET GOING, OKAY?
Y-YOU'RE LEAVING ALREADY? CAN'T YOU STAY A BIT LONGER?
WAI--
PLEASE... DON'T GO...
I HAVE CLASS TOMORROW, REMEMBER? DON'T WORRY, I PROMISE I'LL DROP BACK BY
SEE YOU LATER, OKAY?
するっ…
AH...

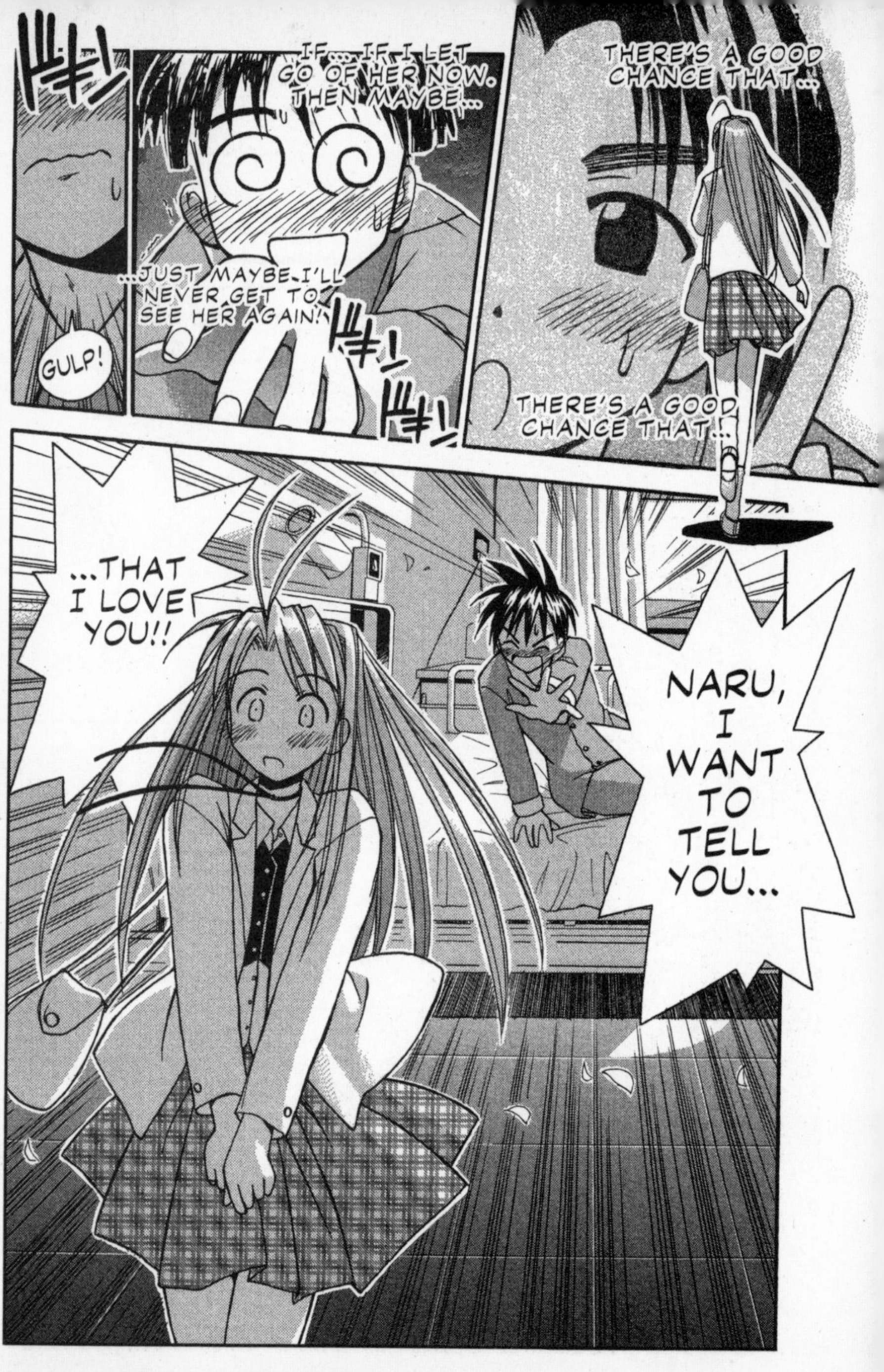
THERE'S A GOOD CHANCE THAT...
THERE'S A GOOD CHANCE THAT...
IF... IF I LET GO OF HER NOW. THEN MAYBE...
...JUST MAYBE I'LL NEVER GET TO SEE HER AGAIN!
GULP!
NARU, I WANT TO TELL YOU...
...THAT I LOVE YOU!!

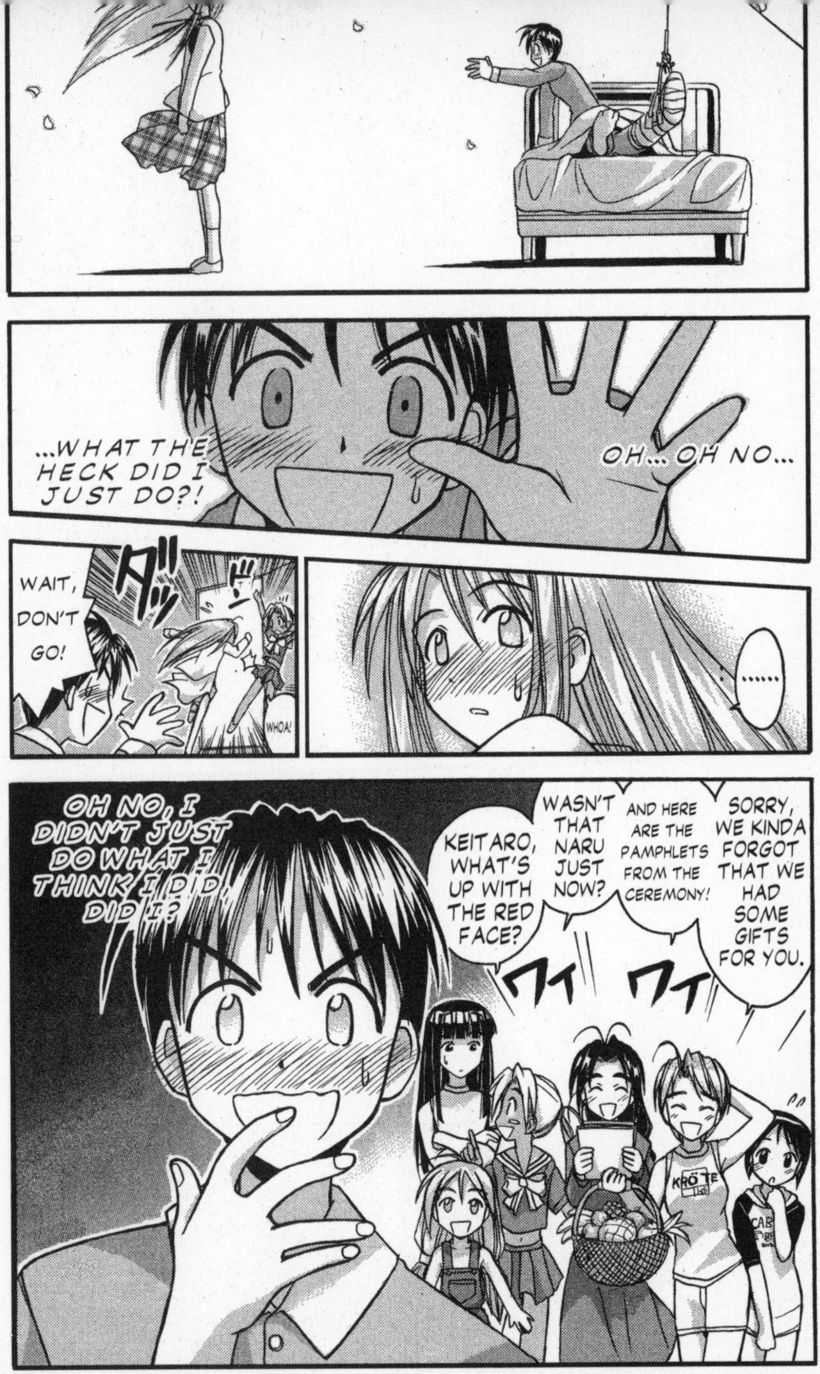
OH... OH NO...
...WHAT THE HECK DID I JUST DO?!
......
WAIT, DON'T GO!
WHOA!
SORRY, WE KINDA FORGOT THAT WE HAD SOME GIFTS FOR YOU.
AND HERE ARE THE PAMPHLETS FROM THE CEREMONY!
WASN'T THAT NARU JUST NOW?
KEITARO, WHAT'S UP WITH THE RED FACE?
ワイ ワイ
OH NO, I DIDN'T JUST DO WHAT I THINK I DID, DID I?

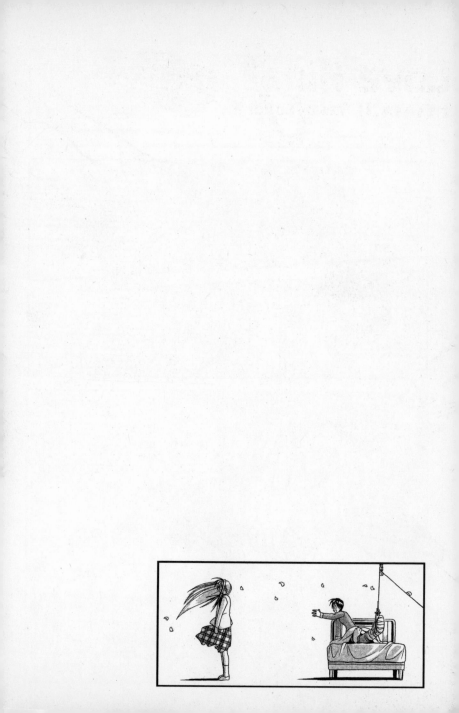

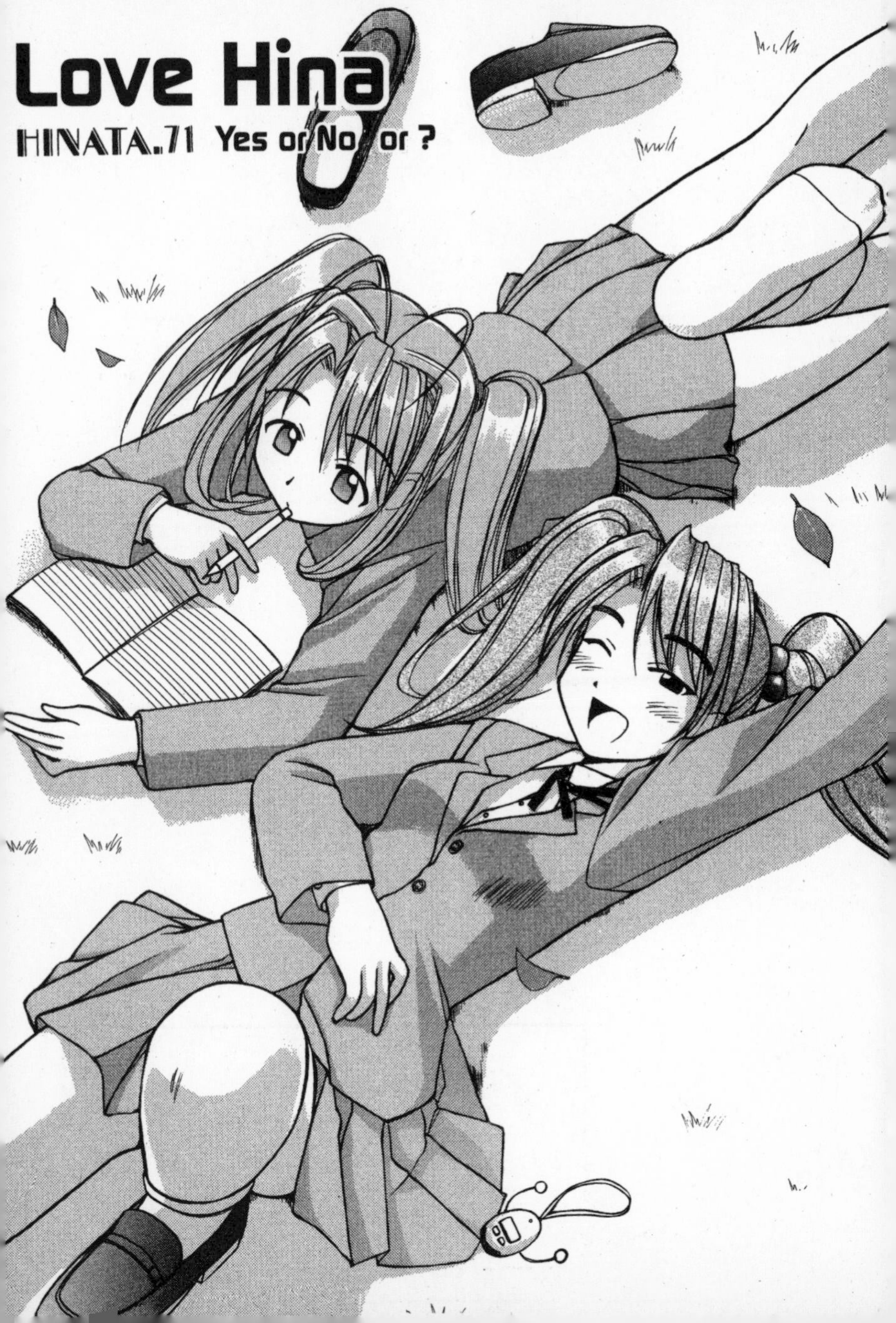
Love Hina
HINATA.71 Yes or No or ?

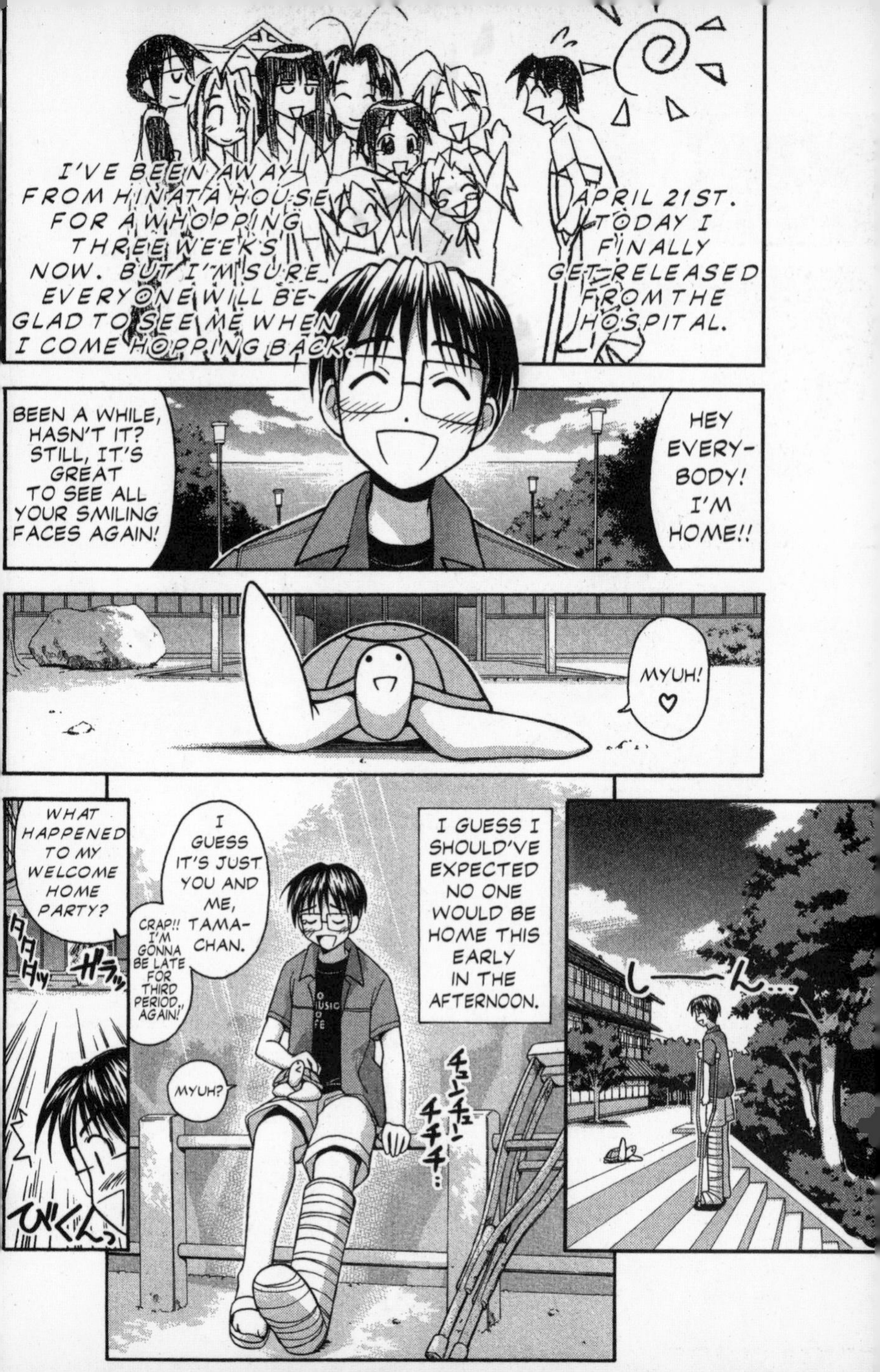
APRIL 21ST. TODAY I FINALLY GET RELEASED FROM THE HOSPITAL.
I'VE BEEN AWAY FROM HINATA HOUSE FOR A WHOPPING THREE WEEKS NOW. BUT I'M SURE EVERYONE WILL BE GLAD TO SEE ME WHEN I COME HOPPING BACK.
HEY EVERY-BODY! I'M HOME!!
BEEN A WHILE, HASN'T IT? STILL, IT'S GREAT TO SEE ALL YOUR SMILING FACES AGAIN!
MYUH! ♡
し――ん…
I GUESS I SHOULD'VE EXPECTED NO ONE WOULD BE HOME THIS EARLY IN THE AFTERNOON.
I GUESS IT'S JUST YOU AND ME, TAMA-CHAN.
MYUH?
CRAP!! I'M GONNA BE LATE FOR THIRD PERIOD, AGAIN!
WHAT HAPPENED TO MY WELCOME HOME PARTY?
タタタッ
ガラッ
びくんっ

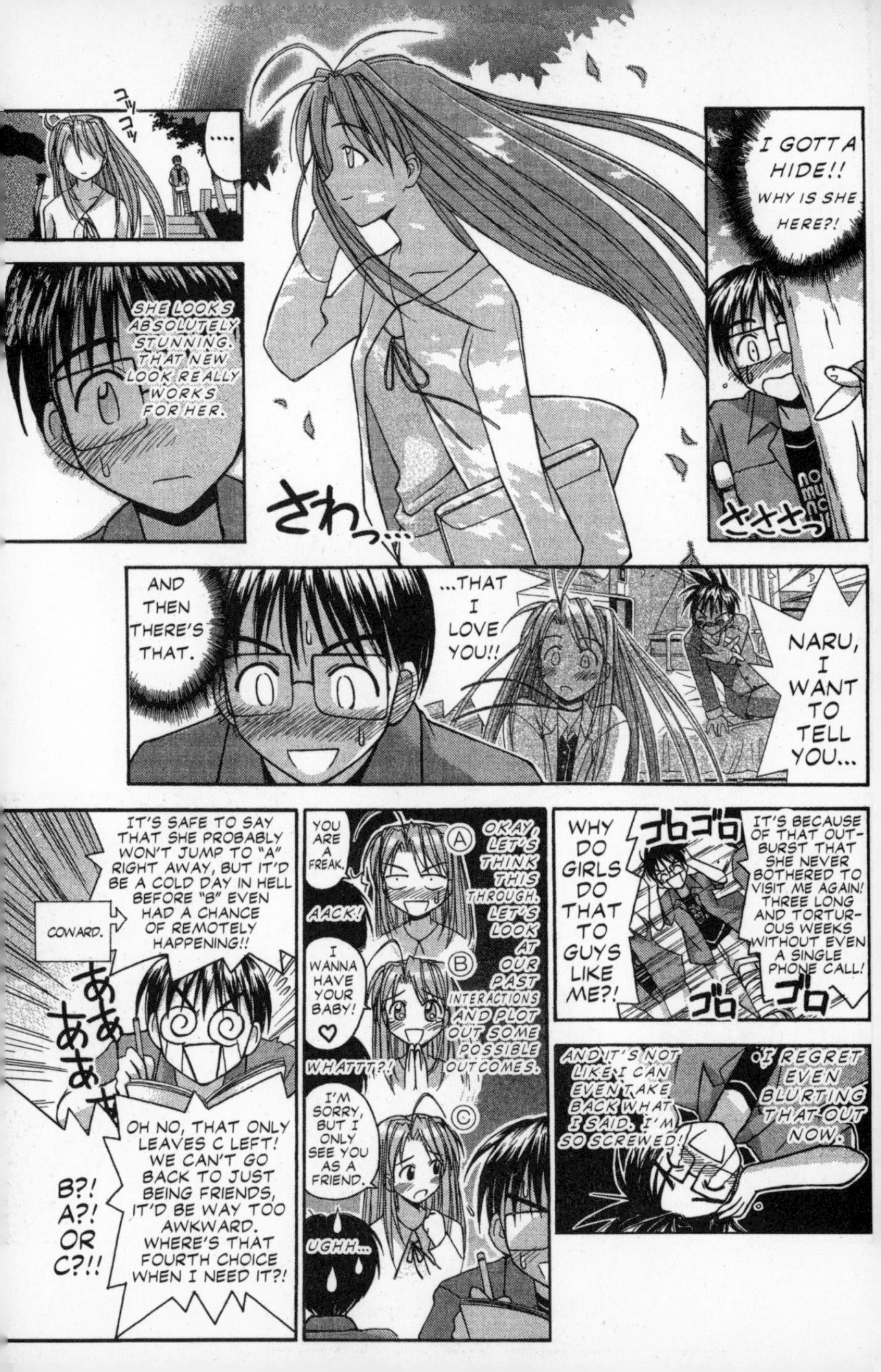
I GOTTA HIDE!! WHY IS SHE HERE?!
ささささっ
さわっ...
コツコツ
.....
SHE LOOKS ABSOLUTELY STUNNING. THAT NEW LOOK REALLY WORKS FOR HER.
NARU, I WANT TO TELL YOU...
...THAT I LOVE YOU!!
AND THEN THERE'S THAT.
IT'S BECAUSE OF THAT OUT-BURST THAT SHE NEVER BOTHERED TO VISIT ME AGAIN! THREE LONG AND TORTUR-OUS WEEKS WITHOUT EVEN A SINGLE PHONE CALL!
ゴロゴロ
WHY DO GIRLS DO THAT TO GUYS LIKE ME?!
ゴロ ゴロ
I REGRET EVEN BLURTING THAT OUT NOW.
AND IT'S NOT LIKE I CAN EVEN TAKE BACK WHAT I SAID. I'M SO SCREWED!
OKAY, LET'S THINK THIS THROUGH. LET'S LOOK AT OUR PAST INTERACTIONS AND PLOT OUT SOME POSSIBLE OUTCOMES.
A
YOU ARE A FREAK.
AACK!
B
I WANNA HAVE YOUR BABY! ♥
WHATTT?!
C
I'M SORRY, BUT I ONLY SEE YOU AS A FRIEND.
UGHH...
IT'S SAFE TO SAY THAT SHE PROBABLY WON'T JUMP TO "A" RIGHT AWAY, BUT IT'D BE A COLD DAY IN HELL BEFORE "B" EVEN HAD A CHANCE OF REMOTELY HAPPENING!!
COWARD.
ああああ
OH NO, THAT ONLY LEAVES C LEFT! WE CAN'T GO BACK TO JUST BEING FRIENDS, IT'D BE WAY TOO AWKWARD. WHERE'S THAT FOURTH CHOICE WHEN I NEED IT?!
B?! A?! OR C?!!

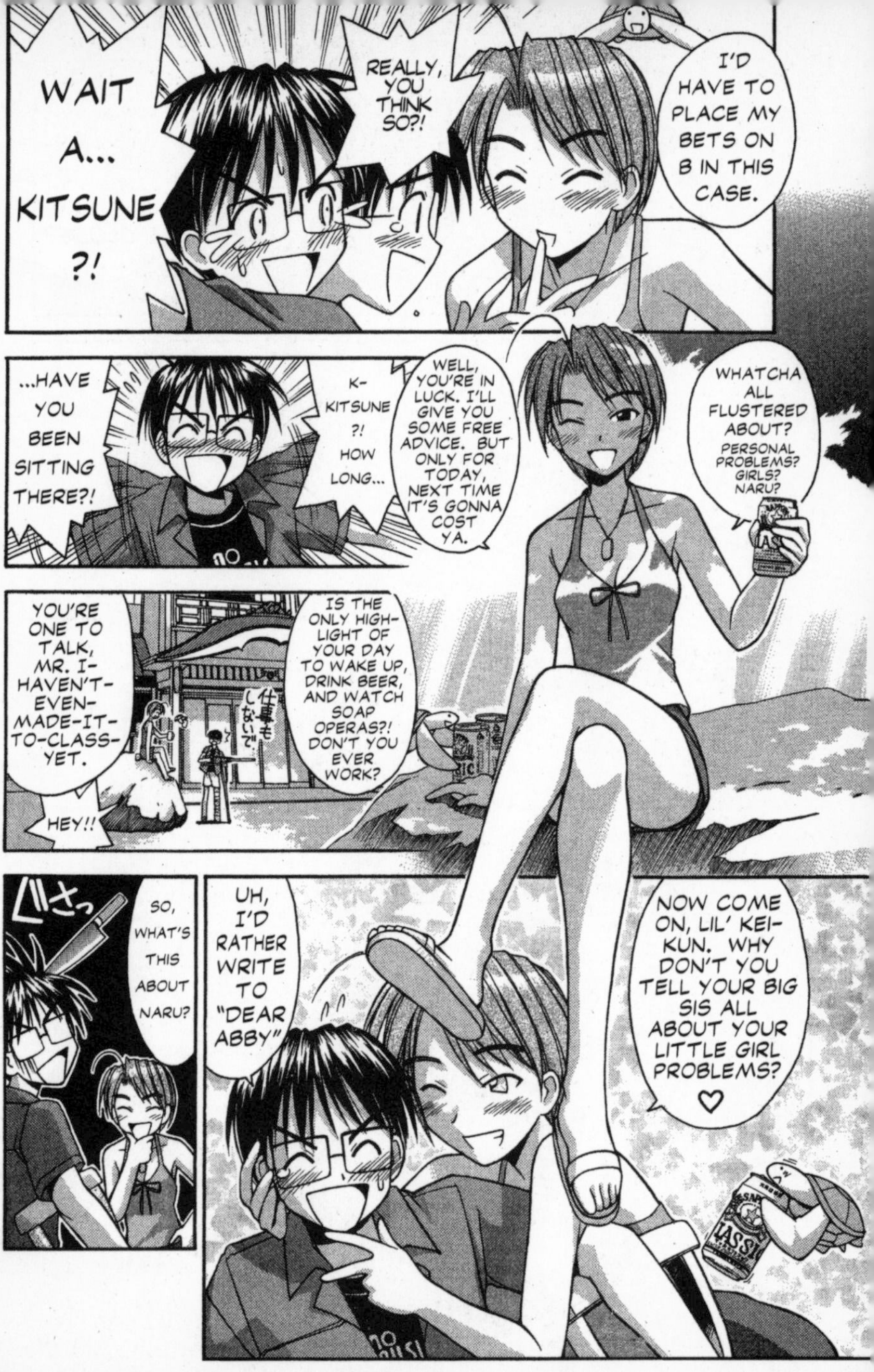
I'D HAVE TO PLACE MY BETS ON B IN THIS CASE.
REALLY, YOU THINK SO?!
WAIT A... KITSUNE ?!
WHATCHA ALL FLUSTERED ABOUT? PERSONAL PROBLEMS? GIRLS? NARU?
WELL, YOU'RE IN LUCK. I'LL GIVE YOU SOME FREE ADVICE. BUT ONLY FOR TODAY, NEXT TIME IT'S GONNA COST YA.
K-KITSUNE ?! HOW LONG...
...HAVE YOU BEEN SITTING THERE?!
IS THE ONLY HIGH-LIGHT OF YOUR DAY TO WAKE UP, DRINK BEER, AND WATCH SOAP OPERAS?! DON'T YOU EVER WORK?
仕事もしないで
YOU'RE ONE TO TALK, MR. I-HAVEN'T-EVEN-MADE-IT-TO-CLASS-YET.
HEY!!
NOW COME ON, LIL' KEI-KUN. WHY DON'T YOU TELL YOUR BIG SIS ALL ABOUT YOUR LITTLE GIRL PROBLEMS? ♡
UH, I'D RATHER WRITE TO "DEAR ABBY"
SO, WHAT'S THIS ABOUT NARU?
ぐさっ

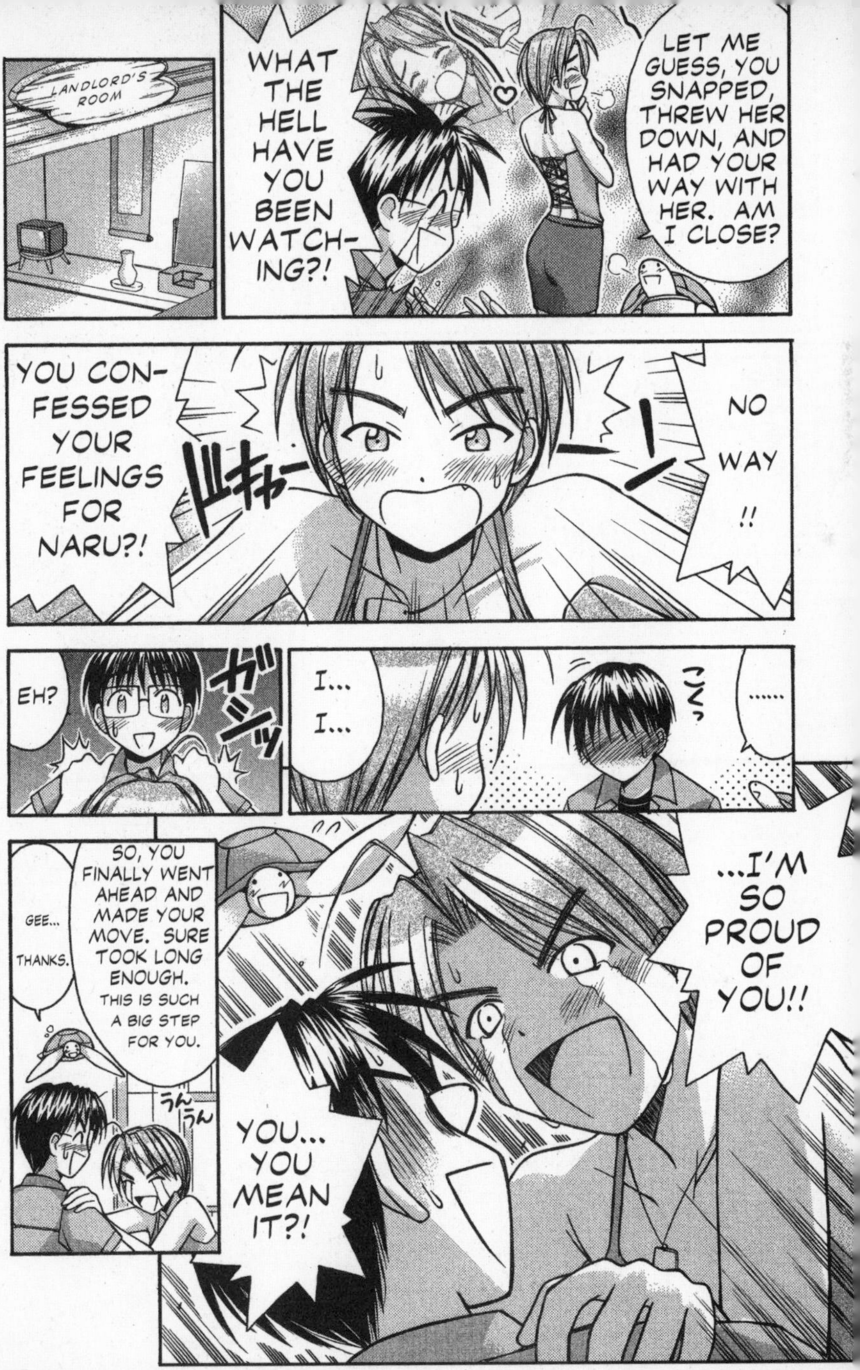
LET ME GUESS, YOU SNAPPED, THREW HER DOWN, AND HAD YOUR WAY WITH HER. AM I CLOSE?
WHAT THE HELL HAVE YOU BEEN WATCH-ING?!
LANDLORD'S ROOM
NO WAY!!
ドキャー
YOU CON-FESSED YOUR FEELINGS FOR NARU?!
......
I... I...
ガシッ
EH?
...I'M SO PROUD OF YOU!!
YOU... YOU MEAN IT?!
SO, YOU FINALLY WENT AHEAD AND MADE YOUR MOVE. SURE TOOK LONG ENOUGH. THIS IS SUCH A BIG STEP FOR YOU.
GEE... THANKS.
うんうん

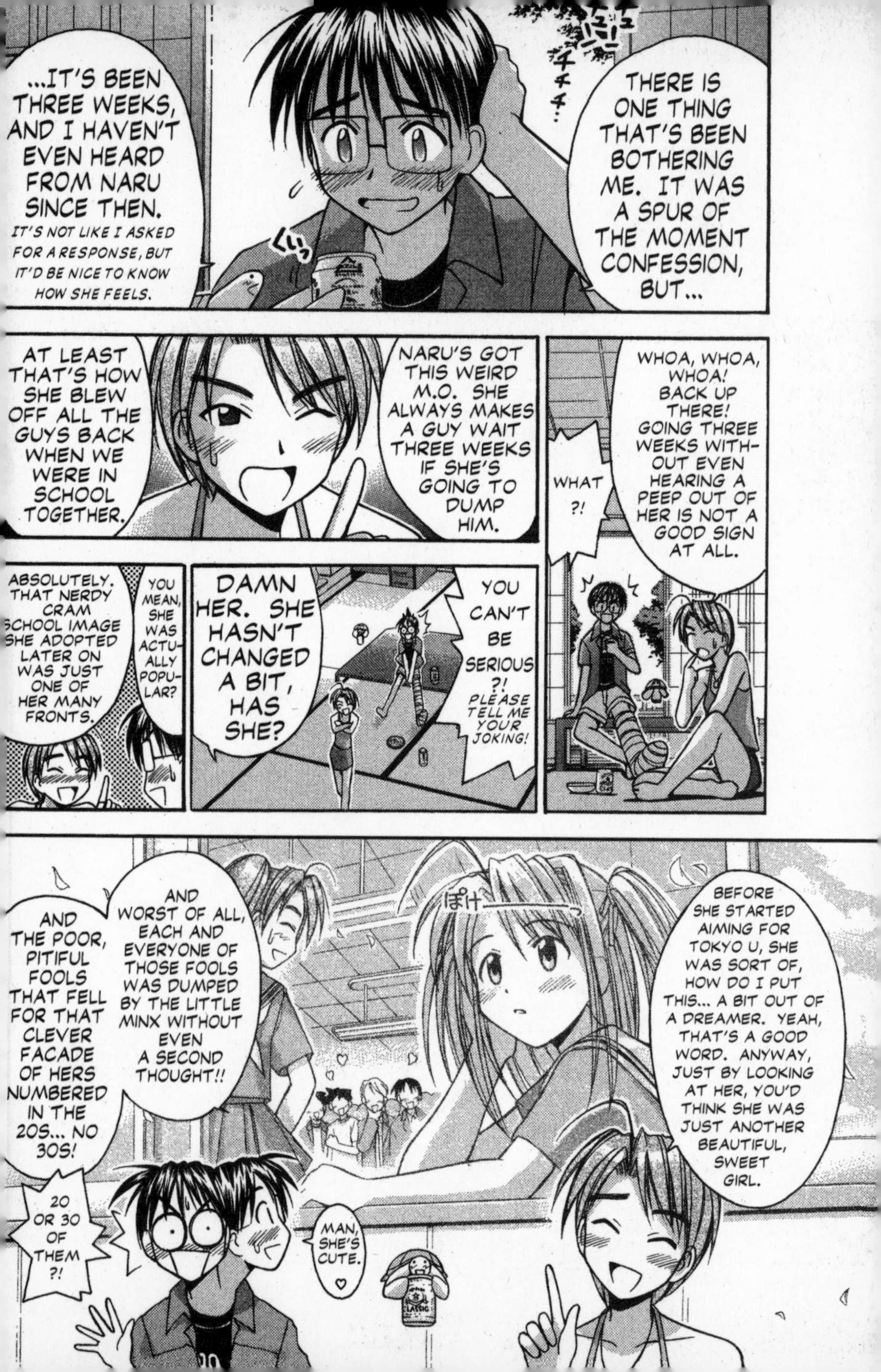
THERE IS ONE THING THAT'S BEEN BOTHERING ME. IT WAS A SPUR OF THE MOMENT CONFESSION, BUT...
...IT'S BEEN THREE WEEKS, AND I HAVEN'T EVEN HEARD FROM NARU SINCE THEN.
IT'S NOT LIKE I ASKED FOR A RESPONSE, BUT IT'D BE NICE TO KNOW HOW SHE FEELS.
WHOA, WHOA, WHOA! BACK UP THERE! GOING THREE WEEKS WITH-OUT EVEN HEARING A PEEP OUT OF HER IS NOT A GOOD SIGN AT ALL.
WHAT ?!
NARU'S GOT THIS WEIRD M.O. SHE ALWAYS MAKES A GUY WAIT THREE WEEKS IF SHE'S GOING TO DUMP HIM.
AT LEAST THAT'S HOW SHE BLEW OFF ALL THE GUYS BACK WHEN WE WERE IN SCHOOL TOGETHER.
YOU CAN'T BE SERIOUS ?!
PLEASE TELL ME YOUR JOKING!
DAMN HER. SHE HASN'T CHANGED A BIT, HAS SHE?
YOU MEAN, SHE WAS ACTU-ALLY POPU-LAR?
ABSOLUTELY. THAT NERDY CRAM SCHOOL IMAGE SHE ADOPTED LATER ON WAS JUST ONE OF HER MANY FRONTS.
BEFORE SHE STARTED AIMING FOR TOKYO U, SHE WAS SORT OF, HOW DO I PUT THIS... A BIT OUT OF A DREAMER. YEAH, THAT'S A GOOD WORD. ANYWAY, JUST BY LOOKING AT HER, YOU'D THINK SHE WAS JUST ANOTHER BEAUTIFUL, SWEET GIRL.
AND WORST OF ALL, EACH AND EVERYONE OF THOSE FOOLS WAS DUMPED BY THE LITTLE MINX WITHOUT EVEN A SECOND THOUGHT!!
AND THE POOR, PITIFUL FOOLS THAT FELL FOR THAT CLEVER FACADE OF HERS NUMBERED IN THE 20S... NO 30S!
MAN, SHE'S CUTE. ♡
20 OR 30 OF THEM ?!

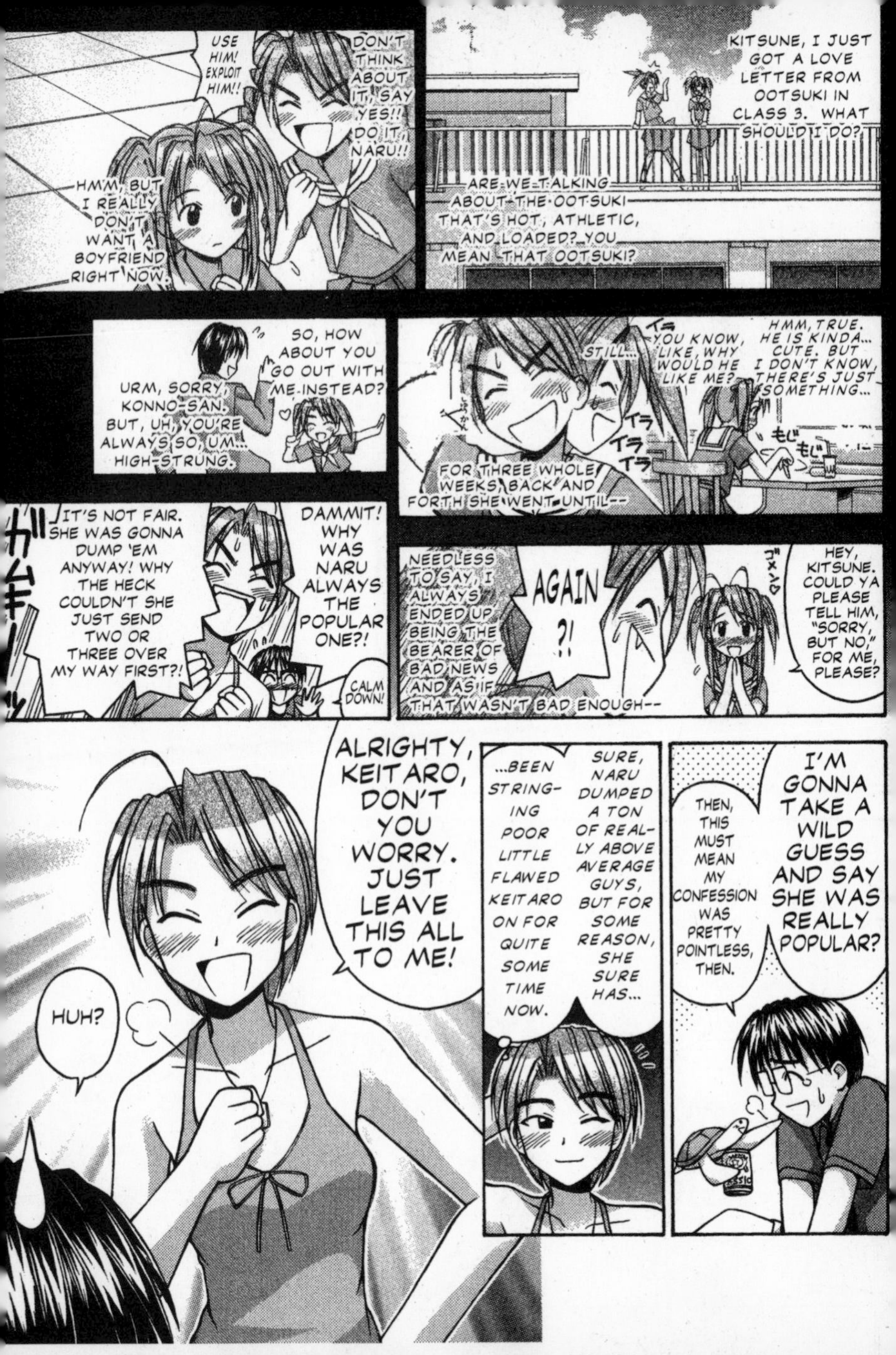
KITSUNE, I JUST GOT A LOVE LETTER FROM OOTSUKI IN CLASS 3. WHAT SHOULD I DO?
ARE WE TALKING ABOUT THE OOTSUKI THAT'S HOT, ATHLETIC, AND LOADED? YOU MEAN THAT OOTSUKI?
DON'T THINK ABOUT IT, SAY YES!! DO IT, NARU!!
USE HIM! EXPLOIT HIM!!
HM'M, BUT I REALLY DON'T WANT A BOYFRIEND RIGHT NOW.
HMM, TRUE. HE IS KINDA... CUTE. BUT I DON'T KNOW, THERE'S JUST SOMETHING...
YOU KNOW, LIKE, WHY WOULD HE LIKE ME?
STILL...
FOR THREE WHOLE WEEKS, BACK AND FORTH SHE WENT UNTIL--
SO, HOW ABOUT YOU GO OUT WITH ME INSTEAD?
URM, SORRY, KONNO-SAN. BUT, UH, YOU'RE ALWAYS SO, UM... HIGH-STRUNG.
HEY, KITSUNE. COULD YA PLEASE TELL HIM, "SORRY, BUT NO," FOR ME, PLEASE?
AGAIN ?!
NEEDLESS TO SAY, I ALWAYS ENDED UP BEING THE BEARER OF BAD NEWS AND AS IF THAT WASN'T BAD ENOUGH--
DAMMIT! WHY WAS NARU ALWAYS THE POPULAR ONE?!
IT'S NOT FAIR. SHE WAS GONNA DUMP 'EM ANYWAY! WHY THE HECK COULDN'T SHE JUST SEND TWO OR THREE OVER MY WAY FIRST?!
CALM DOWN!
I'M GONNA TAKE A WILD GUESS AND SAY SHE WAS REALLY POPULAR?
THEN, THIS MUST MEAN MY CONFESSION WAS PRETTY POINTLESS, THEN.
SURE, NARU DUMPED A TON OF REAL-LY ABOVE AVERAGE GUYS, BUT FOR SOME REASON, SHE SURE HAS...
...BEEN STRING-ING POOR LITTLE FLAWED KEITARO ON FOR QUITE SOME TIME NOW.
ALRIGHTY, KEITARO, DON'T YOU WORRY. JUST LEAVE THIS ALL TO ME!
HUH?

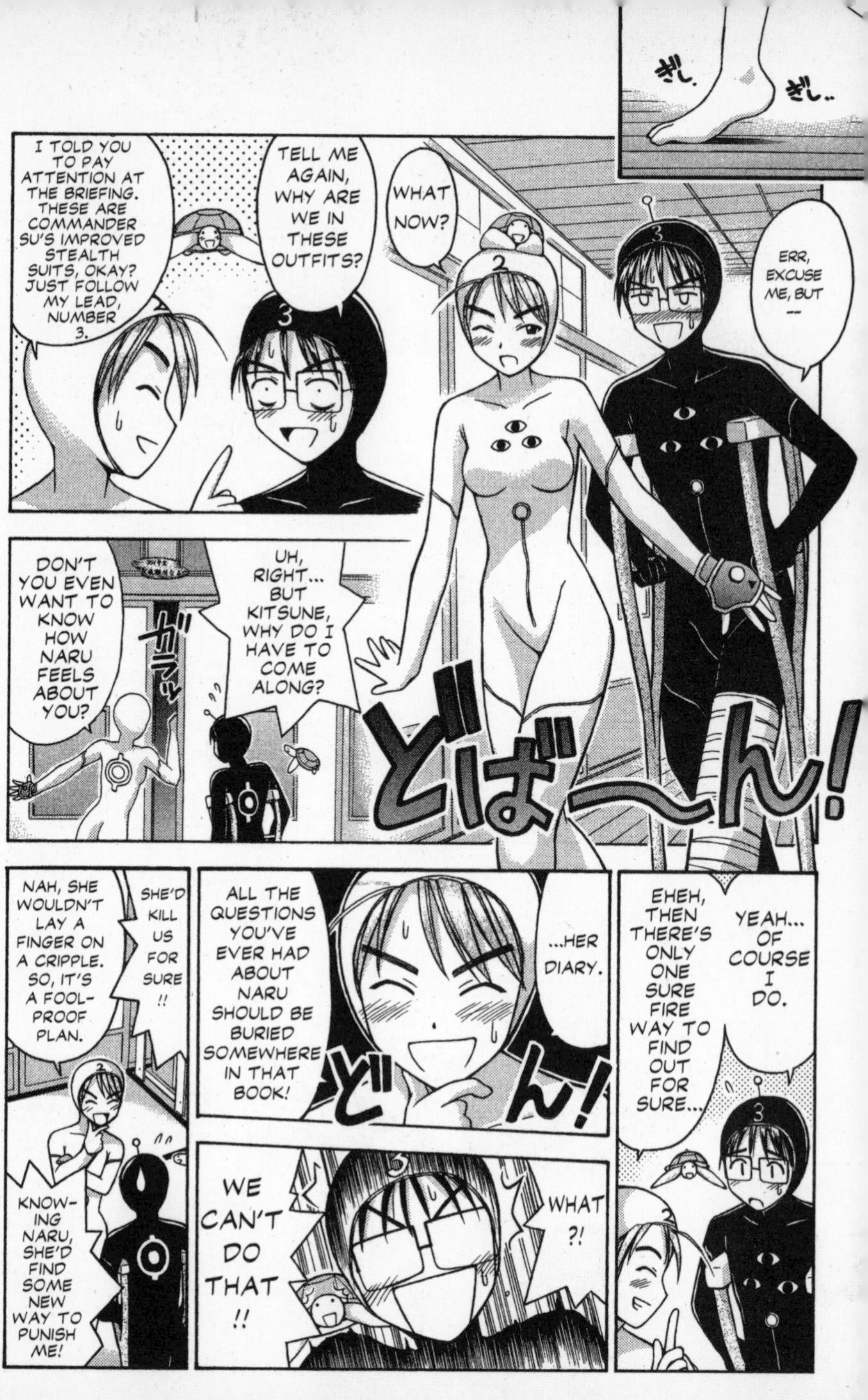
ぎし、
ぎし..
ERR, EXCUSE ME, BUT --
WHAT NOW?
どば〜ん!
TELL ME AGAIN, WHY ARE WE IN THESE OUTFITS?
I TOLD YOU TO PAY ATTENTION AT THE BRIEFING. THESE ARE COMMANDER SU'S IMPROVED STEALTH SUITS, OKAY? JUST FOLLOW MY LEAD, NUMBER 3.
UH, RIGHT... BUT KITSUNE, WHY DO I HAVE TO COME ALONG?
ガラッ
DON'T YOU EVEN WANT TO KNOW HOW NARU FEELS ABOUT YOU?
YEAH... OF COURSE I DO.
EHEH, THEN THERE'S ONLY ONE SURE FIRE WAY TO FIND OUT FOR SURE...
...HER DIARY.
ALL THE QUESTIONS YOU'VE EVER HAD ABOUT NARU SHOULD BE BURIED SOMEWHERE IN THAT BOOK!
どん!
WHAT ?!
WE CAN'T DO THAT !!
SHE'D KILL US FOR SURE !!
NAH, SHE WOULDN'T LAY A FINGER ON A CRIPPLE. SO, IT'S A FOOL-PROOF PLAN.
KNOW-ING NARU, SHE'D FIND SOME NEW WAY TO PUNISH ME!

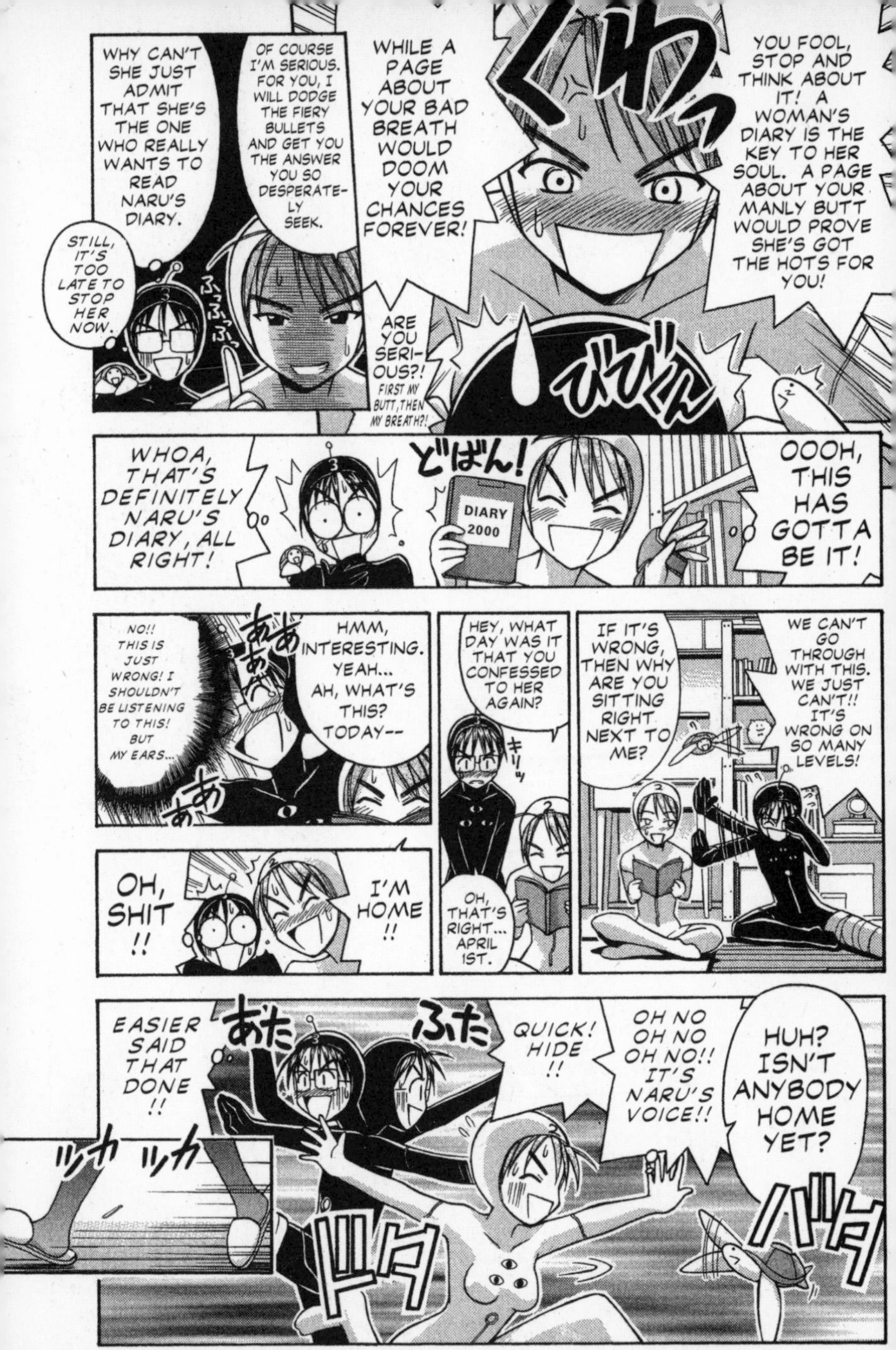
くわっ
YOU FOOL, STOP AND THINK ABOUT IT! A WOMAN'S DIARY IS THE KEY TO HER SOUL. A PAGE ABOUT YOUR MANLY BUTT WOULD PROVE SHE'S GOT THE HOTS FOR YOU!
WHILE A PAGE ABOUT YOUR BAD BREATH WOULD DOOM YOUR CHANCES FOREVER!
ARE YOU SERI-OUS?! FIRST MY BUTT, THEN MY BREATH?!
OF COURSE I'M SERIOUS. FOR YOU, I WILL DODGE THE FIERY BULLETS AND GET YOU THE ANSWER YOU SO DESPERATE-LY SEEK.
WHY CAN'T SHE JUST ADMIT THAT SHE'S THE ONE WHO REALLY WANTS TO READ NARU'S DIARY.
ふっふっふっ
STILL, IT'S TOO LATE TO STOP HER NOW.
OOOH, THIS HAS GOTTA BE IT!
どばん!
DIARY 2000
WHOA, THAT'S DEFINITELY NARU'S DIARY, ALL RIGHT!
WE CAN'T GO THROUGH WITH THIS. WE JUST CAN'T!! IT'S WRONG ON SO MANY LEVELS!
IF IT'S WRONG, THEN WHY ARE YOU SITTING RIGHT NEXT TO ME?
HEY, WHAT DAY WAS IT THAT YOU CONFESSED TO HER AGAIN?
OH, THAT'S RIGHT... APRIL 1ST.
HMM, INTERESTING. YEAH... AH, WHAT'S THIS? TODAY--
NO!! THIS IS JUST WRONG! I SHOULDN'T BE LISTENING TO THIS! BUT MY EARS...
I'M HOME!!
OH, SHIT!!
HUH? ISN'T ANYBODY HOME YET?
バタ
OH NO OH NO OH NO!! IT'S NARU'S VOICE!!
QUICK! HIDE!!
ふた
あた
ドタ
EASIER SAID THAT DONE!!
ツカ ツカ

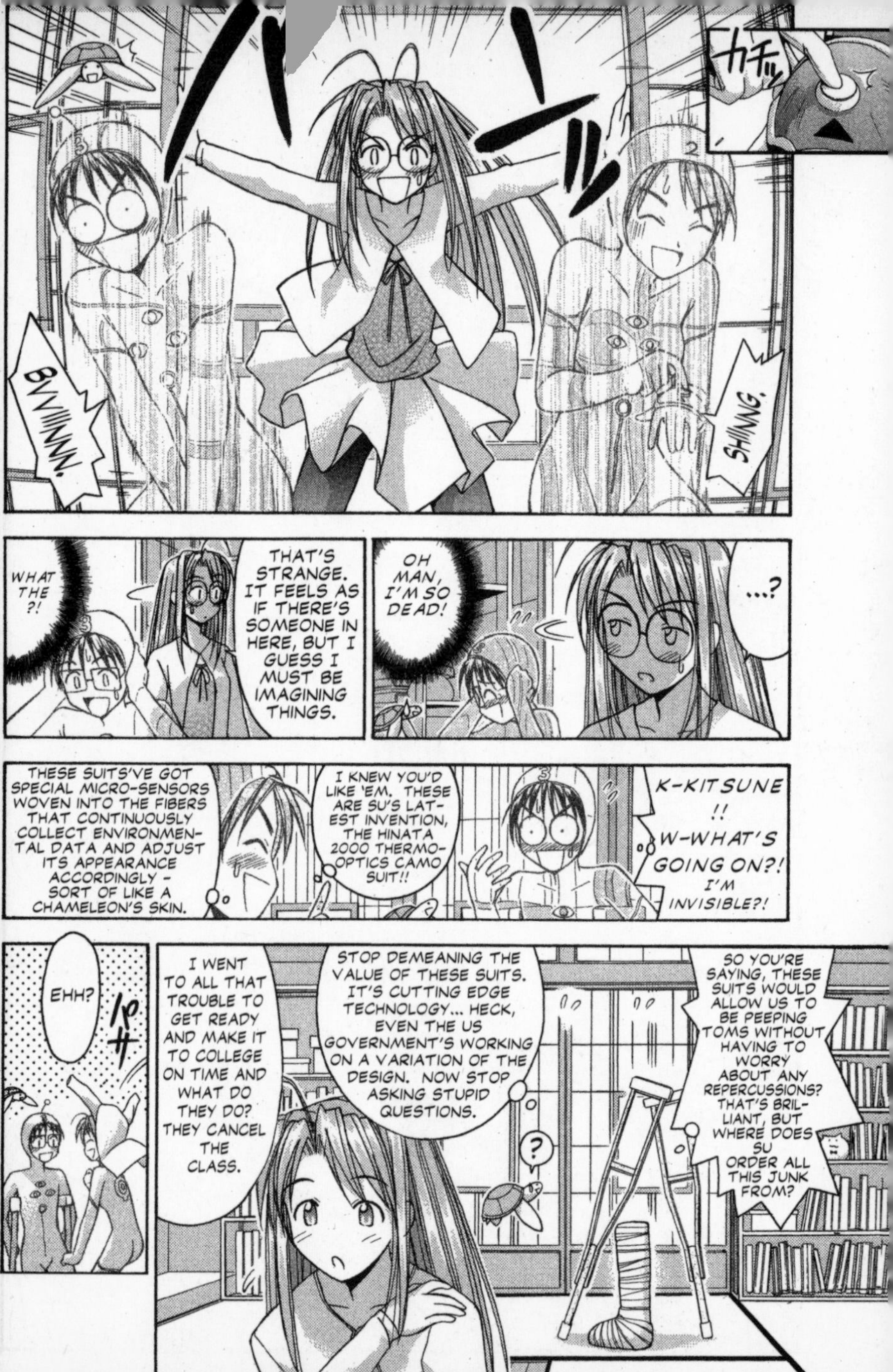
カチッ
SHINNG.
BVVIIINNN.
...?
OH MAN, I'M SO DEAD!
THAT'S STRANGE. IT FEELS AS IF THERE'S SOMEONE IN HERE, BUT I GUESS I MUST BE IMAGINING THINGS.
WHAT THE ?!
K-KITSUNE !! W-WHAT'S GOING ON?! I'M INVISIBLE?!
I KNEW YOU'D LIKE 'EM. THESE ARE SU'S LATEST INVENTION, THE HINATA 2000 THERMO-OPTICS CAMO SUIT!!
THESE SUITS'VE GOT SPECIAL MICRO-SENSORS WOVEN INTO THE FIBERS THAT CONTINUOUSLY COLLECT ENVIRONMENTAL DATA AND ADJUST ITS APPEARANCE ACCORDINGLY - SORT OF LIKE A CHAMELEON'S SKIN.
SO YOU'RE SAYING, THESE SUITS WOULD ALLOW US TO BE PEEPING TOMS WITHOUT HAVING TO WORRY ABOUT ANY REPERCUSSIONS? THAT'S BRILLIANT, BUT WHERE DOES SU ORDER ALL THIS JUNK FROM?
STOP DEMEANING THE VALUE OF THESE SUITS. IT'S CUTTING EDGE TECHNOLOGY... HECK, EVEN THE US GOVERNMENT'S WORKING ON A VARIATION OF THE DESIGN. NOW STOP ASKING STUPID QUESTIONS.
?
I WENT TO ALL THAT TROUBLE TO GET READY AND MAKE IT TO COLLEGE ON TIME AND WHAT DO THEY DO? THEY CANCEL THE CLASS.
ハッ
EHH?

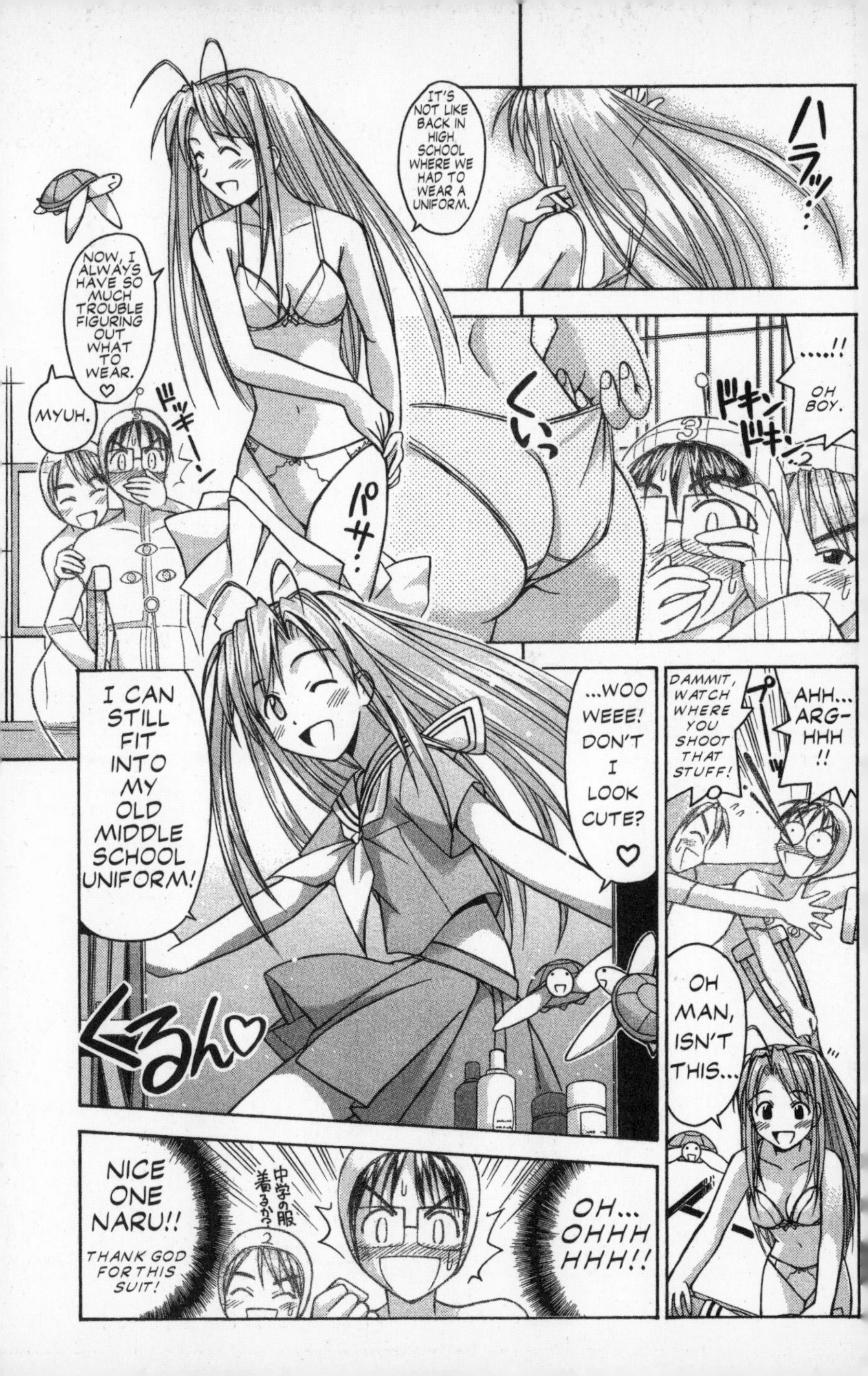

ハラッ…
IT'S NOT LIKE BACK IN HIGH SCHOOL WHERE WE HAD TO WEAR A UNIFORM.
....!!
OH BOY.
ドキン ドキン
くいっ
NOW, I ALWAYS HAVE SO MUCH TROUBLE FIGURING OUT WHAT TO WEAR. ♡
ドッキーン
MYUH.
パサ…
...WOO WEEE! DON'T I LOOK CUTE? ♡
I CAN STILL FIT INTO MY OLD MIDDLE SCHOOL UNIFORM!
くるん♡
AHH... ARG-HHH!!
DAMMIT, WATCH WHERE YOU SHOOT THAT STUFF!
OH MAN, ISN'T THIS...
OH... OHHHHHH!!
中学の服着るかっ
NICE ONE NARU!!
THANK GOD FOR THIS SUIT!

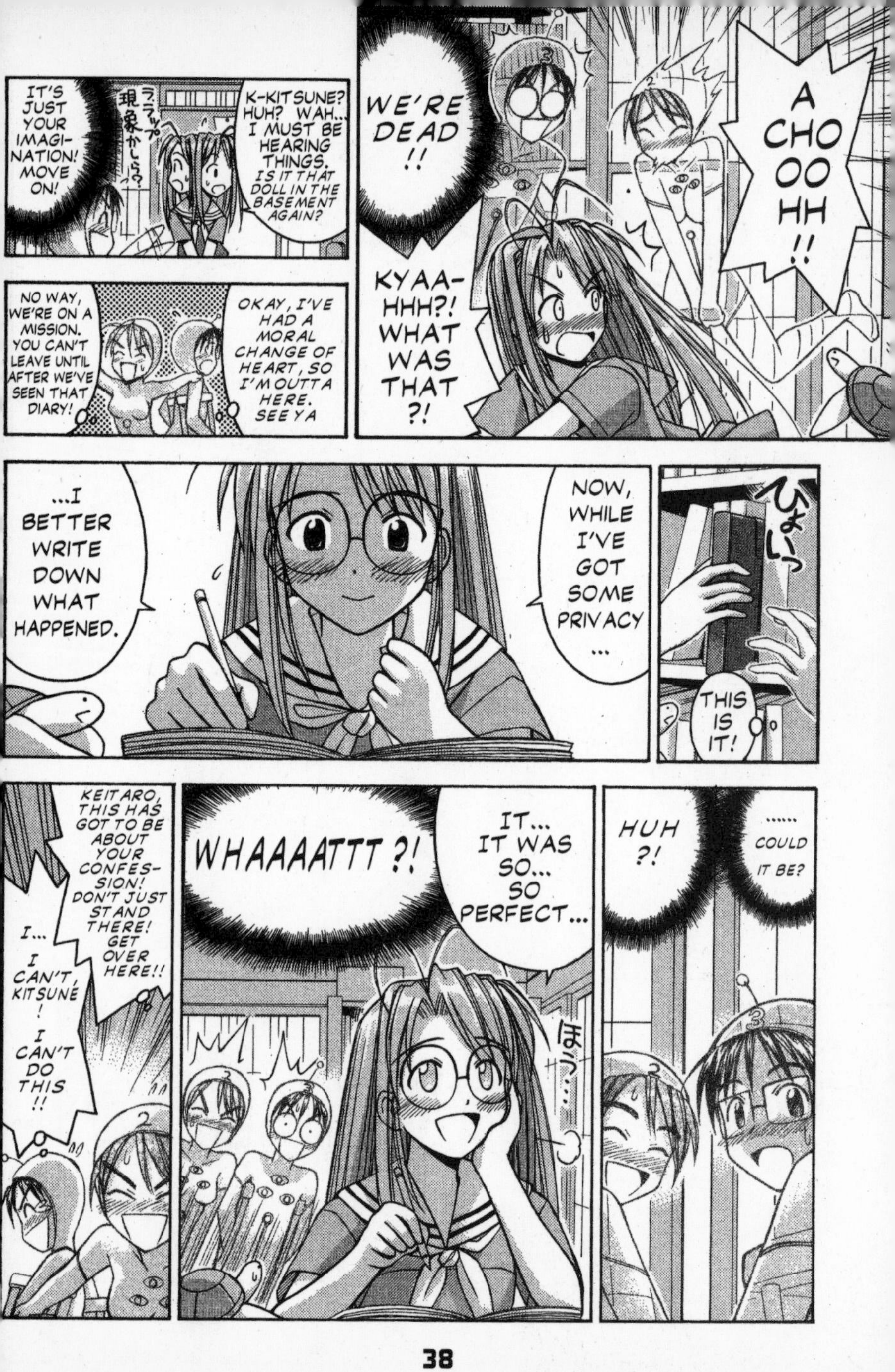
A CHOOOHH!!
WE'RE DEAD!!
KYAA-HHH?! WHAT WAS THAT?!
K-KITSUNE? HUH? WAH... I MUST BE HEARING THINGS. IS IT THAT DOLL IN THE BASEMENT AGAIN?
ラ、ラップ現象かしら?
IT'S JUST YOUR IMAGINATION! MOVE ON!
OKAY, I'VE HAD A MORAL CHANGE OF HEART, SO I'M OUTTA HERE. SEE YA
NO WAY, WE'RE ON A MISSION. YOU CAN'T LEAVE UNTIL AFTER WE'VE SEEN THAT DIARY!
ひょいっ
THIS IS IT!
NOW, WHILE I'VE GOT SOME PRIVACY...
...I BETTER WRITE DOWN WHAT HAPPENED.
......COULD IT BE?
HUH?!
IT... IT WAS SO... SO PERFECT...
ほう…
WHAAAATTT?!
KEITARO, THIS HAS GOT TO BE ABOUT YOUR CONFESSION! DON'T JUST STAND THERE! GET OVER HERE!!
I... I CAN'T, KITSUNE! I CAN'T DO THIS!!

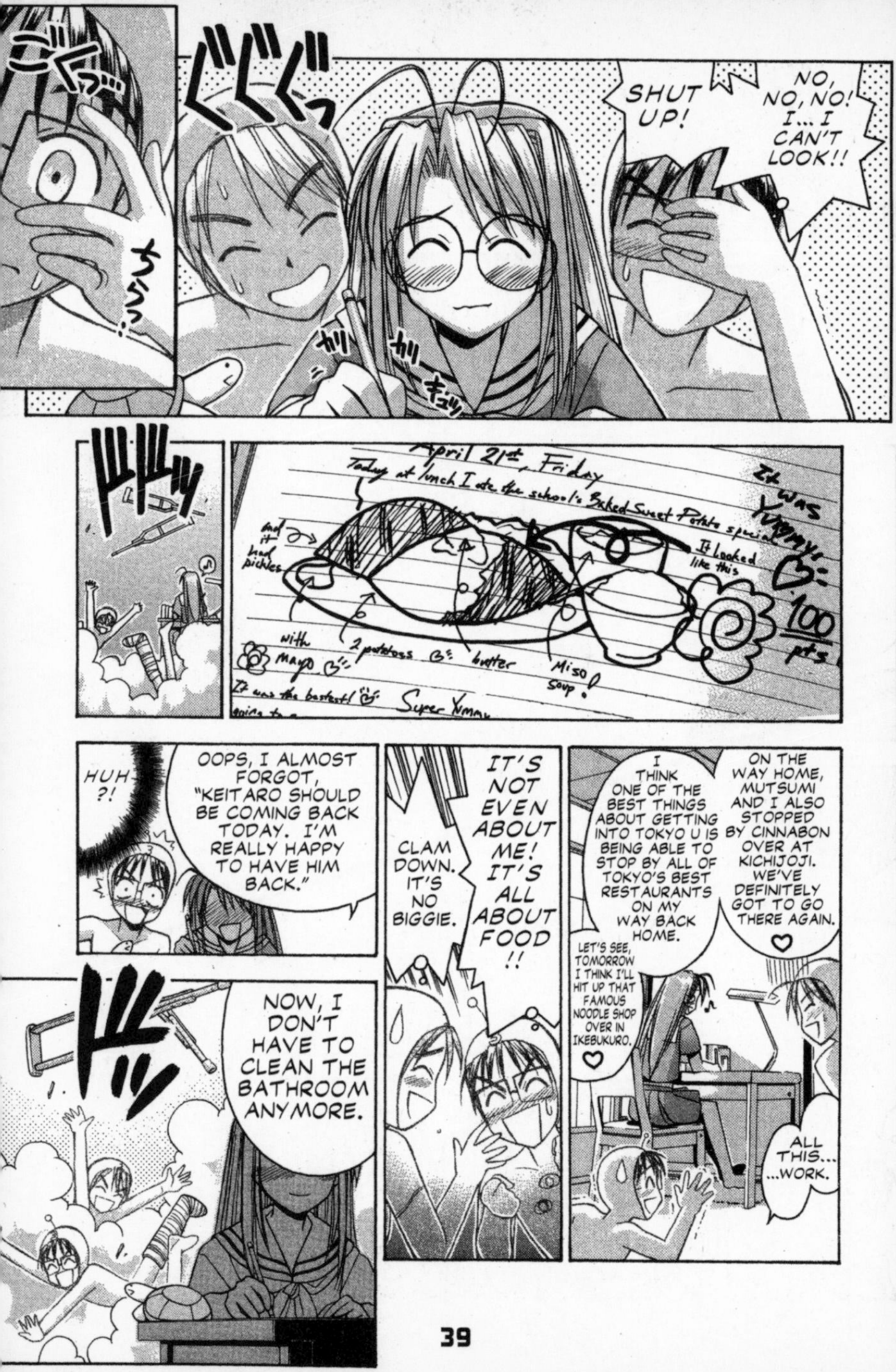
NO, NO, NO! I... I CAN'T LOOK!!
SHUT UP!
April 21st, Friday
Today at lunch I ate the school's Baked Sweet Potato special
It was Yummy!
It looked like this
100 pts
And it had pickles
with mayo
2 potatoes
butter
Miso soup!
It was the bestest!
Super Yummy
ON THE WAY HOME, MUTSUMI AND I ALSO STOPPED BY CINNABON OVER AT KICHIJOJI. WE'VE DEFINITELY GOT TO GO THERE AGAIN. ♡
I THINK ONE OF THE BEST THINGS ABOUT GETTING INTO TOKYO U IS BEING ABLE TO STOP BY ALL OF TOKYO'S BEST RESTAURANTS ON MY WAY BACK HOME.
LET'S SEE, TOMORROW I THINK I'LL HIT UP THAT FAMOUS NOODLE SHOP OVER IN IKEBUKURO. ♡
ALL THIS... ...WORK.
IT'S NOT EVEN ABOUT ME! IT'S ALL ABOUT FOOD!!
CLAM DOWN. IT'S NO BIGGIE.
OOPS, I ALMOST FORGOT, "KEITARO SHOULD BE COMING BACK TODAY. I'M REALLY HAPPY TO HAVE HIM BACK."
HUH?!
NOW, I DON'T HAVE TO CLEAN THE BATHROOM ANYMORE.

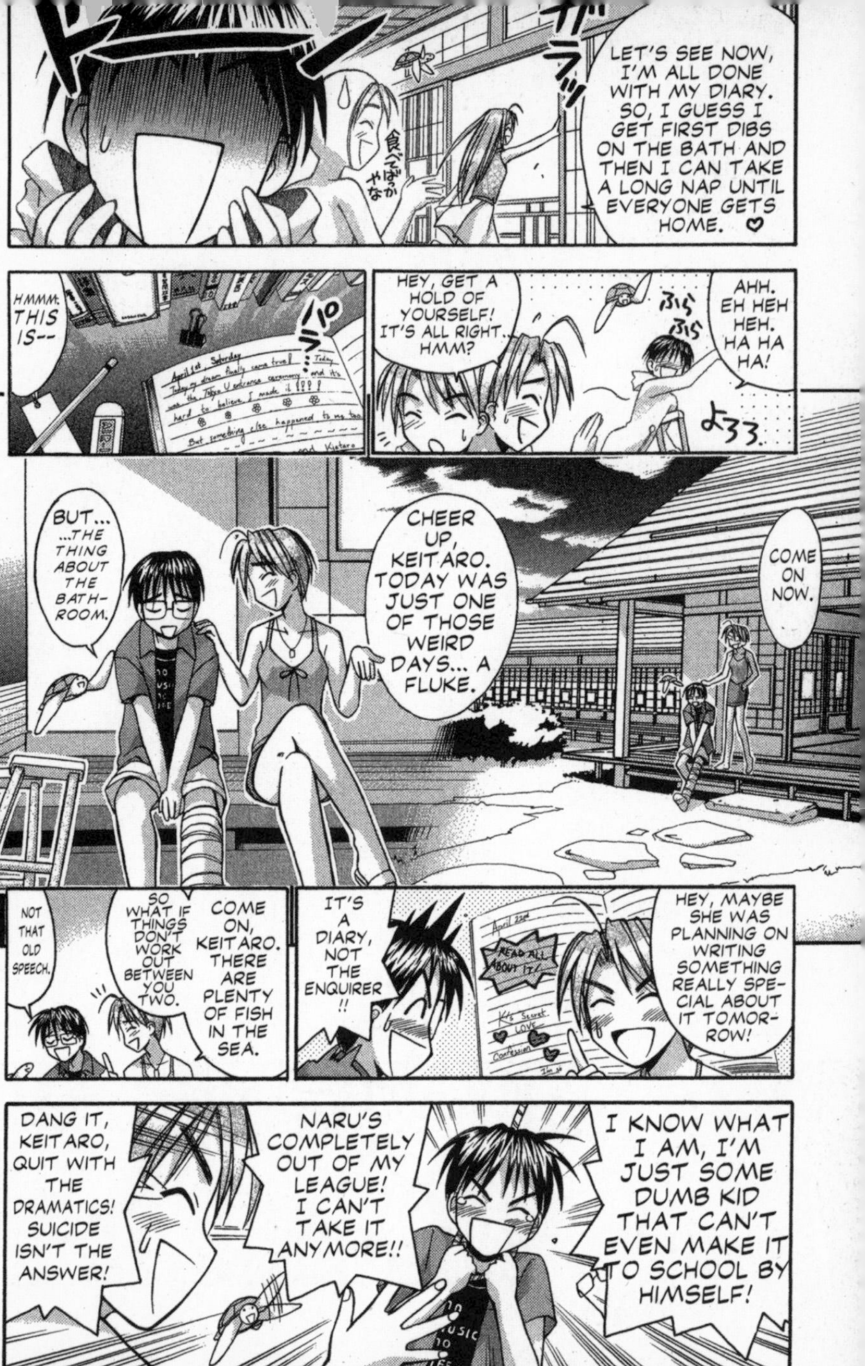
LET'S SEE NOW, I'M ALL DONE WITH MY DIARY. SO, I GUESS I GET FIRST DIBS ON THE BATH AND THEN I CAN TAKE A LONG NAP UNTIL EVERYONE GETS HOME. ♡
食べてばっかやな
AHH. EH HEH HEH. HA HA HA!
ふらふら
HEY, GET A HOLD OF YOURSELF! IT'S ALL RIGHT.. HMM?
よろろ
パラ
HMMM. THIS IS--
COME ON NOW.
CHEER UP, KEITARO. TODAY WAS JUST ONE OF THOSE WEIRD DAYS... A FLUKE.
BUT... ...THE THING ABOUT THE BATHROOM.
HEY, MAYBE SHE WAS PLANNING ON WRITING SOMETHING REALLY SPECIAL ABOUT IT TOMORROW!
April 22nd
READ ALL ABOUT IT!
K's Secret LOVE Confession
IT'S A DIARY, NOT THE ENQUIRER!!
COME ON, KEITARO. THERE ARE PLENTY OF FISH IN THE SEA.
SO WHAT IF THINGS DON'T WORK OUT BETWEEN YOU TWO.
NOT THAT OLD SPEECH.
I KNOW WHAT I AM, I'M JUST SOME DUMB KID THAT CAN'T EVEN MAKE IT TO SCHOOL BY HIMSELF!
NARU'S COMPLETELY OUT OF MY LEAGUE! I CAN'T TAKE IT ANYMORE!!
DANG IT, KEITARO, QUIT WITH THE DRAMATICS! SUICIDE ISN'T THE ANSWER!

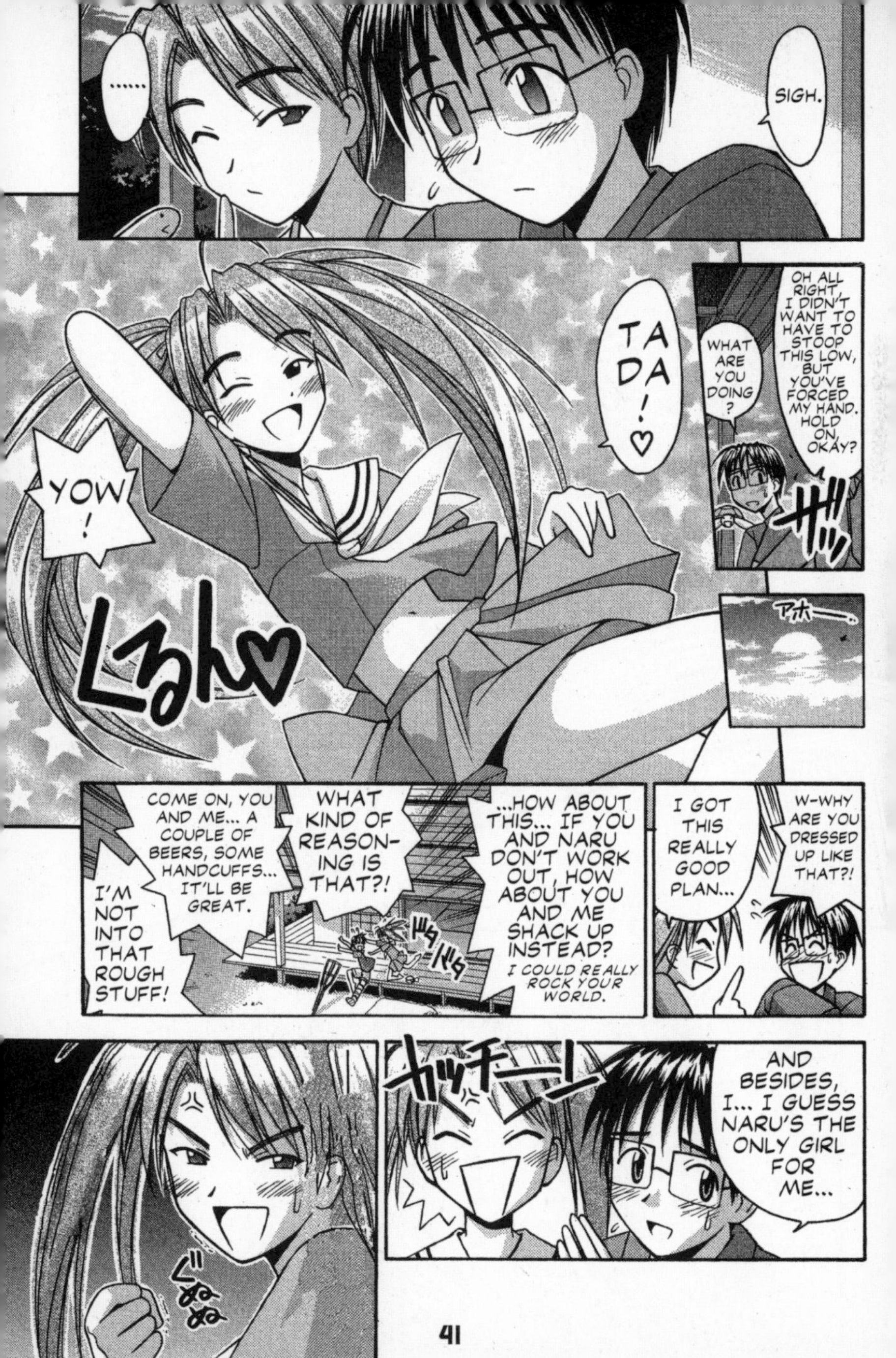

SIGH.
......
OH ALL RIGHT, I DIDN'T WANT TO HAVE TO STOOP THIS LOW, BUT YOU'VE FORCED MY HAND. HOLD ON, OKAY?
WHAT ARE YOU DOING?
ザッ
アホー...
TA DA! ♡
YOW!
くるん♡
W-WHY ARE YOU DRESSED UP LIKE THAT?!
I GOT THIS REALLY GOOD PLAN...
...HOW ABOUT THIS... IF YOU AND NARU DON'T WORK OUT, HOW ABOUT YOU AND ME SHACK UP INSTEAD?
I COULD REALLY ROCK YOUR WORLD.
WHAT KIND OF REASONING IS THAT?!
COME ON, YOU AND ME... A COUPLE OF BEERS, SOME HANDCUFFS... IT'LL BE GREAT.
I'M NOT INTO THAT ROUGH STUFF!
バタ バタ
AND BESIDES, I... I GUESS NARU'S THE ONLY GIRL FOR ME...
カッチーン!
ぐぬぬぬ

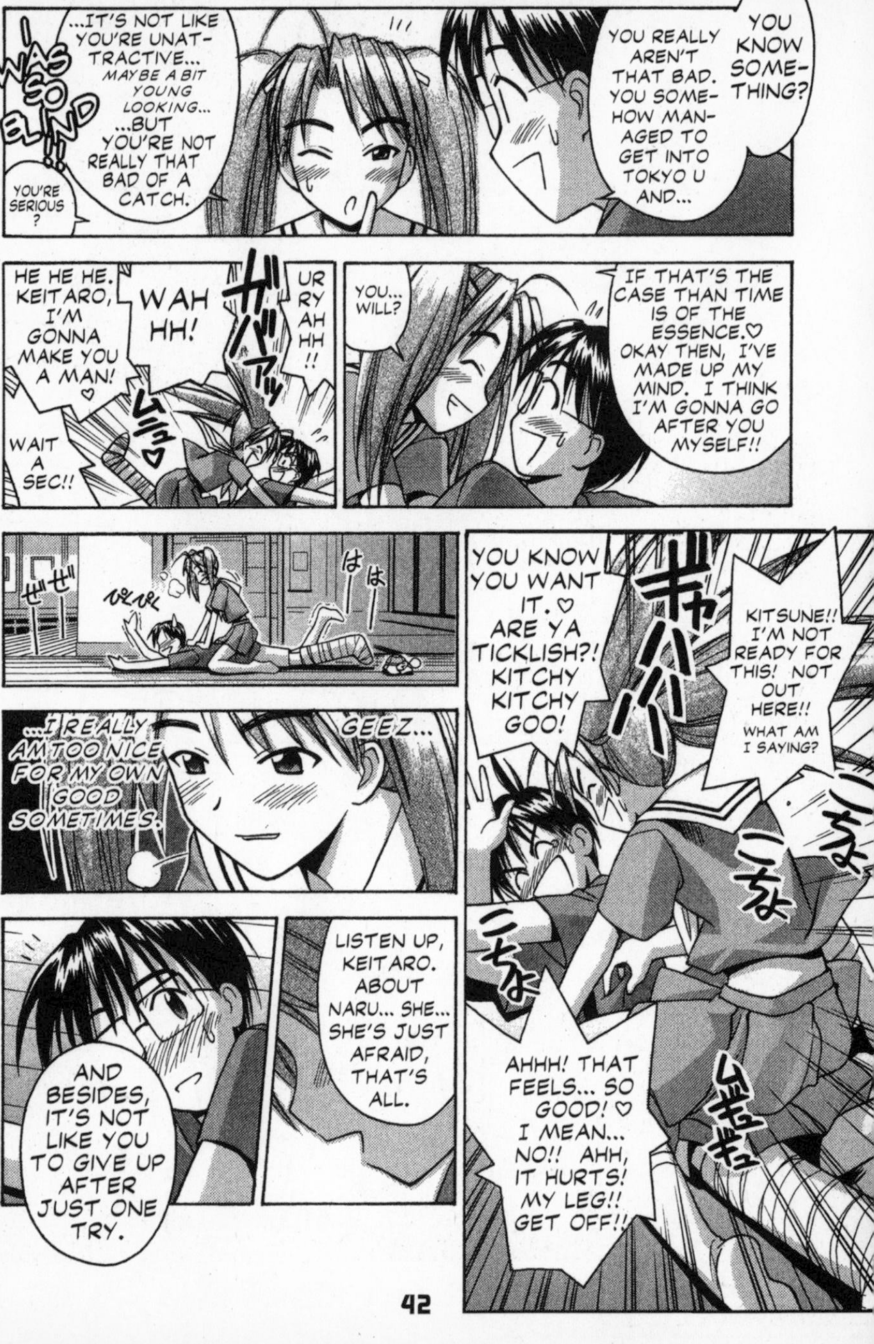
YOU KNOW SOME-THING?
YOU REALLY AREN'T THAT BAD. YOU SOME-HOW MAN-AGED TO GET INTO TOKYO U AND...
...IT'S NOT LIKE YOU'RE UNAT-TRACTIVE... MAYBE A BIT YOUNG LOOKING... ...BUT YOU'RE NOT REALLY THAT BAD OF A CATCH.
I WAS SO BLIND!!
YOU'RE SERIOUS?
IF THAT'S THE CASE THAN TIME IS OF THE ESSENCE.♡ OKAY THEN, I'VE MADE UP MY MIND. I THINK I'M GONNA GO AFTER YOU MYSELF!!
YOU... WILL?
URRYAHHH!!
ガバァッ
WAH HH!
HE HE HE. KEITARO, I'M GONNA MAKE YOU A MAN! ♡
ムニュ♡
WAIT A SEC!!
KITSUNE!! I'M NOT READY FOR THIS! NOT OUT HERE!!
WHAT AM I SAYING?
ギャハハハ
YOU KNOW YOU WANT IT.♡ ARE YA TICKLISH?! KITCHY KITCHY GOO!
こちょ
こちょ
こちょ
AHHH! THAT FEELS... SO GOOD! ♡ I MEAN... NO!! AHH, IT HURTS! MY LEG!! GET OFF!!
はーはー
ぜーぜー
ぴくぴく
GEEZ...
...I REALLY AM TOO NICE FOR MY OWN GOOD SOMETIMES.
LISTEN UP, KEITARO. ABOUT NARU... SHE... SHE'S JUST AFRAID, THAT'S ALL.
AND BESIDES, IT'S NOT LIKE YOU TO GIVE UP AFTER JUST ONE TRY.

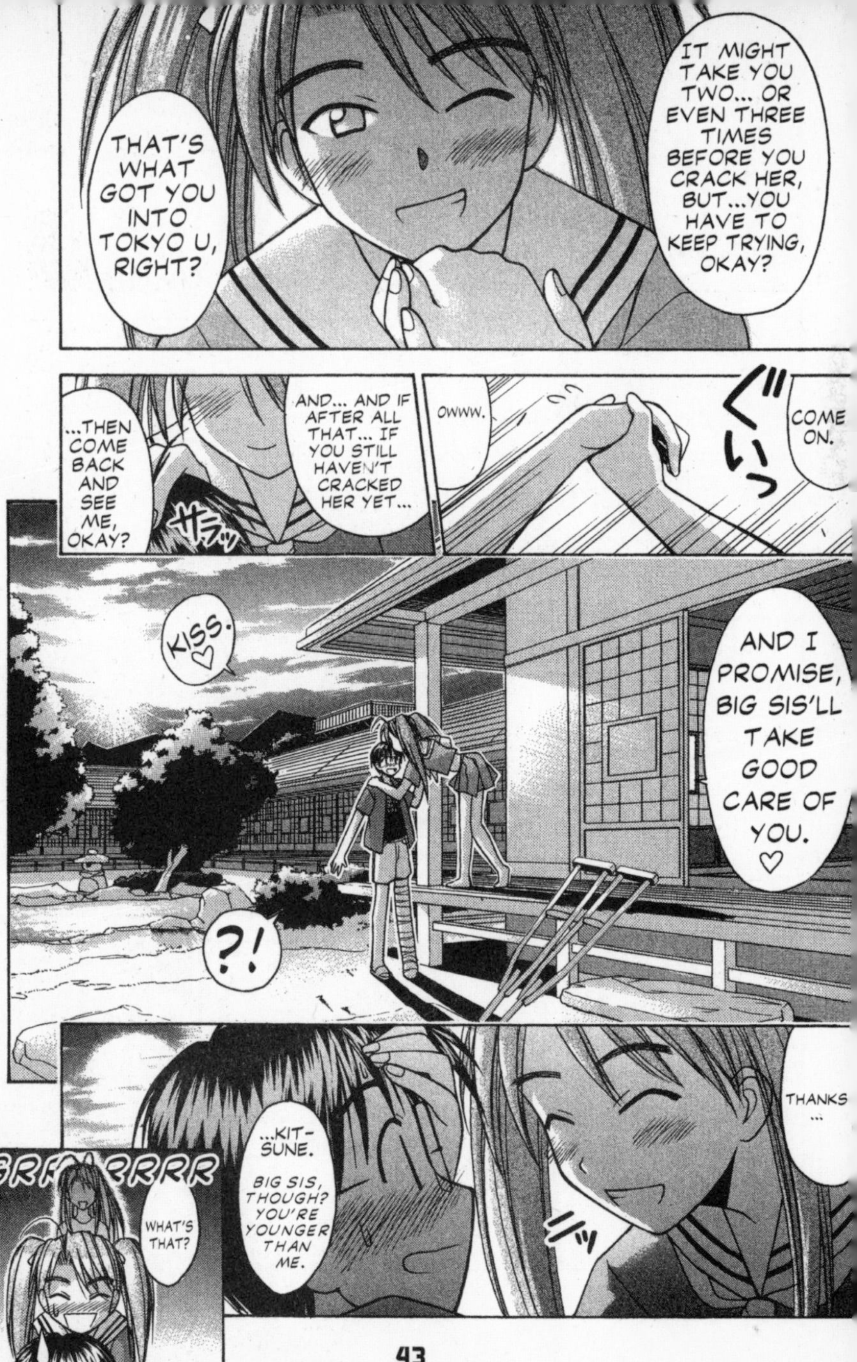
IT MIGHT TAKE YOU TWO... OR EVEN THREE TIMES BEFORE YOU CRACK HER, BUT...YOU HAVE TO KEEP TRYING, OKAY?
THAT'S WHAT GOT YOU INTO TOKYO U, RIGHT?
COME ON.
ぐいっ
OWWW.
AND... AND IF AFTER ALL THAT... IF YOU STILL HAVEN'T CRACKED HER YET...
...THEN COME BACK AND SEE ME, OKAY?
AND I PROMISE, BIG SIS'LL TAKE GOOD CARE OF YOU. ♡
KISS. ♡
?!
THANKS...
...KIT-SUNE.
BIG SIS, THOUGH? YOU'RE YOUNGER THAN ME.
WHAT'S THAT?

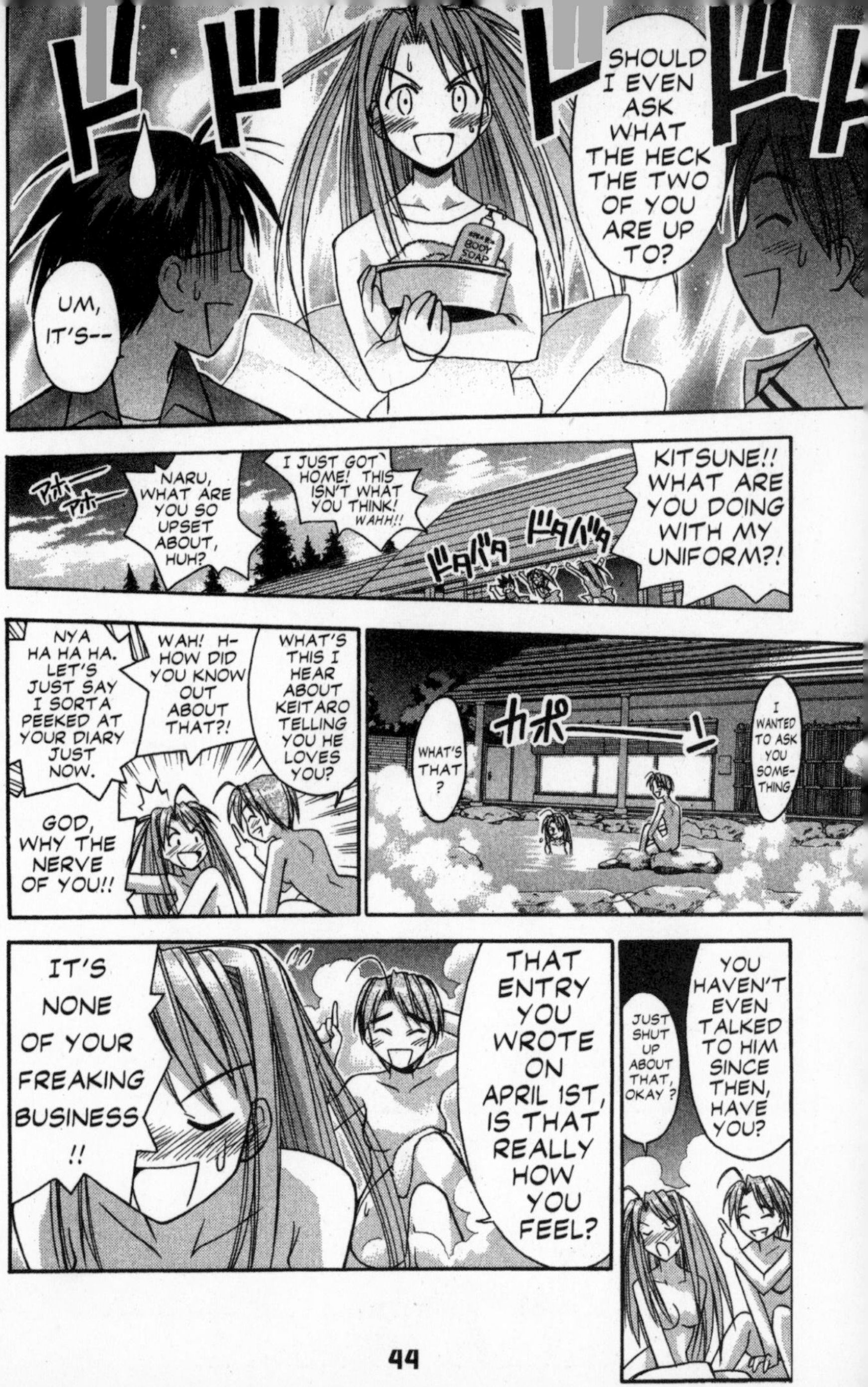
ドドドド
SHOULD I EVEN ASK WHAT THE HECK THE TWO OF YOU ARE UP TO?
UM, IT'S--
KITSUNE!! WHAT ARE YOU DOING WITH MY UNIFORM?!
ドタバタ
ドタバタ
I JUST GOT HOME! THIS ISN'T WHAT YOU THINK! WAHH!!
NARU, WHAT ARE YOU SO UPSET ABOUT, HUH?
アホー アホー
I WANTED TO ASK YOU SOME-THING
カポー
WHAT'S THAT?
WHAT'S THIS I HEAR ABOUT KEITARO TELLING YOU HE LOVES YOU?
WAH! H-HOW DID YOU KNOW OUT ABOUT THAT?!
NYA HA HA HA. LET'S JUST SAY I SORTA PEEKED AT YOUR DIARY JUST NOW.
GOD, WHY THE NERVE OF YOU!!
YOU HAVEN'T EVEN TALKED TO HIM SINCE THEN, HAVE YOU?
JUST SHUT UP ABOUT THAT, OKAY?
THAT ENTRY YOU WROTE ON APRIL 1ST, IS THAT REALLY HOW YOU FEEL?
IT'S NONE OF YOUR FREAKING BUSINESS!!

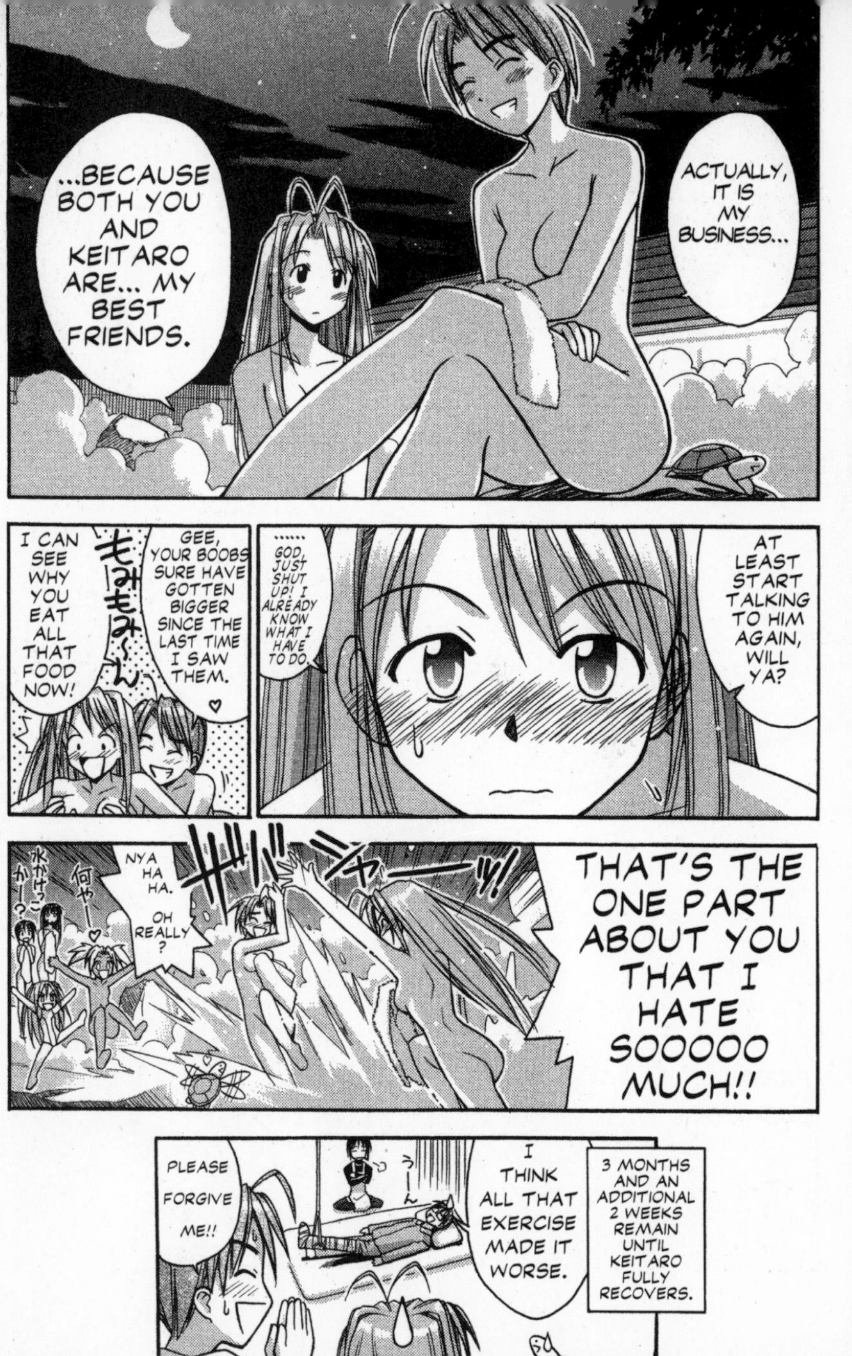
ACTUALLY, IT IS MY BUSINESS...
...BECAUSE BOTH YOU AND KEITARO ARE... MY BEST FRIENDS.
AT LEAST START TALKING TO HIM AGAIN, WILL YA?
...... GOD, JUST SHUT UP! I ALREADY KNOW WHAT I HAVE TO DO.
GEE, YOUR BOOBS SURE HAVE GOTTEN BIGGER SINCE THE LAST TIME I SAW THEM. ♡
もみもみ～ん
I CAN SEE WHY YOU EAT ALL THAT FOOD NOW!
THAT'S THE ONE PART ABOUT YOU THAT I HATE SOOOOO MUCH!!
ザバシャーーッ!
NYA HA HA.
OH REALLY?
何やー♡
水かけっこかー?
3 MONTHS AND AN ADDITIONAL 2 WEEKS REMAIN UNTIL KEITARO FULLY RECOVERS.
I THINK ALL THAT EXERCISE MADE IT WORSE.
うーん
PLEASE FORGIVE ME!!

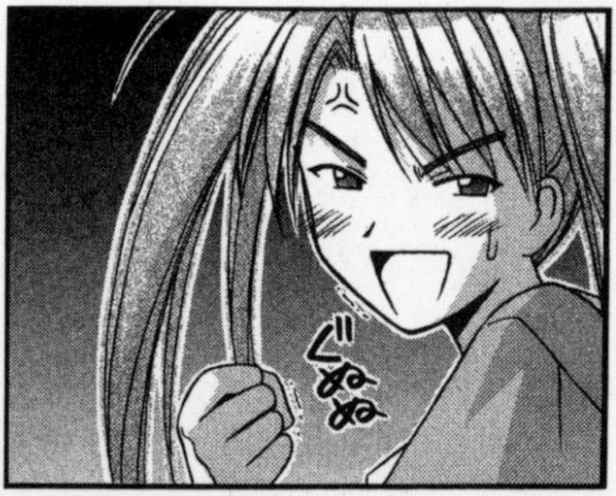
ぐぬぬ

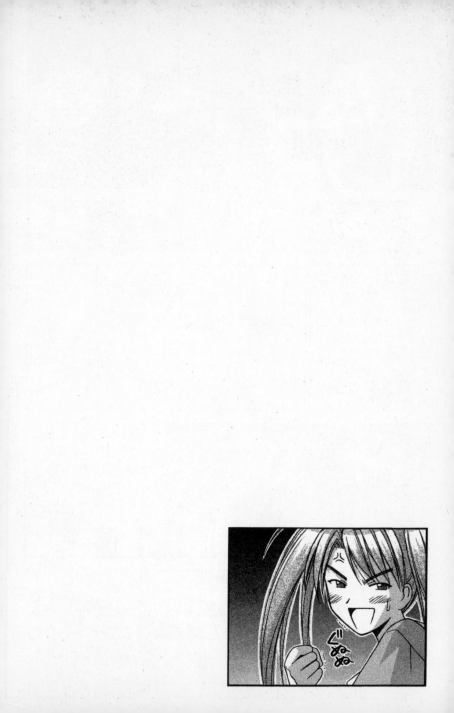

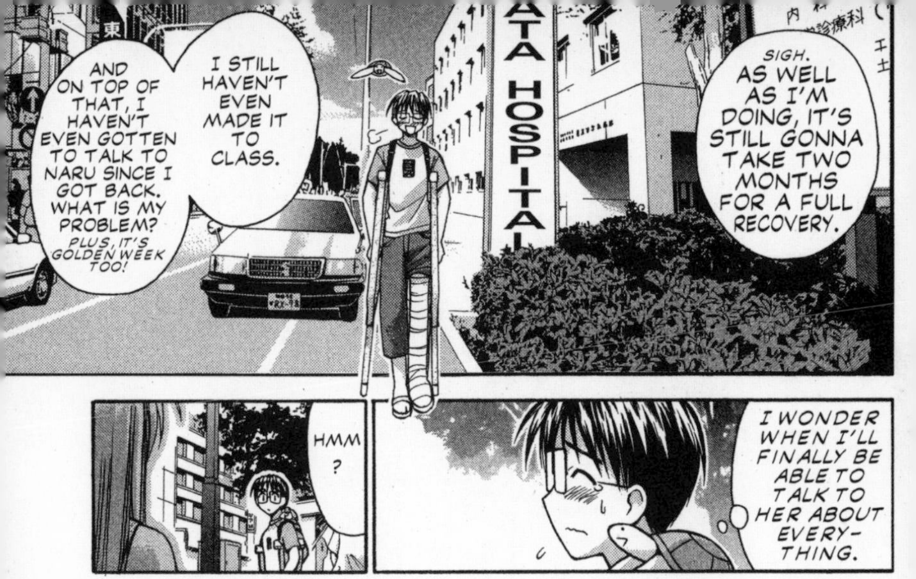
ATA HOSPITAL
SIGH. AS WELL AS I'M DOING, IT'S STILL GONNA TAKE TWO MONTHS FOR A FULL RECOVERY.
I STILL HAVEN'T EVEN MADE IT TO CLASS.
AND ON TOP OF THAT, I HAVEN'T EVEN GOTTEN TO TALK TO NARU SINCE I GOT BACK. WHAT IS MY PROBLEM?
PLUS, IT'S GOLDEN WEEK TOO!
I WONDER WHEN I'LL FINALLY BE ABLE TO TALK TO HER ABOUT EVERY-THING.
HMM ?

HINATA.72 Burn Up Blade: Part 1

Big Sister Comes to Tokyo!

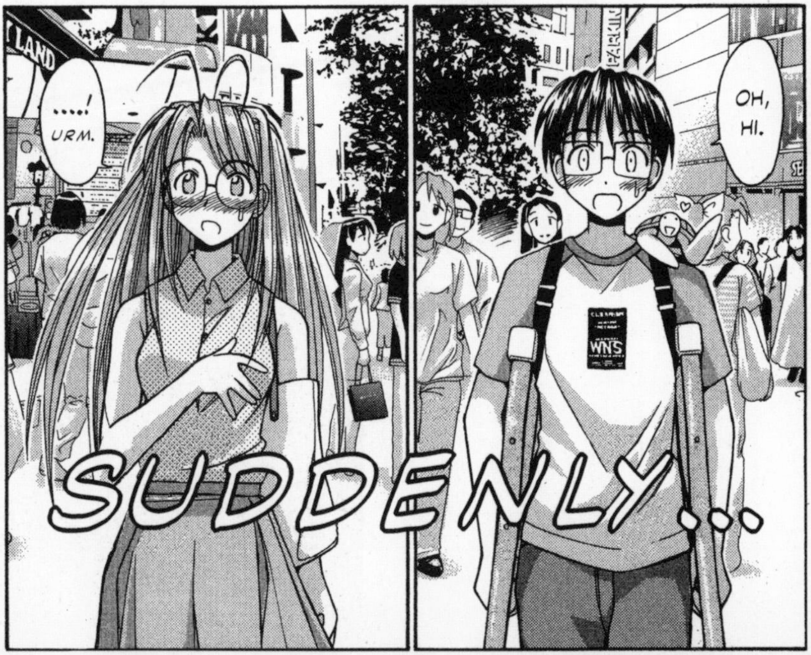
OH, HI.
....! URM.
SUDDENLY...

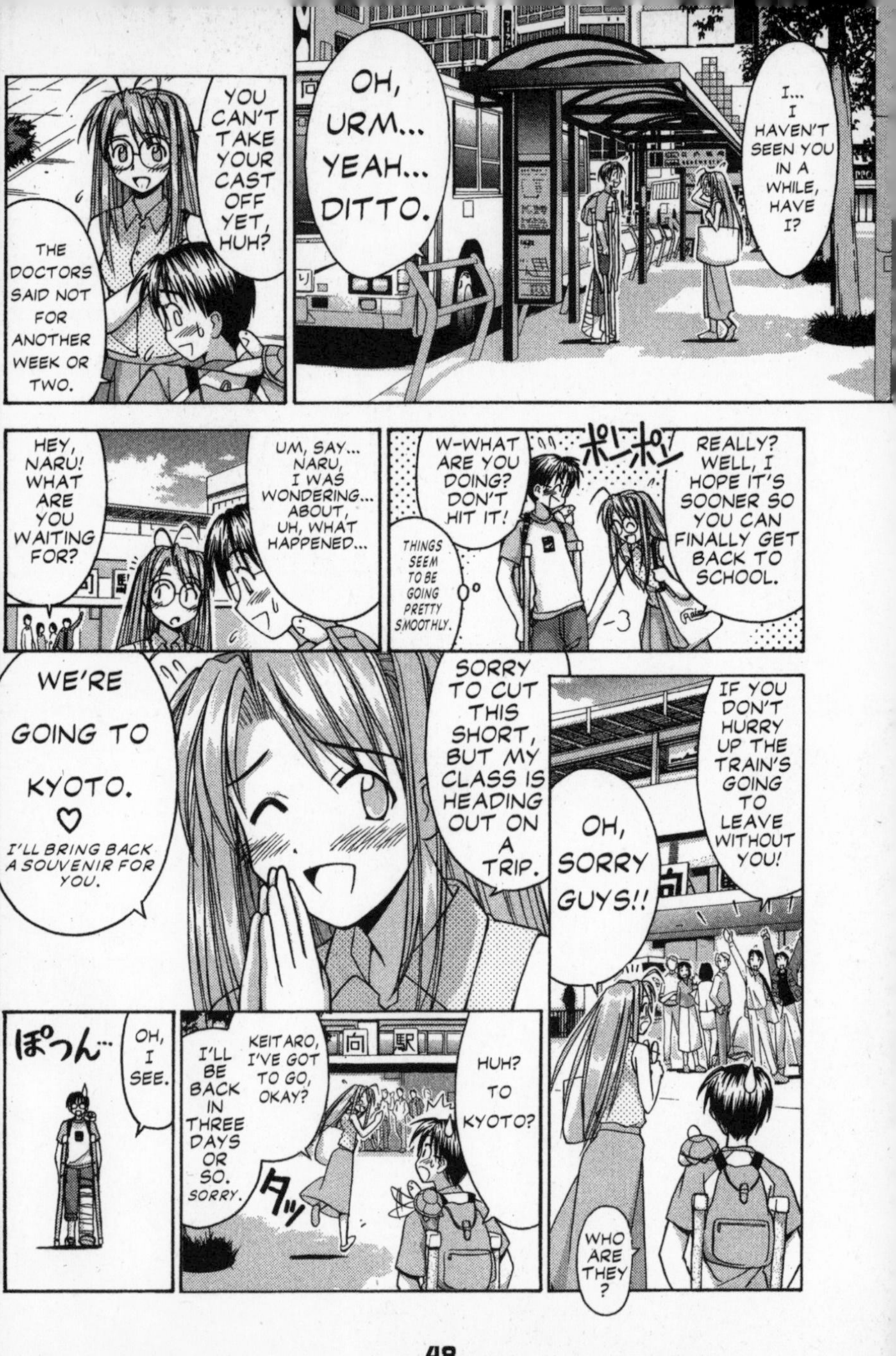
I... I HAVEN'T SEEN YOU IN A WHILE, HAVE I?
OH, URM... YEAH... DITTO.
YOU CAN'T TAKE YOUR CAST OFF YET, HUH?
THE DOCTORS SAID NOT FOR ANOTHER WEEK OR TWO.
REALLY? WELL, I HOPE IT'S SOONER SO YOU CAN FINALLY GET BACK TO SCHOOL.
ポンポン
W-WHAT ARE YOU DOING? DON'T HIT IT!
THINGS SEEM TO BE GOING PRETTY SMOOTHLY.
UM, SAY... NARU, I WAS WONDERING... ABOUT, UH, WHAT HAPPENED...
HEY, NARU! WHAT ARE YOU WAITING FOR?
IF YOU DON'T HURRY UP THE TRAIN'S GOING TO LEAVE WITHOUT YOU!
OH, SORRY GUYS!!
WHO ARE THEY?
SORRY TO CUT THIS SHORT, BUT MY CLASS IS HEADING OUT ON A TRIP.
WE'RE GOING TO KYOTO. ♡
I'LL BRING BACK A SOUVENIR FOR YOU.
HUH? TO KYOTO?
KEITARO, I'VE GOT TO GO, OKAY?
I'LL BE BACK IN THREE DAYS OR SO. SORRY.
タッ
OH, I SEE.
ぽつん…

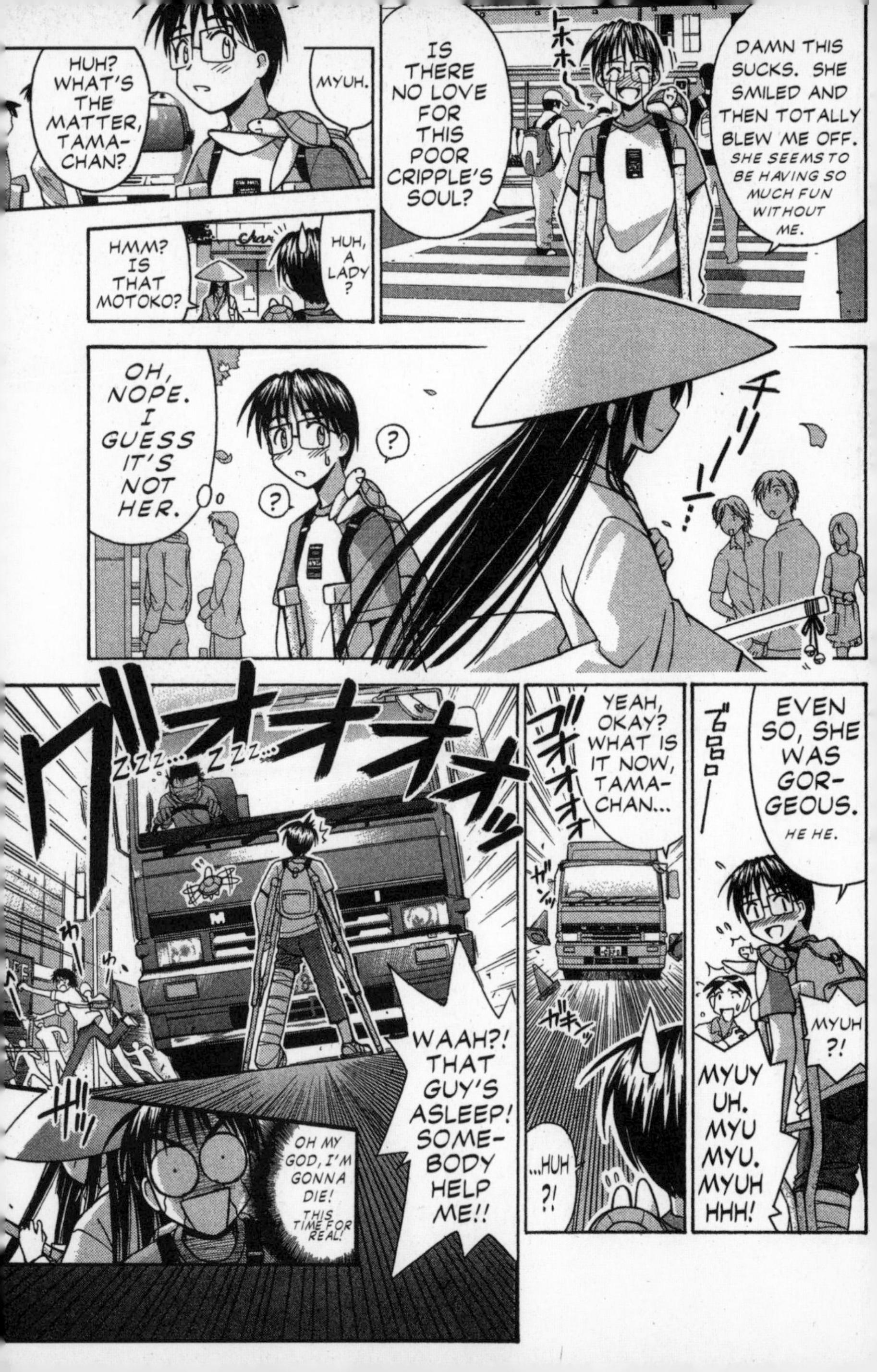
DAMN THIS SUCKS. SHE SMILED AND THEN TOTALLY BLEW ME OFF. SHE SEEMS TO BE HAVING SO MUCH FUN WITHOUT ME.
トホホ
IS THERE NO LOVE FOR THIS POOR CRIPPLE'S SOUL?
MYUH.
HUH? WHAT'S THE MATTER, TAMA-CHAN?
HUH, A LADY?
HMM? IS THAT MOTOKO?
チリーン
OH, NOPE. I GUESS IT'S NOT HER.
?
?
EVEN SO, SHE WAS GORGEOUS. HE HE.
MYUH ?!
MYUY UH. MYU MYU. MYUH HHH!
YEAH, OKAY? WHAT IS IT NOW, TAMA-CHAN...
...HUH ?!
ZZZ... ZZZ...
WAAH?! THAT GUY'S ASLEEP! SOMEBODY HELP ME!!
OH MY GOD, I'M GONNA DIE! THIS TIME FOR REAL!

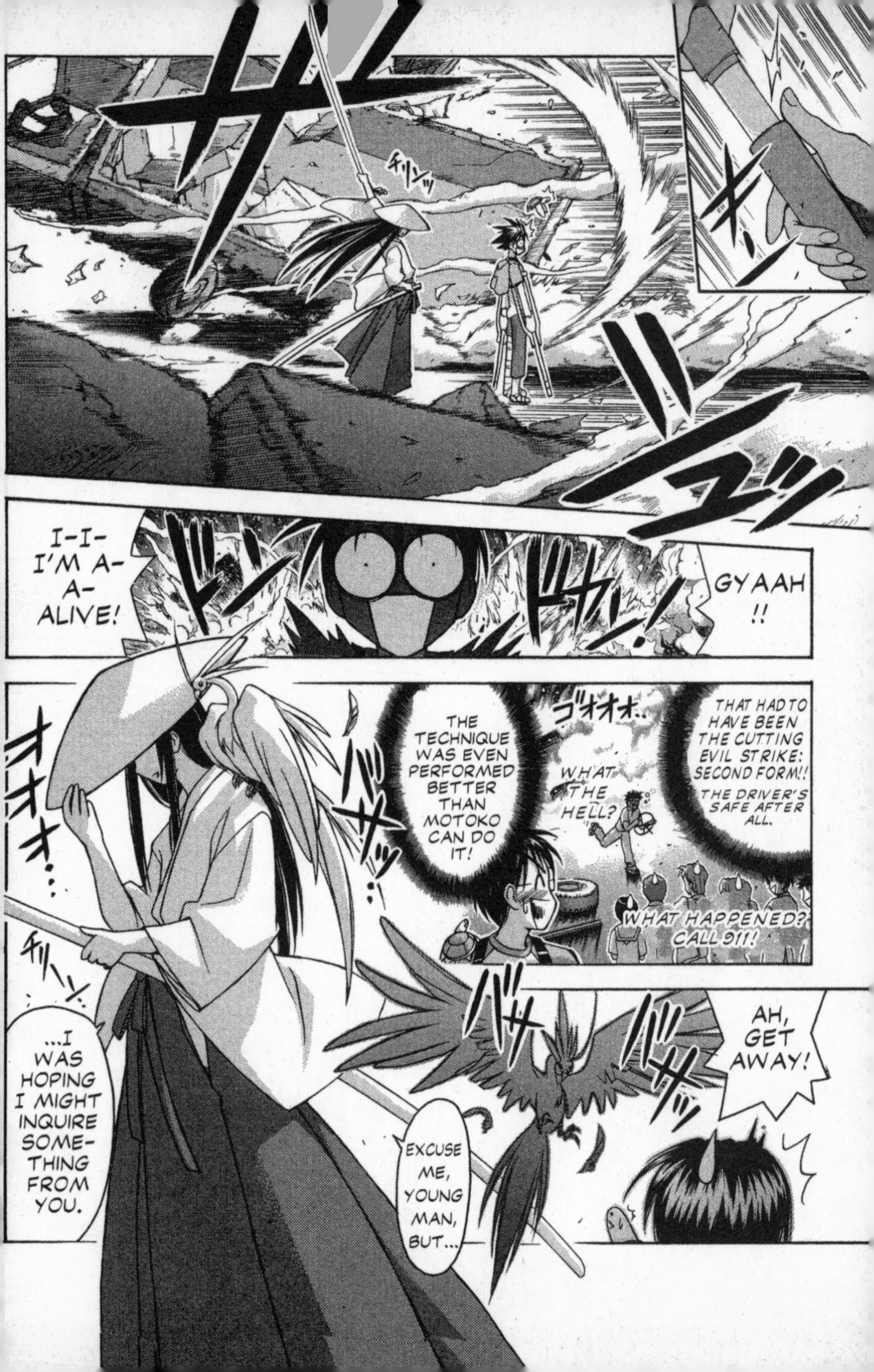

チリンッ
GYAAH !!
I-I-I'M A-A-ALIVE!
THAT HAD TO HAVE BEEN THE CUTTING EVIL STRIKE: SECOND FORM!!
THE DRIVER'S SAFE AFTER ALL.
ゴオオオ..
WHAT THE HELL?
THE TECHNIQUE WAS EVEN PERFORMED BETTER THAN MOTOKO CAN DO IT!
WHAT HAPPENED? CALL 911!
AH, GET AWAY!
EXCUSE ME, YOUNG MAN, BUT...
...I WAS HOPING I MIGHT INQUIRE SOMETHING FROM YOU.

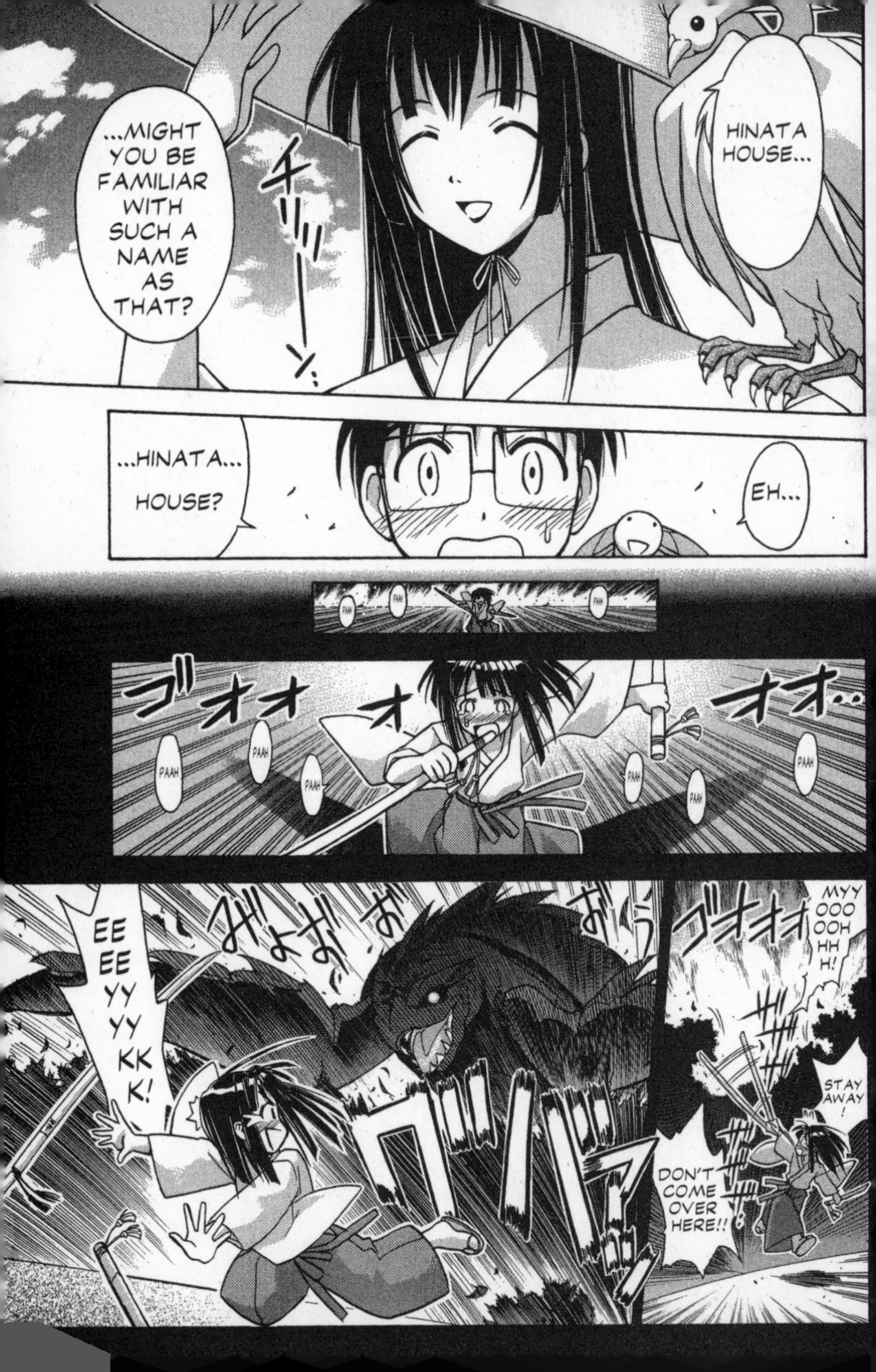
HINATA HOUSE...
...MIGHT YOU BE FAMILIAR WITH SUCH A NAME AS THAT?
EH...
...HINATA... HOUSE?
PAAH
PAAH
PAAH
PAAH
PAAH
PAAH
PAAH
PAAH
PAAH
MYYOOOOOHHHH!
STAY AWAY!
DON'T COME OVER HERE!!
EEEEYYYYKKK!

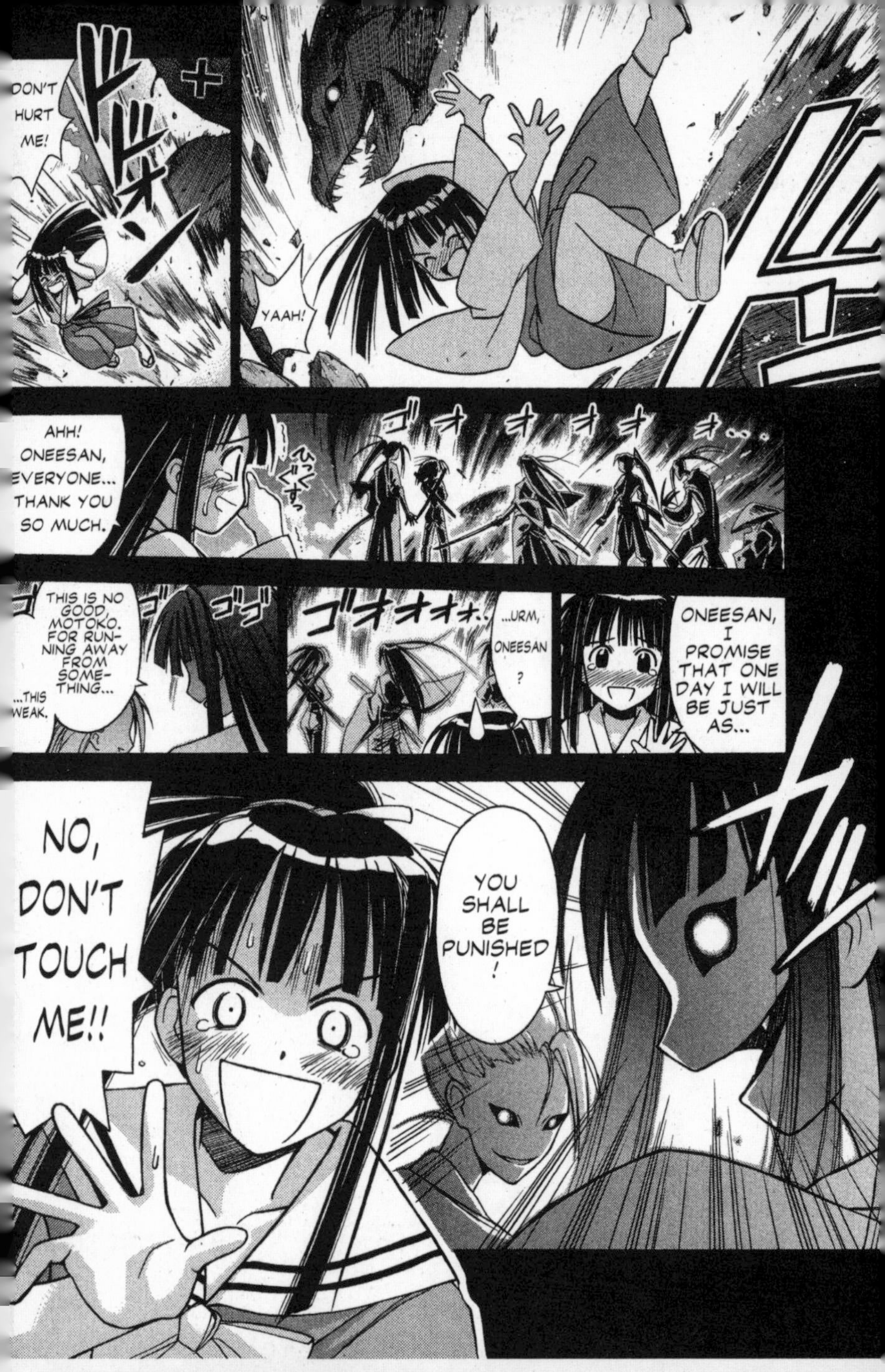
YAAH!
DON'T HURT ME!
ゴオオオオオ...
ひっくぐずっ
AHH! ONEESAN, EVERYONE... THANK YOU SO MUCH.
ONEESAN, I PROMISE THAT ONE DAY I WILL BE JUST AS...
ゴオオオォ...
...URM, ONEESAN ?
THIS IS NO GOOD, MOTOKO. FOR RUNNING AWAY FROM SOMETHING...
...THIS WEAK.
YOU SHALL BE PUNISHED !
NO, DON'T TOUCH ME!!

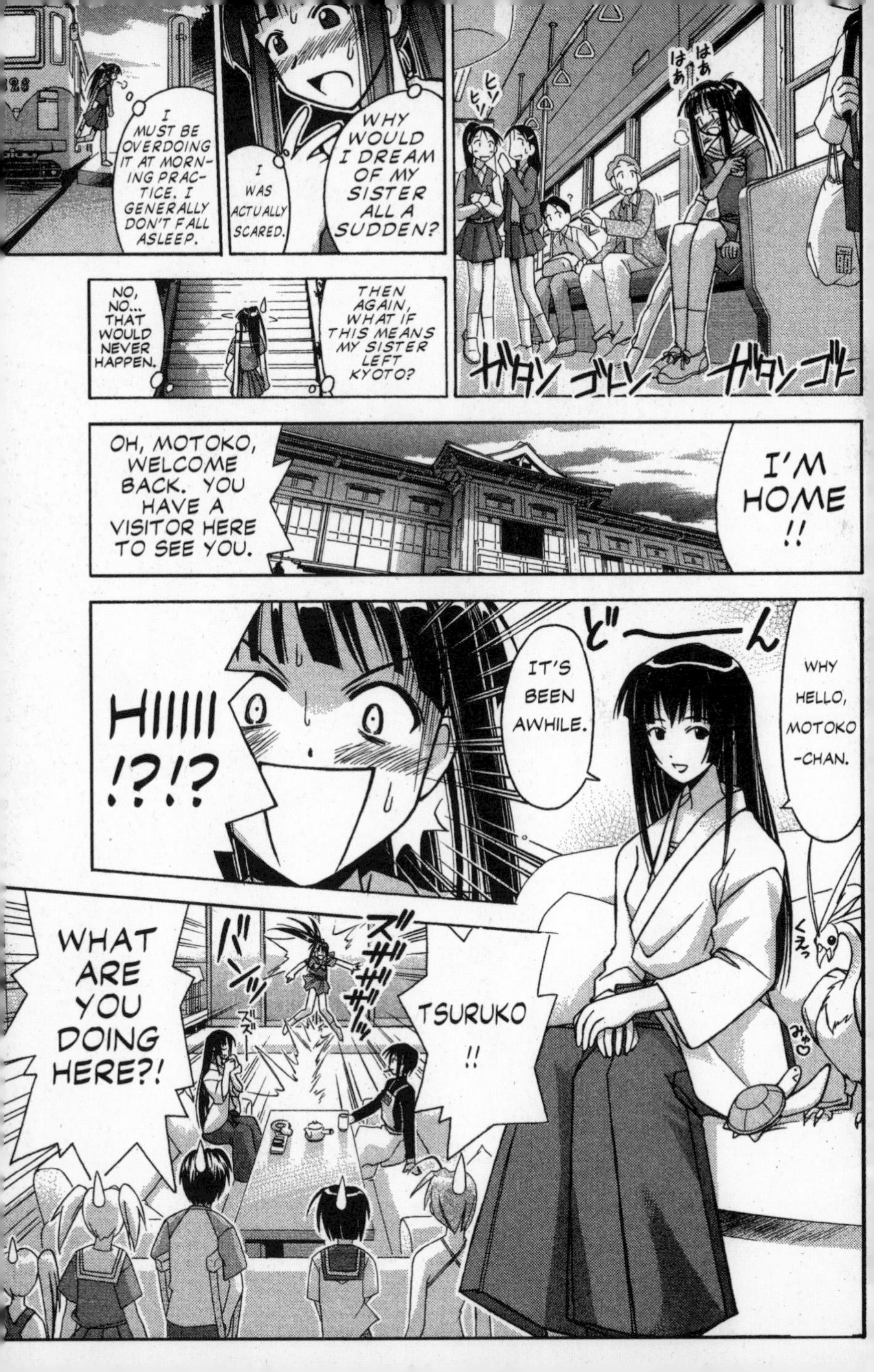
はぁ はぁ
ヒソ ヒソ
ガタン ゴトン ガタン ゴト
WHY WOULD I DREAM OF MY SISTER ALL A SUDDEN?
I WAS ACTUALLY SCARED.
I MUST BE OVERDOING IT AT MORNING PRACTICE. I GENERALLY DON'T FALL ASLEEP.
THEN AGAIN, WHAT IF THIS MEANS MY SISTER LEFT KYOTO?
NO, NO... THAT WOULD NEVER HAPPEN.
I'M HOME!!
OH, MOTOKO, WELCOME BACK. YOU HAVE A VISITOR HERE TO SEE YOU.
どーーん
WHY HELLO, MOTOKO-CHAN.
IT'S BEEN AWHILE.
HIIIII!?!?
くえっ
みゅ♡
TSURUKO!!
ズザザザッ
バンッ
ズズー
WHAT ARE YOU DOING HERE?!

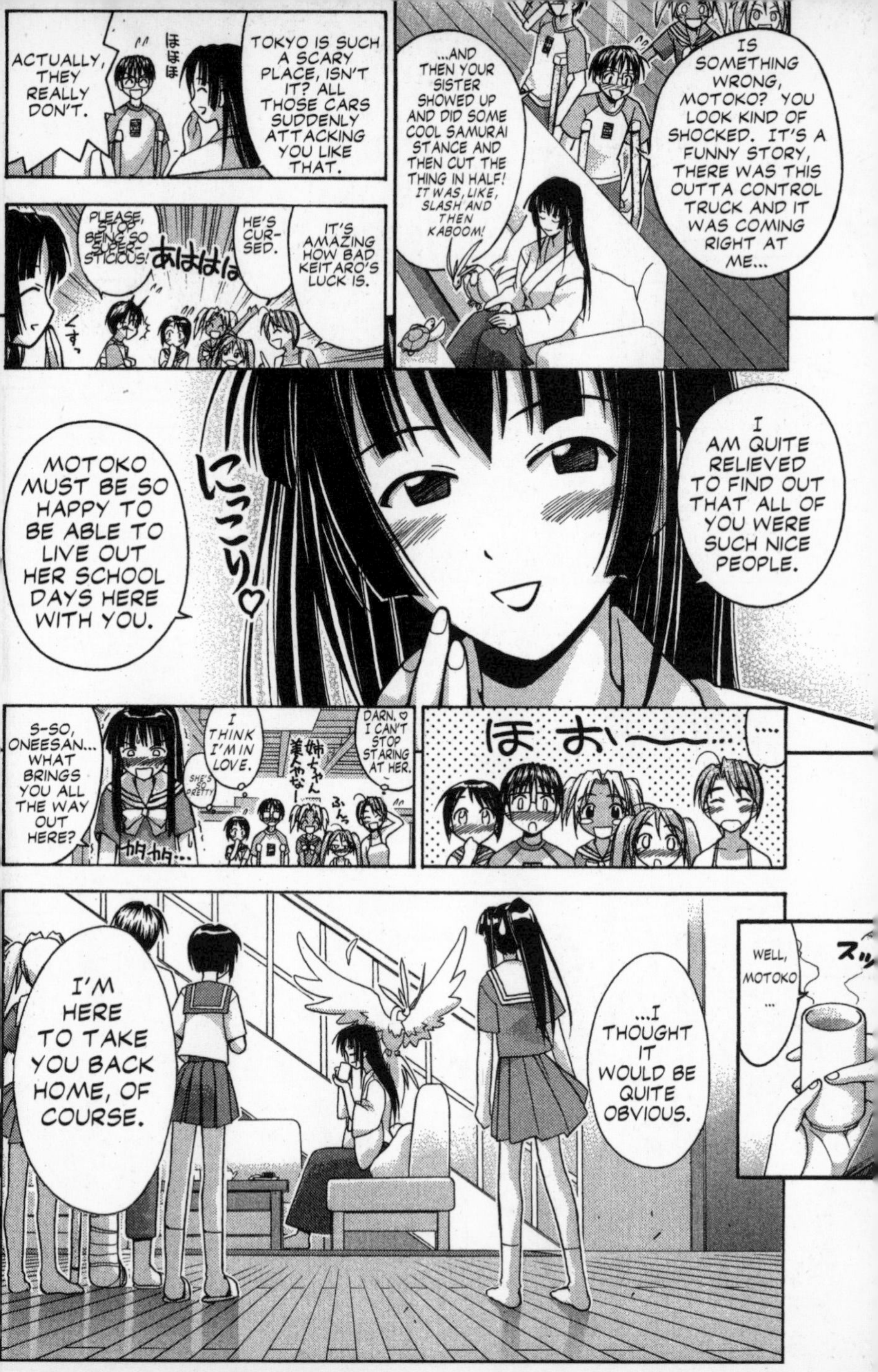
IS SOMETHING WRONG, MOTOKO? YOU LOOK KIND OF SHOCKED. IT'S A FUNNY STORY, THERE WAS THIS OUTTA CONTROL TRUCK AND IT WAS COMING RIGHT AT ME...
...AND THEN YOUR SISTER SHOWED UP AND DID SOME COOL SAMURAI STANCE AND THEN CUT THE THING IN HALF! IT WAS, LIKE, SLASH AND THEN KABOOM!
TOKYO IS SUCH A SCARY PLACE, ISN'T IT? ALL THOSE CARS SUDDENLY ATTACKING YOU LIKE THAT.
ほほほ
ACTUALLY, THEY REALLY DON'T.
IT'S AMAZING HOW BAD KEITARO'S LUCK IS.
HE'S CURSED.
あははは
PLEASE, STOP BEING SO SUPERSTICIOUS!
くすっ
I AM QUITE RELIEVED TO FIND OUT THAT ALL OF YOU WERE SUCH NICE PEOPLE.
にっこり♡
MOTOKO MUST BE SO HAPPY TO BE ABLE TO LIVE OUT HER SCHOOL DAYS HERE WITH YOU.
ほぉ～～…
....
DARN. ♡ I CAN'T STOP STARING AT HER.
姉ちゃん美人やなー
I THINK I'M IN LOVE.
SHE'S SO PRETTY.
S-SO, ONEESAN... WHAT BRINGS YOU ALL THE WAY OUT HERE?
WELL, MOTOKO...
...I THOUGHT IT WOULD BE QUITE OBVIOUS.
I'M HERE TO TAKE YOU BACK HOME, OF COURSE.

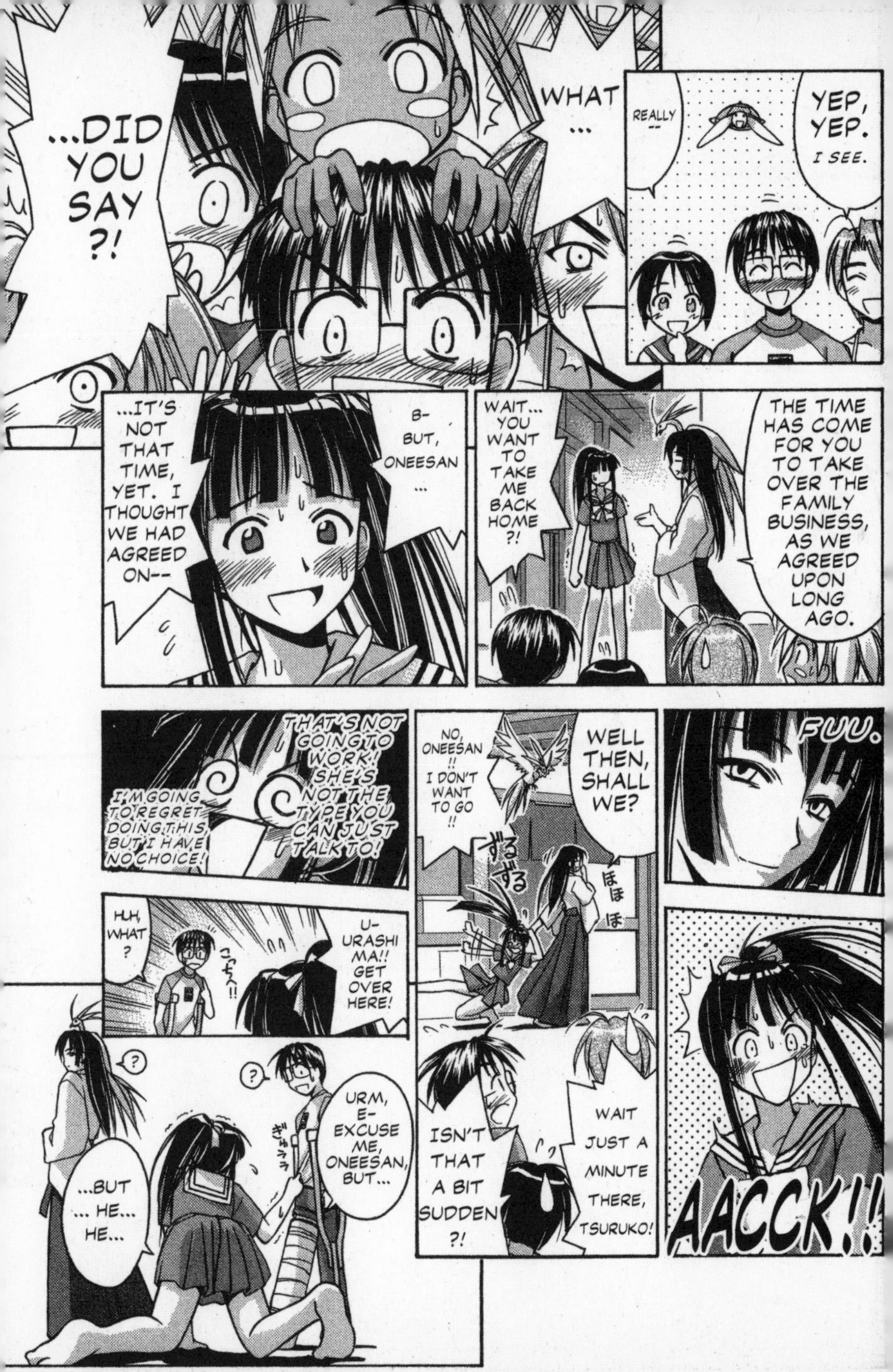
YEP, YEP.
I SEE.
REALLY --
WHAT ...
...DID YOU SAY ?!
THE TIME HAS COME FOR YOU TO TAKE OVER THE FAMILY BUSINESS, AS WE AGREED UPON LONG AGO.
WAIT... YOU WANT TO TAKE ME BACK HOME ?!
B- BUT, ONEESAN ...
...IT'S NOT THAT TIME, YET. I THOUGHT WE HAD AGREED ON--
FUU.
WELL THEN, SHALL WE?
NO, ONEESAN !! I DON'T WANT TO GO !!
ずるずる
ほほほ
THAT'S NOT GOING TO WORK! SHE'S NOT THE TYPE YOU CAN JUST TALK TO!
I'M GOING TO REGRET DOING THIS, BUT I HAVE NO CHOICE!
AACCK!!
WAIT JUST A MINUTE THERE, TSURUKO!
ISN'T THAT A BIT SUDDEN ?!
U- URASHIMA!! GET OVER HERE!
HUH, WHAT ?
URM, E- EXCUSE ME, ONEESAN, BUT...
?
?
...BUT ... HE... HE...

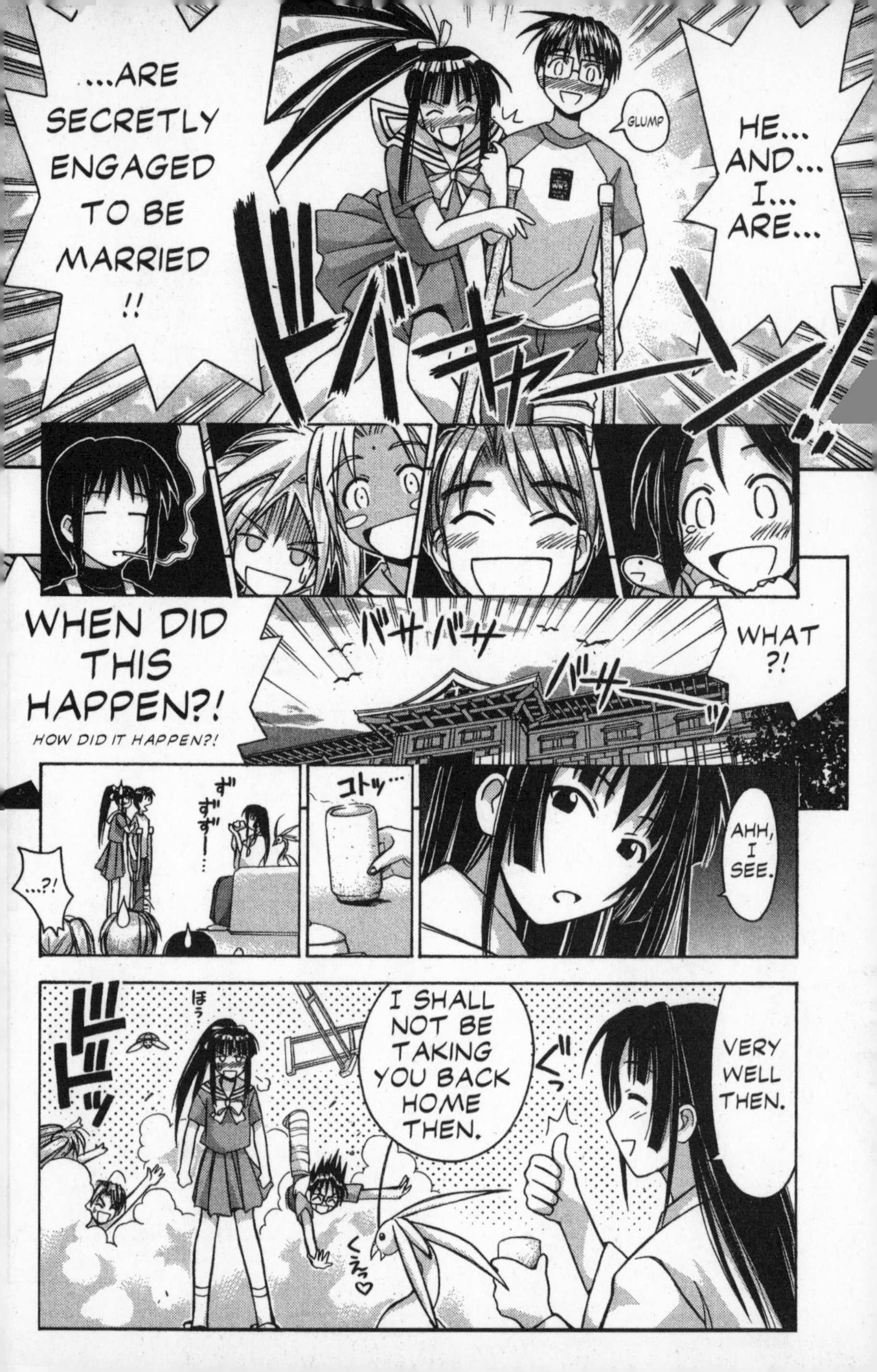
HE... AND... I... ARE...
GLUMP
...ARE SECRETLY ENGAGED TO BE MARRIED !!
WHAT ?!
バサバサ
バサ
WHEN DID THIS HAPPEN?!
HOW DID IT HAPPEN?!
AHH, I SEE.
コトッ…
ずずずー…
...?!
VERY WELL THEN.
ぐっ
I SHALL NOT BE TAKING YOU BACK HOME THEN.
ほう
くえっ♡
ドドッ

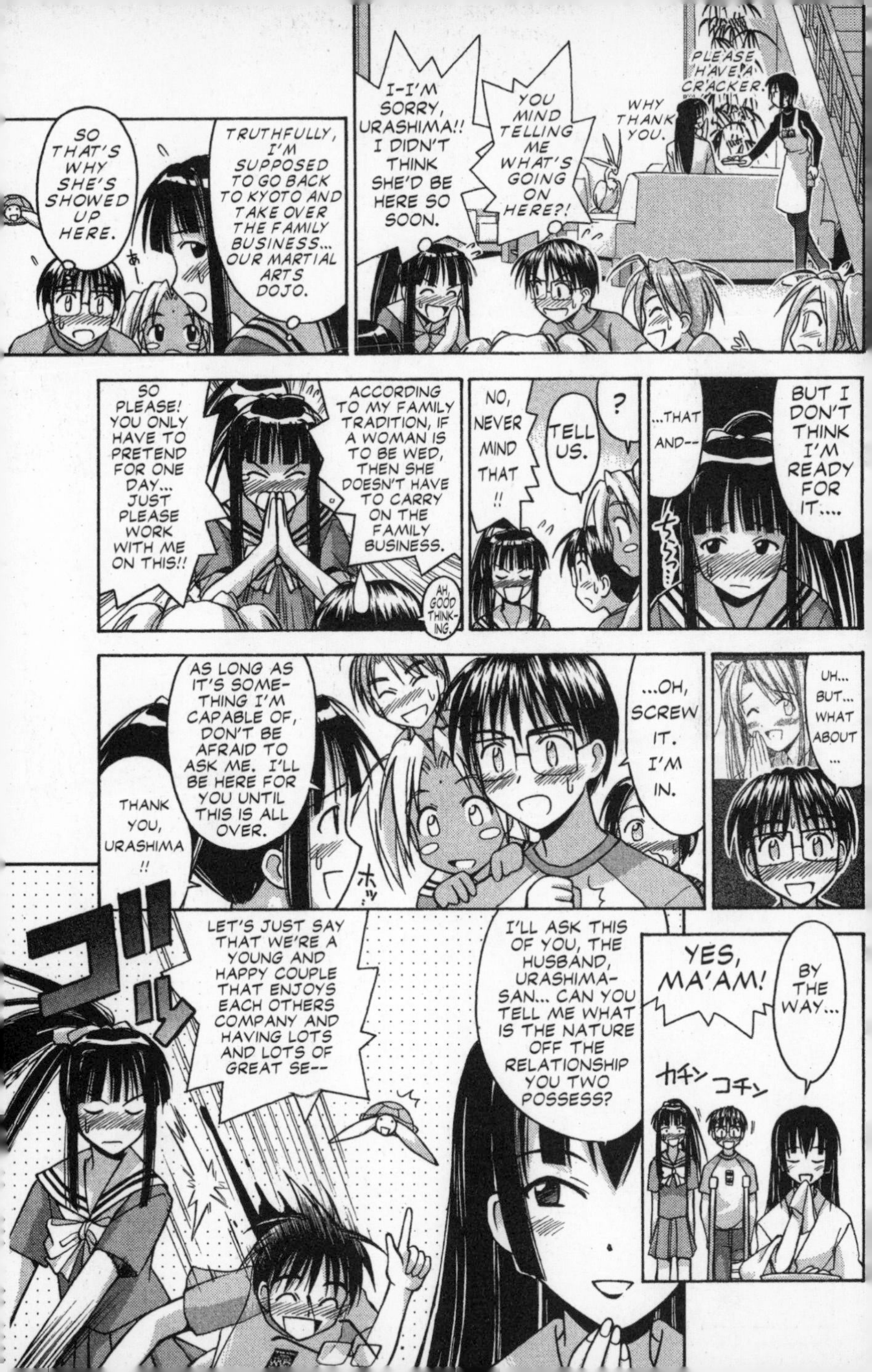
PLEASE HAVE A CRACKER.
WHY THANK YOU.
YOU MIND TELLING ME WHAT'S GOING ON HERE?!
I-I'M SORRY, URASHIMA!! I DIDN'T THINK SHE'D BE HERE SO SOON.
TRUTHFULLY, I'M SUPPOSED TO GO BACK TO KYOTO AND TAKE OVER THE FAMILY BUSINESS... OUR MARTIAL ARTS DOJO.
SO THAT'S WHY SHE'S SHOWED UP HERE.
BUT I DON'T THINK I'M READY FOR IT....
...THAT AND--
?
TELL US.
NO, NEVER MIND THAT !!
ACCORDING TO MY FAMILY TRADITION, IF A WOMAN IS TO BE WED, THEN SHE DOESN'T HAVE TO CARRY ON THE FAMILY BUSINESS.
SO PLEASE! YOU ONLY HAVE TO PRETEND FOR ONE DAY... JUST PLEASE WORK WITH ME ON THIS!!
AH, GOOD THINKING.
UH... BUT... WHAT ABOUT ...
...OH, SCREW IT. I'M IN.
AS LONG AS IT'S SOMETHING I'M CAPABLE OF, DON'T BE AFRAID TO ASK ME. I'LL BE HERE FOR YOU UNTIL THIS IS ALL OVER.
THANK YOU, URASHIMA !!
ホッ
BY THE WAY...
YES, MA'AM!
カチン コチン
I'LL ASK THIS OF YOU, THE HUSBAND, URASHIMA-SAN... CAN YOU TELL ME WHAT IS THE NATURE OFF THE RELATIONSHIP YOU TWO POSSESS?
LET'S JUST SAY THAT WE'RE A YOUNG AND HAPPY COUPLE THAT ENJOYS EACH OTHERS COMPANY AND HAVING LOTS AND LOTS OF GREAT SE--
ゴッ

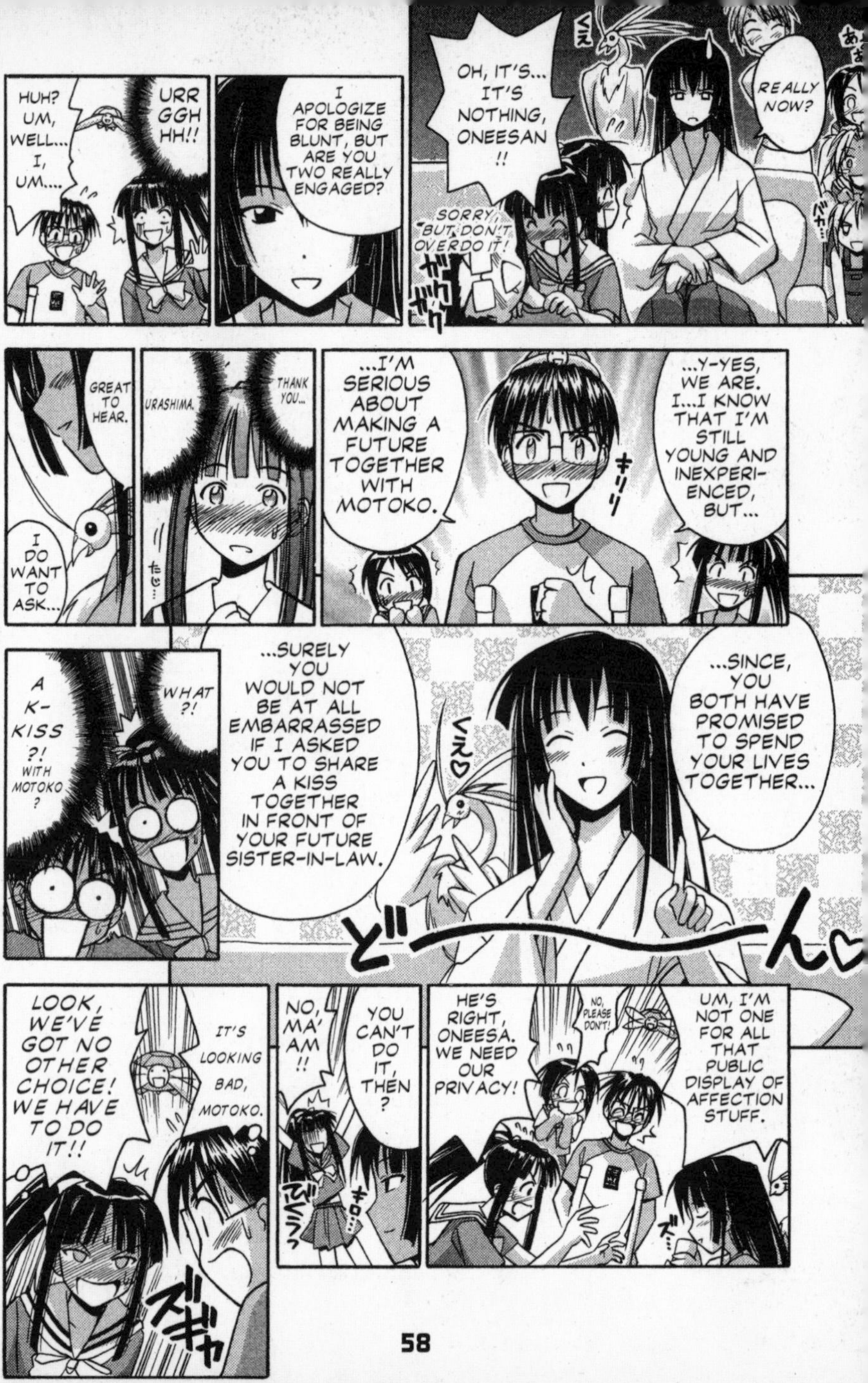
REALLY NOW?
OH, IT'S... IT'S NOTHING, ONEESAN!!
SORRY, BUT DON'T OVERDO IT!
I APOLOGIZE FOR BEING BLUNT, BUT ARE YOU TWO REALLY ENGAGED?
URRGGHH!!
HUH? UM, WELL... I, UM....
...Y-YES, WE ARE. I...I KNOW THAT I'M STILL YOUNG AND INEXPERIENCED, BUT...
...I'M SERIOUS ABOUT MAKING A FUTURE TOGETHER WITH MOTOKO.
THANK YOU...
URASHIMA.
GREAT TO HEAR.
I DO WANT TO ASK...
...SINCE, YOU BOTH HAVE PROMISED TO SPEND YOUR LIVES TOGETHER...
...SURELY YOU WOULD NOT BE AT ALL EMBARRASSED IF I ASKED YOU TO SHARE A KISS TOGETHER IN FRONT OF YOUR FUTURE SISTER-IN-LAW.
ど————ん♡
WHAT?!
A K-KISS?! WITH MOTOKO?
UM, I'M NOT ONE FOR ALL THAT PUBLIC DISPLAY OF AFFECTION STUFF.
NO, PLEASE DON'T!
HE'S RIGHT, ONEESA. WE NEED OUR PRIVACY!
YOU CAN'T DO IT, THEN?
NO, MA'AM!!
IT'S LOOKING BAD, MOTOKO.
LOOK, WE'VE GOT NO OTHER CHOICE! WE HAVE TO DO IT!!

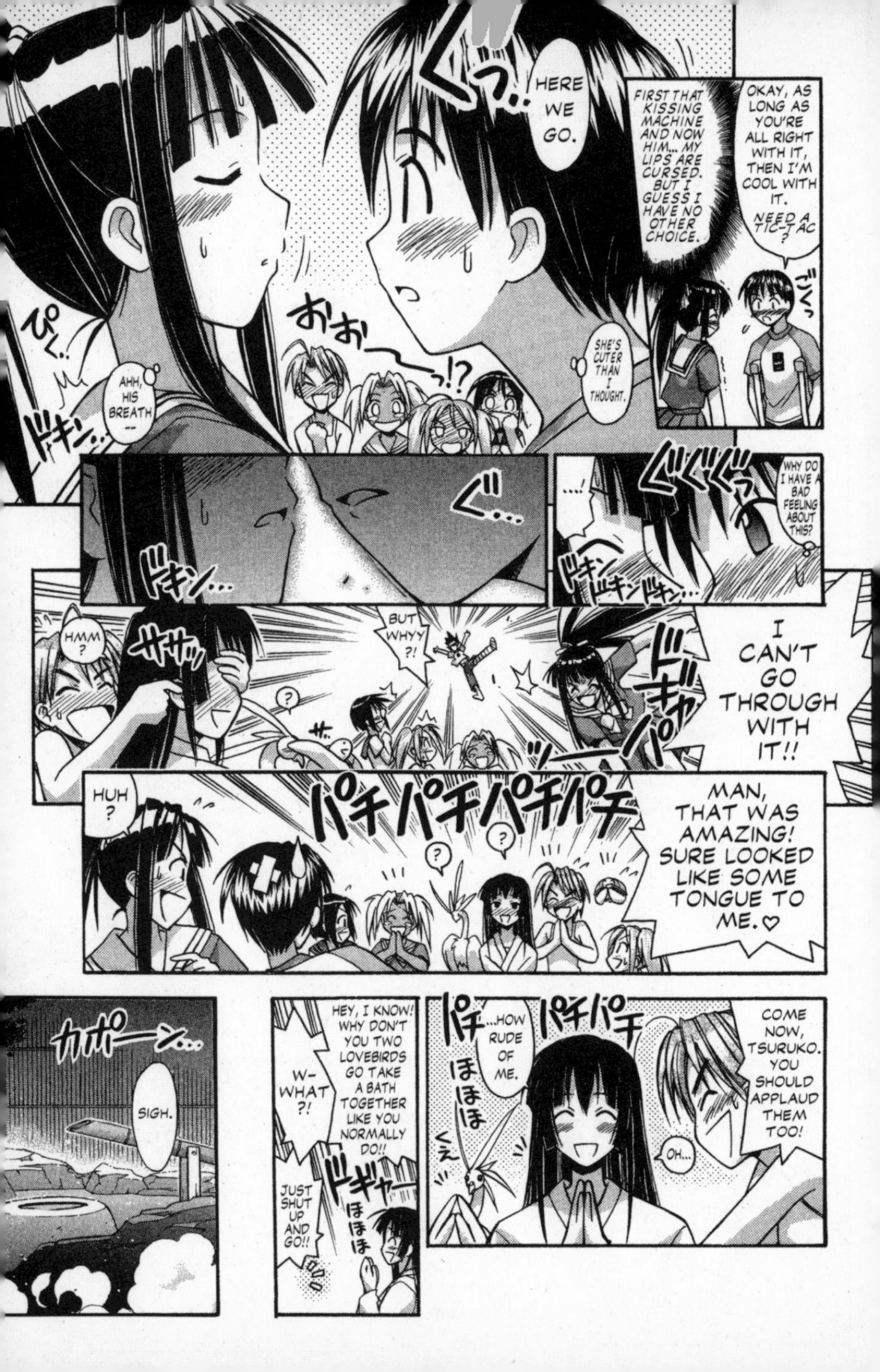
OKAY, AS LONG AS YOU'RE ALL RIGHT WITH IT, THEN I'M COOL WITH IT. NEED A TIC-TAC?
FIRST THAT KISSING MACHINE AND NOW HIM... MY LIPS ARE CURSED. BUT I GUESS I HAVE NO OTHER CHOICE.
HERE WE GO.
SHE'S CUTER THAN I THOUGHT.
AHH, HIS BREATH--
...!
WHY DO I HAVE A BAD FEELING ABOUT THIS?
I CAN'T GO THROUGH WITH IT!!
BUT WHYY?!
?
HMM?
MAN, THAT WAS AMAZING! SURE LOOKED LIKE SOME TONGUE TO ME.♡
?
?
HUH?
COME NOW, TSURUKO. YOU SHOULD APPLAUD THEM TOO!
OH...
...HOW RUDE OF ME.
HEY, I KNOW! WHY DON'T YOU TWO LOVEBIRDS GO TAKE A BATH TOGETHER LIKE YOU NORMALLY DO!!
W-WHAT?!
JUST SHUT UP AND GO!!
SIGH.

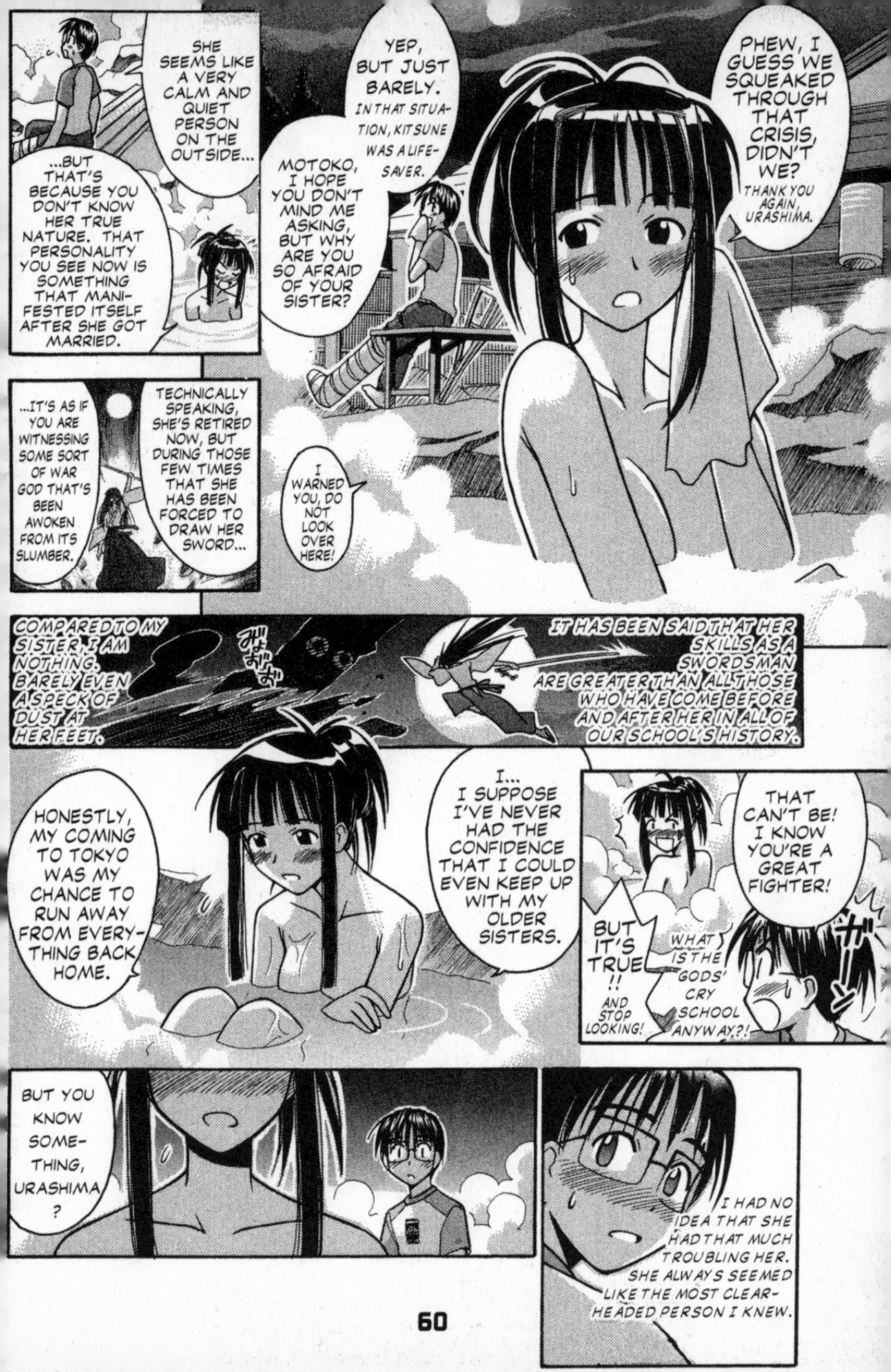
PHEW, I GUESS WE SQUEAKED THROUGH THAT CRISIS, DIDN'T WE?
THANK YOU AGAIN, URASHIMA.
YEP, BUT JUST BARELY.
IN THAT SITUATION, KITSUNE WAS A LIFE-SAVER.
MOTOKO, I HOPE YOU DON'T MIND ME ASKING, BUT WHY ARE YOU SO AFRAID OF YOUR SISTER?
I WARNED YOU, DO NOT LOOK OVER HERE!
SHE SEEMS LIKE A VERY CALM AND QUIET PERSON ON THE OUTSIDE...
...BUT THAT'S BECAUSE YOU DON'T KNOW HER TRUE NATURE. THAT PERSONALITY YOU SEE NOW IS SOMETHING THAT MANI-FESTED ITSELF AFTER SHE GOT MARRIED.
TECHNICALLY SPEAKING, SHE'S RETIRED NOW, BUT DURING THOSE FEW TIMES THAT SHE HAS BEEN FORCED TO DRAW HER SWORD...
...IT'S AS IF YOU ARE WITNESSING SOME SORT OF WAR GOD THAT'S BEEN AWOKEN FROM ITS SLUMBER.
IT HAS BEEN SAID THAT HER SKILLS AS A SWORDSMAN ARE GREATER THAN ALL THOSE WHO HAVE COME BEFORE AND AFTER HER IN ALL OF OUR SCHOOL'S HISTORY.
COMPARED TO MY SISTER, I AM NOTHING. BARELY EVEN A SPECK OF DUST AT HER FEET.
THAT CAN'T BE! I KNOW YOU'RE A GREAT FIGHTER!
WHAT IS THE GODS' CRY SCHOOL ANYWAY?!
BUT IT'S TRUE!!
AND STOP LOOKING!
I... I SUPPOSE I'VE NEVER HAD THE CONFIDENCE THAT I COULD EVEN KEEP UP WITH MY OLDER SISTERS.
HONESTLY, MY COMING TO TOKYO WAS MY CHANCE TO RUN AWAY FROM EVERY-THING BACK HOME.
I HAD NO IDEA THAT SHE HAD THAT MUCH TROUBLING HER. SHE ALWAYS SEEMED LIKE THE MOST CLEAR-HEADED PERSON I KNEW.
BUT YOU KNOW SOME-THING, URASHIMA?

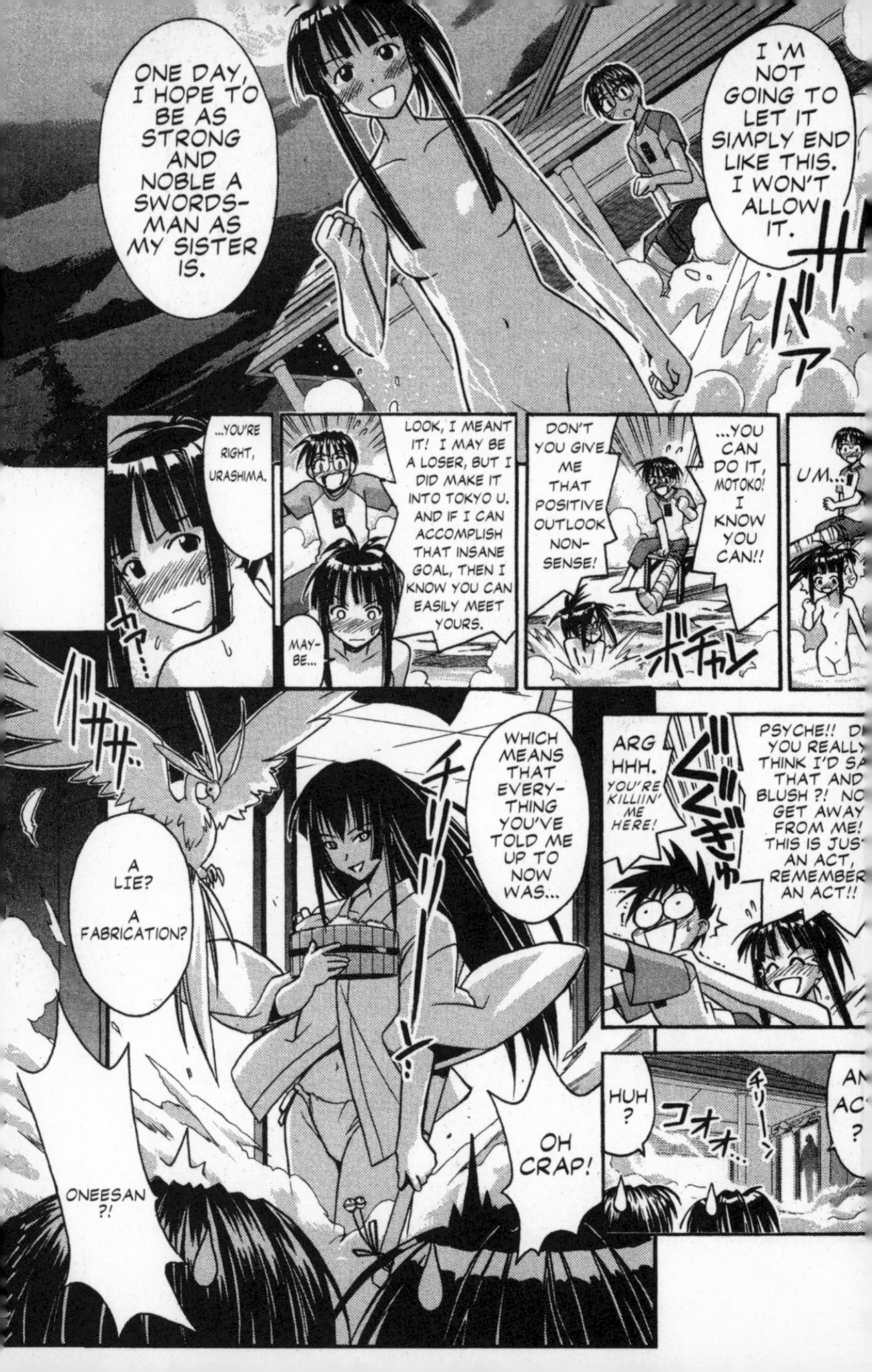
I'M NOT GOING TO LET IT SIMPLY END LIKE THIS. I WON'T ALLOW IT.
ザバア
ONE DAY, I HOPE TO BE AS STRONG AND NOBLE A SWORDS-MAN AS MY SISTER IS.
UM...
...YOU CAN DO IT, MOTOKO! I KNOW YOU CAN!!
DON'T YOU GIVE ME THAT POSITIVE OUTLOOK NON-SENSE!
ボチャン
LOOK, I MEANT IT! I MAY BE A LOSER, BUT I DID MAKE IT INTO TOKYO U. AND IF I CAN ACCOMPLISH THAT INSANE GOAL, THEN I KNOW YOU CAN EASILY MEET YOURS.
MAY-BE...
...YOU'RE RIGHT, URASHIMA.
カァ...
PSYCHE!! D YOU REALLY THINK I'D SA THAT AND BLUSH ?! NO GET AWAY FROM ME! THIS IS JUS AN ACT, REMEMBER AN ACT!!
ぐぐぎゅ
ARG HHH.
YOU'RE KILLIIN' ME HERE!
AN ACT ?
HUH ?
チリーン
コオオ...
WHICH MEANS THAT EVERY-THING YOU'VE TOLD ME UP TO NOW WAS...
チリーン
OH CRAP!
バササ
A LIE? A FABRICATION?
ONEESAN ?!

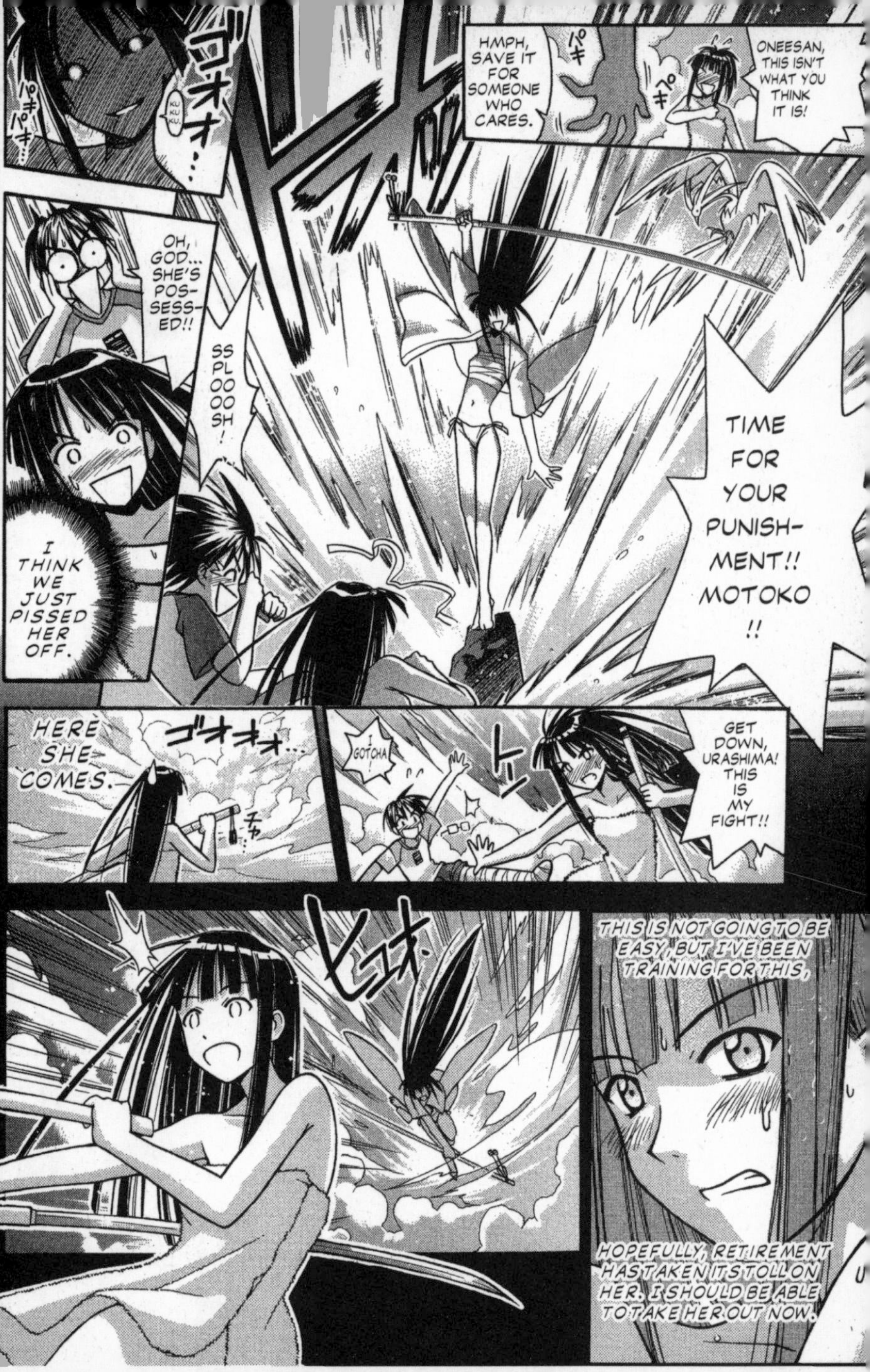

ONEESAN, THIS ISN'T WHAT YOU THINK IT IS!
ペキ
パキ
HMPH, SAVE IT FOR SOMEONE WHO CARES.
ゴオオ…
KU KU KU.
パキパキ…
TIME FOR YOUR PUNISHMENT!! MOTOKO!!
SSPLOOOOSH!
OH, GOD... SHE'S POSSESSED!!
I THINK WE JUST PISSED HER OFF.
GET DOWN, URASHIMA! THIS IS MY FIGHT!!
トン
I GOTCHA!
ゴオオオ…
HERE SHE COMES.
チャ
THIS IS NOT GOING TO BE EASY, BUT I'VE BEEN TRAINING FOR THIS,
HOPEFULLY, RETIREMENT HAS TAKEN ITS TOLL ON HER. I SHOULD BE ABLE TO TAKE HER OUT NOW.
ヒュオ

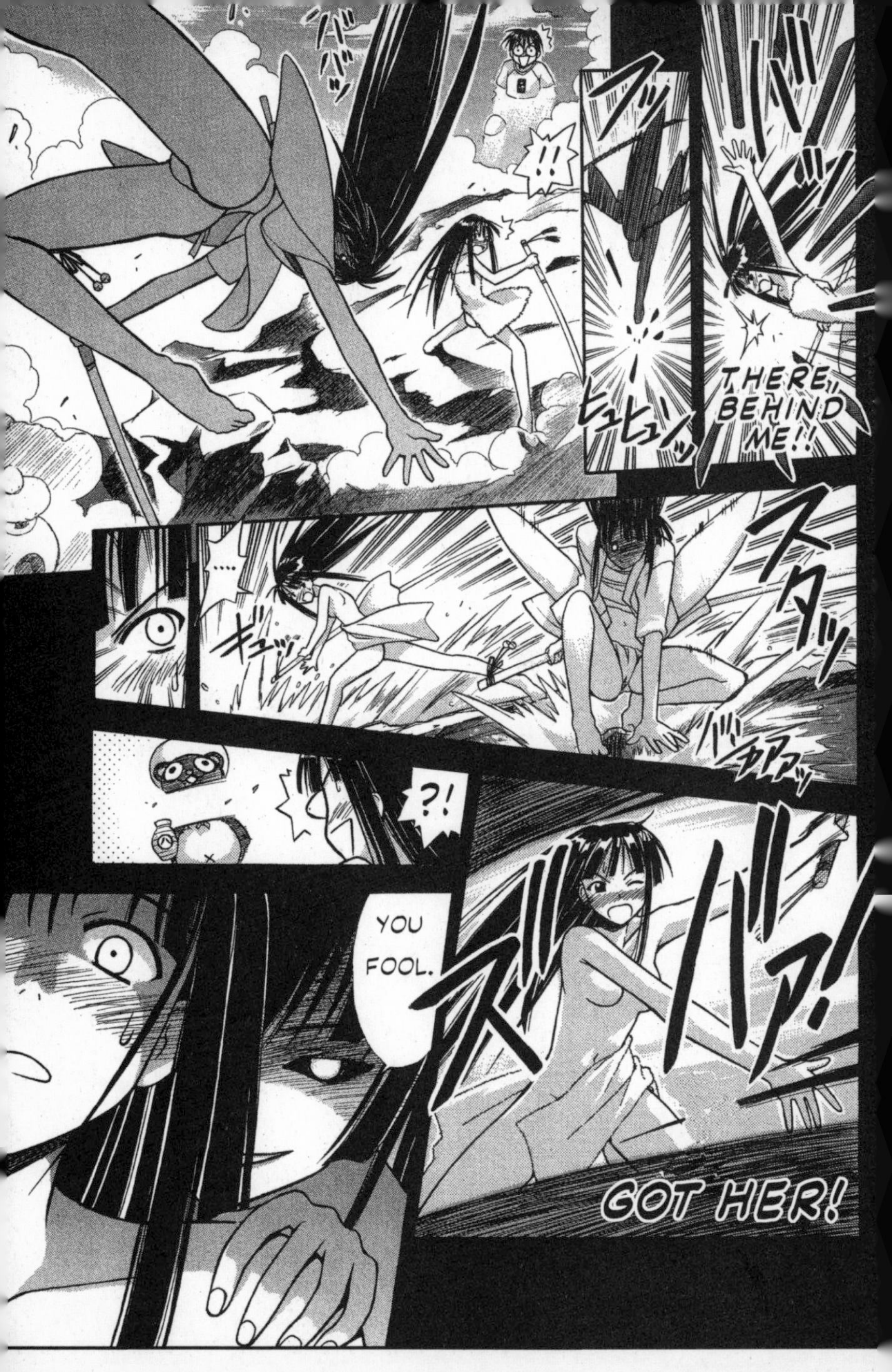
!!
THERE, BEHIND ME!!
?!
YOU FOOL.
GOT HER!

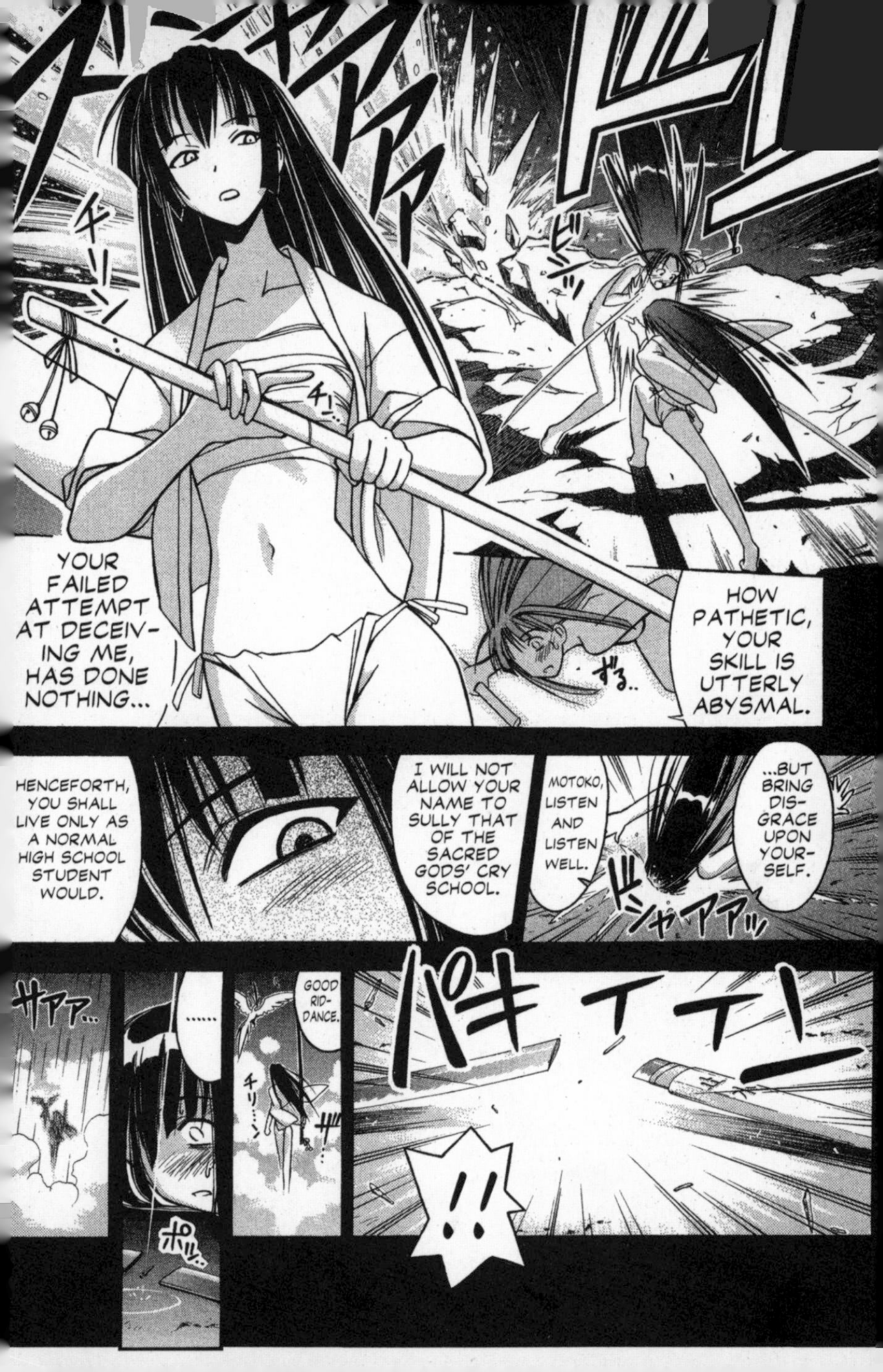
HOW PATHETIC, YOUR SKILL IS UTTERLY ABYSMAL.
ずる..
YOUR FAILED ATTEMPT AT DECEIV-ING ME, HAS DONE NOTHING...
...BUT BRING DIS-GRACE UPON YOUR-SELF.
MOTOKO, LISTEN AND LISTEN WELL.
I WILL NOT ALLOW YOUR NAME TO SULLY THAT OF THE SACRED GODS' CRY SCHOOL.
HENCEFORTH, YOU SHALL LIVE ONLY AS A NORMAL HIGH SCHOOL STUDENT WOULD.
パキィィー
!!
GOOD RID-DANCE.
チリ...ン
......
サァァ...

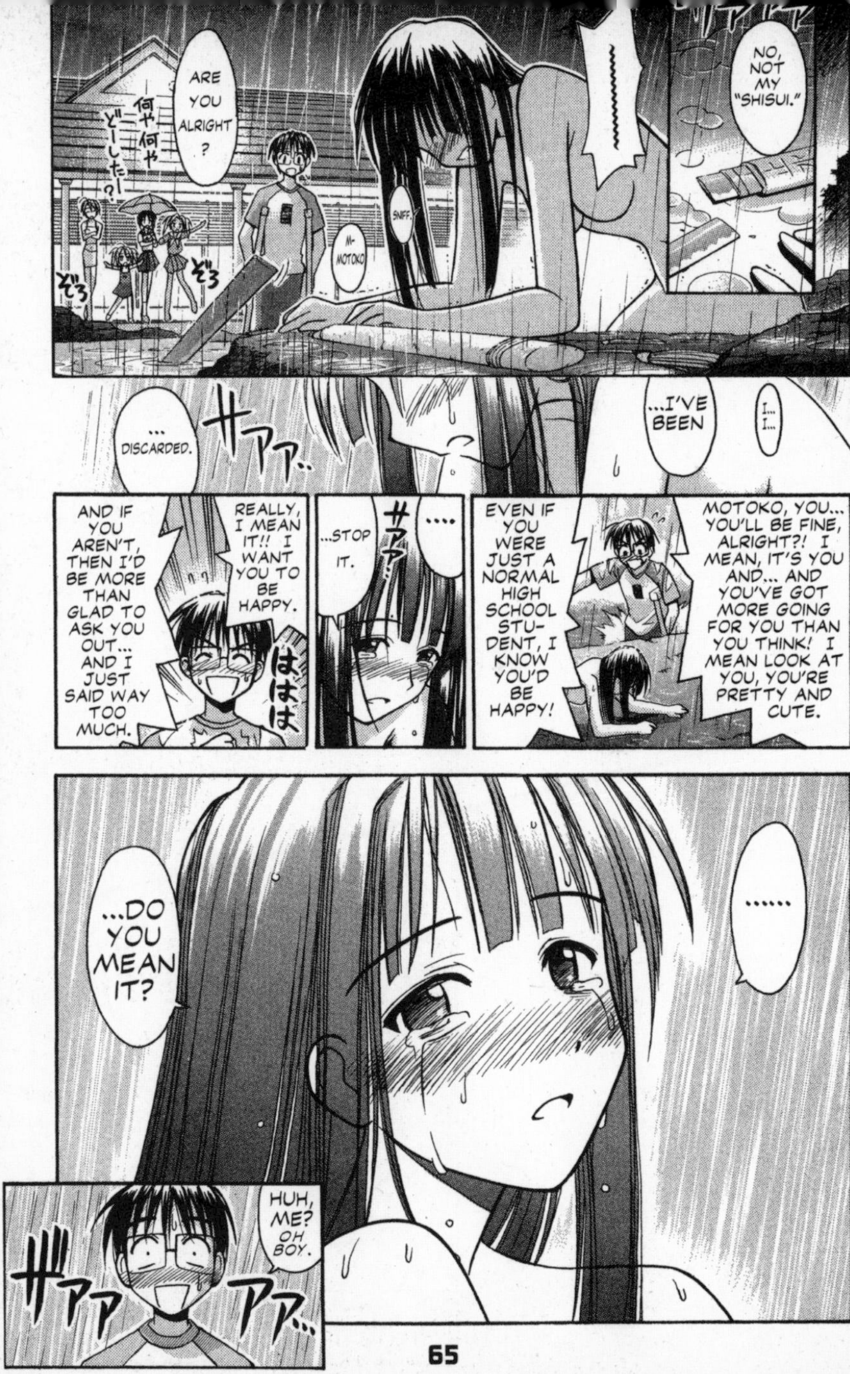
NO, NOT MY "SHISUI."
~~~~~~~~
ARE YOU ALRIGHT?
何や何やどーしたー?
SNIFF.
M-MOTOKO
ぞろ
ぞろ
I... I...
...I'VE BEEN
...DISCARDED.
ザァア..
MOTOKO, YOU... YOU'LL BE FINE, ALRIGHT?! I MEAN, IT'S YOU AND... AND YOU'VE GOT MORE GOING FOR YOU THAN YOU THINK! I MEAN LOOK AT YOU, YOU'RE PRETTY AND CUTE.
EVEN IF YOU WERE JUST A NORMAL HIGH SCHOOL STU-DENT, I KNOW YOU'D BE HAPPY!
....
...STOP IT.
ザァ..
REALLY, I MEAN IT!! I WANT YOU TO BE HAPPY.
AND IF YOU AREN'T, THEN I'D BE MORE THAN GLAD TO ASK YOU OUT... AND I JUST SAID WAY TOO MUCH.
ははは
......
...DO YOU MEAN IT?
HUH, ME? OH BOY.
ザァァ
アァ...
~~~~~~~~

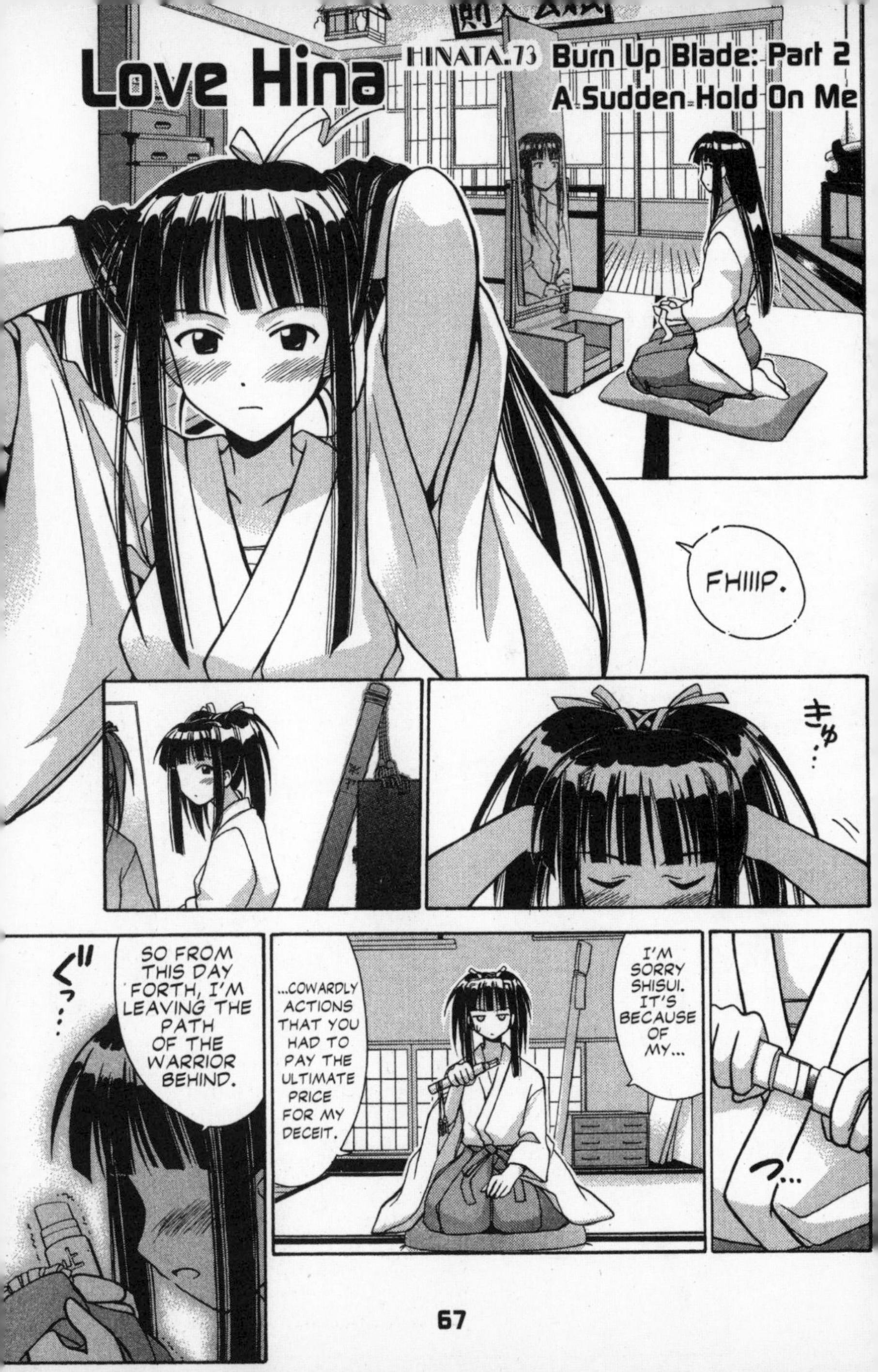
Love Hina
HINATA.73 Burn Up Blade: Part 2
A Sudden Hold On Me
FHIIIP.
きゅ...
つ...
I'M SORRY SHISUI. IT'S BECAUSE OF MY...
...COWARDLY ACTIONS THAT YOU HAD TO PAY THE ULTIMATE PRICE FOR MY DECEIT.
SO FROM THIS DAY FORTH, I'M LEAVING THE PATH OF THE WARRIOR BEHIND.
ぐっ...

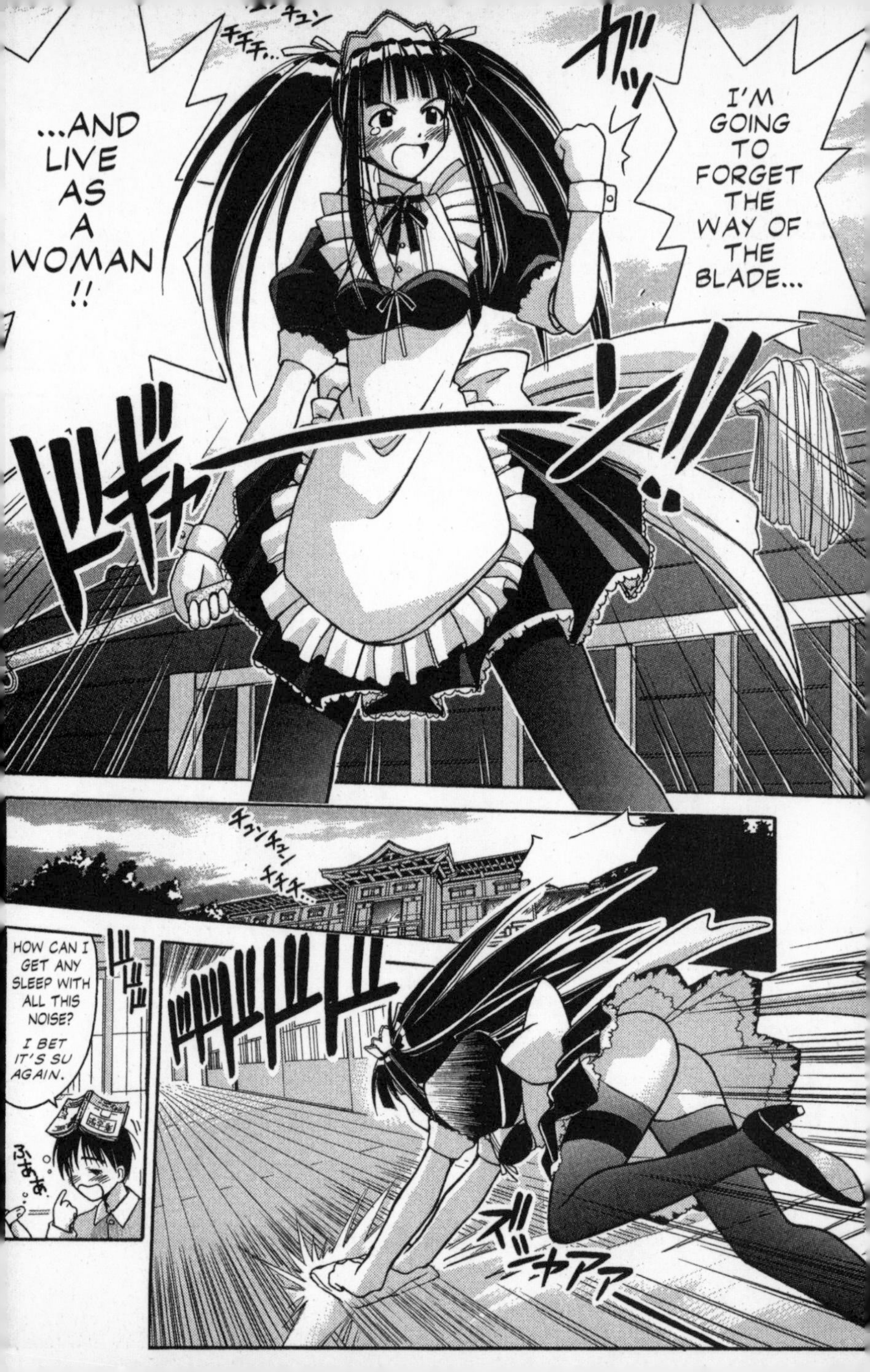
I'M GOING TO FORGET THE WAY OF THE BLADE...
...AND LIVE AS A WOMAN!!
HOW CAN I GET ANY SLEEP WITH ALL THIS NOISE?
I BET IT'S SU AGAIN.

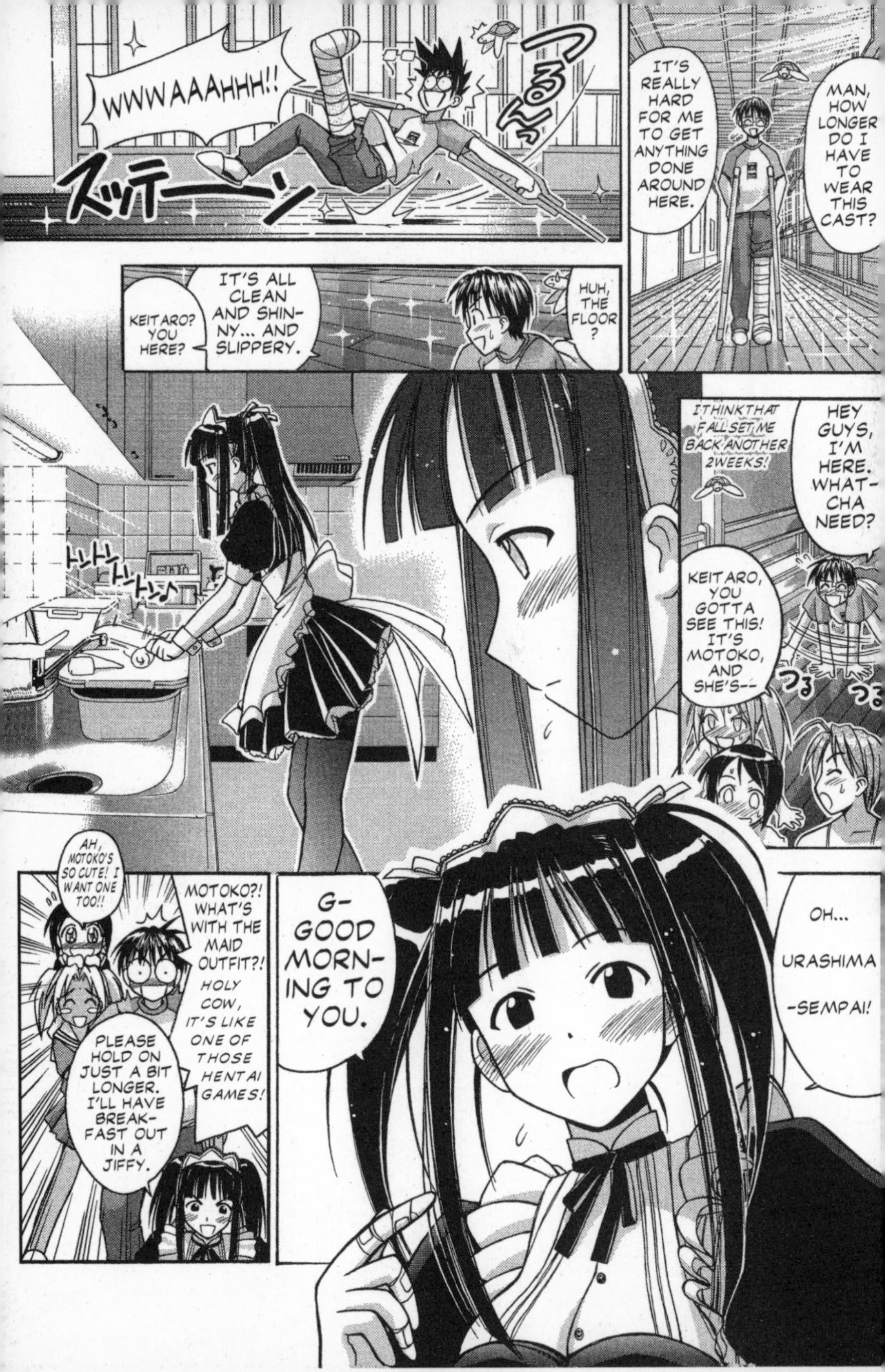
MAN, HOW LONGER DO I HAVE TO WEAR THIS CAST?
IT'S REALLY HARD FOR ME TO GET ANYTHING DONE AROUND HERE.
つるん
WWWAAAHHH!!
ステーン
HUH, THE FLOOR?
IT'S ALL CLEAN AND SHINNY... AND SLIPPERY.
KEITARO? YOU HERE?
HEY GUYS, I'M HERE. WHATCHA NEED?
I THINK THAT FALL SET ME BACK ANOTHER 2WEEKS!
KEITARO, YOU GOTTA SEE THIS! IT'S MOTOKO, AND SHE'S--
つる つる
トントン トントン♪
OH... URASHIMA -SEMPAI!
G-GOOD MORNING TO YOU.
MOTOKO?! WHAT'S WITH THE MAID OUTFIT?!
HOLY COW, IT'S LIKE ONE OF THOSE HENTAI GAMES!
AH, MOTOKO'S SO CUTE! I WANT ONE TOO!!
PLEASE HOLD ON JUST A BIT LONGER. I'LL HAVE BREAKFAST OUT IN A JIFFY.

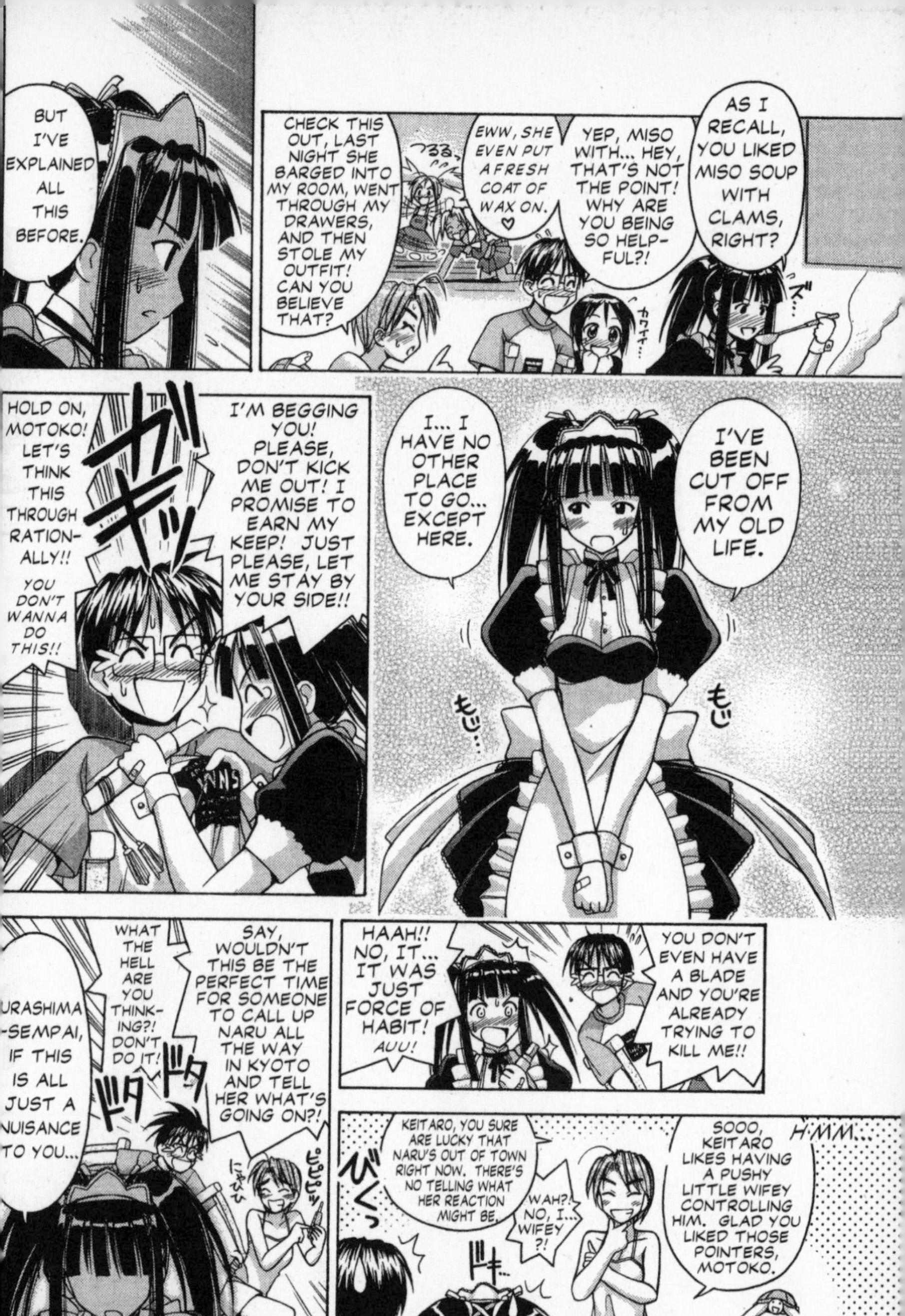
AS I RECALL, YOU LIKED MISO SOUP WITH CLAMS, RIGHT?
ズ…
YEP, MISO WITH... HEY, THAT'S NOT THE POINT! WHY ARE YOU BEING SO HELP-FUL?!
EWW, SHE EVEN PUT A FRESH COAT OF WAX ON. ♡
CHECK THIS OUT, LAST NIGHT SHE BARGED INTO MY ROOM, WENT THROUGH MY DRAWERS, AND THEN STOLE MY OUTFIT! CAN YOU BELIEVE THAT?
BUT I'VE EXPLAINED ALL THIS BEFORE.
I'VE BEEN CUT OFF FROM MY OLD LIFE.
I... I HAVE NO OTHER PLACE TO GO... EXCEPT HERE.
もじ
もじ…
I'M BEGGING YOU! PLEASE, DON'T KICK ME OUT! I PROMISE TO EARN MY KEEP! JUST PLEASE, LET ME STAY BY YOUR SIDE!!
ガギッ
HOLD ON, MOTOKO! LET'S THINK THIS THROUGH RATION-ALLY!!
YOU DON'T WANNA DO THIS!!
YOU DON'T EVEN HAVE A BLADE AND YOU'RE ALREADY TRYING TO KILL ME!!
HAAH!! NO, IT... IT WAS JUST FORCE OF HABIT!
AUU!
HMMM...
SOOO, KEITARO LIKES HAVING A PUSHY LITTLE WIFEY CONTROLLING HIM. GLAD YOU LIKED THOSE POINTERS, MOTOKO.
WAH?! NO, I... WIFEY?!
KEITARO, YOU SURE ARE LUCKY THAT NARU'S OUT OF TOWN RIGHT NOW. THERE'S NO TELLING WHAT HER REACTION MIGHT BE.
びくっ
ドキ…
SAY, WOULDN'T THIS BE THE PERFECT TIME FOR SOMEONE TO CALL UP NARU ALL THE WAY IN KYOTO AND TELL HER WHAT'S GOING ON?!
WHAT THE HELL ARE YOU THINKING?! DON'T DO IT!
ドタ
ドタ
URASHIMA-SEMPAI, IF THIS IS ALL JUST A NUISANCE TO YOU...

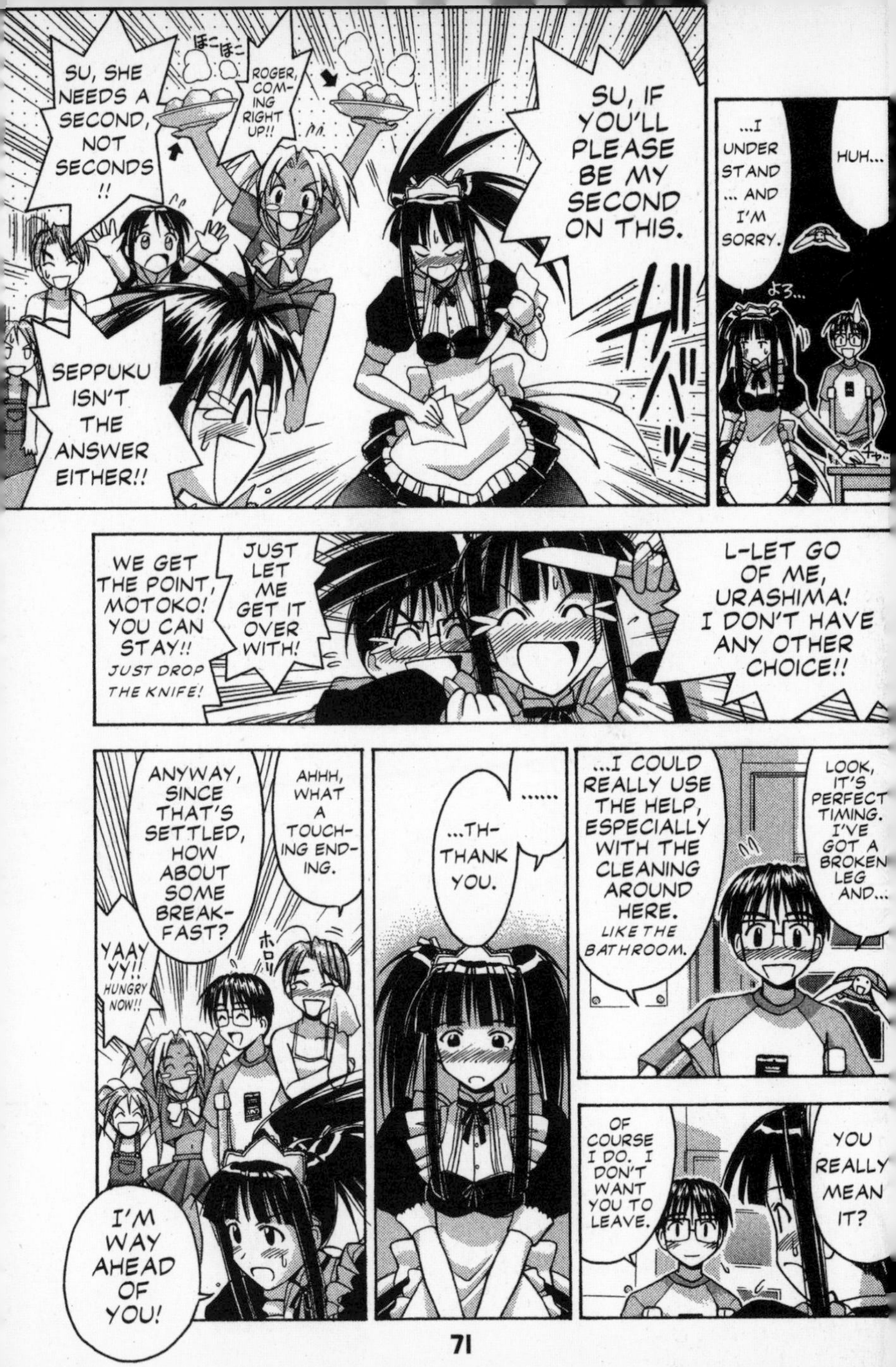
HUH...
...I UNDERSTAND ... AND I'M SORRY.
よろ...
SU, IF YOU'LL PLEASE BE MY SECOND ON THIS.
ガバッ
ほこほこ
ROGER, COMING RIGHT UP!!
SU, SHE NEEDS A SECOND, NOT SECONDS!!
SEPPUKU ISN'T THE ANSWER EITHER!!
L-LET GO OF ME, URASHIMA! I DON'T HAVE ANY OTHER CHOICE!!
JUST LET ME GET IT OVER WITH!
WE GET THE POINT, MOTOKO! YOU CAN STAY!!
JUST DROP THE KNIFE!
LOOK, IT'S PERFECT TIMING. I'VE GOT A BROKEN LEG AND...
...I COULD REALLY USE THE HELP, ESPECIALLY WITH THE CLEANING AROUND HERE.
LIKE THE BATHROOM.
YOU REALLY MEAN IT?
OF COURSE I DO. I DON'T WANT YOU TO LEAVE.
......
...TH-THANK YOU.
AHHH, WHAT A TOUCHING ENDING.
ANYWAY, SINCE THAT'S SETTLED, HOW ABOUT SOME BREAKFAST?
ホロリ
YAAAYY!!
HUNGRY NOW!!
I'M WAY AHEAD OF YOU!

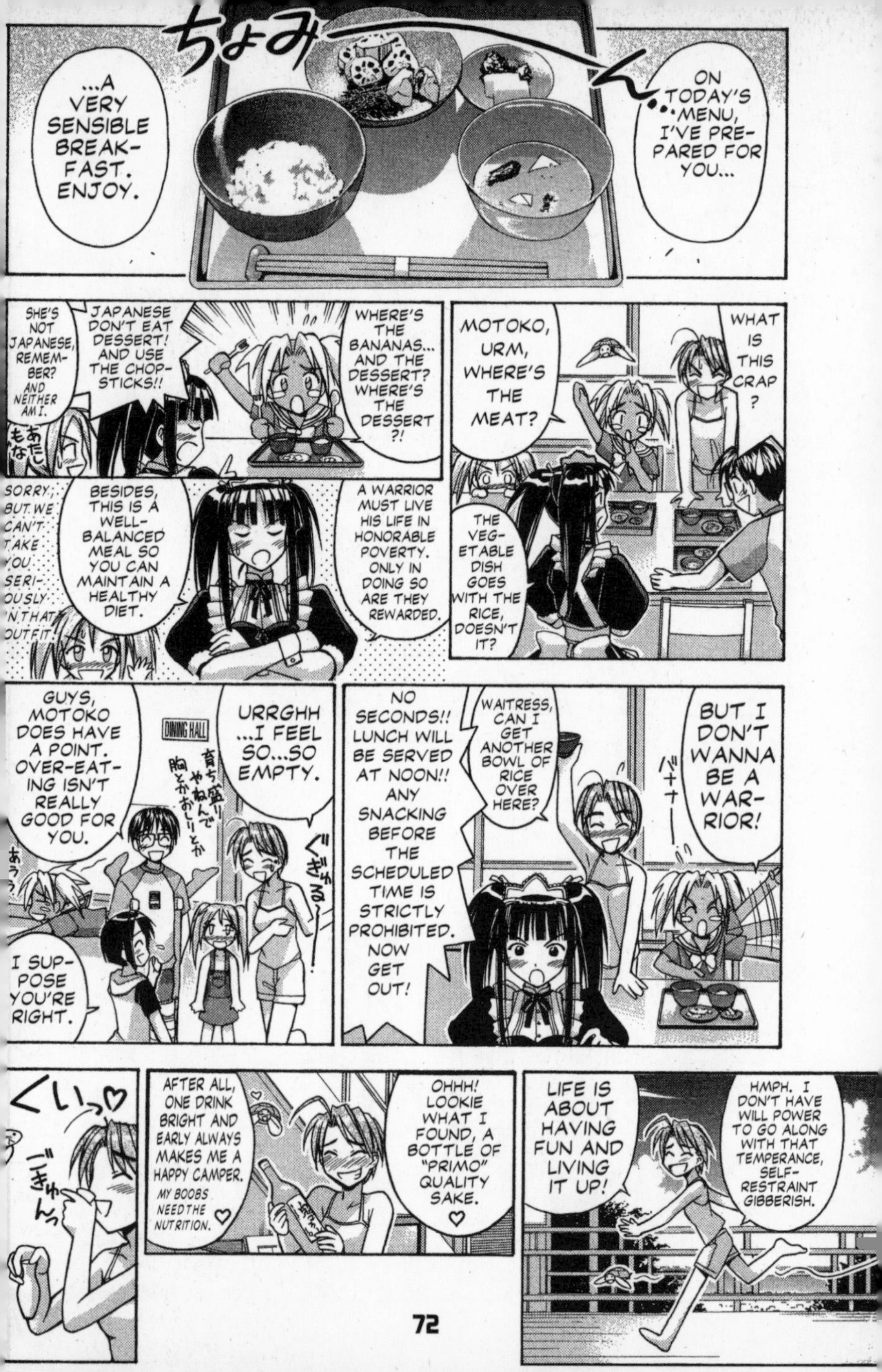

ON TODAY'S MENU, I'VE PREPARED FOR YOU...
ちょみーーん...
...A VERY SENSIBLE BREAK-FAST. ENJOY.
WHAT IS THIS CRAP?
MOTOKO, URM, WHERE'S THE MEAT?
THE VEG-ETABLE DISH GOES WITH THE RICE, DOESN'T IT?
WHERE'S THE BANANAS... AND THE DESSERT? WHERE'S THE DESSERT?!
JAPANESE DON'T EAT DESSERT! AND USE THE CHOP-STICKS!!
SHE'S NOT JAPANESE, REMEM-BER? AND NEITHER AM I.
あたしもな
A WARRIOR MUST LIVE HIS LIFE IN HONORABLE POVERTY. ONLY IN DOING SO ARE THEY REWARDED.
BESIDES, THIS IS A WELL-BALANCED MEAL SO YOU CAN MAINTAIN A HEALTHY DIET.
SORRY, BUT WE CAN'T TAKE YOU SERI-OUSLY IN THAT OUTFIT.
BUT I DON'T WANNA BE A WAR-RIOR!
バナナーー
WAITRESS, CAN I GET ANOTHER BOWL OF RICE OVER HERE?
NO SECONDS!! LUNCH WILL BE SERVED AT NOON!! ANY SNACKING BEFORE THE SCHEDULED TIME IS STRICTLY PROHIBITED. NOW GET OUT!
URRGHH ...I FEEL SO...SO EMPTY.
DINING HALL
育ち盛りやねんで胸とかおしりとか
ぐぎゅる～
GUYS, MOTOKO DOES HAVE A POINT. OVER-EAT-ING ISN'T REALLY GOOD FOR YOU.
あうう
I SUP-POSE YOU'RE RIGHT.
HMPH. I DON'T HAVE WILL POWER TO GO ALONG WITH THAT TEMPERANCE, SELF-RESTRAINT GIBBERISH.
LIFE IS ABOUT HAVING FUN AND LIVING IT UP!
OHHH! LOOKIE WHAT I FOUND, A BOTTLE OF "PRIMO" QUALITY SAKE. ♡
AFTER ALL, ONE DRINK BRIGHT AND EARLY ALWAYS MAKES ME A HAPPY CAMPER.
MY BOOBS NEED THE NUTRITION. ♡
くいっ♡
ごきゅんっ

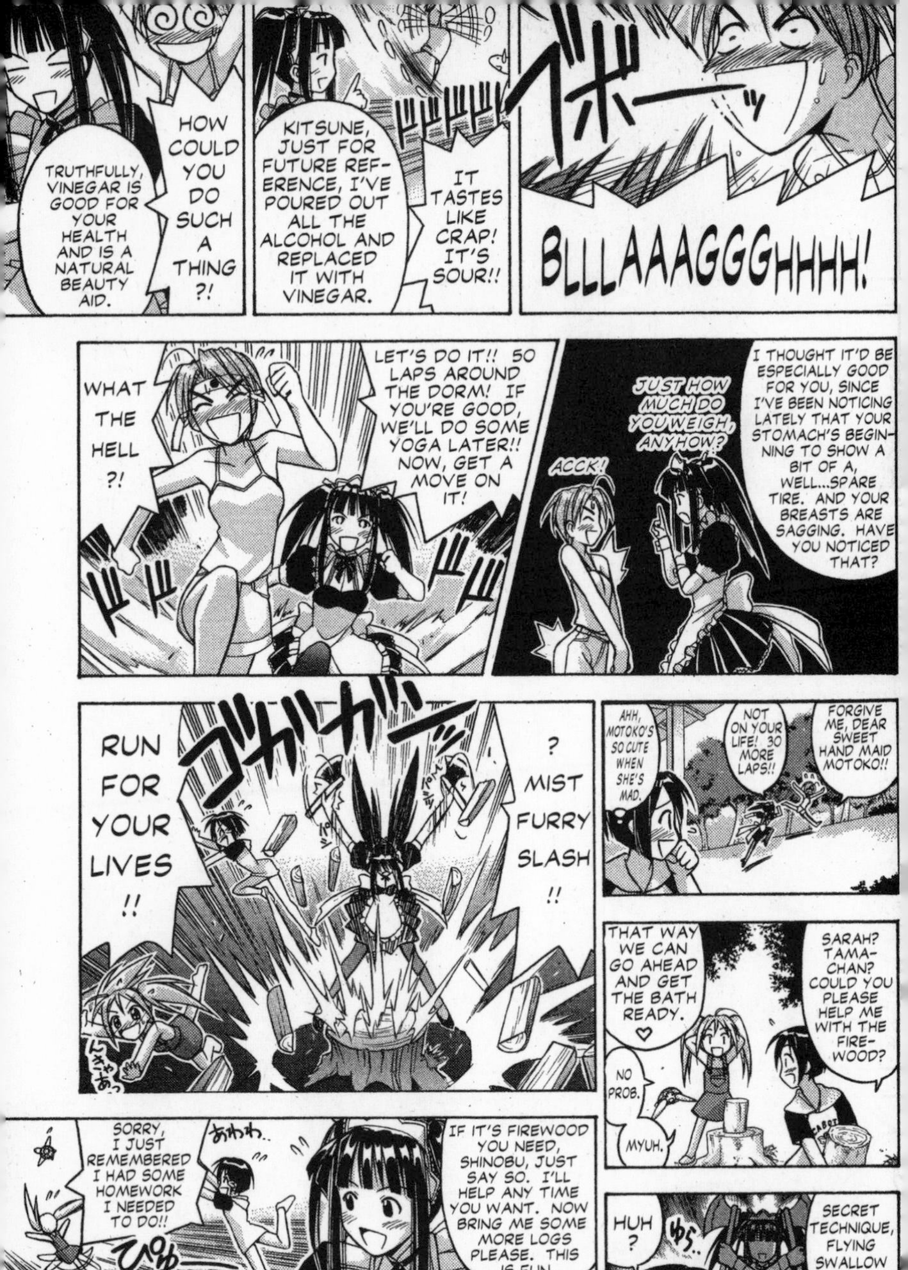
ブボーッ
BLLLAAAGGGHHHH!
ドドドドド
IT TASTES LIKE CRAP! IT'S SOUR!!
KITSUNE, JUST FOR FUTURE REFERENCE, I'VE POURED OUT ALL THE ALCOHOL AND REPLACED IT WITH VINEGAR.
HOW COULD YOU DO SUCH A THING?!
TRUTHFULLY, VINEGAR IS GOOD FOR YOUR HEALTH AND IS A NATURAL BEAUTY AID.
I THOUGHT IT'D BE ESPECIALLY GOOD FOR YOU, SINCE I'VE BEEN NOTICING LATELY THAT YOUR STOMACH'S BEGINNING TO SHOW A BIT OF A, WELL...SPARE TIRE. AND YOUR BREASTS ARE SAGGING. HAVE YOU NOTICED THAT?
JUST HOW MUCH DO YOU WEIGH, ANYHOW?
ACCK!
LET'S DO IT!! 50 LAPS AROUND THE DORM! IF YOU'RE GOOD, WE'LL DO SOME YOGA LATER!! NOW, GET A MOVE ON IT!
WHAT THE HELL?!
ドドドド
FORGIVE ME, DEAR SWEET HAND MAID MOTOKO!!
NOT ON YOUR LIFE! 30 MORE LAPS!!
AHH, MOTOKO'S SO CUTE WHEN SHE'S MAD.
SARAH? TAMA-CHAN? COULD YOU PLEASE HELP ME WITH THE FIRE-WOOD?
THAT WAY WE CAN GO AHEAD AND GET THE BATH READY. ♡
NO PROB.
MYUH.
IF IT'S FIREWOOD YOU NEED, SHINOBU, JUST SAY SO. I'LL HELP ANY TIME YOU WANT. NOW BRING ME SOME MORE LOGS PLEASE. THIS IS FUN.
あわわ..
SORRY, I JUST REMEMBERED I HAD SOME HOMEWORK I NEEDED TO DO!!
ぴゅー
SECRET TECHNIQUE, FLYING SWALLOW DRAWING SWORD!
ゆら..
HUH?
ゴガガーッ
? MIST FURRY SLASH!!
RUN FOR YOUR LIVES!!

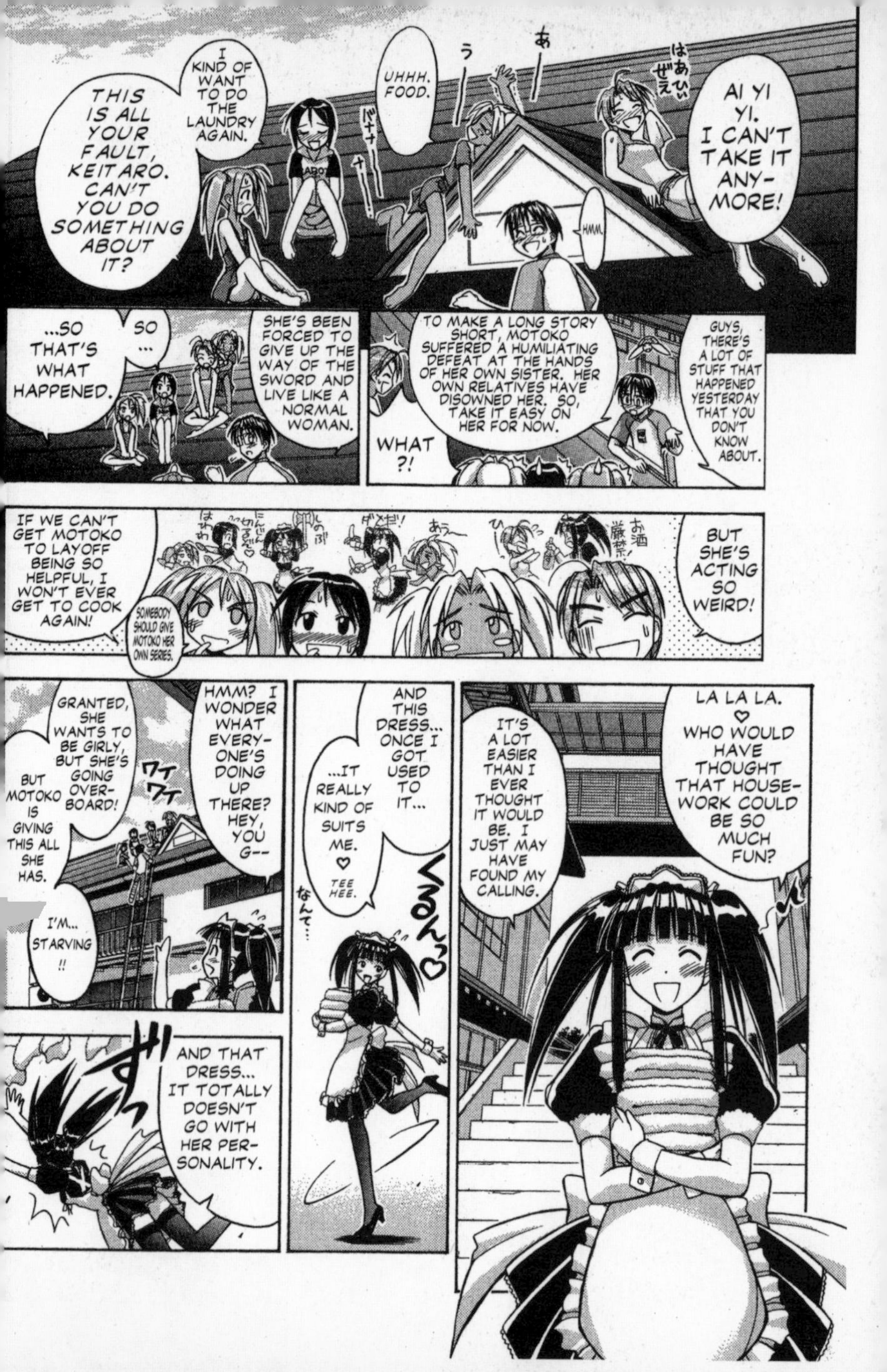
AI YI YI. I CAN'T TAKE IT ANYMORE!
あー
うー
UHHH. FOOD.
HMM.
I KIND OF WANT TO DO THE LAUNDRY AGAIN.
THIS IS ALL YOUR FAULT, KEITARO. CAN'T YOU DO SOMETHING ABOUT IT?
GUYS, THERE'S A LOT OF STUFF THAT HAPPENED YESTERDAY THAT YOU DON'T KNOW ABOUT.
TO MAKE A LONG STORY SHORT, MOTOKO SUFFERED A HUMILIATING DEFEAT AT THE HANDS OF HER OWN SISTER. HER OWN RELATIVES HAVE DISOWNED HER. SO, TAKE IT EASY ON HER FOR NOW.
WHAT ?!
SHE'S BEEN FORCED TO GIVE UP THE WAY OF THE SWORD AND LIVE LIKE A NORMAL WOMAN.
SO ...
...SO THAT'S WHAT HAPPENED.
BUT SHE'S ACTING SO WEIRD!
お酒厳禁!
IF WE CAN'T GET MOTOKO TO LAYOFF BEING SO HELPFUL, I WON'T EVER GET TO COOK AGAIN!
SOMEBODY SHOULD GIVE MOTOKO HER OWN SERIES.
LA LA LA. ♡ WHO WOULD HAVE THOUGHT THAT HOUSE-WORK COULD BE SO MUCH FUN?
IT'S A LOT EASIER THAN I EVER THOUGHT IT WOULD BE. I JUST MAY HAVE FOUND MY CALLING.
AND THIS DRESS... ONCE I GOT USED TO IT...
...IT REALLY KIND OF SUITS ME. ♡
TEE HEE.
なんて…
くるんっ♡
HMM? I WONDER WHAT EVERY-ONE'S DOING UP THERE? HEY, YOU G--
GRANTED, SHE WANTS TO BE GIRLY, BUT SHE'S GOING OVER-BOARD!
ワイワイ
BUT MOTOKO IS GIVING THIS ALL SHE HAS.
I'M... STARVING !!
AND THAT DRESS... IT TOTALLY DOESN'T GO WITH HER PER-SONALITY.
ずっ

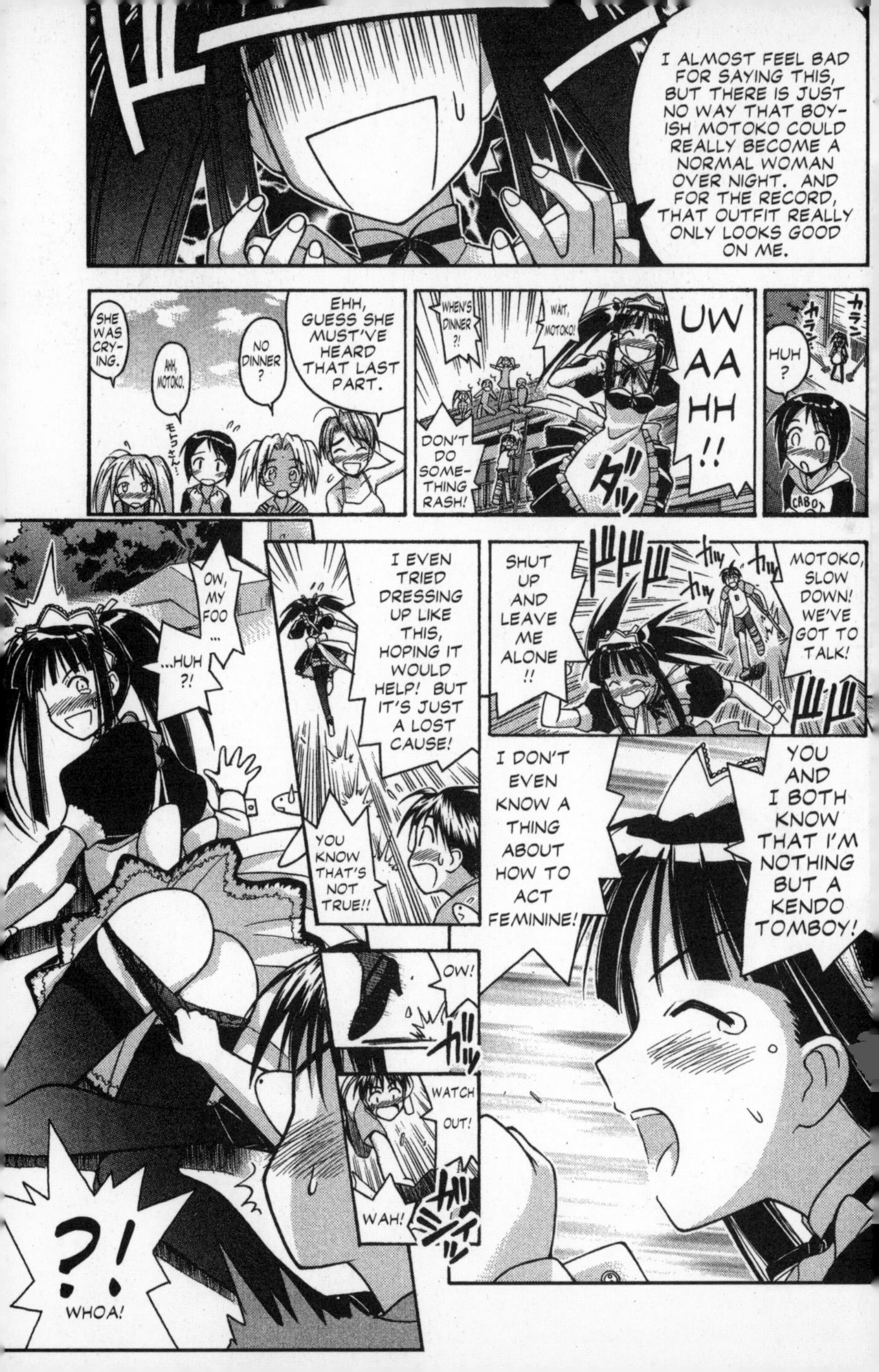
I ALMOST FEEL BAD FOR SAYING THIS, BUT THERE IS JUST NO WAY THAT BOY-ISH MOTOKO COULD REALLY BECOME A NORMAL WOMAN OVER NIGHT. AND FOR THE RECORD, THAT OUTFIT REALLY ONLY LOOKS GOOD ON ME.
HUH?
UW AA HH!!
WAIT, MOTOKO!
WHEN'S DINNER?!
DON'T DO SOME-THING RASH!
EHH, GUESS SHE MUST'VE HEARD THAT LAST PART.
NO DINNER?
AHH, MOTOKO.
SHE WAS CRY-ING.
MOTOKO, SLOW DOWN! WE'VE GOT TO TALK!
SHUT UP AND LEAVE ME ALONE!!
I EVEN TRIED DRESSING UP LIKE THIS, HOPING IT WOULD HELP! BUT IT'S JUST A LOST CAUSE!
YOU KNOW THAT'S NOT TRUE!!
YOU AND I BOTH KNOW THAT I'M NOTHING BUT A KENDO TOMBOY!
I DON'T EVEN KNOW A THING ABOUT HOW TO ACT FEMININE!
OW!
WATCH OUT!
WAH!
OW, MY FOO...
...HUH?!
?!
WHOA!

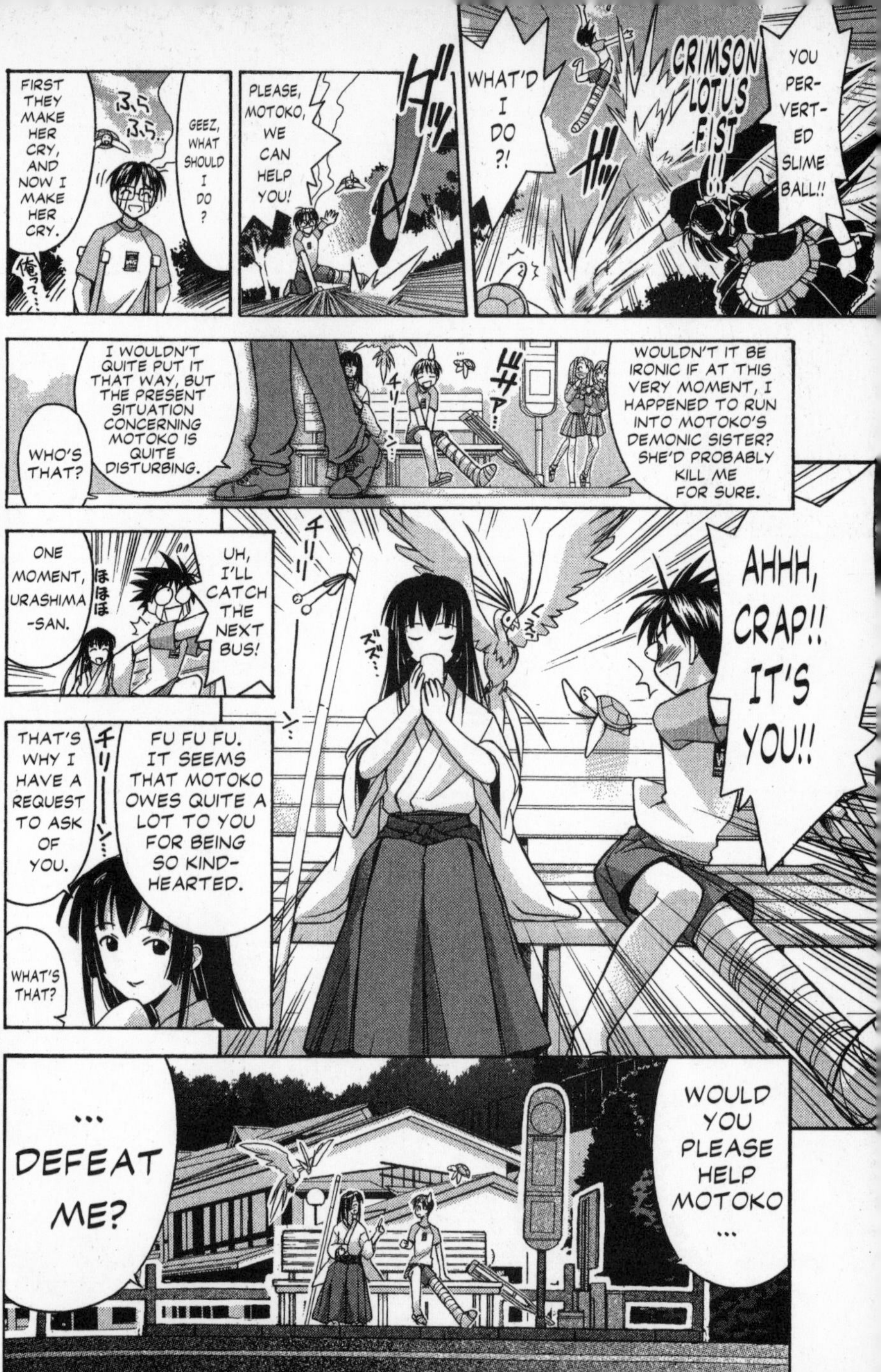
YOU PERVERTED SLIME BALL!!
CRIMSON LOTUS FIST!!
ガッ
ガッ
WHAT'D I DO?!
PLEASE, MOTOKO, WE CAN HELP YOU!
ふらふら..
GEEZ, WHAT SHOULD I DO?
FIRST THEY MAKE HER CRY, AND NOW I MAKE HER CRY.
俺って…
WOULDN'T IT BE IRONIC IF AT THIS VERY MOMENT, I HAPPENED TO RUN INTO MOTOKO'S DEMONIC SISTER? SHE'D PROBABLY KILL ME FOR SURE.
ザァ…
チリーン…
I WOULDN'T QUITE PUT IT THAT WAY, BUT THE PRESENT SITUATION CONCERNING MOTOKO IS QUITE DISTURBING.
WHO'S THAT?
AHHH, CRAP!! IT'S YOU!!
ズズ…
チリリ
UH, I'LL CATCH THE NEXT BUS!
ほほほ
ONE MOMENT, URASHIMA-SAN.
FU FU FU. IT SEEMS THAT MOTOKO OWES QUITE A LOT TO YOU FOR BEING SO KIND-HEARTED.
チリーン…
THAT'S WHY I HAVE A REQUEST TO ASK OF YOU.
WHAT'S THAT?
WOULD YOU PLEASE HELP MOTOKO…
… DEFEAT ME?

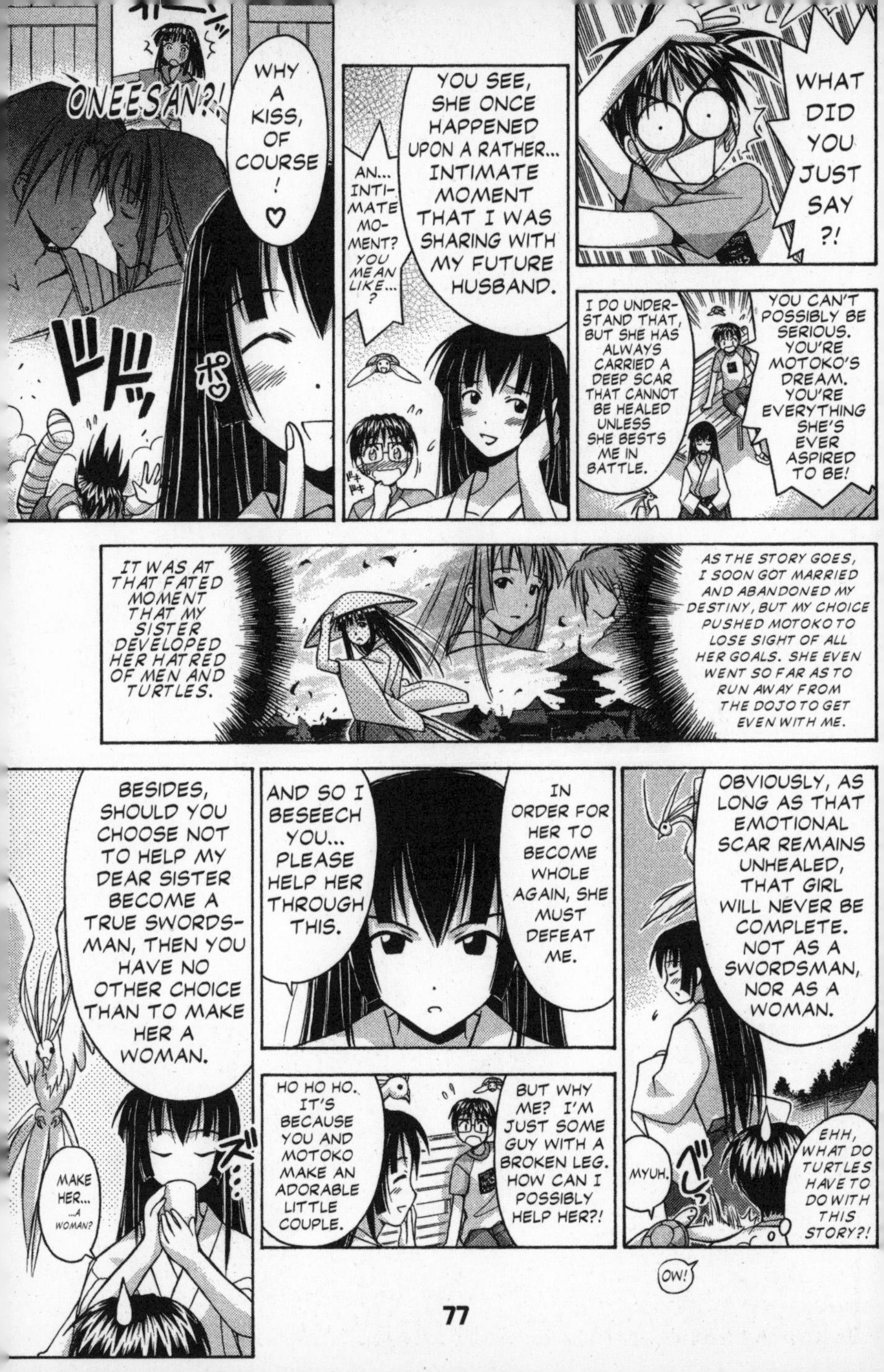
WHAT DID YOU JUST SAY?!
YOU CAN'T POSSIBLY BE SERIOUS. YOU'RE MOTOKO'S DREAM. YOU'RE EVERYTHING SHE'S EVER ASPIRED TO BE!
I DO UNDERSTAND THAT, BUT SHE HAS ALWAYS CARRIED A DEEP SCAR THAT CANNOT BE HEALED UNLESS SHE BESTS ME IN BATTLE.
YOU SEE, SHE ONCE HAPPENED UPON A RATHER... INTIMATE MOMENT THAT I WAS SHARING WITH MY FUTURE HUSBAND.
AN... INTIMATE MOMENT? YOU MEAN LIKE...?
WHY A KISS, OF COURSE! ♥
ONEESAN?!
ドドッ
ポ♡
AS THE STORY GOES, I SOON GOT MARRIED AND ABANDONED MY DESTINY, BUT MY CHOICE PUSHED MOTOKO TO LOSE SIGHT OF ALL HER GOALS. SHE EVEN WENT SO FAR AS TO RUN AWAY FROM THE DOJO TO GET EVEN WITH ME.
IT WAS AT THAT FATED MOMENT THAT MY SISTER DEVELOPED HER HATRED OF MEN AND TURTLES.
OBVIOUSLY, AS LONG AS THAT EMOTIONAL SCAR REMAINS UNHEALED, THAT GIRL WILL NEVER BE COMPLETE. NOT AS A SWORDSMAN, NOR AS A WOMAN.
EHH, WHAT DO TURTLES HAVE TO DO WITH THIS STORY?!
MYUH.
OW!
IN ORDER FOR HER TO BECOME WHOLE AGAIN, SHE MUST DEFEAT ME.
AND SO I BESEECH YOU... PLEASE HELP HER THROUGH THIS.
BUT WHY ME? I'M JUST SOME GUY WITH A BROKEN LEG. HOW CAN I POSSIBLY HELP HER?!
HO HO HO. IT'S BECAUSE YOU AND MOTOKO MAKE AN ADORABLE LITTLE COUPLE.
BESIDES, SHOULD YOU CHOOSE NOT TO HELP MY DEAR SISTER BECOME A TRUE SWORDSMAN, THEN YOU HAVE NO OTHER CHOICE THAN TO MAKE HER A WOMAN.
ズ...
MAKE HER... ...A WOMAN?

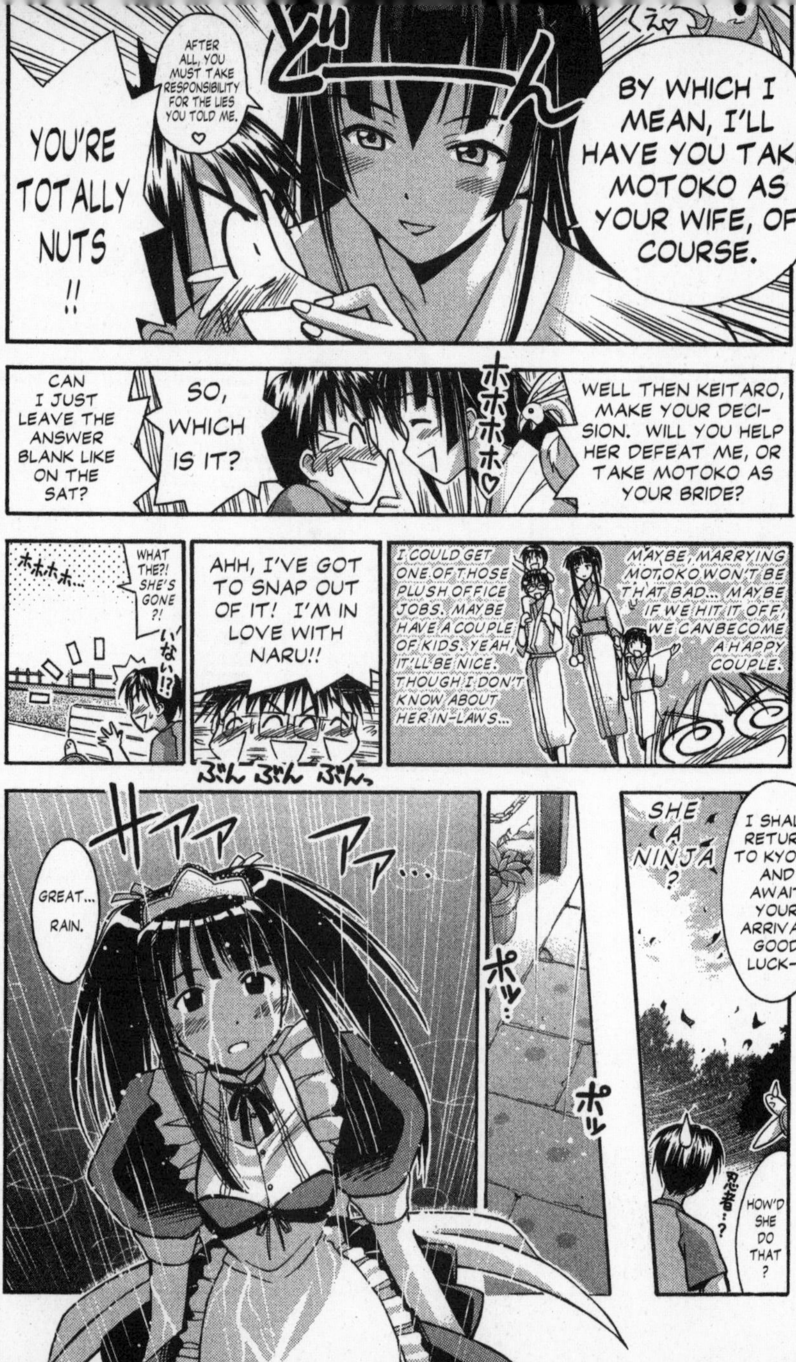

くえ♡
BY WHICH I MEAN, I'LL HAVE YOU TAKE MOTOKO AS YOUR WIFE, OF COURSE.
どーん
AFTER ALL, YOU MUST TAKE RESPONSIBILITY FOR THE LIES YOU TOLD ME. ♡
YOU'RE TOTALLY NUTS !!
WELL THEN KEITARO, MAKE YOUR DECI-SION. WILL YOU HELP HER DEFEAT ME, OR TAKE MOTOKO AS YOUR BRIDE?
ホホホホ♡
SO, WHICH IS IT?
CAN I JUST LEAVE THE ANSWER BLANK LIKE ON THE SAT?
MAYBE, MARRYING MOTOKO WON'T BE THAT BAD... MAYBE IF WE HIT IT OFF, WE CAN BECOME A HAPPY COUPLE.
I COULD GET ONE OF THOSE PLUSH OFFICE JOBS. MAYBE HAVE A COUPLE OF KIDS. YEAH, IT'LL BE NICE. THOUGH I DON'T KNOW ABOUT HER IN-LAWS...
AHH, I'VE GOT TO SNAP OUT OF IT! I'M IN LOVE WITH NARU!!
ぶん ぶん ぶんっ
WHAT THE?! SHE'S GONE ?!
いない!?
ホホホホ...
I SHALL RETURN TO KYOTO AND AWAIT YOUR ARRIVAL. GOOD LUCK--
SHE A NINJA?
忍者…?
HOW'D SHE DO THAT?
ポツ
ポツ
ザァァ ァ...
GREAT... RAIN.

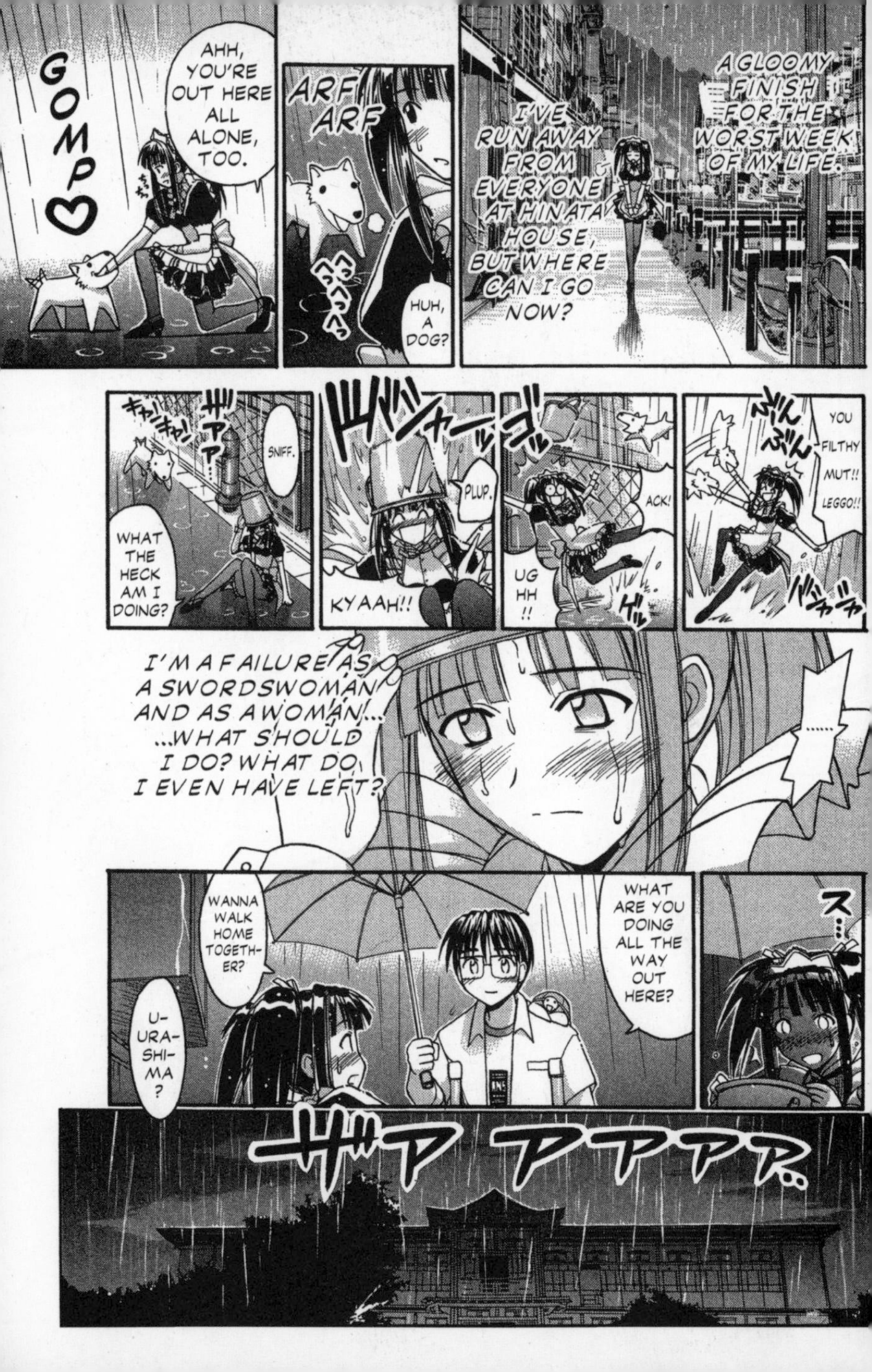
A GLOOMY FINISH FOR THE WORST WEEK OF MY LIFE.
I'VE RUN AWAY FROM EVERYONE AT HINATA HOUSE, BUT WHERE CAN I GO NOW?
ARF ARF
HUH, A DOG?
AHH, YOU'RE OUT HERE ALL ALONE, TOO.
GOMP♡
YOU FILTHY MUT!! LEGGO!!
ACK!
UGH HH!!
PLUP.
KYAAH!!
SNIFF.
WHAT THE HECK AM I DOING?
I'M A FAILURE AS A SWORDSWOMAN AND AS A WOMAN!... ...WHAT SHOULD I DO? WHAT DO I EVEN HAVE LEFT?
......
WHAT ARE YOU DOING ALL THE WAY OUT HERE?
WANNA WALK HOME TOGETH-ER?
U-URA-SHI-MA?

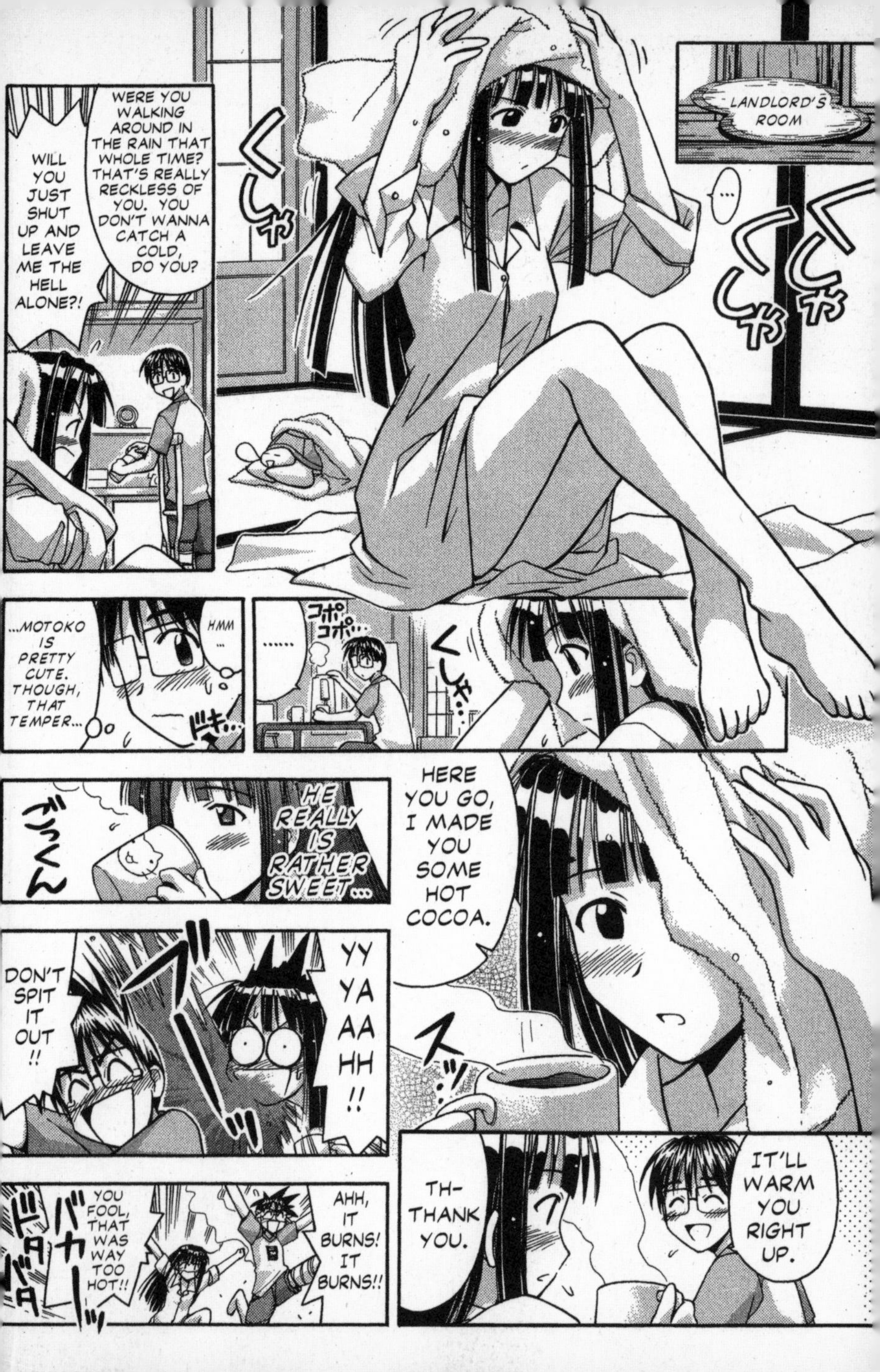
LANDLORD'S ROOM
...
くしゃくしゃ
くしゃ
WERE YOU WALKING AROUND IN THE RAIN THAT WHOLE TIME? THAT'S REALLY RECKLESS OF YOU. YOU DON'T WANNA CATCH A COLD, DO YOU?
WILL YOU JUST SHUT UP AND LEAVE ME THE HELL ALONE?!
くしゅ...
コポコポ...
......
HMM...
...MOTOKO IS PRETTY CUTE. THOUGH, THAT TEMPER...
ドキ...
HERE YOU GO, I MADE YOU SOME HOT COCOA.
スッ
TH-THANK YOU.
IT'LL WARM YOU RIGHT UP.
ごっくん
HE REALLY IS RATHER SWEET...
YYYAAAHH!!
DON'T SPIT IT OUT!!
AHH, IT BURNS! IT BURNS!!
YOU FOOL, THAT WAS WAY TOO HOT!!
バカー
ドタバタ

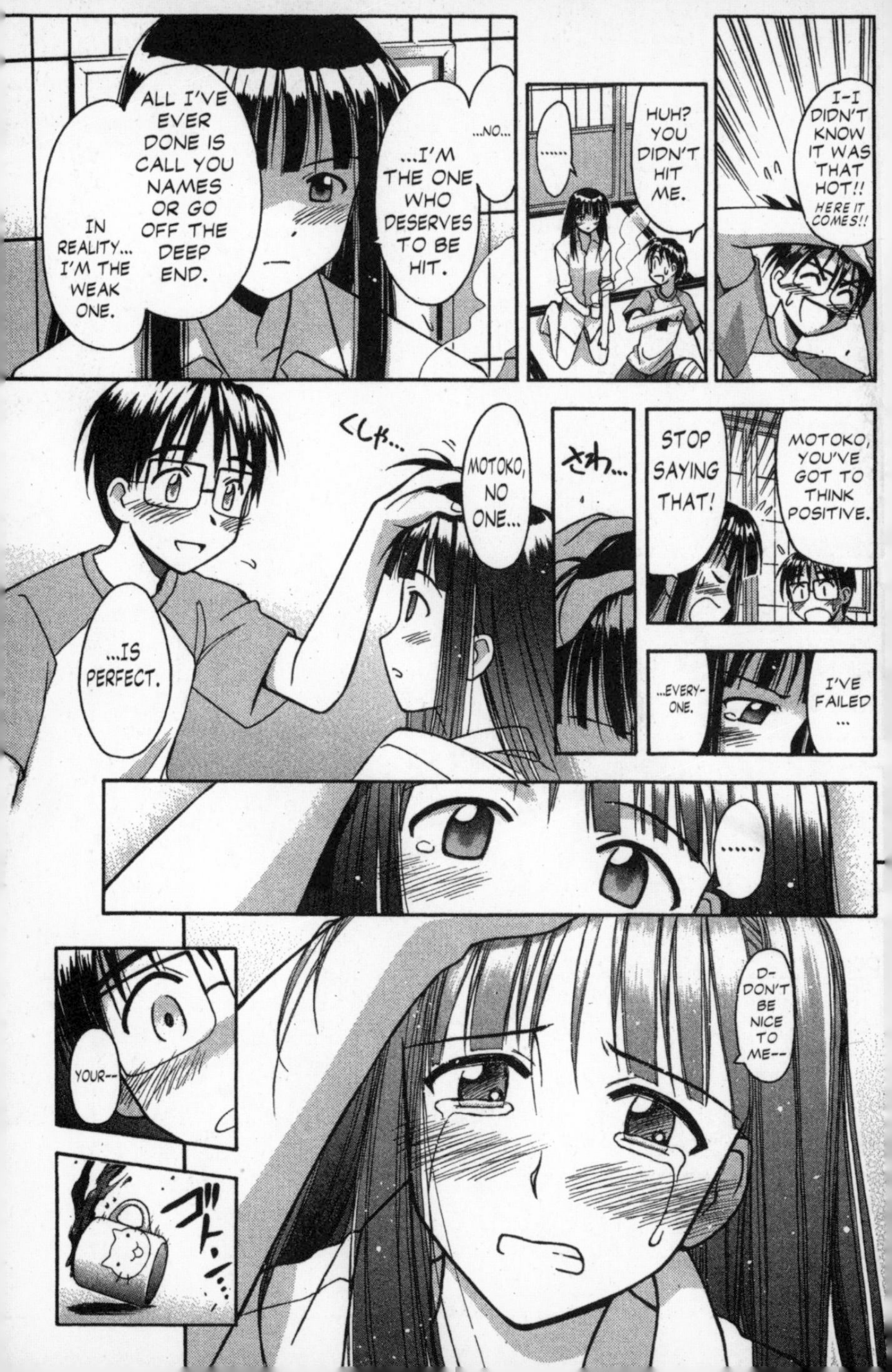
I-I DIDN'T KNOW IT WAS THAT HOT!!
HERE IT COMES!!
HUH? YOU DIDN'T HIT ME.
......
...NO...
...I'M THE ONE WHO DESERVES TO BE HIT.
ALL I'VE EVER DONE IS CALL YOU NAMES OR GO OFF THE DEEP END.
IN REALITY... I'M THE WEAK ONE.
MOTOKO, YOU'VE GOT TO THINK POSITIVE.
STOP SAYING THAT!
さわ...
I'VE FAILED ...
...EVERY-ONE.
くしゃ...
MOTOKO, NO ONE...
...IS PERFECT.
......
D-DON'T BE NICE TO ME--
YOUR--
ゴトッ...

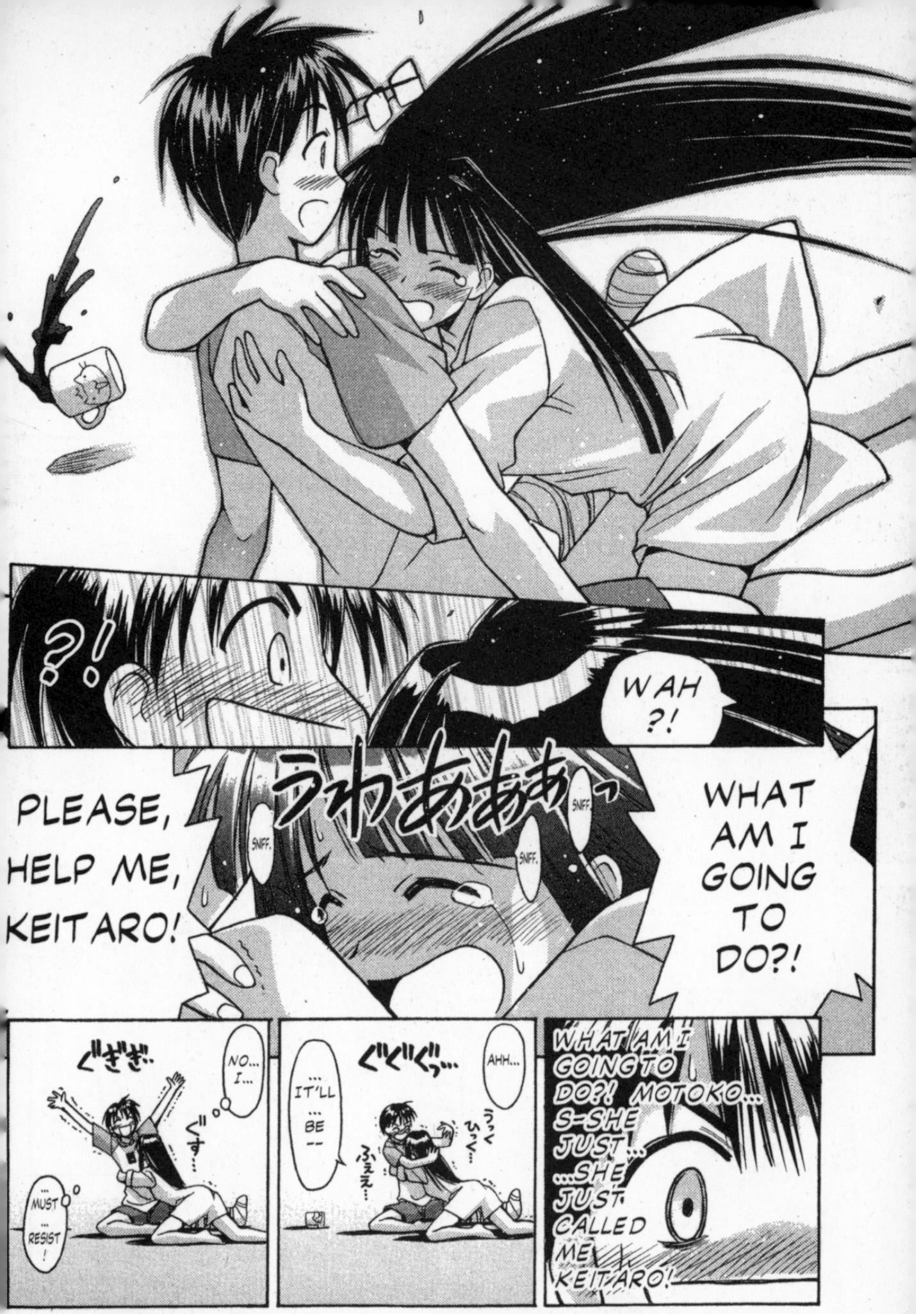
?!
WAH ?!
WHAT AM I GOING TO DO?!
うわあああっ
SNIFF.
SNIFF.
SNIFF.
PLEASE, HELP ME, KEITARO!
WHAT AM I GOING TO DO?! MOTOKO... S-SHE JUST... ...SHE JUST CALLED ME KEITARO!
AHH...
ぐぐぐっ...
うっく ひっく...
ふぇぇ...
... IT'LL ... BE --
NO... I...
ぐぎぎ
ぐす...
... MUST ... RESIST!

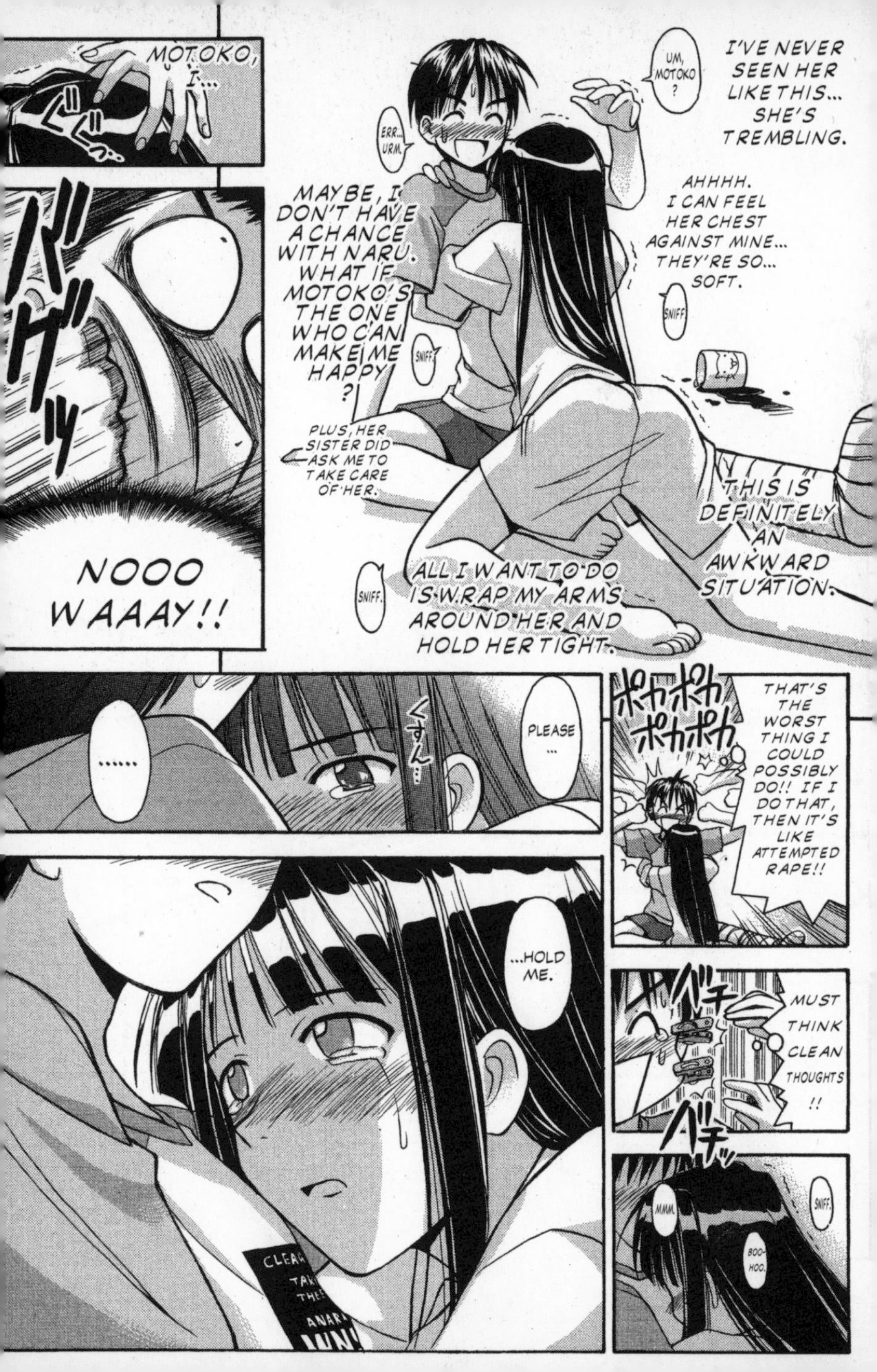
I'VE NEVER SEEN HER LIKE THIS... SHE'S TREMBLING.
UM, MOTOKO?
ERR... URM.
AHHHH. I CAN FEEL HER CHEST AGAINST MINE... THEY'RE SO... SOFT.
SNIFF
MAYBE, I DON'T HAVE A CHANCE WITH NARU. WHAT IF MOTOKO'S THE ONE WHO CAN MAKE ME HAPPY?
SNIFF.
PLUS, HER SISTER DID ASK ME TO TAKE CARE OF HER.
THIS IS DEFINITELY AN AWKWARD SITUATION.
ALL I WANT TO DO IS WRAP MY ARMS AROUND HER AND HOLD HER TIGHT.
SNIFF.
MOTOKO, I...
NOOO WAAAY!!
ポカポカ ポカポカ
THAT'S THE WORST THING I COULD POSSIBLY DO!! IF I DO THAT, THEN IT'S LIKE ATTEMPTED RAPE!!
MUST THINK CLEAN THOUGHTS!!
SNIFF.
MMM.
BOO-HOO.
PLEASE...
くすん...
......
...HOLD ME.

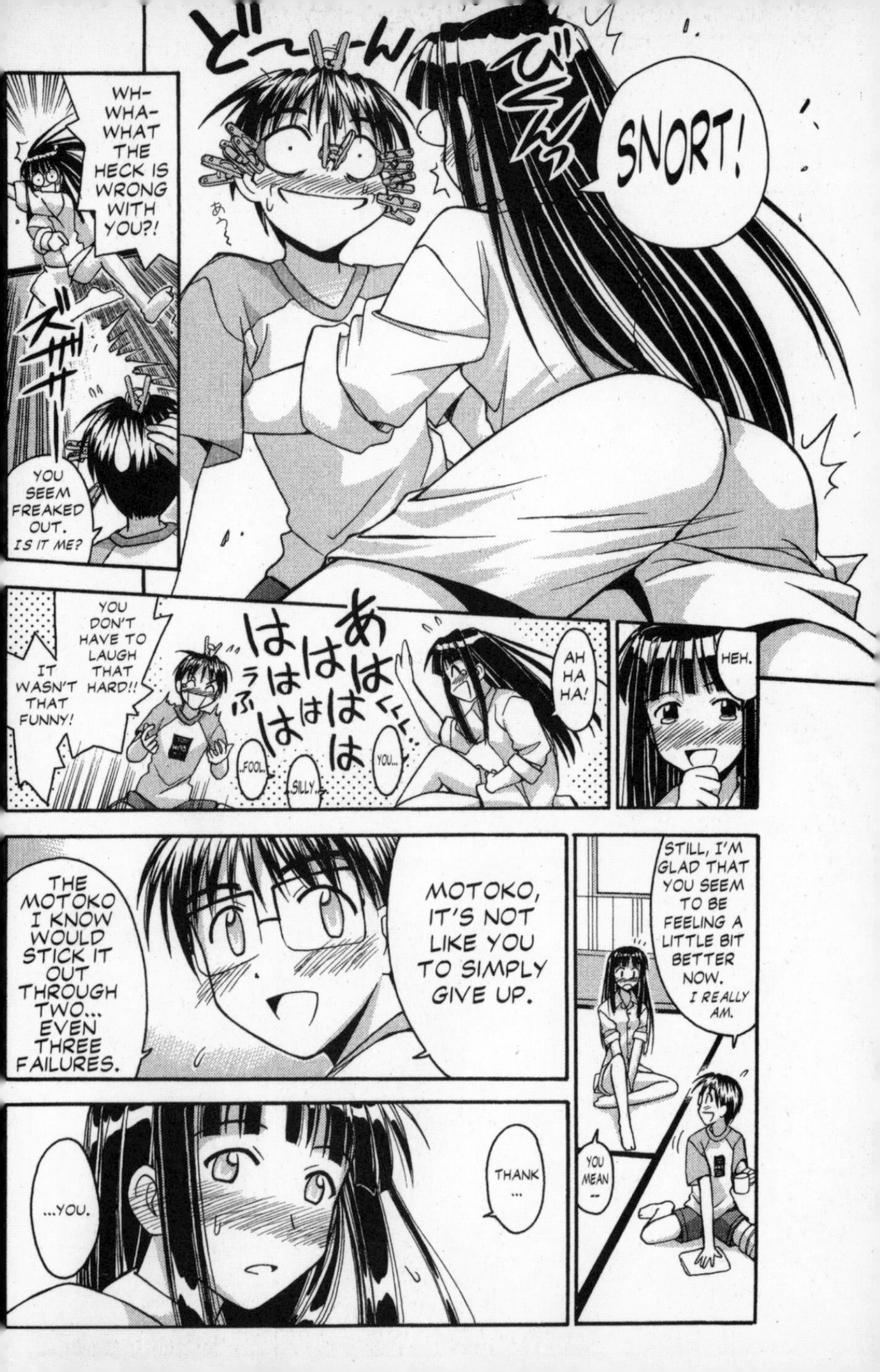
SNORT!
WH- WHA- WHAT THE HECK IS WRONG WITH YOU?!
YOU SEEM FREAKED OUT. IS IT ME?
HEH.
AH HA HA!
YOU...
...SILLY...
...FOOL...
YOU DON'T HAVE TO LAUGH THAT HARD!!
IT WASN'T THAT FUNNY!
STILL, I'M GLAD THAT YOU SEEM TO BE FEELING A LITTLE BIT BETTER NOW. I REALLY AM.
YOU MEAN --
MOTOKO, IT'S NOT LIKE YOU TO SIMPLY GIVE UP.
THE MOTOKO I KNOW WOULD STICK IT OUT THROUGH TWO... EVEN THREE FAILURES.
THANK ...
...YOU.

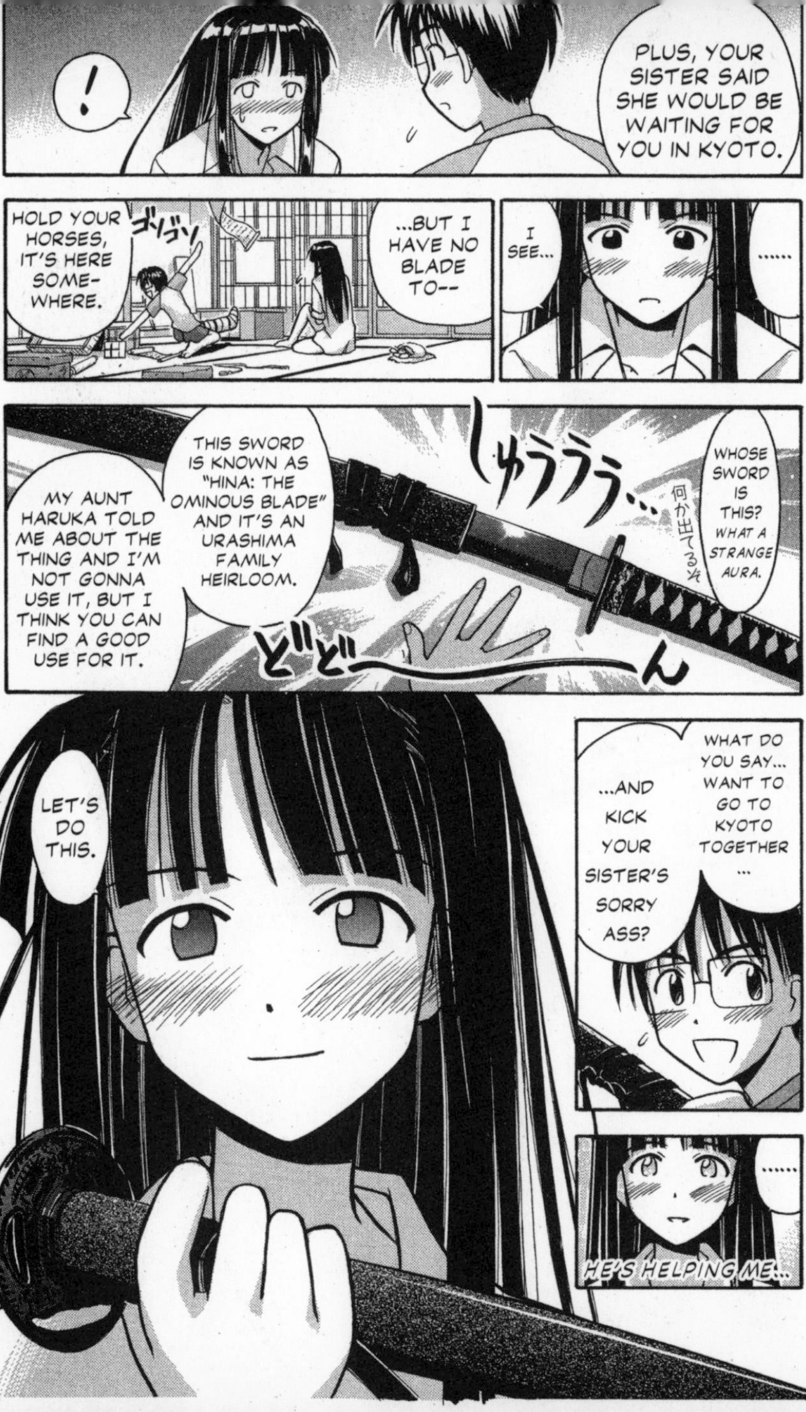
PLUS, YOUR SISTER SAID SHE WOULD BE WAITING FOR YOU IN KYOTO.
!
......
I SEE...
...BUT I HAVE NO BLADE TO--
ゴソゴソ
HOLD YOUR HORSES, IT'S HERE SOME-WHERE.
WHOSE SWORD IS THIS? WHAT A STRANGE AURA.
何か出てる
しゅううう...
THIS SWORD IS KNOWN AS "HINA: THE OMINOUS BLADE" AND IT'S AN URASHIMA FAMILY HEIRLOOM.
MY AUNT HARUKA TOLD ME ABOUT THE THING AND I'M NOT GONNA USE IT, BUT I THINK YOU CAN FIND A GOOD USE FOR IT.
どどーーーん
WHAT DO YOU SAY... WANT TO GO TO KYOTO TOGETHER...
...AND KICK YOUR SISTER'S SORRY ASS?
......
HE'S HELPING ME...
LET'S DO THIS.

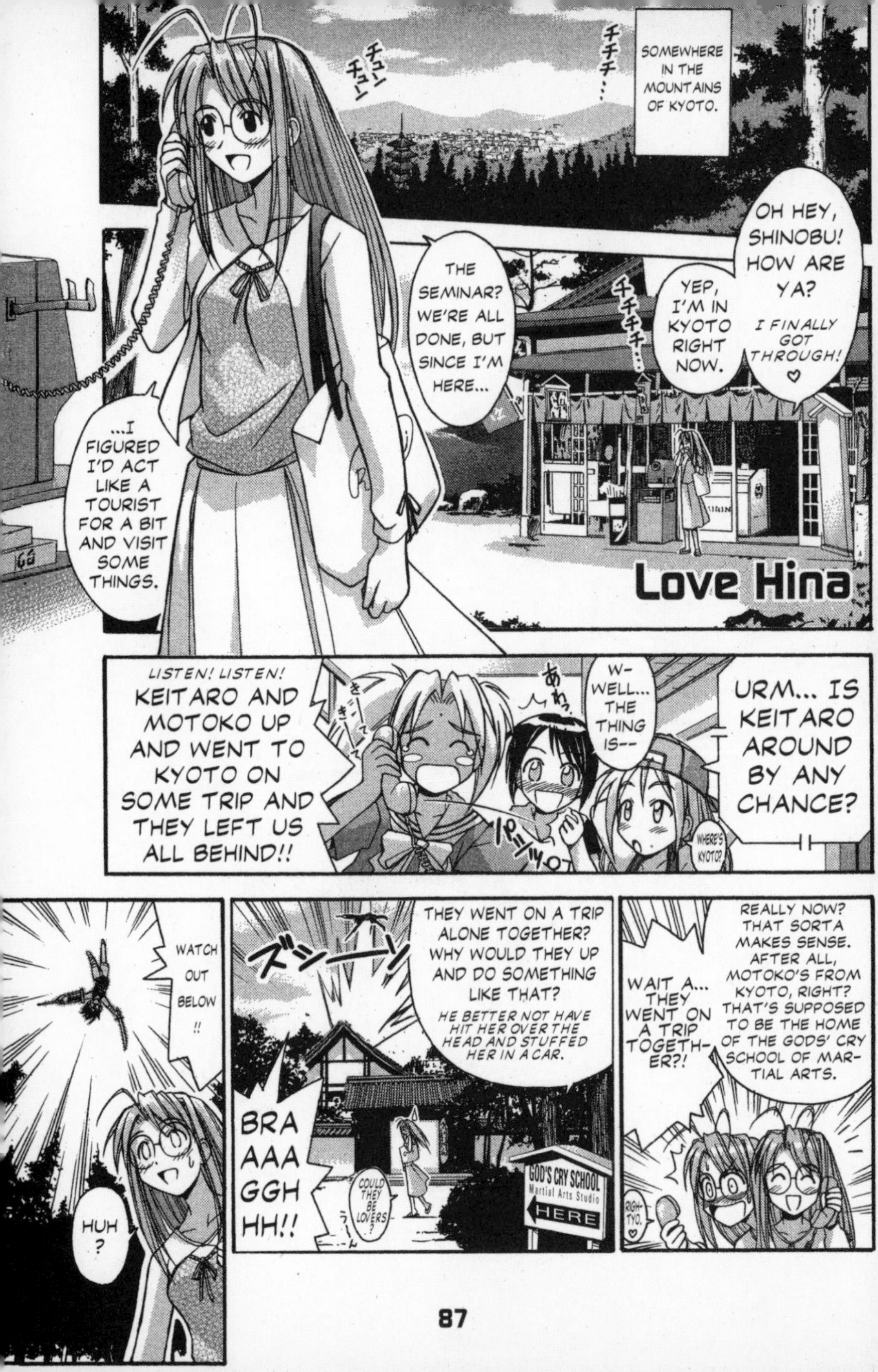
SOMEWHERE IN THE MOUNTAINS OF KYOTO.
チチチ…
チュンチュン
OH HEY, SHINOBU! HOW ARE YA?
I FINALLY GOT THROUGH! ♡
YEP, I'M IN KYOTO RIGHT NOW.
チチチチ…
THE SEMINAR? WE'RE ALL DONE, BUT SINCE I'M HERE...
...I FIGURED I'D ACT LIKE A TOURIST FOR A BIT AND VISIT SOME THINGS.
Love Hina
URM... IS KEITARO AROUND BY ANY CHANCE?
WHERE'S KYOTO?
W-WELL... THE THING IS--
あわっ
LISTEN! LISTEN!
KEITARO AND MOTOKO UP AND WENT TO KYOTO ON SOME TRIP AND THEY LEFT US ALL BEHIND!!
REALLY NOW? THAT SORTA MAKES SENSE. AFTER ALL, MOTOKO'S FROM KYOTO, RIGHT? THAT'S SUPPOSED TO BE THE HOME OF THE GODS' CRY SCHOOL OF MARTIAL ARTS.
WAIT A... THEY WENT ON A TRIP TOGETHER?!
RIGHTYO. ♡
THEY WENT ON A TRIP ALONE TOGETHER? WHY WOULD THEY UP AND DO SOMETHING LIKE THAT?
HE BETTER NOT HAVE HIT HER OVER THE HEAD AND STUFFED HER IN A CAR.
ズシーン
BRAAAAGGHHH!!
COULD THEY BE LOVERS?
GOD'S CRY SCHOOL
Martial Arts Studio
HERE
WATCH OUT BELOW !!
HUH ?

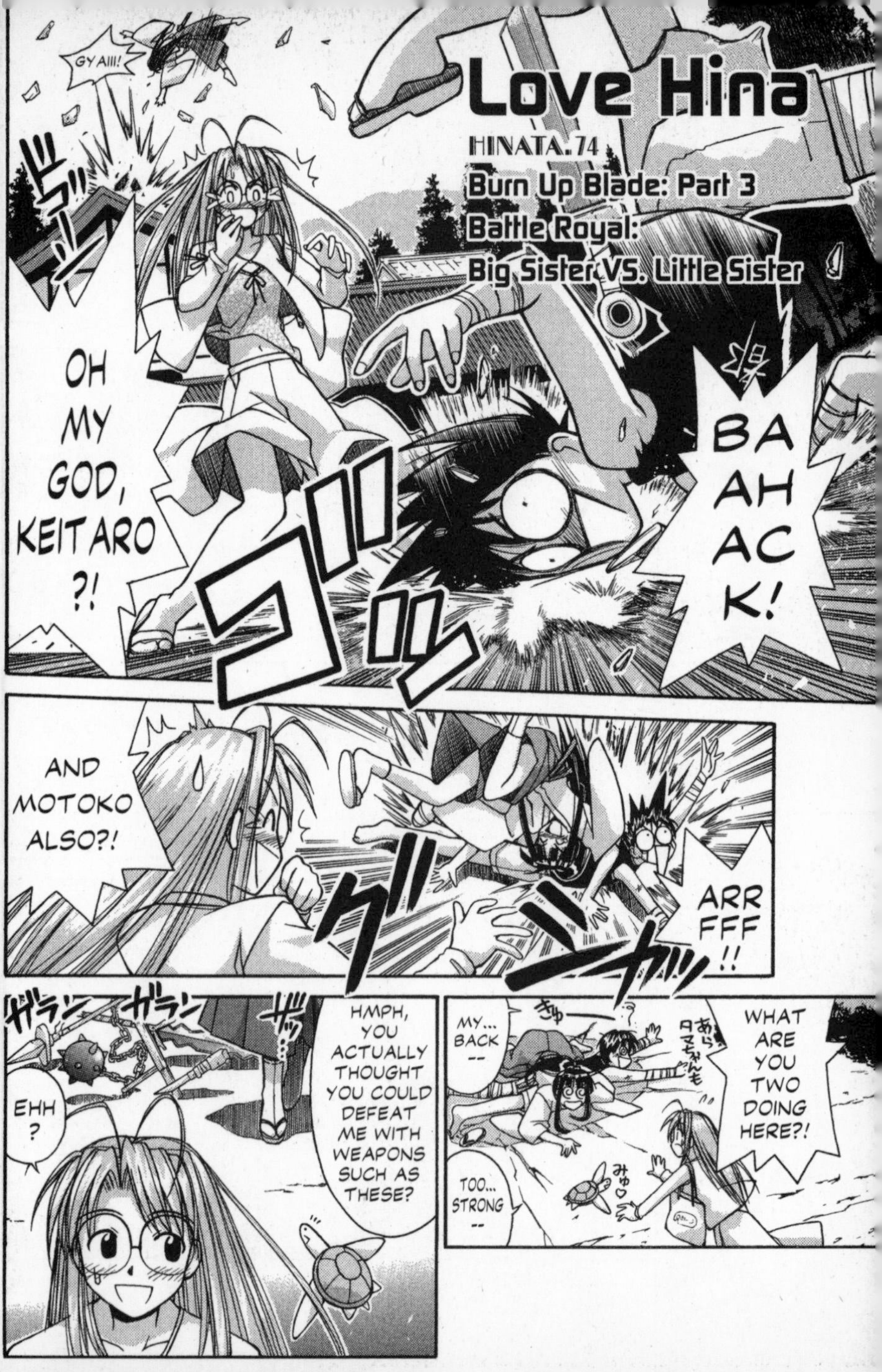
Love Hina
HINATA.74
Burn Up Blade: Part 3
Battle Royal:
Big Sister VS. Little Sister
BA AH AC K!
GYAIII!
OH MY GOD, KEITARO ?!
ARR FFF !!
AND MOTOKO ALSO?!
WHAT ARE YOU TWO DOING HERE?!
あら タマちゃんも
MY... BACK --
TOO... STRONG --
みゅ♡
HMPH, YOU ACTUALLY THOUGHT YOU COULD DEFEAT ME WITH WEAPONS SUCH AS THESE?
ガラン
ガラン
EHH ?

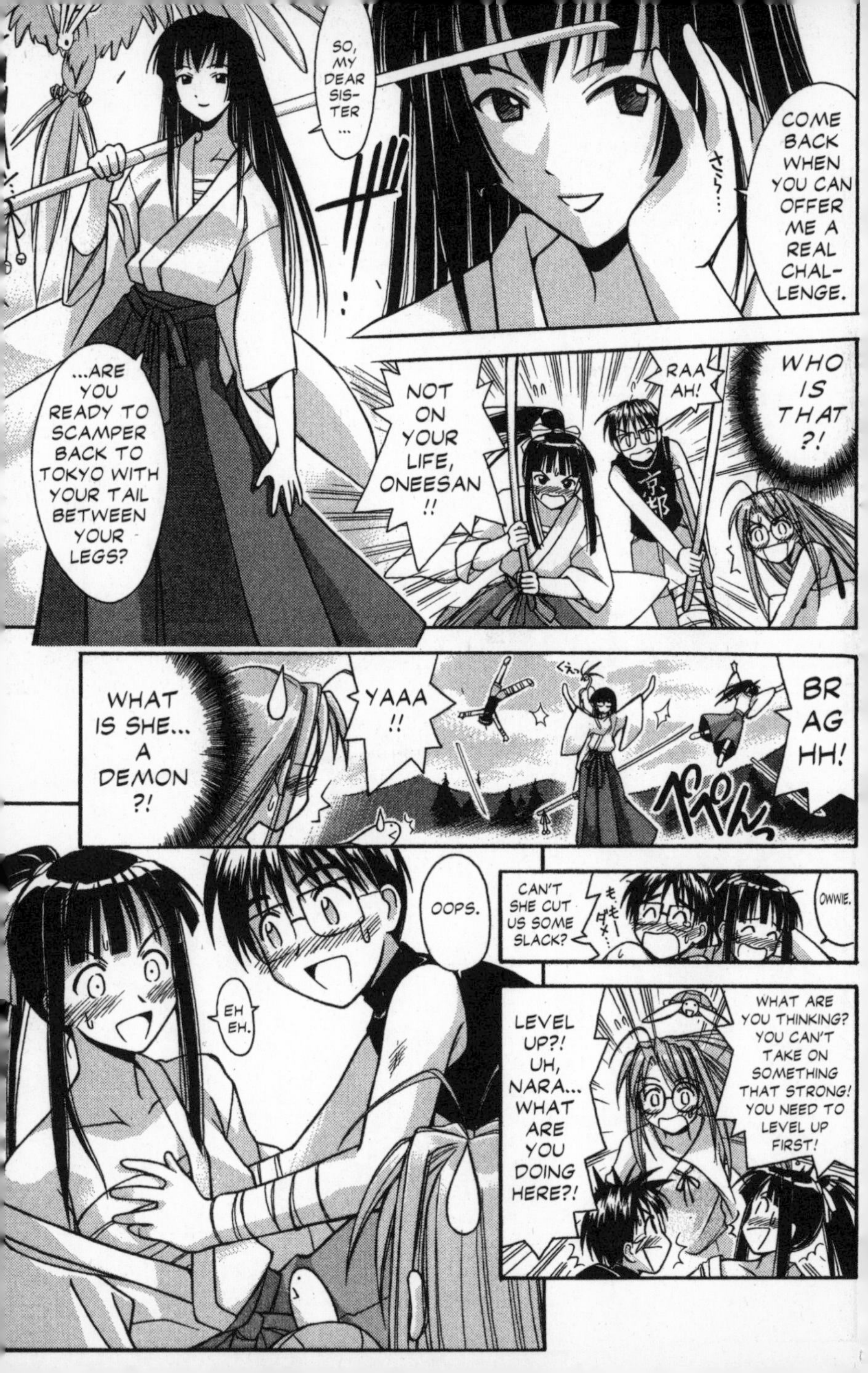
SO, MY DEAR SISTER...
COME BACK WHEN YOU CAN OFFER ME A REAL CHALLENGE.
さら…
WHO IS THAT?!
RAAAH!
NOT ON YOUR LIFE, ONEESAN!!
...ARE YOU READY TO SCAMPER BACK TO TOKYO WITH YOUR TAIL BETWEEN YOUR LEGS?
BRAGHH!
ぺぺん
YAAA!!
WHAT IS SHE... A DEMON?!
OWWIE.
も、もーダメ…
CAN'T SHE CUT US SOME SLACK?
WHAT ARE YOU THINKING? YOU CAN'T TAKE ON SOMETHING THAT STRONG! YOU NEED TO LEVEL UP FIRST!
LEVEL UP?! UH, NARA... WHAT ARE YOU DOING HERE?!
OOPS.
EH EH.

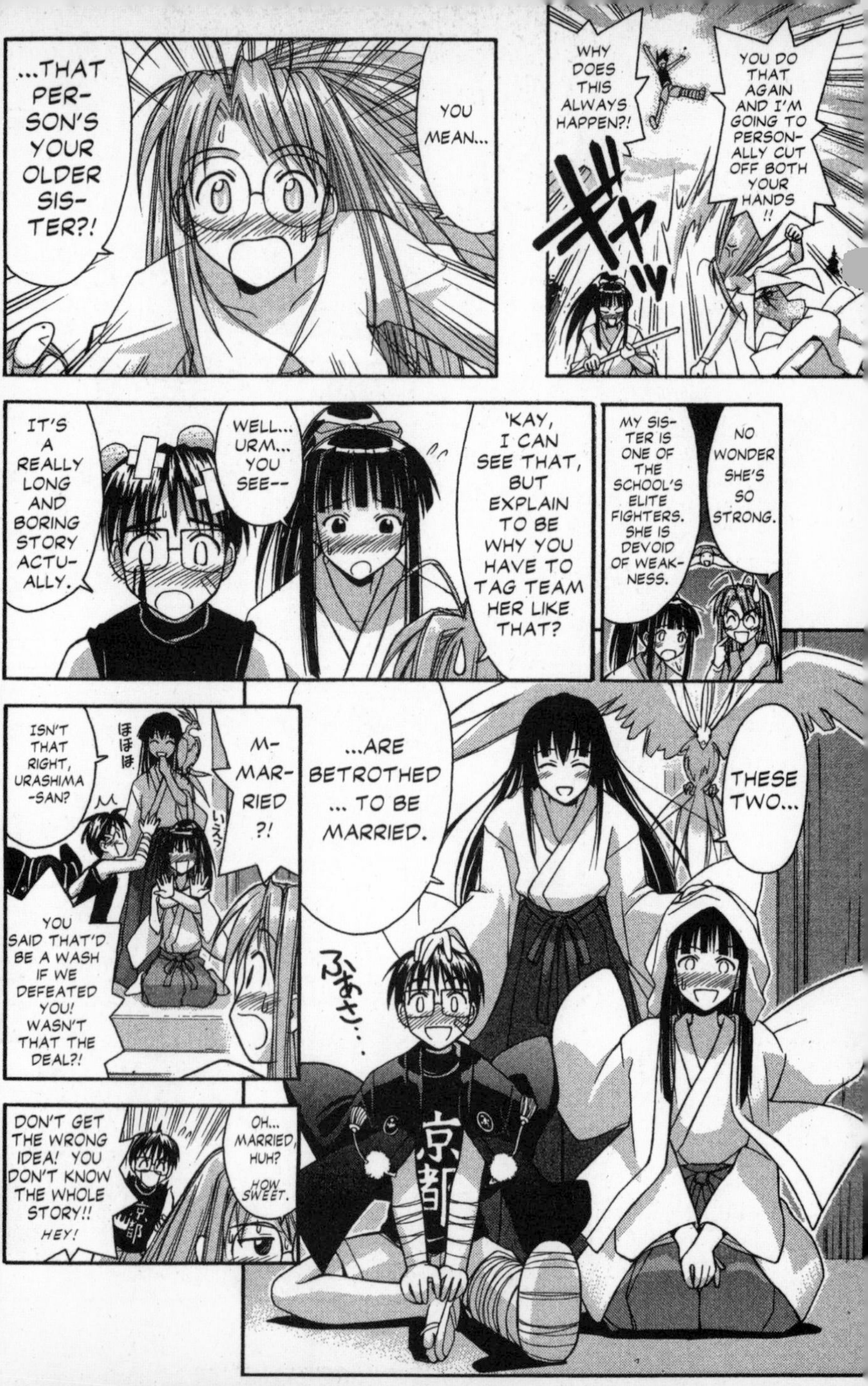
YOU DO THAT AGAIN AND I'M GOING TO PERSONALLY CUT OFF BOTH YOUR HANDS !!
WHY DOES THIS ALWAYS HAPPEN?!
ギャッ
YOU MEAN...
...THAT PERSON'S YOUR OLDER SISTER?!
NO WONDER SHE'S SO STRONG.
MY SISTER IS ONE OF THE SCHOOL'S ELITE FIGHTERS. SHE IS DEVOID OF WEAKNESS.
'KAY, I CAN SEE THAT, BUT EXPLAIN TO BE WHY YOU HAVE TO TAG TEAM HER LIKE THAT?
WELL... URM... YOU SEE--
IT'S A REALLY LONG AND BORING STORY ACTUALLY.
THESE TWO...
...ARE BETROTHED ... TO BE MARRIED.
ふあさ...
M-MARRIED?!
ほほほ
ISN'T THAT RIGHT, URASHIMA-SAN?
いえっ
YOU SAID THAT'D BE A WASH IF WE DEFEATED YOU! WASN'T THAT THE DEAL?!
OH... MARRIED, HUH? HOW SWEET.
DON'T GET THE WRONG IDEA! YOU DON'T KNOW THE WHOLE STORY!!
HEY!

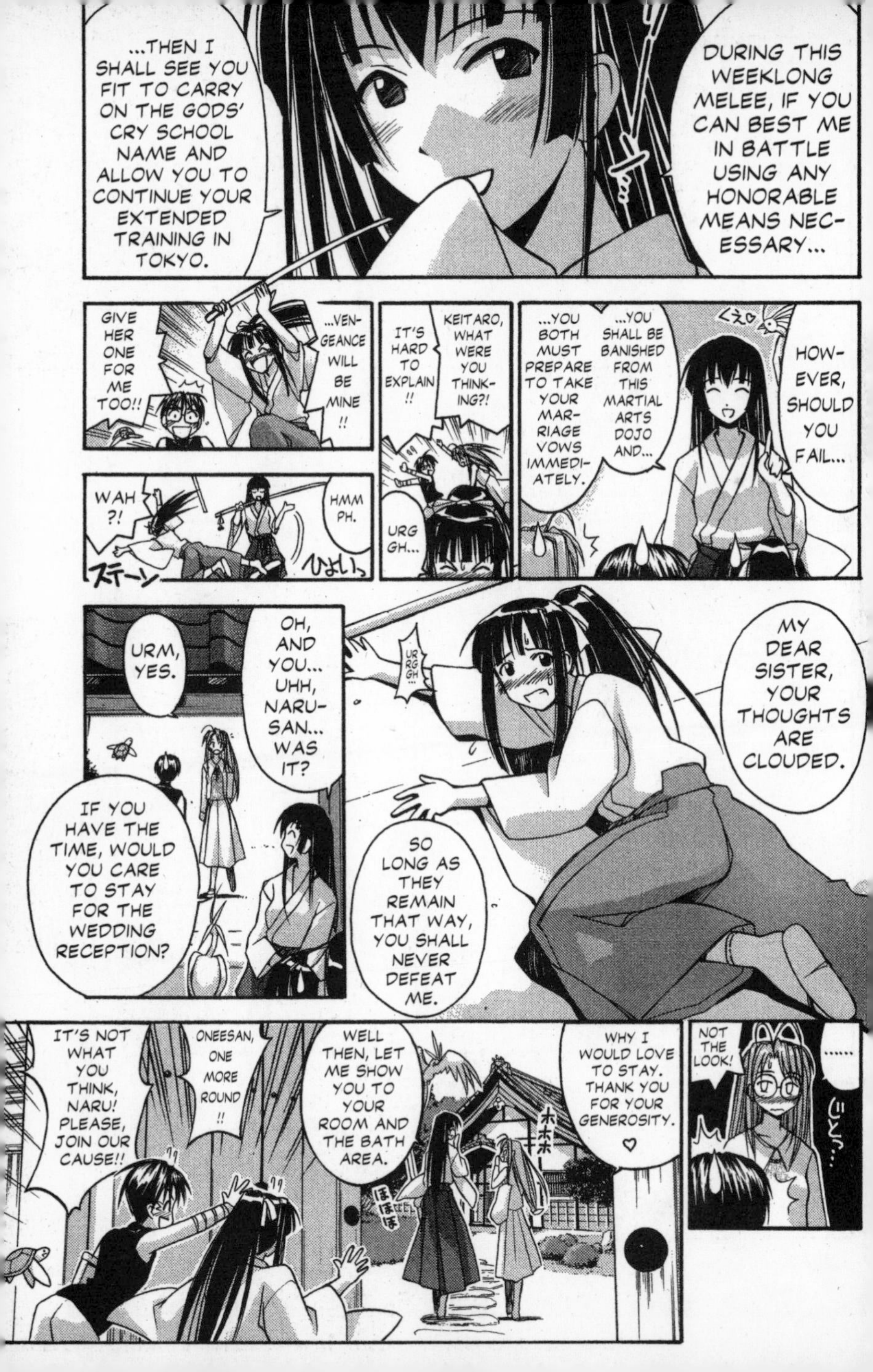
DURING THIS WEEKLONG MELEE, IF YOU CAN BEST ME IN BATTLE USING ANY HONORABLE MEANS NECESSARY...
...THEN I SHALL SEE YOU FIT TO CARRY ON THE GODS' CRY SCHOOL NAME AND ALLOW YOU TO CONTINUE YOUR EXTENDED TRAINING IN TOKYO.
HOWEVER, SHOULD YOU FAIL...
...YOU SHALL BE BANISHED FROM THIS MARTIAL ARTS DOJO AND...
...YOU BOTH MUST PREPARE TO TAKE YOUR MARRIAGE VOWS IMMEDIATELY.
KEITARO, WHAT WERE YOU THINKING?!
IT'S HARD TO EXPLAIN!!
URGGH...
...VENGEANCE WILL BE MINE!!
GIVE HER ONE FOR ME TOO!!
HMMPH.
WAH?!
MY DEAR SISTER, YOUR THOUGHTS ARE CLOUDED.
URRGGH...
SO LONG AS THEY REMAIN THAT WAY, YOU SHALL NEVER DEFEAT ME.
OH, AND YOU... UHH, NARU-SAN... WAS IT?
URM, YES.
IF YOU HAVE THE TIME, WOULD YOU CARE TO STAY FOR THE WEDDING RECEPTION?
......
NOT THE LOOK!
WHY I WOULD LOVE TO STAY. THANK YOU FOR YOUR GENEROSITY. ♡
WELL THEN, LET ME SHOW YOU TO YOUR ROOM AND THE BATH AREA.
ONEESAN, ONE MORE ROUND!!
IT'S NOT WHAT YOU THINK, NARU! PLEASE, JOIN OUR CAUSE!!

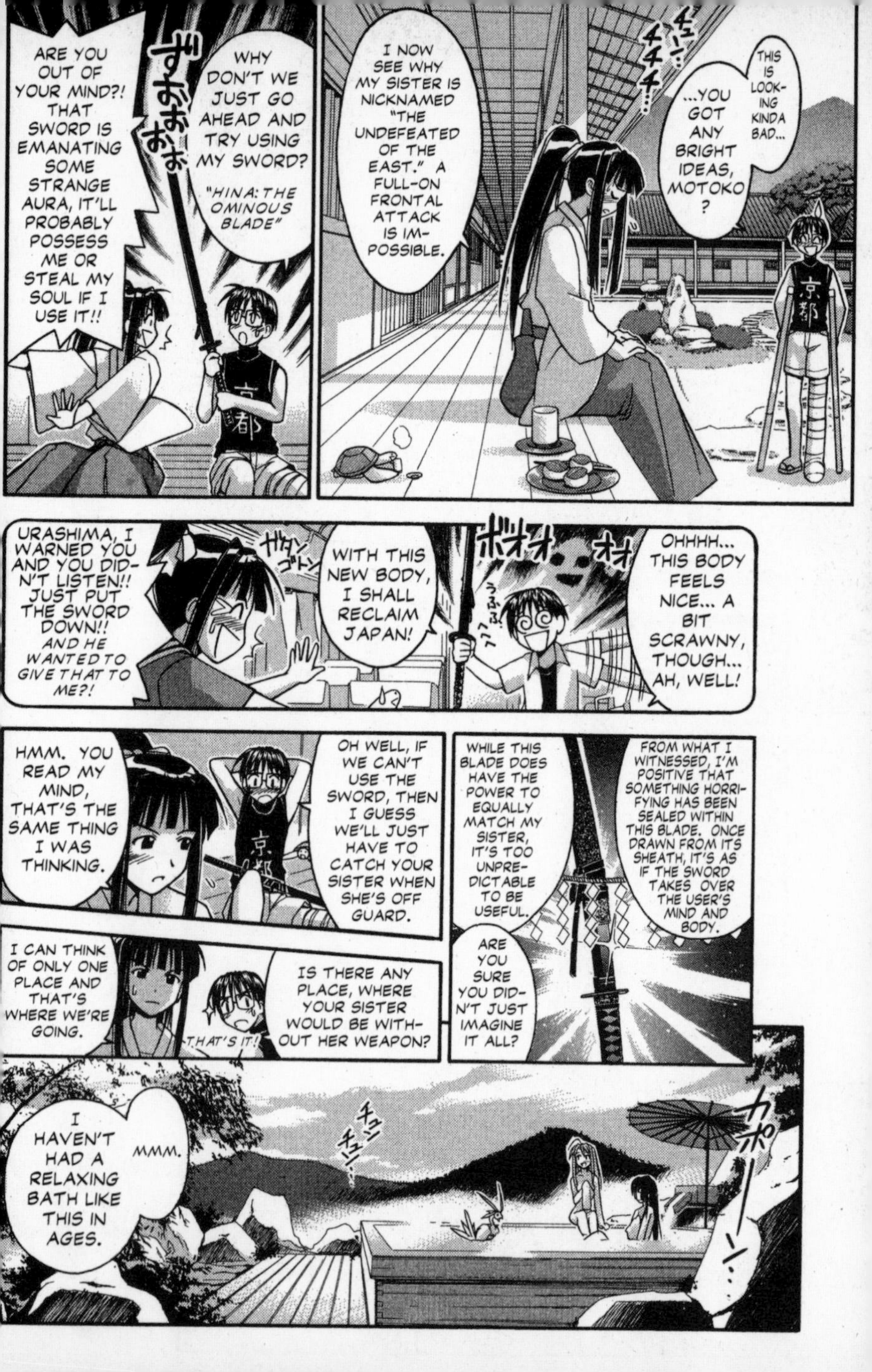
チュン チチチ…
THIS IS LOOKING KINDA BAD...
...YOU GOT ANY BRIGHT IDEAS, MOTOKO?
I NOW SEE WHY MY SISTER IS NICKNAMED "THE UNDEFEATED OF THE EAST." A FULL-ON FRONTAL ATTACK IS IMPOSSIBLE.
WHY DON'T WE JUST GO AHEAD AND TRY USING MY SWORD?
"HINA: THE OMINOUS BLADE"
ずおおおお
ARE YOU OUT OF YOUR MIND?! THAT SWORD IS EMANATING SOME STRANGE AURA, IT'LL PROBABLY POSSESS ME OR STEAL MY SOUL IF I USE IT!!
OHHHH... THIS BODY FEELS NICE... A BIT SCRAWNY, THOUGH... AH, WELL!
ボオオオ オオ
うふふふ
WITH THIS NEW BODY, I SHALL RECLAIM JAPAN!
ガタン ゴトン
URASHIMA, I WARNED YOU AND YOU DIDN'T LISTEN!! JUST PUT THE SWORD DOWN!!
AND HE WANTED TO GIVE THAT TO ME?!
FROM WHAT I WITNESSED, I'M POSITIVE THAT SOMETHING HORRIFYING HAS BEEN SEALED WITHIN THIS BLADE. ONCE DRAWN FROM ITS SHEATH, IT'S AS IF THE SWORD TAKES OVER THE USER'S MIND AND BODY.
WHILE THIS BLADE DOES HAVE THE POWER TO EQUALLY MATCH MY SISTER, IT'S TOO UNPREDICTABLE TO BE USEFUL.
ARE YOU SURE YOU DIDN'T JUST IMAGINE IT ALL?
OH WELL, IF WE CAN'T USE THE SWORD, THEN I GUESS WE'LL JUST HAVE TO CATCH YOUR SISTER WHEN SHE'S OFF GUARD.
HMM. YOU READ MY MIND, THAT'S THE SAME THING I WAS THINKING.
IS THERE ANY PLACE, WHERE YOUR SISTER WOULD BE WITHOUT HER WEAPON?
THAT'S IT!
I CAN THINK OF ONLY ONE PLACE AND THAT'S WHERE WE'RE GOING.
カポーン…
チュン チュン…
MMM.
I HAVEN'T HAD A RELAXING BATH LIKE THIS IN AGES.

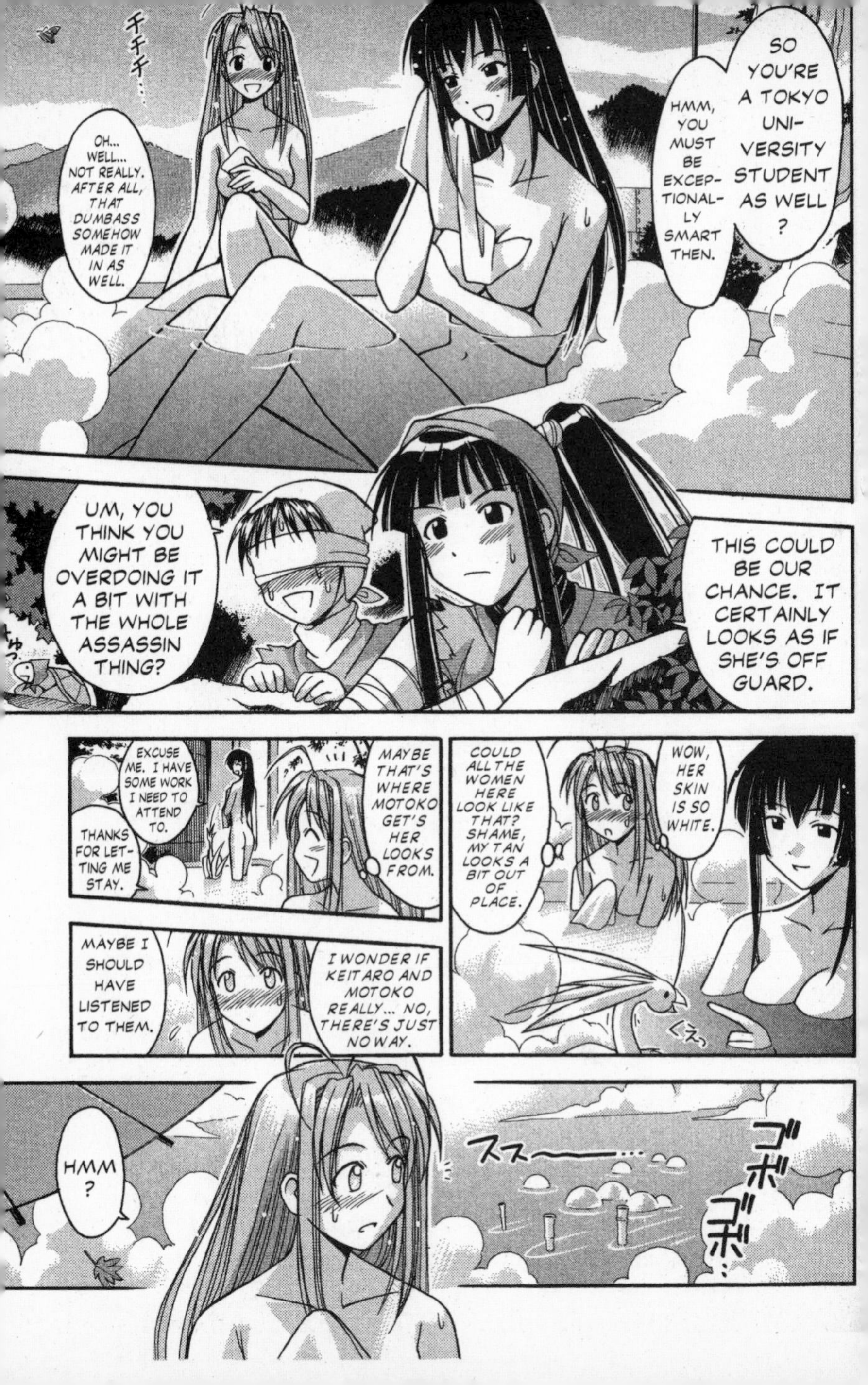
SO YOU'RE A TOKYO UNIVERSITY STUDENT AS WELL?
HMM, YOU MUST BE EXCEPTIONALLY SMART THEN.
チチチ...
OH... WELL... NOT REALLY. AFTER ALL, THAT DUMBASS SOMEHOW MADE IT IN AS WELL.
THIS COULD BE OUR CHANCE. IT CERTAINLY LOOKS AS IF SHE'S OFF GUARD.
UM, YOU THINK YOU MIGHT BE OVERDOING IT A BIT WITH THE WHOLE ASSASSIN THING?
WOW, HER SKIN IS SO WHITE.
COULD ALL THE WOMEN HERE LOOK LIKE THAT? SHAME, MY TAN LOOKS A BIT OUT OF PLACE.
くえっ
MAYBE THAT'S WHERE MOTOKO GET'S HER LOOKS FROM.
EXCUSE ME. I HAVE SOME WORK I NEED TO ATTEND TO.
THANKS FOR LETTING ME STAY.
I WONDER IF KEITARO AND MOTOKO REALLY... NO, THERE'S JUST NO WAY.
MAYBE I SHOULD HAVE LISTENED TO THEM.
ゴボゴボ...
ススー...
HMM?

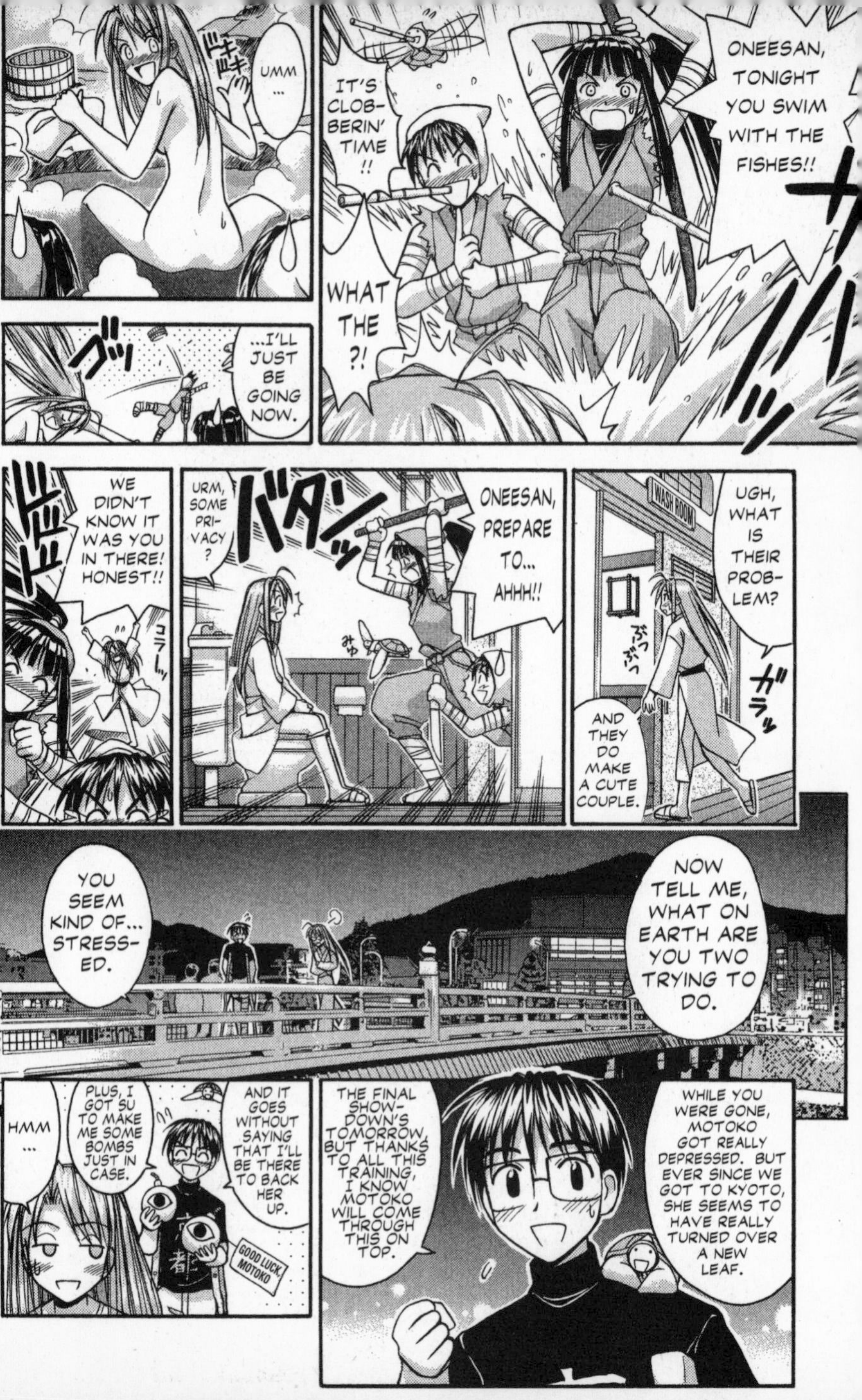
ONEESAN, TONIGHT YOU SWIM WITH THE FISHES!!
IT'S CLOBBERIN' TIME!!
WHAT THE ?!
UMM ...
...I'LL JUST BE GOING NOW.
WASH ROOM
UGH, WHAT IS THEIR PROBLEM?
AND THEY DO MAKE A CUTE COUPLE.
ONEESAN, PREPARE TO... AHHH!!
URM, SOME PRIVACY?
WE DIDN'T KNOW IT WAS YOU IN THERE! HONEST!!
NOW TELL ME, WHAT ON EARTH ARE YOU TWO TRYING TO DO.
YOU SEEM KIND OF... STRESSED.
WHILE YOU WERE GONE, MOTOKO GOT REALLY DEPRESSED. BUT EVER SINCE WE GOT TO KYOTO, SHE SEEMS TO HAVE REALLY TURNED OVER A NEW LEAF.
THE FINAL SHOWDOWN'S TOMORROW, BUT THANKS TO ALL THIS TRAINING, I KNOW MOTOKO WILL COME THROUGH THIS ON TOP.
AND IT GOES WITHOUT SAYING THAT I'LL BE THERE TO BACK HER UP.
PLUS, I GOT SU TO MAKE ME SOME BOMBS JUST IN CASE.
HMM ...
GOOD LUCK, MOTOKO

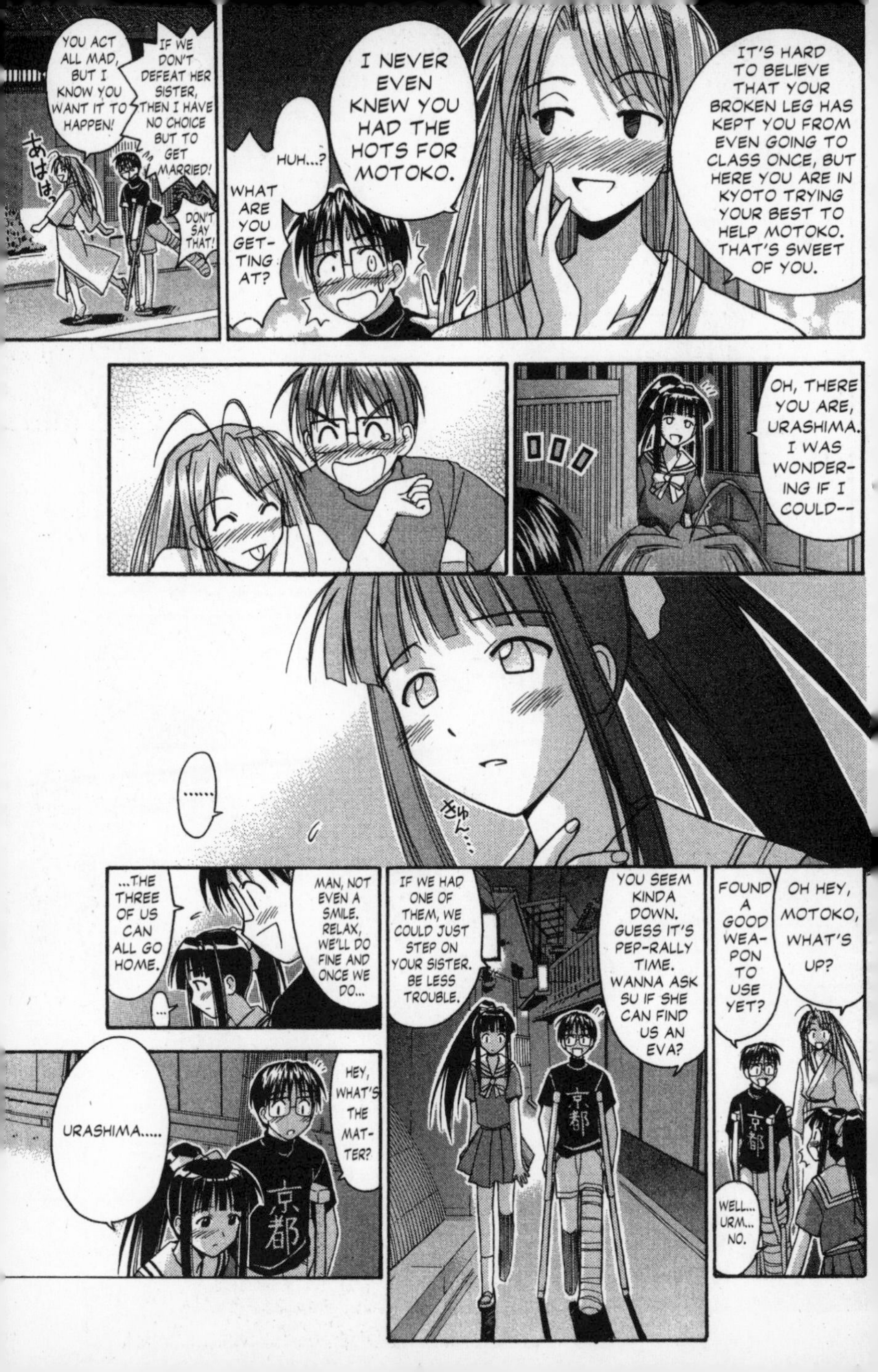
IT'S HARD TO BELIEVE THAT YOUR BROKEN LEG HAS KEPT YOU FROM EVEN GOING TO CLASS ONCE, BUT HERE YOU ARE IN KYOTO TRYING YOUR BEST TO HELP MOTOKO. THAT'S SWEET OF YOU.
I NEVER EVEN KNEW YOU HAD THE HOTS FOR MOTOKO.
HUH...?
WHAT ARE YOU GET-TING AT?
IF WE DON'T DEFEAT HER SISTER, THEN I HAVE NO CHOICE BUT TO GET MARRIED!
YOU ACT ALL MAD, BUT I KNOW YOU WANT IT TO HAPPEN!
あはは
DON'T SAY THAT!
OH, THERE YOU ARE, URASHIMA. I WAS WONDER-ING IF I COULD--
......
きゅん...
OH HEY, MOTOKO, WHAT'S UP?
FOUND A GOOD WEA-PON TO USE YET?
WELL... URM... NO.
YOU SEEM KINDA DOWN. GUESS IT'S PEP-RALLY TIME. WANNA ASK SU IF SHE CAN FIND US AN EVA?
IF WE HAD ONE OF THEM, WE COULD JUST STEP ON YOUR SISTER. BE LESS TROUBLE.
MAN, NOT EVEN A SMILE. RELAX, WE'LL DO FINE AND ONCE WE DO...
...THE THREE OF US CAN ALL GO HOME.
...
HEY, WHAT'S THE MAT-TER?
URASHIMA.....

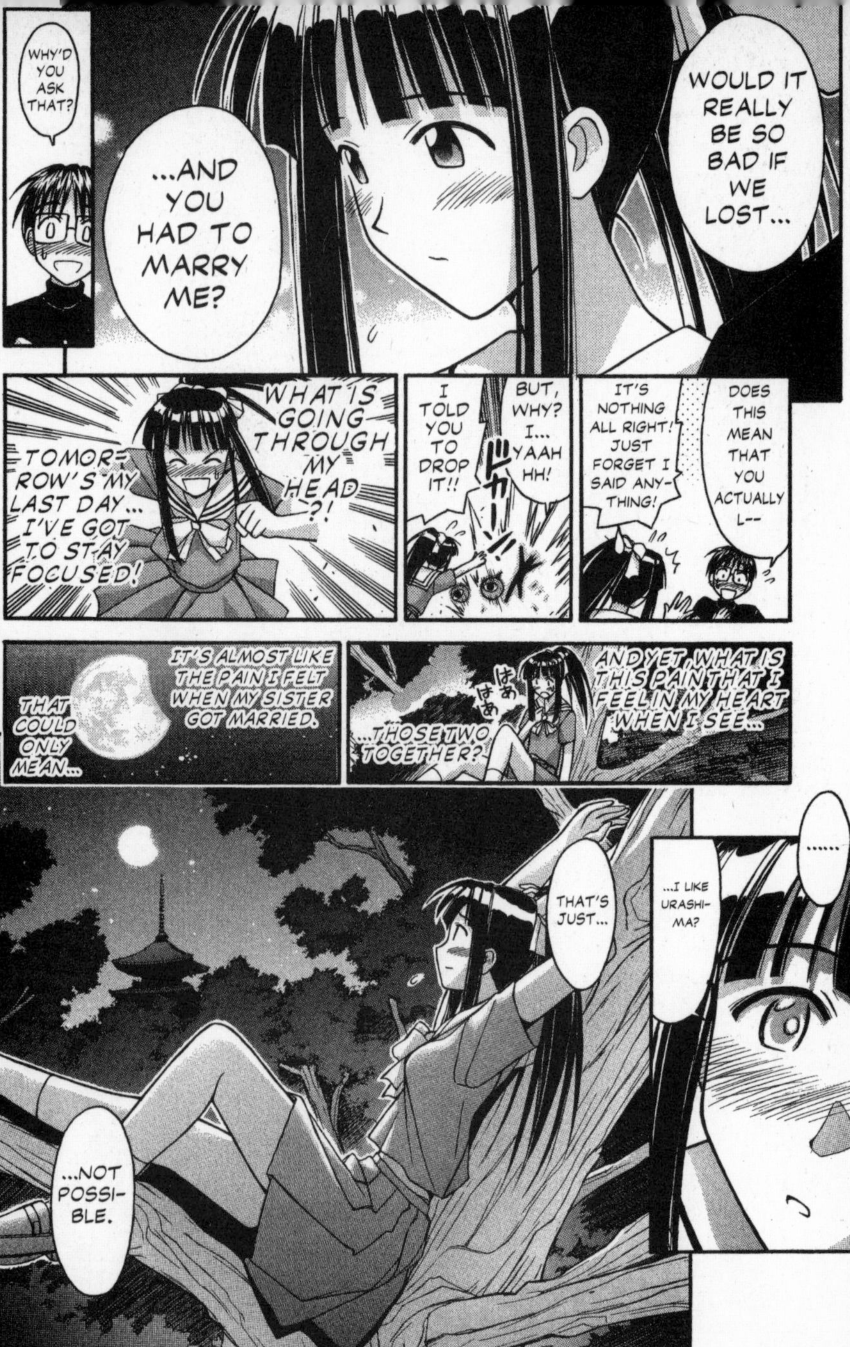
WOULD IT REALLY BE SO BAD IF WE LOST...
...AND YOU HAD TO MARRY ME?
WHY'D YOU ASK THAT?
DOES THIS MEAN THAT YOU ACTUALLY L--
IT'S NOTHING ALL RIGHT! JUST FORGET I SAID ANY-THING!
BUT, WHY? I... YAAHH!
I TOLD YOU TO DROP IT!!
ドカーン
WHAT IS GOING THROUGH MY HEAD?!
TOMOR-ROW'S MY LAST DAY... I'VE GOT TO STAY FOCUSED!
AND YET WHAT IS THIS PAIN THAT I FEEL IN MY HEART WHEN I SEE...
はあ はあ
...THOSE TWO TOGETHER?
IT'S ALMOST LIKE THE PAIN I FELT WHEN MY SISTER GOT MARRIED.
THAT COULD ONLY MEAN...
......
...I LIKE URASHI-MA?
THAT'S JUST...
...NOT POSSI-BLE.

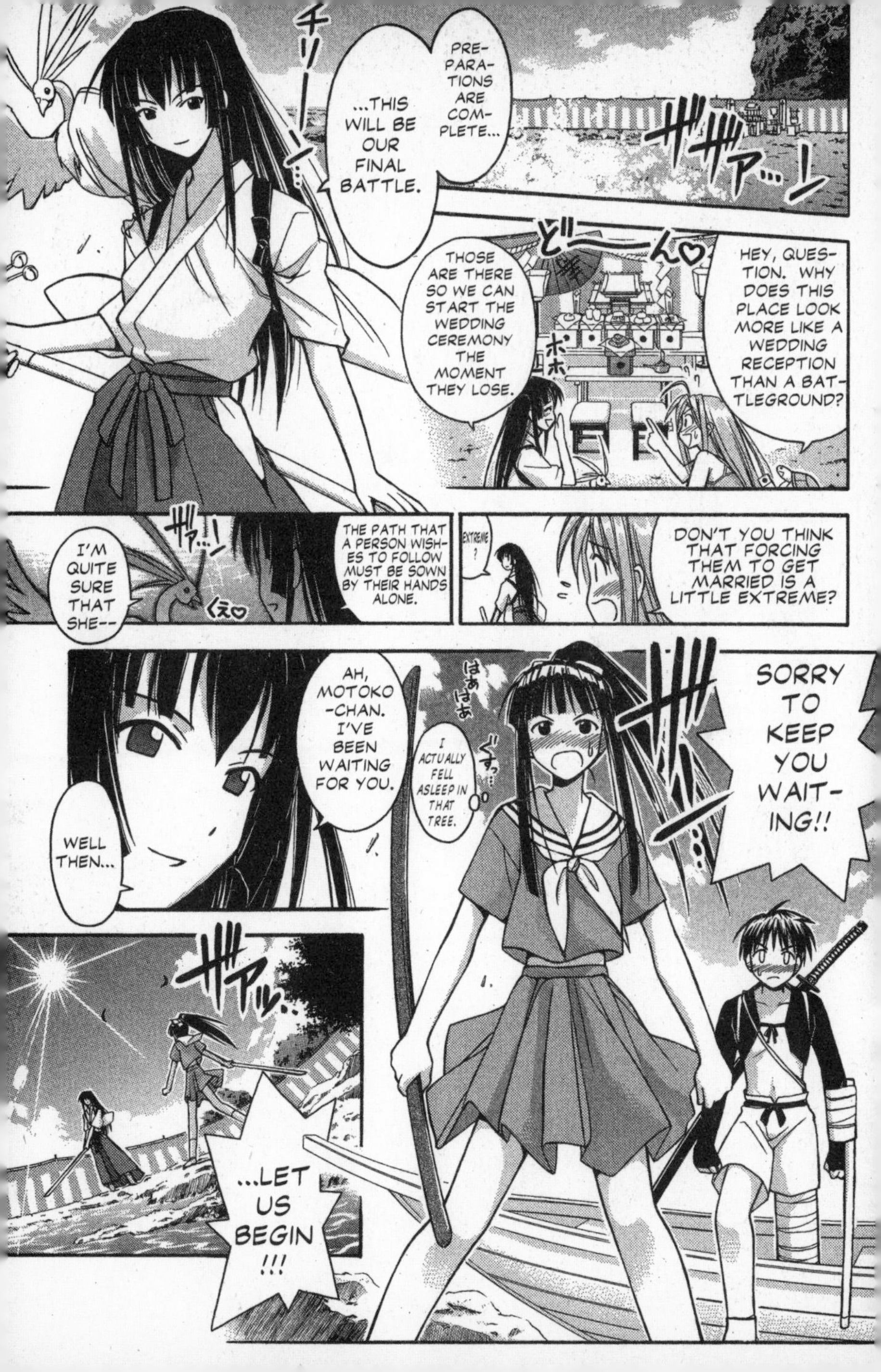
ザザァ…
PRE-PARA-TIONS ARE COM-PLETE...
...THIS WILL BE OUR FINAL BATTLE.
チリー…
どーん♡
HEY, QUES-TION. WHY DOES THIS PLACE LOOK MORE LIKE A WEDDING RECEPTION THAN A BAT-TLEGROUND?
THOSE ARE THERE SO WE CAN START THE WEDDING CEREMONY THE MOMENT THEY LOSE.
DON'T YOU THINK THAT FORCING THEM TO GET MARRIED IS A LITTLE EXTREME?
EXTREME?
THE PATH THAT A PERSON WISH-ES TO FOLLOW MUST BE SOWN BY THEIR HANDS ALONE.
ザァ…
I'M QUITE SURE THAT SHE--
くえ♡
SORRY TO KEEP YOU WAIT-ING!!
はあはあ
ぐすっ…
I ACTUALLY FELL ASLEEP IN THAT TREE.
AH, MOTOKO-CHAN. I'VE BEEN WAITING FOR YOU.
WELL THEN...
ザアッ…
...LET US BEGIN!!!

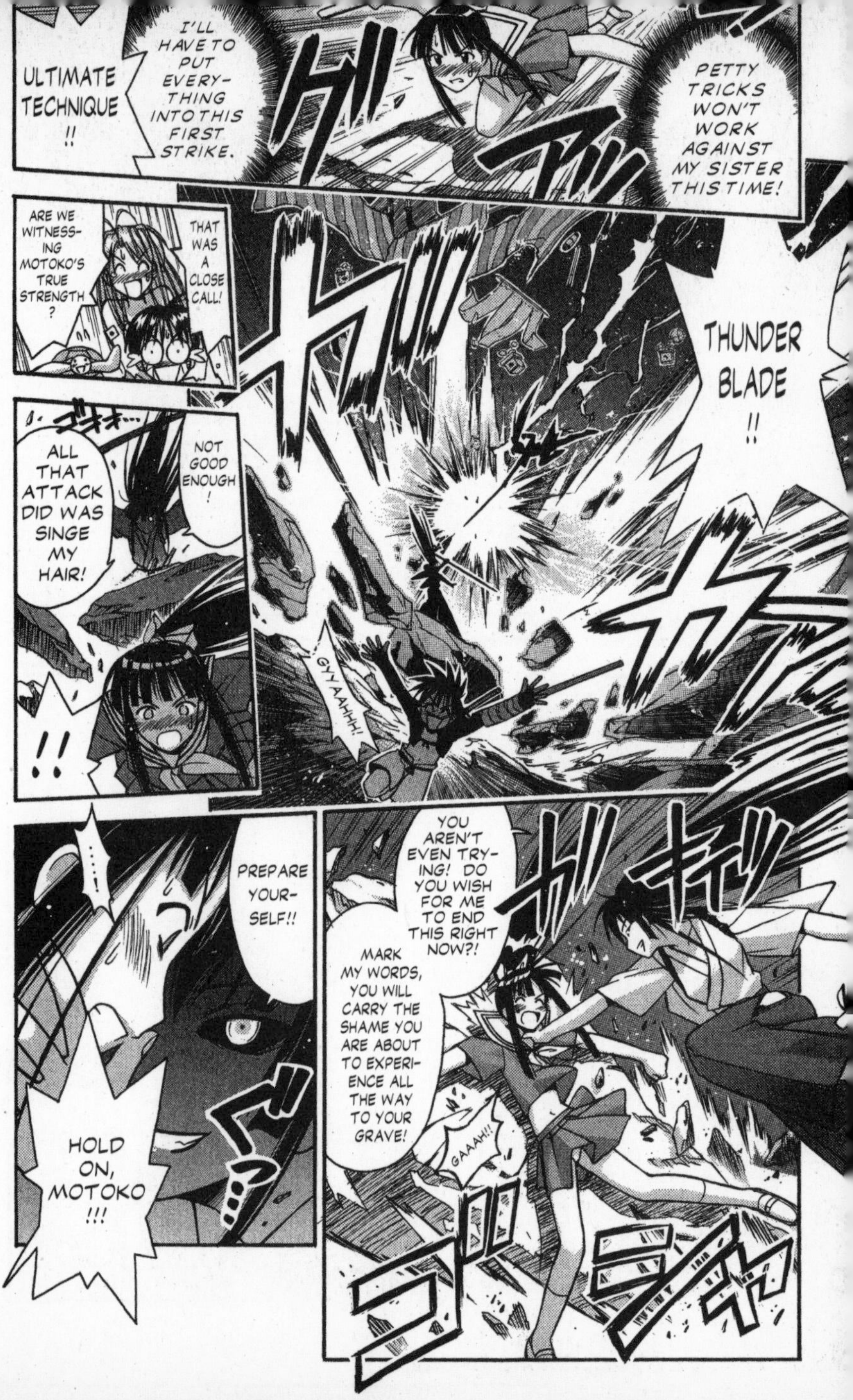
PETTY TRICKS WON'T WORK AGAINST MY SISTER THIS TIME!
I'LL HAVE TO PUT EVERYTHING INTO THIS FIRST STRIKE.
ULTIMATE TECHNIQUE !!
THUNDER BLADE !!
GYYAAHHH!
THAT WAS A CLOSE CALL!
ARE WE WITNESSING MOTOKO'S TRUE STRENGTH?
NOT GOOD ENOUGH!
ALL THAT ATTACK DID WAS SINGE MY HAIR!
!!
YOU AREN'T EVEN TRYING! DO YOU WISH FOR ME TO END THIS RIGHT NOW?!
MARK MY WORDS, YOU WILL CARRY THE SHAME YOU ARE ABOUT TO EXPERIENCE ALL THE WAY TO YOUR GRAVE!
GAAAH!!
PREPARE YOURSELF!!
...!
HOLD ON, MOTOKO !!!

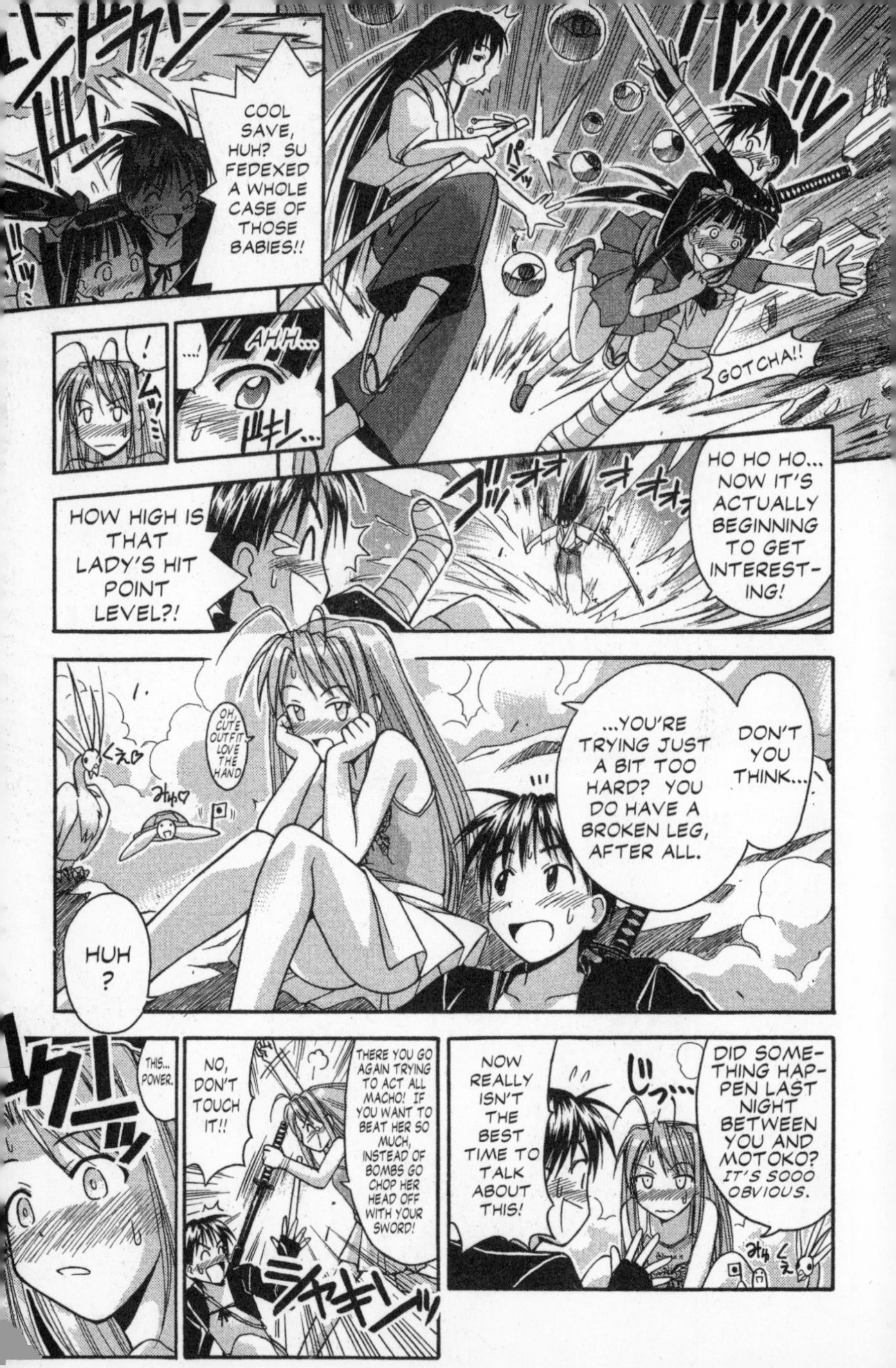
GOTCHA!!
COOL SAVE, HUH? SU FEDEXED A WHOLE CASE OF THOSE BABIES!!
AHH...
...!
!
HO HO HO... NOW IT'S ACTUALLY BEGINNING TO GET INTEREST-ING!
HOW HIGH IS THAT LADY'S HIT POINT LEVEL?!
DON'T YOU THINK...
...YOU'RE TRYING JUST A BIT TOO HARD? YOU DO HAVE A BROKEN LEG, AFTER ALL.
OH, CUTE OUTFIT LOVE THE HAND
HUH?
DID SOME-THING HAP-PEN LAST NIGHT BETWEEN YOU AND MOTOKO? IT'S SOOO OBVIOUS.
NOW REALLY ISN'T THE BEST TIME TO TALK ABOUT THIS!
THERE YOU GO AGAIN TRYING TO ACT ALL MACHO! IF YOU WANT TO BEAT HER SO MUCH, INSTEAD OF BOMBS GO CHOP HER HEAD OFF WITH YOUR SWORD!
NO, DON'T TOUCH IT!!
THIS... POWER.

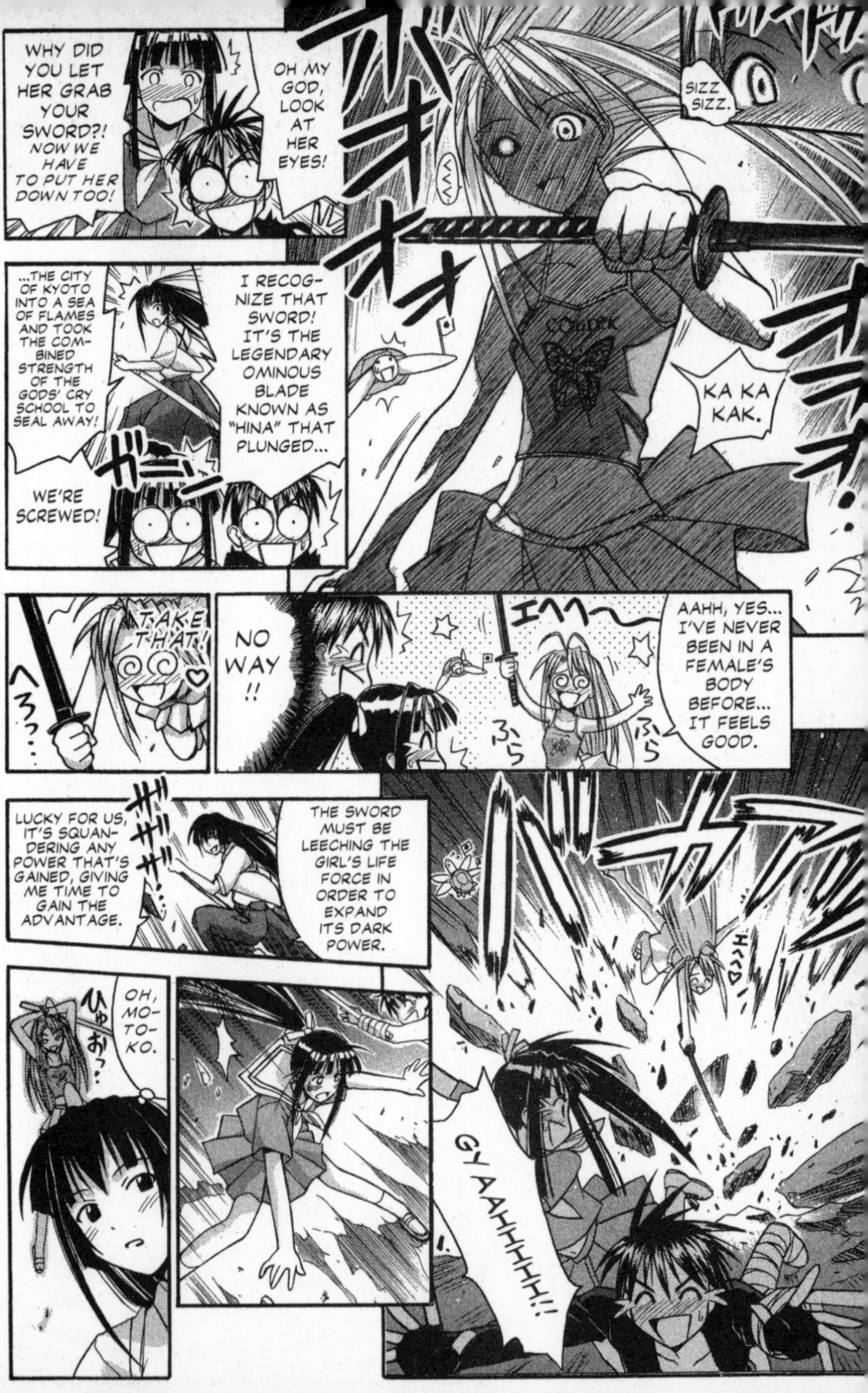
SIZZ SIZZ.
KA KA KAK.
OH MY GOD, LOOK AT HER EYES!
WHY DID YOU LET HER GRAB YOUR SWORD?! NOW WE HAVE TO PUT HER DOWN TOO!
I RECOGNIZE THAT SWORD! IT'S THE LEGENDARY OMINOUS BLADE KNOWN AS "HINA" THAT PLUNGED...
...THE CITY OF KYOTO INTO A SEA OF FLAMES AND TOOK THE COMBINED STRENGTH OF THE GODS' CRY SCHOOL TO SEAL AWAY!
WE'RE SCREWED!
AAHH, YES... I'VE NEVER BEEN IN A FEMALE'S BODY BEFORE... IT FEELS GOOD.
NO WAY!!
TAKE THAT!
THE SWORD MUST BE LEECHING THE GIRL'S LIFE FORCE IN ORDER TO EXPAND ITS DARK POWER.
LUCKY FOR US, IT'S SQUANDERING ANY POWER THAT'S GAINED, GIVING ME TIME TO GAIN THE ADVANTAGE.
GYAAHHHHH!!
OH, MOTOKO.

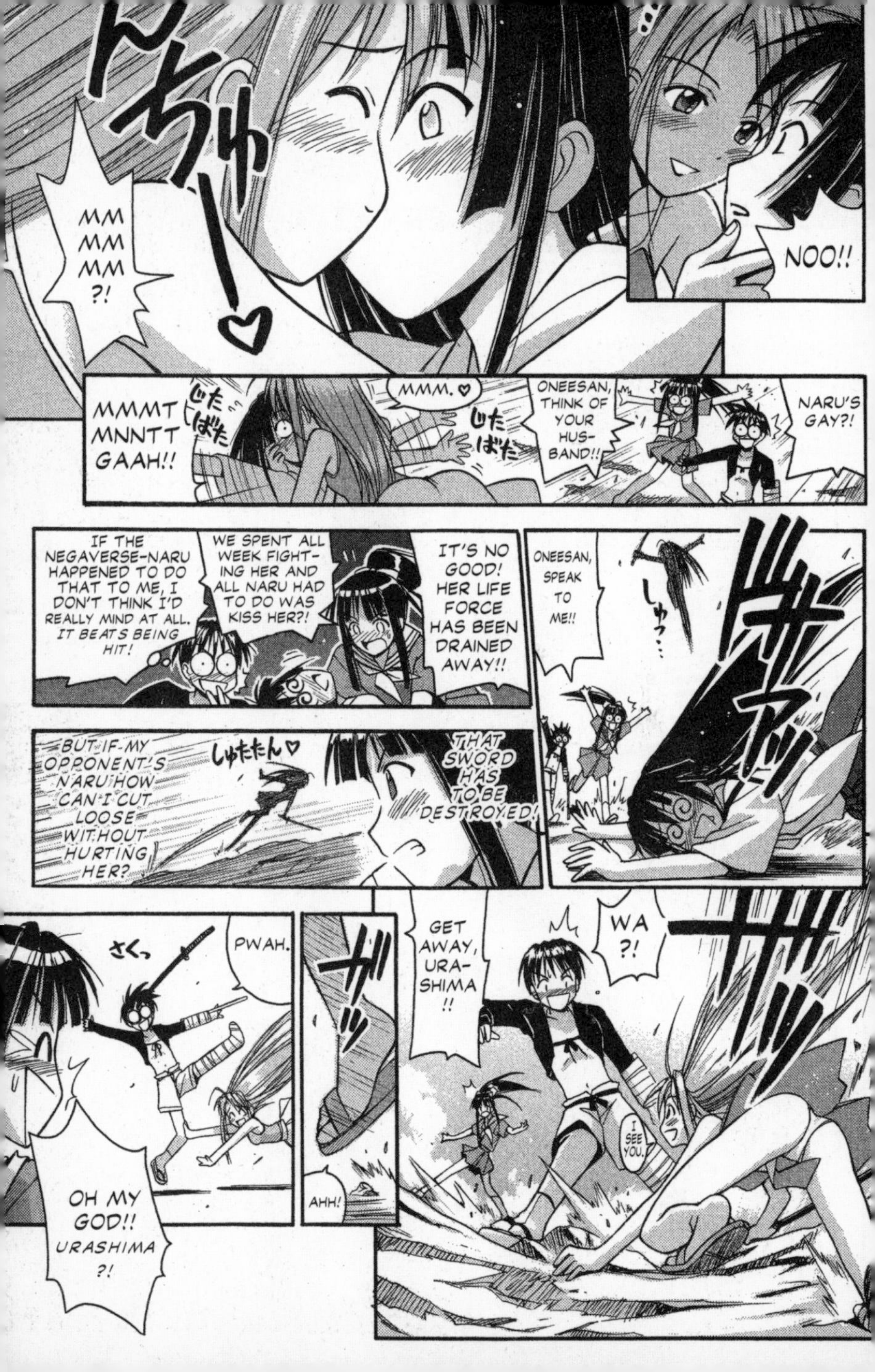
NOO!!
んちゅー♥
MM MM MM ?!
NARU'S GAY?!
ONEESAN, THINK OF YOUR HUS-BAND!!
じたばた
MMM.♥
じたばた
MMMT MNNTT GAAH!!
ドサァッ
ONEESAN, SPEAK TO ME!!
しゅっ…
IT'S NO GOOD! HER LIFE FORCE HAS BEEN DRAINED AWAY!!
WE SPENT ALL WEEK FIGHT-ING HER AND ALL NARU HAD TO DO WAS KISS HER?!
IF THE NEGAVERSE-NARU HAPPENED TO DO THAT TO ME, I DON'T THINK I'D REALLY MIND AT ALL. IT BEATS BEING HIT!
THAT SWORD HAS TO BE DESTROYED!
しゅたたん♥
BUT IF MY OPPONENT'S NARU HOW CAN I CUT LOOSE WITHOUT HURTING HER?
ザッ
WA ?!
GET AWAY, URA-SHIMA !!
I SEE YOU.
ザッ
AHH!
PWAH.
さくっ
OH MY GOD!! URASHIMA ?!

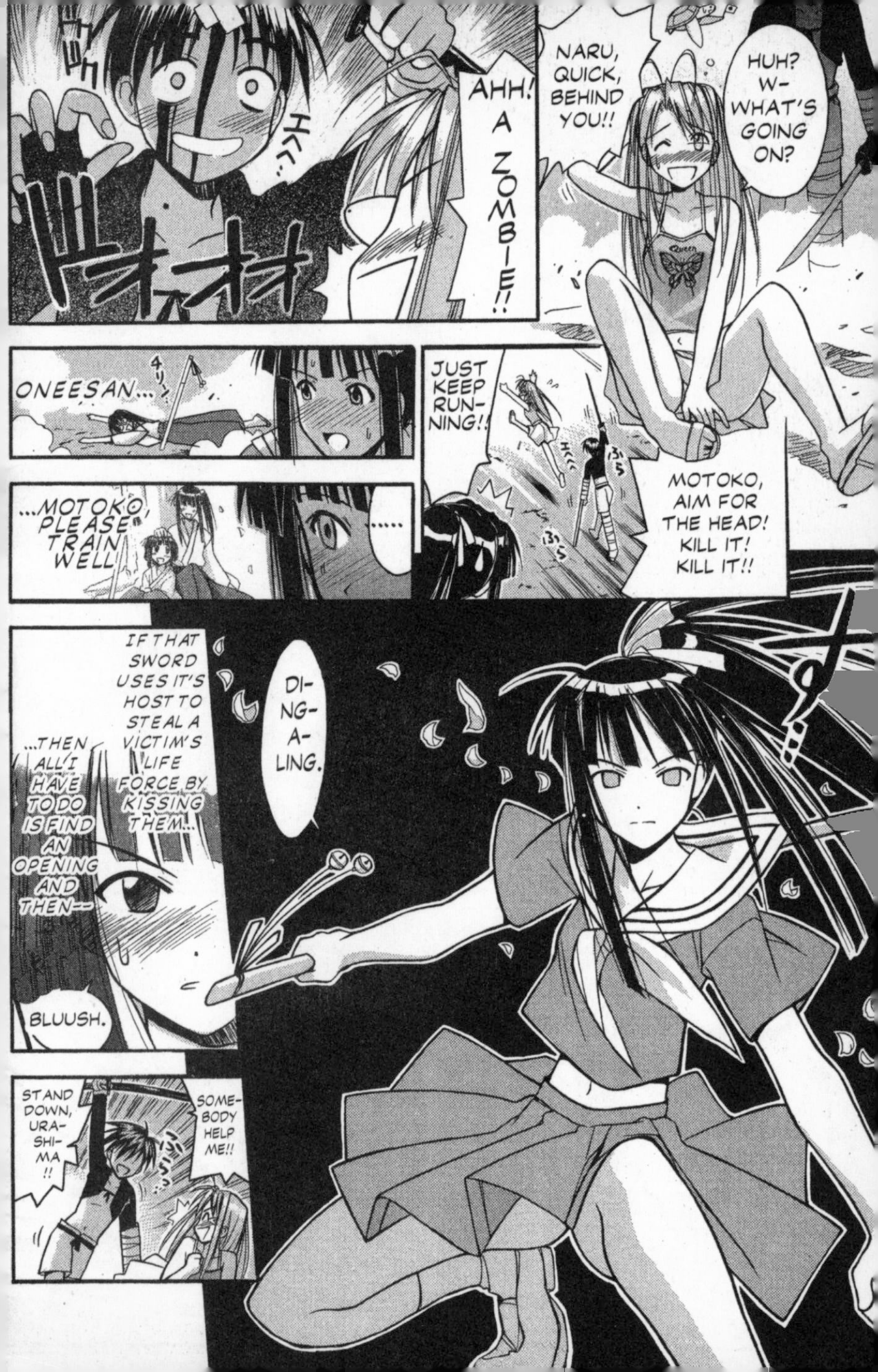
HUH? W-WHAT'S GOING ON?
NARU, QUICK, BEHIND YOU!!
AHH! A ZOMBIE!!
JUST KEEP RUN-NING!!
MOTOKO, AIM FOR THE HEAD! KILL IT! KILL IT!!
ONEESAN...
......
...MOTOKO, PLEASE TRAIN WELL
DI-NG-A-LING.
IF THAT SWORD USES IT'S HOST TO STEAL A VICTIM'S LIFE FORCE BY KISSING THEM...
...THEN ALL I HAVE TO DO IS FIND AN OPENING AND THEN--
BLUUSH.
SOME-BODY HELP ME!!
STAND DOWN, URA-SHI-MA!!

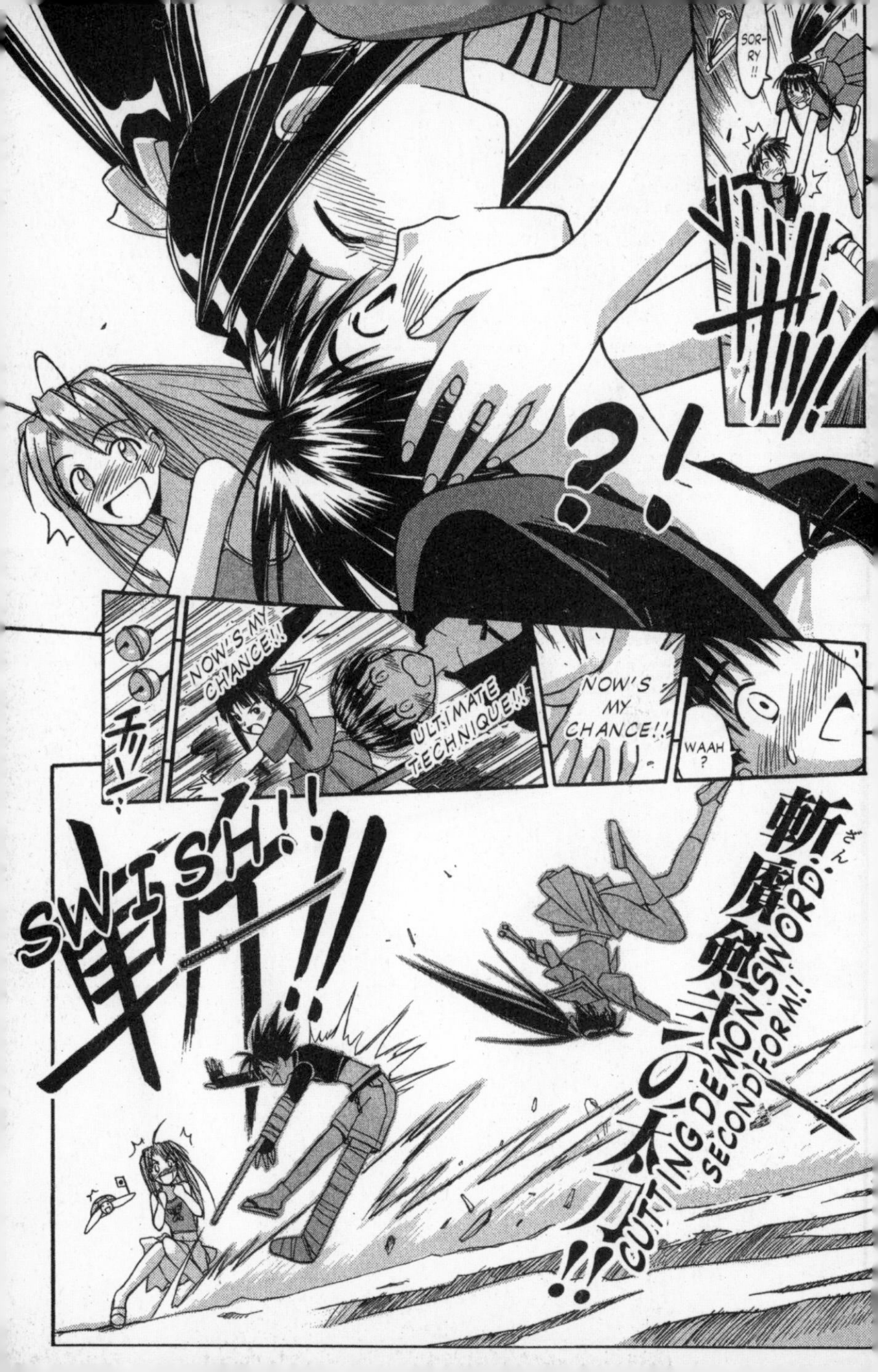
SOR-RY!!
?!
WAAH?
NOW'S MY CHANCE!!
NOW'S MY CHANCE!!
ULTIMATE TECHNIQUE!!
CUTTING DEMON SWORD: SECOND FORM!!
SWISH!!

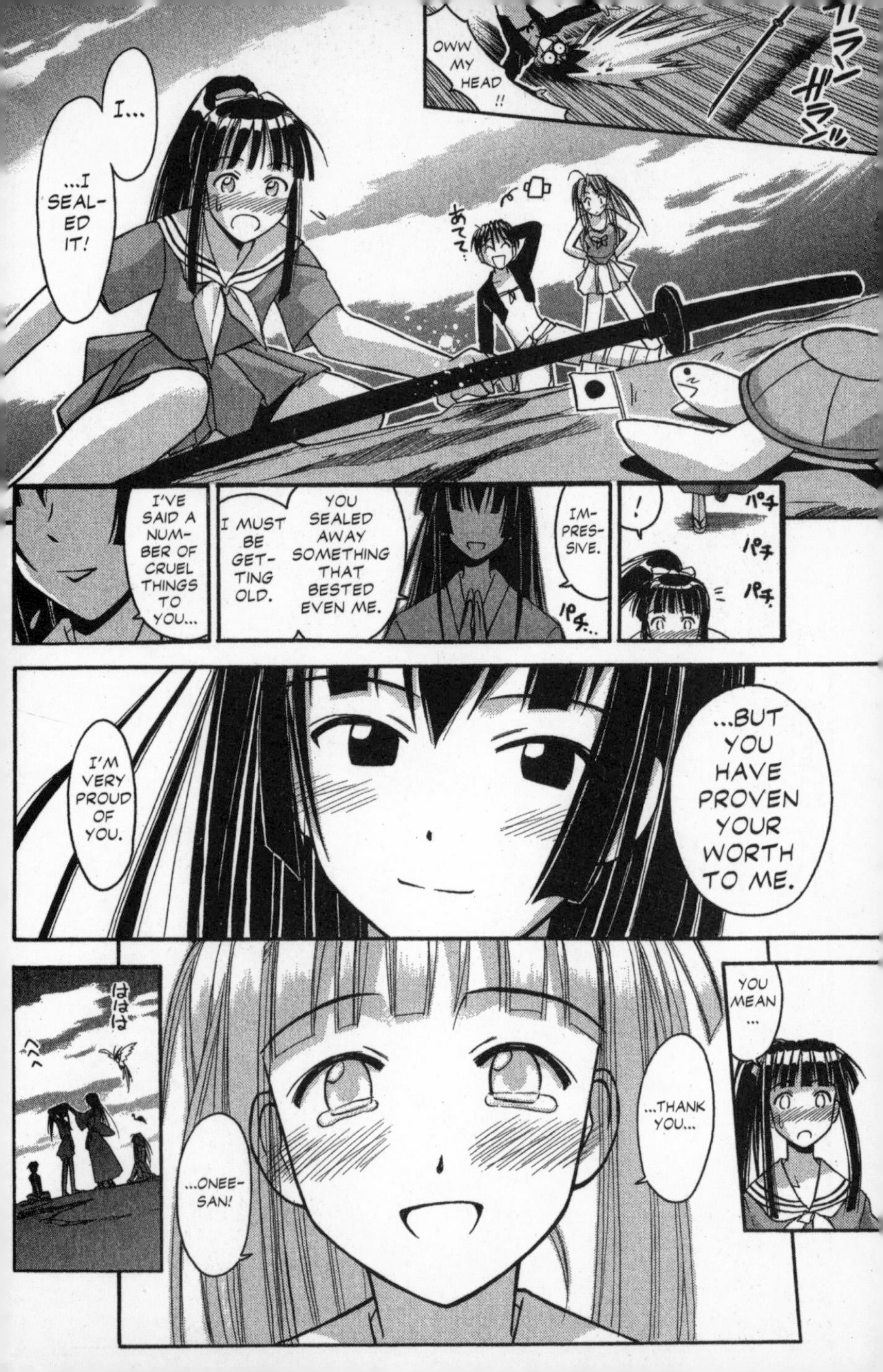
ガランガランッ
OWW MY HEAD !!
I...
...I SEALED IT!
あてて...
!
パチ
パチ
パチ
IM-PRESSIVE.
パチ...
YOU SEALED AWAY SOMETHING THAT BESTED EVEN ME.
I MUST BE GETTING OLD.
I'VE SAID A NUMBER OF CRUEL THINGS TO YOU...
...BUT YOU HAVE PROVEN YOUR WORTH TO ME.
I'M VERY PROUD OF YOU.
YOU MEAN ...
...THANK YOU...
...ONEE-SAN!
ははは
へへ

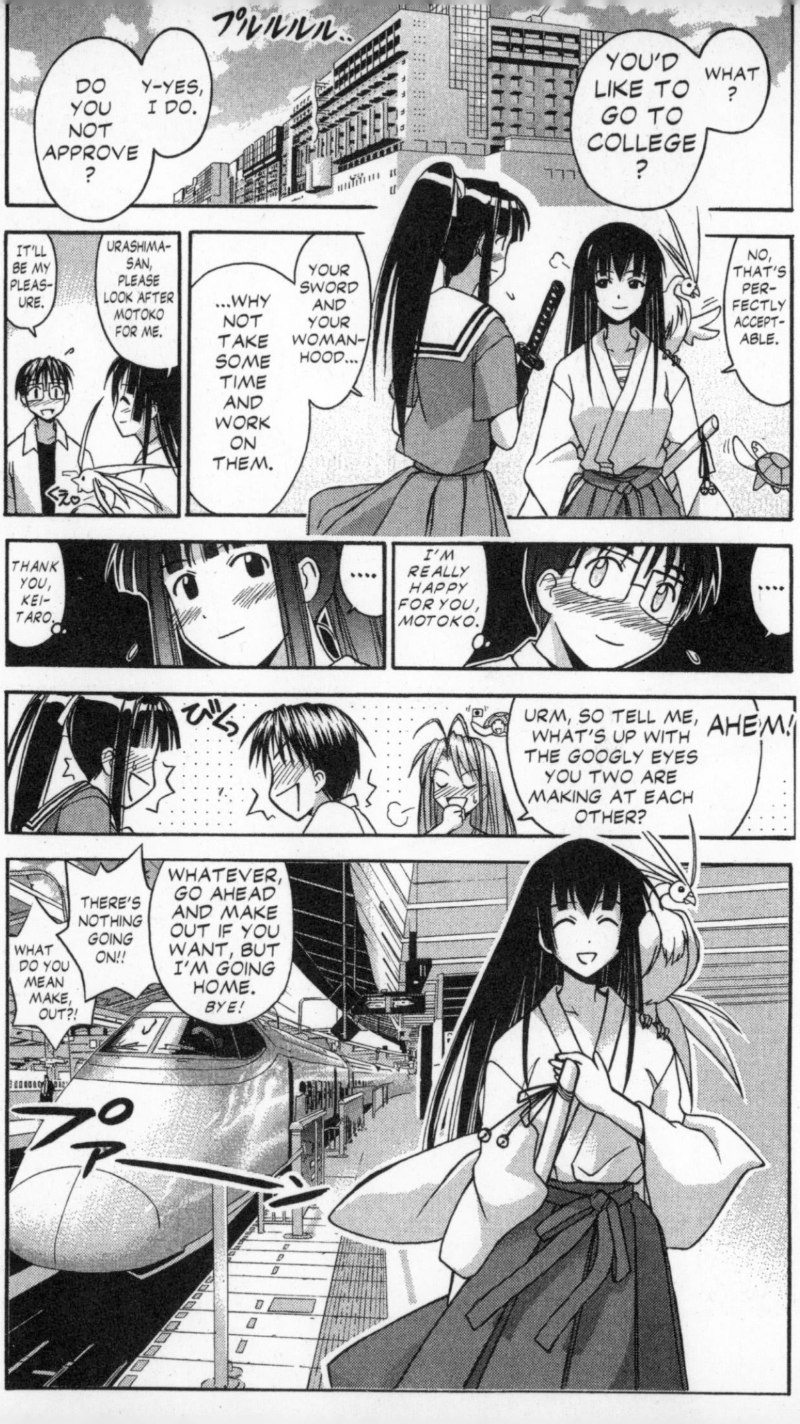
プルルルル..
WHAT?
YOU'D LIKE TO GO TO COLLEGE?
Y-YES, I DO.
DO YOU NOT APPROVE?
NO, THAT'S PERFECTLY ACCEPTABLE.
YOUR SWORD AND YOUR WOMANHOOD...
...WHY NOT TAKE SOME TIME AND WORK ON THEM.
URASHIMA-SAN, PLEASE LOOK AFTER MOTOKO FOR ME.
IT'LL BE MY PLEASURE.
....
I'M REALLY HAPPY FOR YOU, MOTOKO.
....
THANK YOU, KEI-TARO.
AHEM!
URM, SO TELL ME, WHAT'S UP WITH THE GOOGLY EYES YOU TWO ARE MAKING AT EACH OTHER?
びくっ
WHATEVER, GO AHEAD AND MAKE OUT IF YOU WANT, BUT I'M GOING HOME. BYE!
THERE'S NOTHING GOING ON!!
WHAT DO YOU MEAN MAKE, OUT?!
プアーン

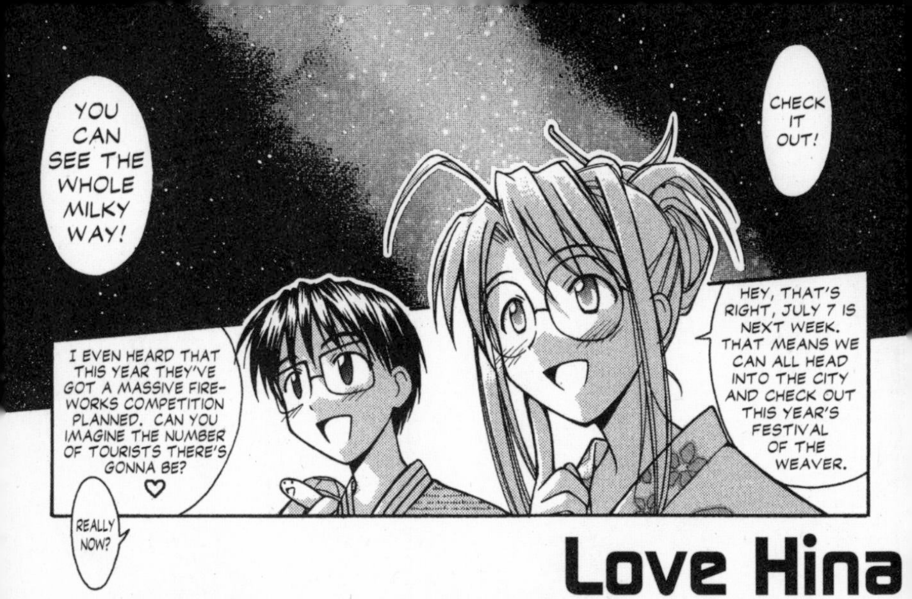
CHECK IT OUT!
YOU CAN SEE THE WHOLE MILKY WAY!
HEY, THAT'S RIGHT, JULY 7 IS NEXT WEEK. THAT MEANS WE CAN ALL HEAD INTO THE CITY AND CHECK OUT THIS YEAR'S FESTIVAL OF THE WEAVER.
I EVEN HEARD THAT THIS YEAR THEY'VE GOT A MASSIVE FIRE-WORKS COMPETITION PLANNED. CAN YOU IMAGINE THE NUMBER OF TOURISTS THERE'S GONNA BE? ♡
REALLY NOW?

Love Hina

HINATA.75 Shinobu's B-Line to Tokyo U ♡

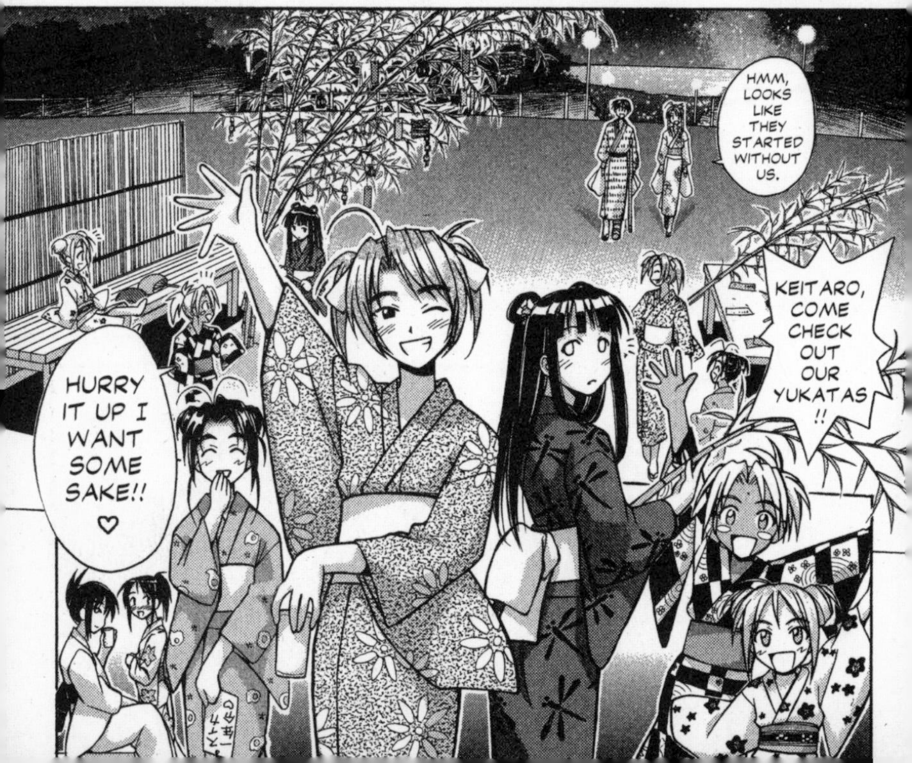
HMM, LOOKS LIKE THEY STARTED WITHOUT US.
KEITARO, COME CHECK OUT OUR YUKATAS !!
HURRY IT UP I WANT SOME SAKE!! ♡

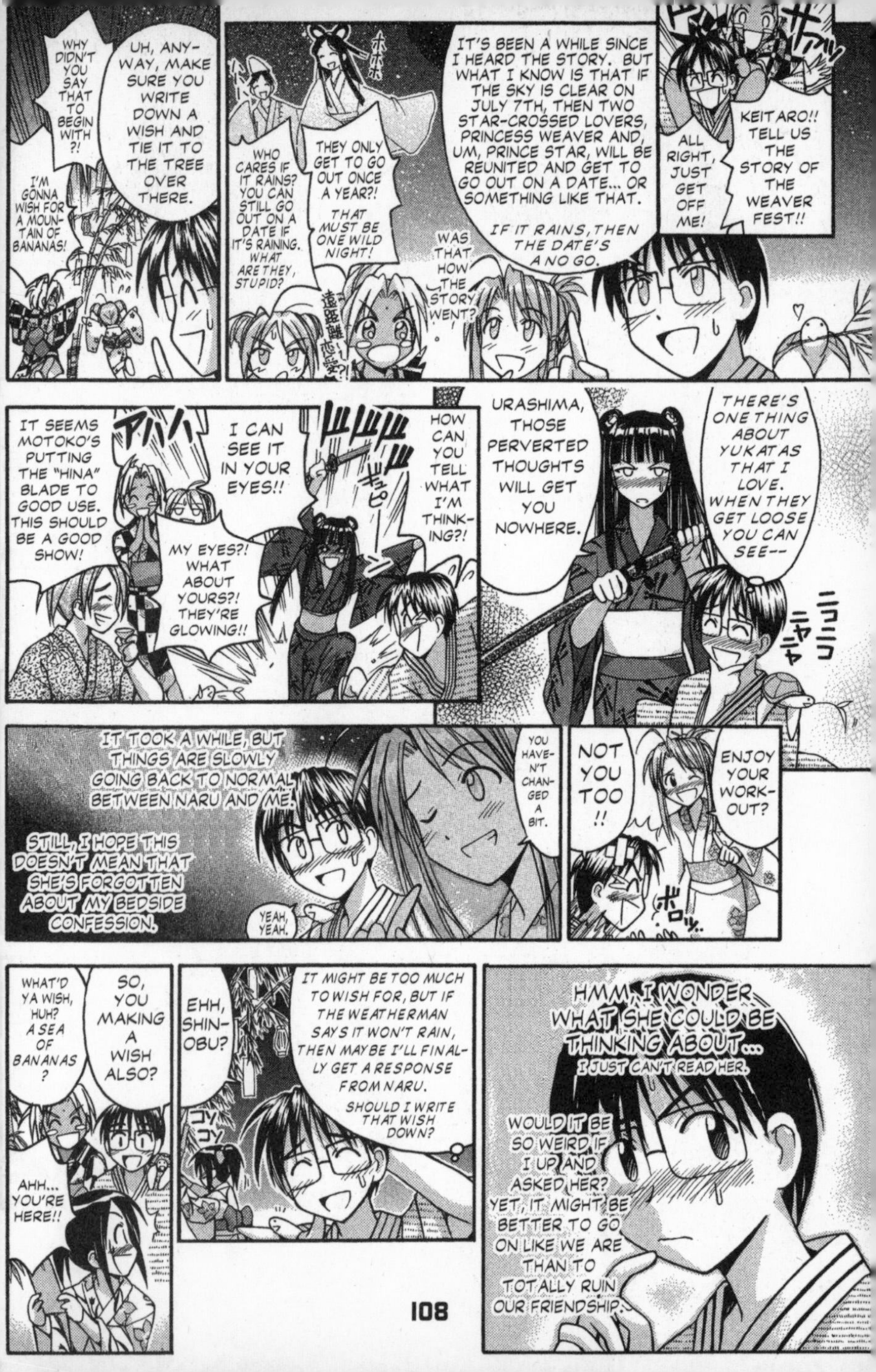

KEITARO!! TELL US THE STORY OF THE WEAVER FEST!!
ALL RIGHT, JUST GET OFF ME!
IT'S BEEN A WHILE SINCE I HEARD THE STORY. BUT WHAT I KNOW IS THAT IF THE SKY IS CLEAR ON JULY 7TH, THEN TWO STAR-CROSSED LOVERS, PRINCESS WEAVER AND, UM, PRINCE STAR, WILL BE REUNITED AND GET TO GO OUT ON A DATE... OR SOMETHING LIKE THAT.
IF IT RAINS, THEN THE DATE'S A NO GO.
WAS THAT HOW THE STORY WENT?
THEY ONLY GET TO GO OUT ONCE A YEAR?!
THAT MUST BE ONE WILD NIGHT!
WHO CARES IF IT RAINS? YOU CAN STILL GO OUT ON A DATE IF IT'S RAINING. WHAT ARE THEY, STUPID?
UH, ANYWAY, MAKE SURE YOU WRITE DOWN A WISH AND TIE IT TO THE TREE OVER THERE.
WHY DIDN'T YOU SAY THAT TO BEGIN WITH ?!
I'M GONNA WISH FOR A MOUNTAIN OF BANANAS!
THERE'S ONE THING ABOUT YUKATAS THAT I LOVE. WHEN THEY GET LOOSE YOU CAN SEE--
URASHIMA, THOSE PERVERTED THOUGHTS WILL GET YOU NOWHERE.
HOW CAN YOU TELL WHAT I'M THINKING?!
I CAN SEE IT IN YOUR EYES!!
MY EYES?! WHAT ABOUT YOURS?! THEY'RE GLOWING!!
IT SEEMS MOTOKO'S PUTTING THE "HINA" BLADE TO GOOD USE. THIS SHOULD BE A GOOD SHOW!
ENJOY YOUR WORK-OUT?
NOT YOU TOO !!
YOU HAVEN'T CHANGED A BIT.
IT TOOK A WHILE, BUT THINGS ARE SLOWLY GOING BACK TO NORMAL BETWEEN NARU AND ME.
STILL, I HOPE THIS DOESN'T MEAN THAT SHE'S FORGOTTEN ABOUT MY BEDSIDE CONFESSION.
YEAH, YEAH.
HMM, I WONDER WHAT SHE COULD BE THINKING ABOUT...
I JUST CAN'T READ HER.
WOULD IT BE SO WEIRD IF I UP AND ASKED HER? YET, IT MIGHT BE BETTER TO GO ON LIKE WE ARE THAN TO TOTALLY RUIN OUR FRIENDSHIP.
IT MIGHT BE TOO MUCH TO WISH FOR, BUT IF THE WEATHERMAN SAYS IT WON'T RAIN, THEN MAYBE I'LL FINALLY GET A RESPONSE FROM NARU.
SHOULD I WRITE THAT WISH DOWN?
EHH, SHINOBU?
SO, YOU MAKING A WISH ALSO?
WHAT'D YA WISH, HUH? A SEA OF BANANAS ?
AHH... YOU'RE HERE!!

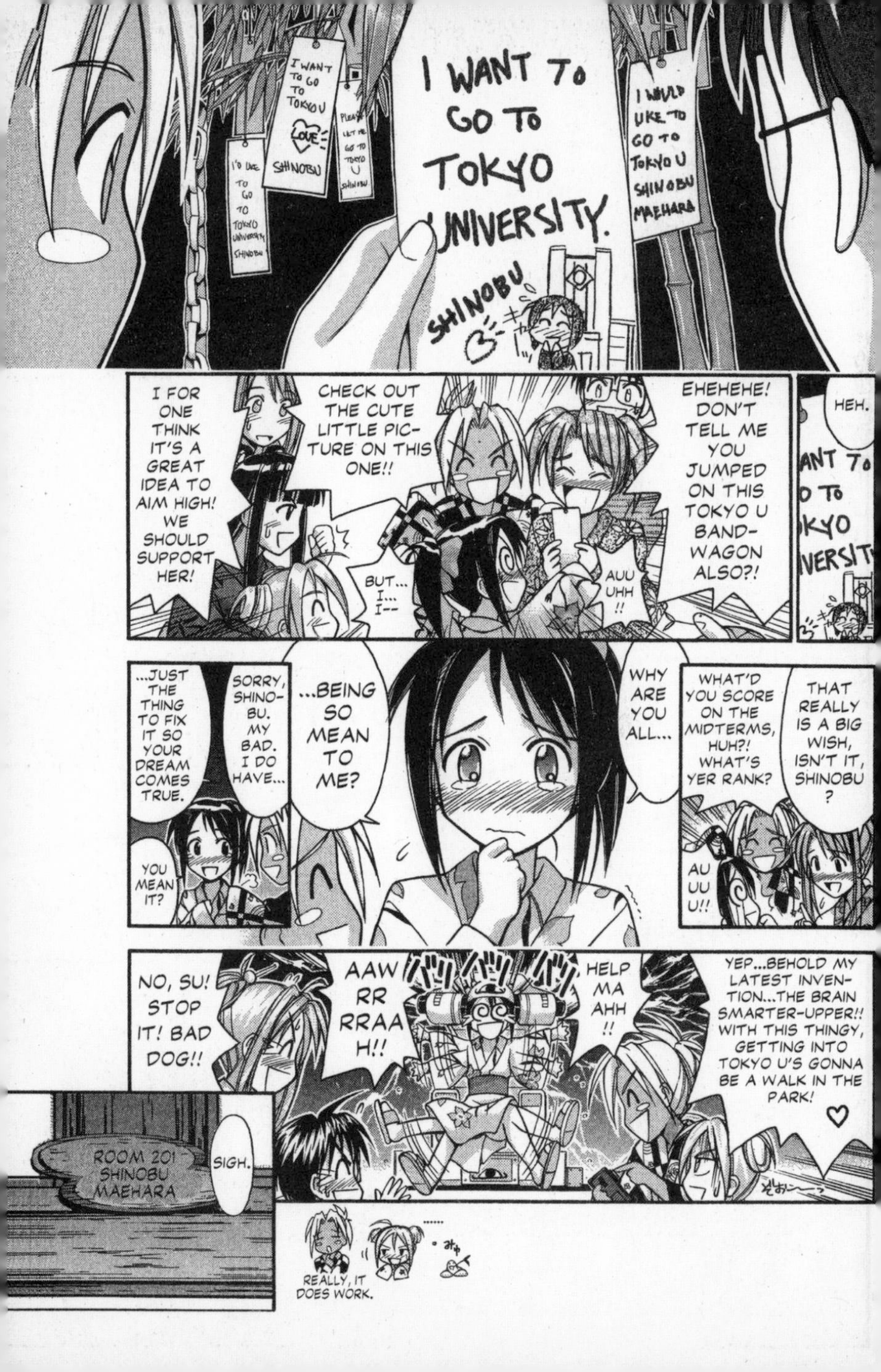

I WOULD LIKE TO GO TO TOKYO U SHINOBU MAEHARA
I WANT TO GO TO TOKYO UNIVERSITY.
SHINOBU
PLEASE LET ME GO TO TOKYO U SHINOBU
I WANT TO GO TO TOKYO U LOVE SHINOBU
I'D LIKE TO GO TO TOKYO UNIVERSITY SHINOBU
HEH.
EHEHEHE! DON'T TELL ME YOU JUMPED ON THIS TOKYO U BAND-WAGON ALSO?!
CHECK OUT THE CUTE LITTLE PIC-TURE ON THIS ONE!!
AUU UHH !!
BUT... I... I--
I FOR ONE THINK IT'S A GREAT IDEA TO AIM HIGH! WE SHOULD SUPPORT HER!
THAT REALLY IS A BIG WISH, ISN'T IT, SHINOBU ?
WHAT'D YOU SCORE ON THE MIDTERMS, HUH?! WHAT'S YER RANK?
AU UU U!!
WHY ARE YOU ALL...
...BEING SO MEAN TO ME?
SORRY, SHINO-BU. MY BAD. I DO HAVE...
...JUST THE THING TO FIX IT SO YOUR DREAM COMES TRUE.
YOU MEAN IT?
YEP...BEHOLD MY LATEST INVEN-TION...THE BRAIN SMARTER-UPPER!! WITH THIS THINGY, GETTING INTO TOKYO U'S GONNA BE A WALK IN THE PARK! ♡
HELP MA AHH !!
AAW RR RRAA H!!
NO, SU! STOP IT! BAD DOG!!
ROOM 201 SHINOBU MAEHARA
SIGH.
......
REALLY, IT DOES WORK.

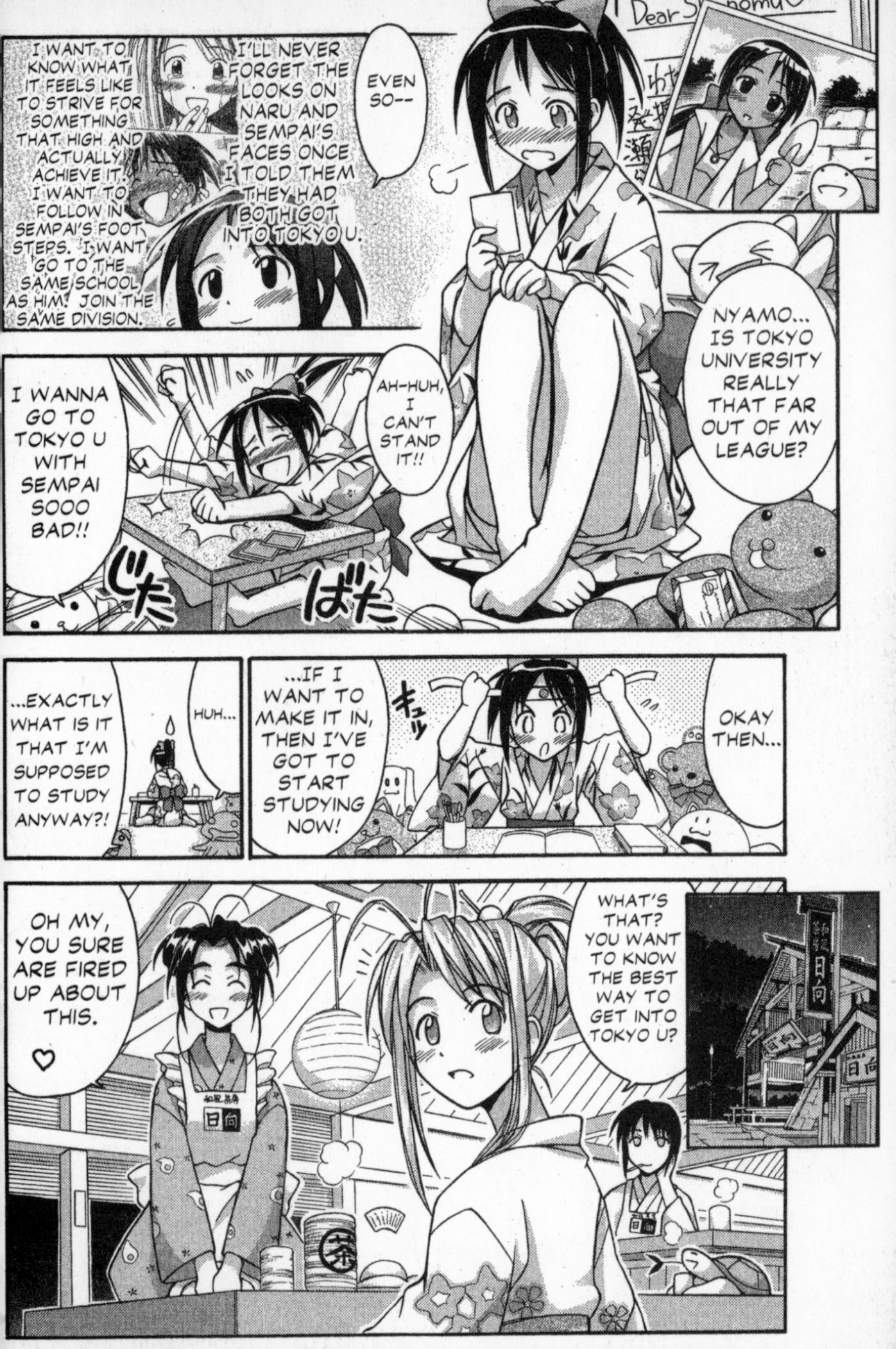

Dear Sh nomu♡
EVEN SO--
NYAMO... IS TOKYO UNIVERSITY REALLY THAT FAR OUT OF MY LEAGUE?
I'LL NEVER FORGET THE LOOKS ON NARU AND SEMPAI'S FACES ONCE I TOLD THEM THEY HAD BOTH GOT INTO TOKYO U.
I WANT TO KNOW WHAT IT FEELS LIKE TO STRIVE FOR SOMETHING THAT HIGH AND ACTUALLY ACHIEVE IT. I WANT TO FOLLOW IN SEMPAI'S FOOT STEPS. I WANT GO TO THE SAME SCHOOL AS HIM. JOIN THE SAME DIVISION.
AH-HUH, I CAN'T STAND IT!!
I WANNA GO TO TOKYO U WITH SEMPAI SOOO BAD!!
じた
ばた
OKAY THEN...
キュッ
...IF I WANT TO MAKE IT IN, THEN I'VE GOT TO START STUDYING NOW!
HUH...
...EXACTLY WHAT IS IT THAT I'M SUPPOSED TO STUDY ANYWAY?!
WHAT'S THAT? YOU WANT TO KNOW THE BEST WAY TO GET INTO TOKYO U?
OH MY, YOU SURE ARE FIRED UP ABOUT THIS. ♡

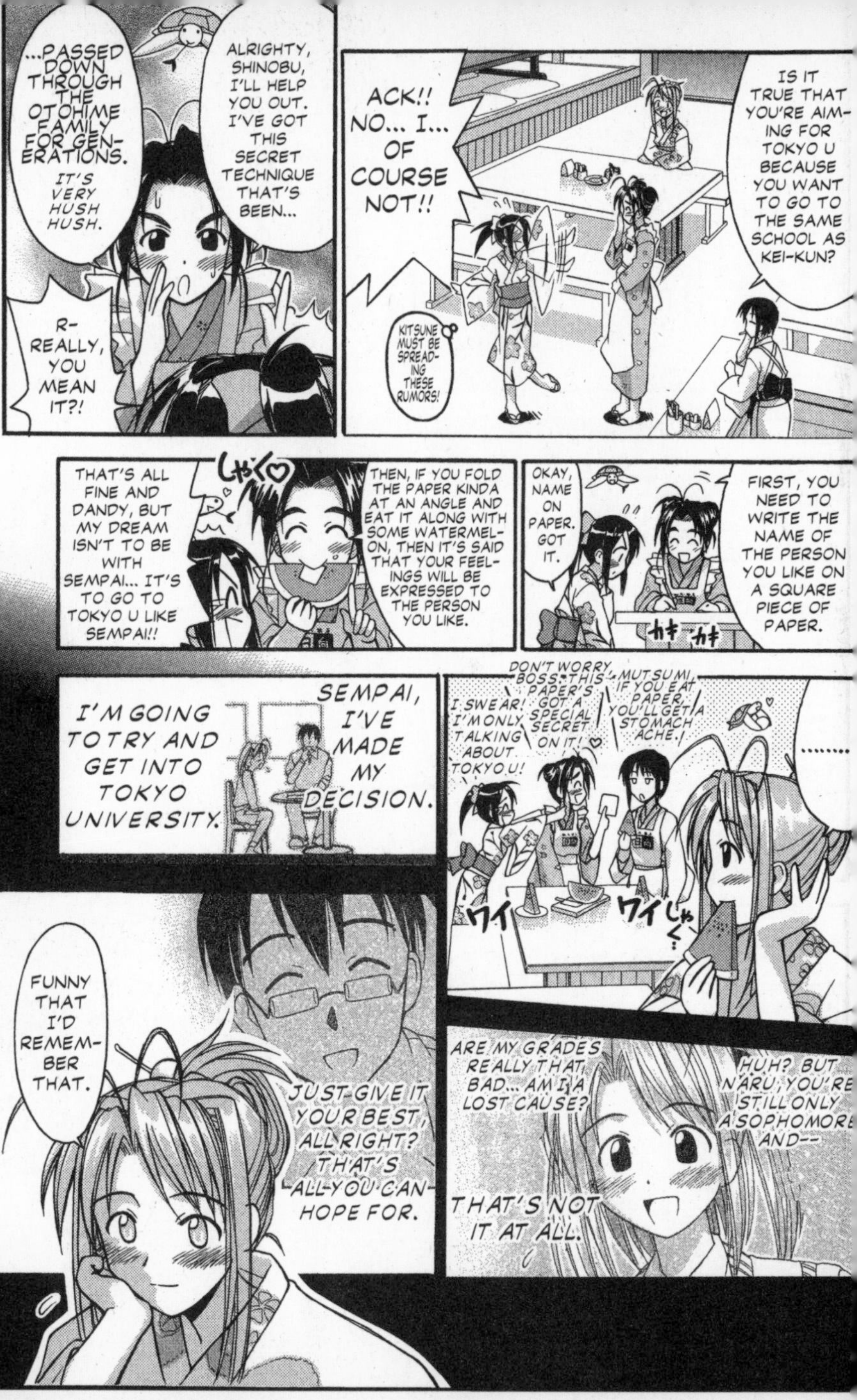
IS IT TRUE THAT YOU'RE AIMING FOR TOKYO U BECAUSE YOU WANT TO GO TO THE SAME SCHOOL AS KEI-KUN?
ACK!! NO... I... OF COURSE NOT!!
KITSUNE MUST BE SPREADING THESE RUMORS!
ALRIGHTY, SHINOBU, I'LL HELP YOU OUT. I'VE GOT THIS SECRET TECHNIQUE THAT'S BEEN...
...PASSED DOWN THROUGH THE OTOHIME FAMILY FOR GENERATIONS.
IT'S VERY HUSH HUSH.
R-REALLY, YOU MEAN IT?!
FIRST, YOU NEED TO WRITE THE NAME OF THE PERSON YOU LIKE ON A SQUARE PIECE OF PAPER.
OKAY, NAME ON PAPER. GOT IT.
カキ カキ
THEN, IF YOU FOLD THE PAPER KINDA AT AN ANGLE AND EAT IT ALONG WITH SOME WATERMELON, THEN IT'S SAID THAT YOUR FEELINGS WILL BE EXPRESSED TO THE PERSON YOU LIKE.
しゃく♡
THAT'S ALL FINE AND DANDY, BUT MY DREAM ISN'T TO BE WITH SEMPAI... IT'S TO GO TO TOKYO U LIKE SEMPAI!!
....
MUTSUMI, IF YOU EAT PAPER, YOU'LL GET A STOMACH ACHE.
DON'T WORRY, BOSS. THIS PAPER'S GOT A SPECIAL SECRET ON IT!
I SWEAR! I'M ONLY TALKING ABOUT TOKYO U!
ワイ ワイ しゃく
SEMPAI, I'VE MADE MY DECISION.
I'M GOING TO TRY AND GET INTO TOKYO UNIVERSITY.
HUH? BUT NARU, YOU'RE STILL ONLY A SOPHOMORE AND--
ARE MY GRADES REALLY THAT BAD... AM I A LOST CAUSE?
THAT'S NOT IT AT ALL.
JUST GIVE IT YOUR BEST, ALL RIGHT? THAT'S ALL YOU CAN HOPE FOR.
FUNNY THAT I'D REMEMBER THAT.

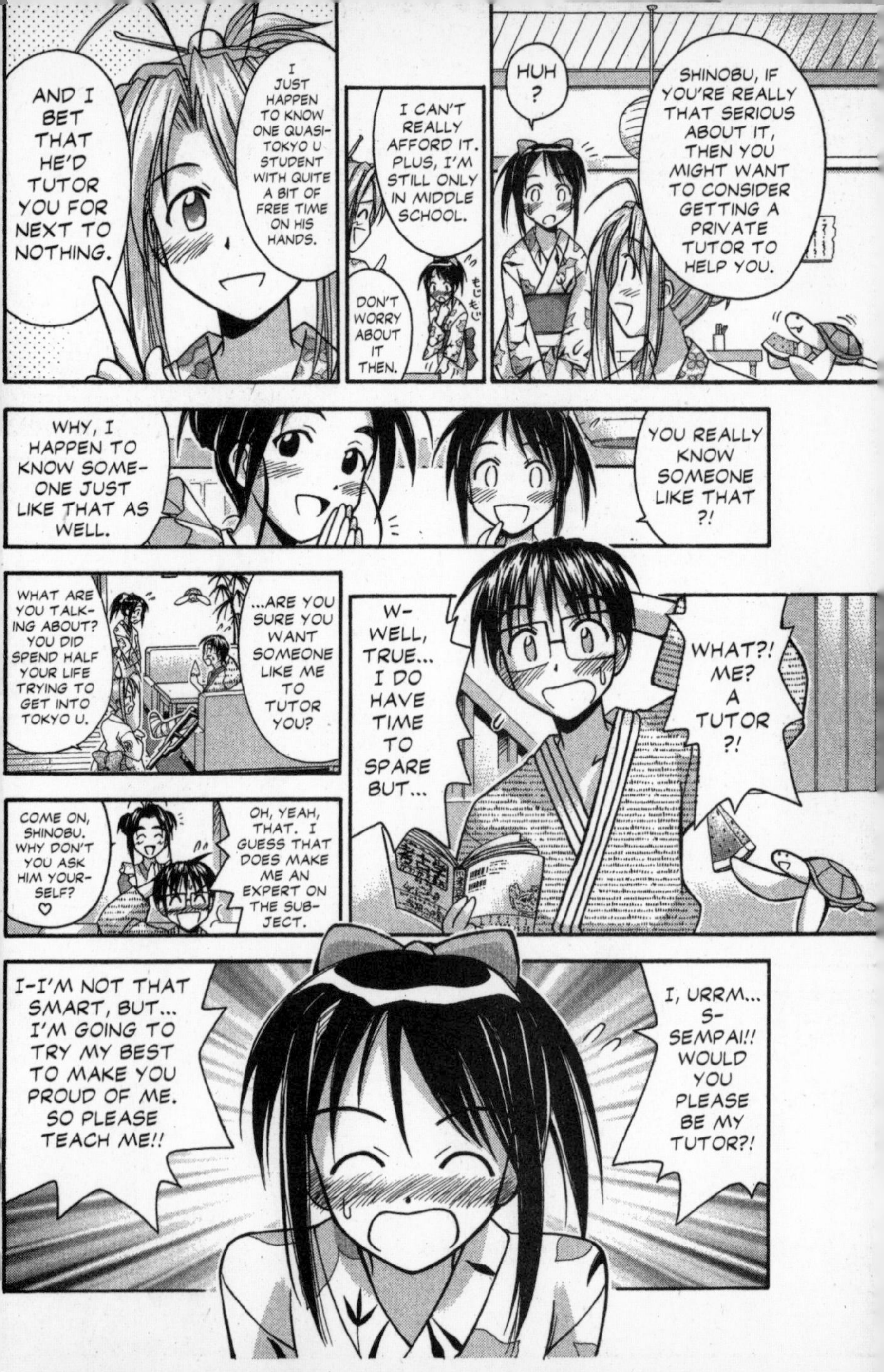
SHINOBU, IF YOU'RE REALLY THAT SERIOUS ABOUT IT, THEN YOU MIGHT WANT TO CONSIDER GETTING A PRIVATE TUTOR TO HELP YOU.
HUH?
I CAN'T REALLY AFFORD IT. PLUS, I'M STILL ONLY IN MIDDLE SCHOOL.
もじもじ
DON'T WORRY ABOUT IT THEN.
I JUST HAPPEN TO KNOW ONE QUASI-TOKYO U STUDENT WITH QUITE A BIT OF FREE TIME ON HIS HANDS.
AND I BET THAT HE'D TUTOR YOU FOR NEXT TO NOTHING.
YOU REALLY KNOW SOMEONE LIKE THAT?!
WHY, I HAPPEN TO KNOW SOME-ONE JUST LIKE THAT AS WELL.
WHAT?! ME? A TUTOR?!
W-WELL, TRUE... I DO HAVE TIME TO SPARE BUT...
...ARE YOU SURE YOU WANT SOMEONE LIKE ME TO TUTOR YOU?
WHAT ARE YOU TALK-ING ABOUT? YOU DID SPEND HALF YOUR LIFE TRYING TO GET INTO TOKYO U.
OH, YEAH, THAT. I GUESS THAT DOES MAKE ME AN EXPERT ON THE SUB-JECT.
COME ON, SHINOBU. WHY DON'T YOU ASK HIM YOUR-SELF? ♡
I, URRM... S-SEMPAI!! WOULD YOU PLEASE BE MY TUTOR?!
I-I'M NOT THAT SMART, BUT... I'M GOING TO TRY MY BEST TO MAKE YOU PROUD OF ME. SO PLEASE TEACH ME!!

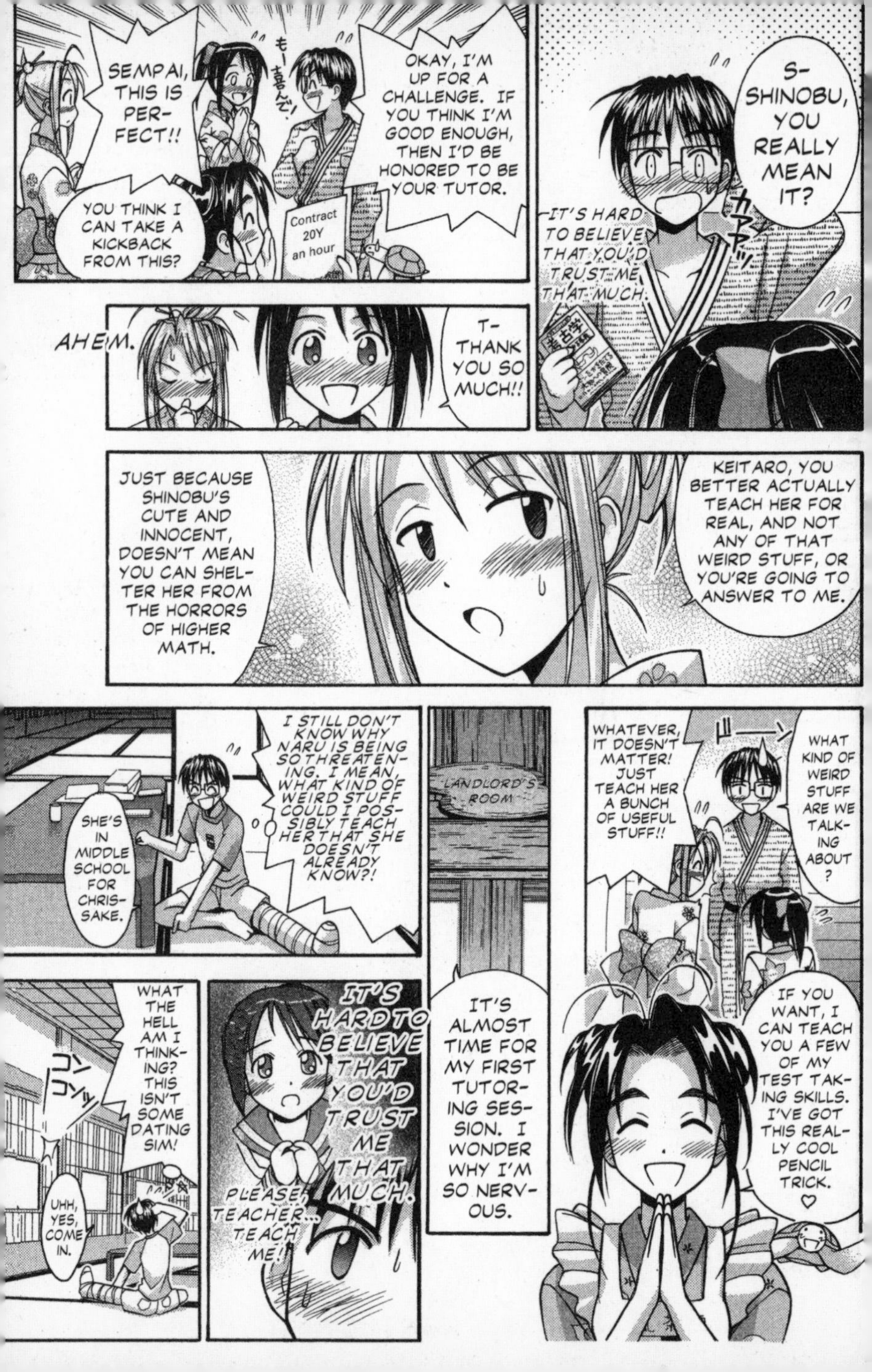
S-SHINOBU, YOU REALLY MEAN IT?
IT'S HARD TO BELIEVE THAT YOU'D TRUST ME THAT MUCH.
OKAY, I'M UP FOR A CHALLENGE. IF YOU THINK I'M GOOD ENOUGH, THEN I'D BE HONORED TO BE YOUR TUTOR.
もー喜んで!
SEMPAI, THIS IS PERFECT!!
Contract 20Y an hour
YOU THINK I CAN TAKE A KICKBACK FROM THIS?
T-THANK YOU SO MUCH!!
AHEM.
KEITARO, YOU BETTER ACTUALLY TEACH HER FOR REAL, AND NOT ANY OF THAT WEIRD STUFF, OR YOU'RE GOING TO ANSWER TO ME.
JUST BECAUSE SHINOBU'S CUTE AND INNOCENT, DOESN'T MEAN YOU CAN SHELTER HER FROM THE HORRORS OF HIGHER MATH.
WHAT KIND OF WEIRD STUFF ARE WE TALKING ABOUT?
WHATEVER, IT DOESN'T MATTER! JUST TEACH HER A BUNCH OF USEFUL STUFF!!
LANDLORD'S ROOM
I STILL DON'T KNOW WHY NARU IS BEING SO THREATENING. I MEAN, WHAT KIND OF WEIRD STUFF COULD I POSSIBLY TEACH HER THAT SHE DOESN'T ALREADY KNOW?!
SHE'S IN MIDDLE SCHOOL FOR CHRIS-SAKE.
IF YOU WANT, I CAN TEACH YOU A FEW OF MY TEST TAKING SKILLS. I'VE GOT THIS REALLY COOL PENCIL TRICK. ♡
IT'S ALMOST TIME FOR MY FIRST TUTORING SESSION. I WONDER WHY I'M SO NERVOUS.
IT'S HARD TO BELIEVE THAT YOU'D TRUST ME THAT MUCH.
PLEASE, TEACHER... TEACH ME!
WHAT THE HELL AM I THINKING? THIS ISN'T SOME DATING SIM!
コンコンッ
UHH, YES, COME IN.

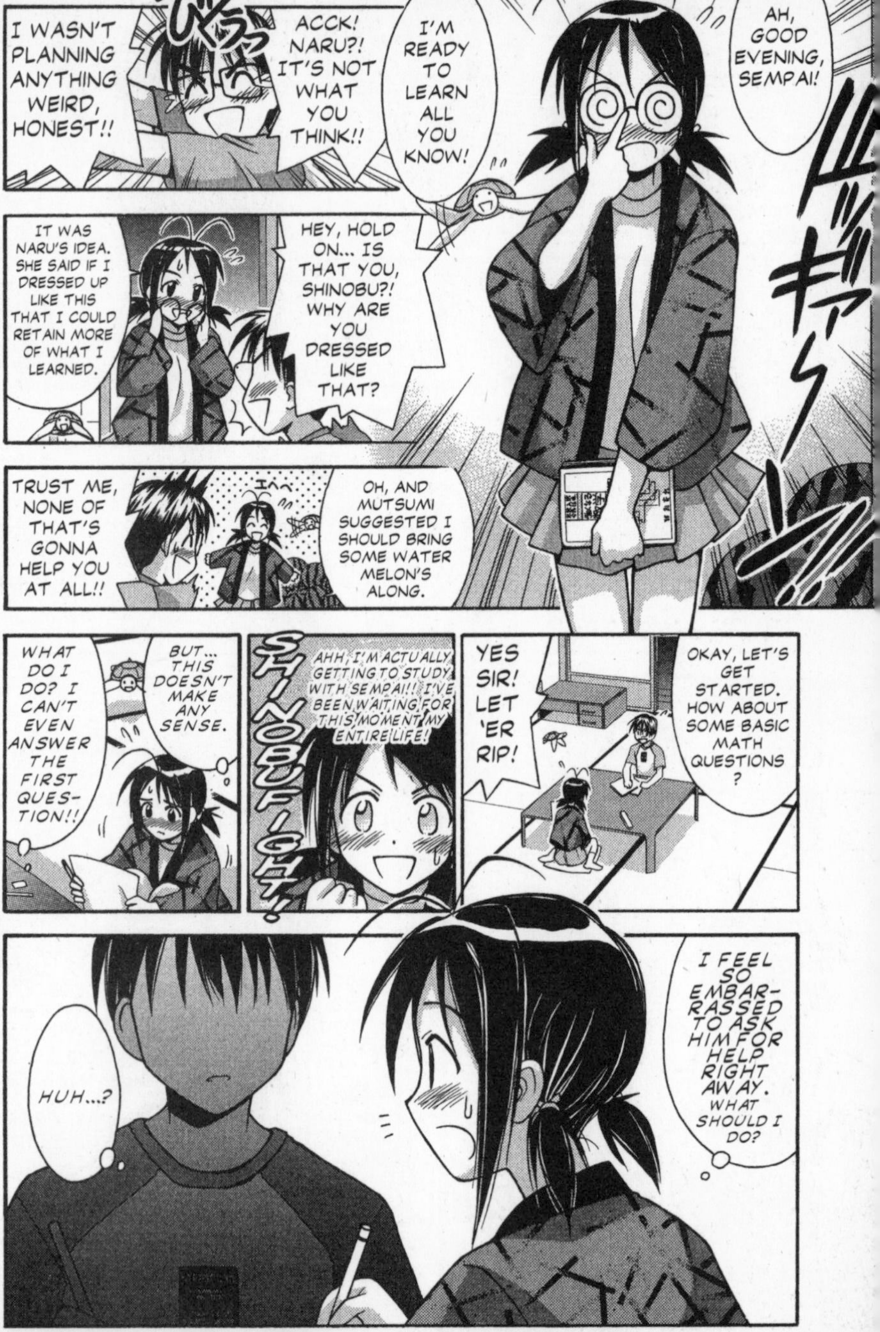
AH, GOOD EVENING, SEMPAI!
I'M READY TO LEARN ALL YOU KNOW!
ACCK! NARU?! IT'S NOT WHAT YOU THINK!!
I WASN'T PLANNING ANYTHING WEIRD, HONEST!!
HEY, HOLD ON... IS THAT YOU, SHINOBU?! WHY ARE YOU DRESSED LIKE THAT?
IT WAS NARU'S IDEA. SHE SAID IF I DRESSED UP LIKE THIS THAT I COULD RETAIN MORE OF WHAT I LEARNED.
OH, AND MUTSUMI SUGGESTED I SHOULD BRING SOME WATER MELON'S ALONG.
TRUST ME, NONE OF THAT'S GONNA HELP YOU AT ALL!!
OKAY, LET'S GET STARTED. HOW ABOUT SOME BASIC MATH QUESTIONS?
YES SIR! LET 'ER RIP!
AHH, I'M ACTUALLY GETTING TO STUDY WITH SEMPAI!! I'VE BEEN WAITING FOR THIS MOMENT MY ENTIRE LIFE!
SHINOBU FIGHT!
BUT... THIS DOESN'T MAKE ANY SENSE.
WHAT DO I DO? I CAN'T EVEN ANSWER THE FIRST QUES-TION!!
I FEEL SO EMBAR-RASSED TO ASK HIM FOR HELP RIGHT AWAY. WHAT SHOULD I DO?
HUH...?

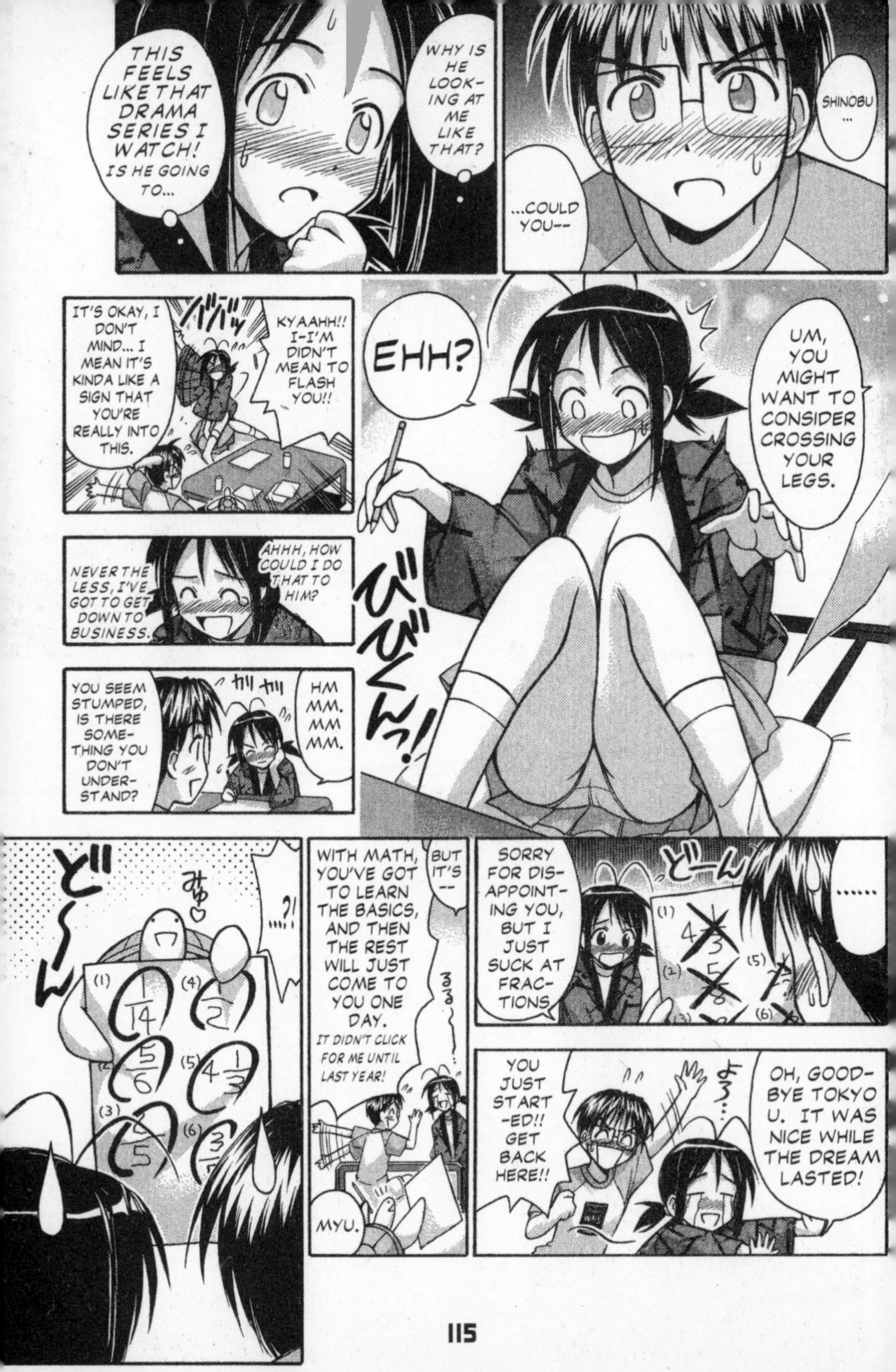
SHINOBU ...
...COULD YOU--
WHY IS HE LOOKING AT ME LIKE THAT?
THIS FEELS LIKE THAT DRAMA SERIES I WATCH! IS HE GOING TO...
UM, YOU MIGHT WANT TO CONSIDER CROSSING YOUR LEGS.
EHH?
びびくんっ!
KYAAHH!! I-I'M DIDN'T MEAN TO FLASH YOU!!
IT'S OKAY, I DON'T MIND... I MEAN IT'S KINDA LIKE A SIGN THAT YOU'RE REALLY INTO THIS.
AHHH, HOW COULD I DO THAT TO HIM?
NEVER THE LESS, I'VE GOT TO GET DOWN TO BUSINESS.
HM MM. MM MM.
YOU SEEM STUMPED, IS THERE SOMETHING YOU DON'T UNDERSTAND?
......
どーん
SORRY FOR DISAPPOINTING YOU, BUT I JUST SUCK AT FRACTIONS.
OH, GOOD-BYE TOKYO U. IT WAS NICE WHILE THE DREAM LASTED!
よろ...
YOU JUST START-ED!! GET BACK HERE!!
BUT IT'S --
WITH MATH, YOU'VE GOT TO LEARN THE BASICS, AND THEN THE REST WILL JUST COME TO YOU ONE DAY.
IT DIDN'T CLICK FOR ME UNTIL LAST YEAR!
るる~...
MYU.
....?!
みゅ♡
どーん

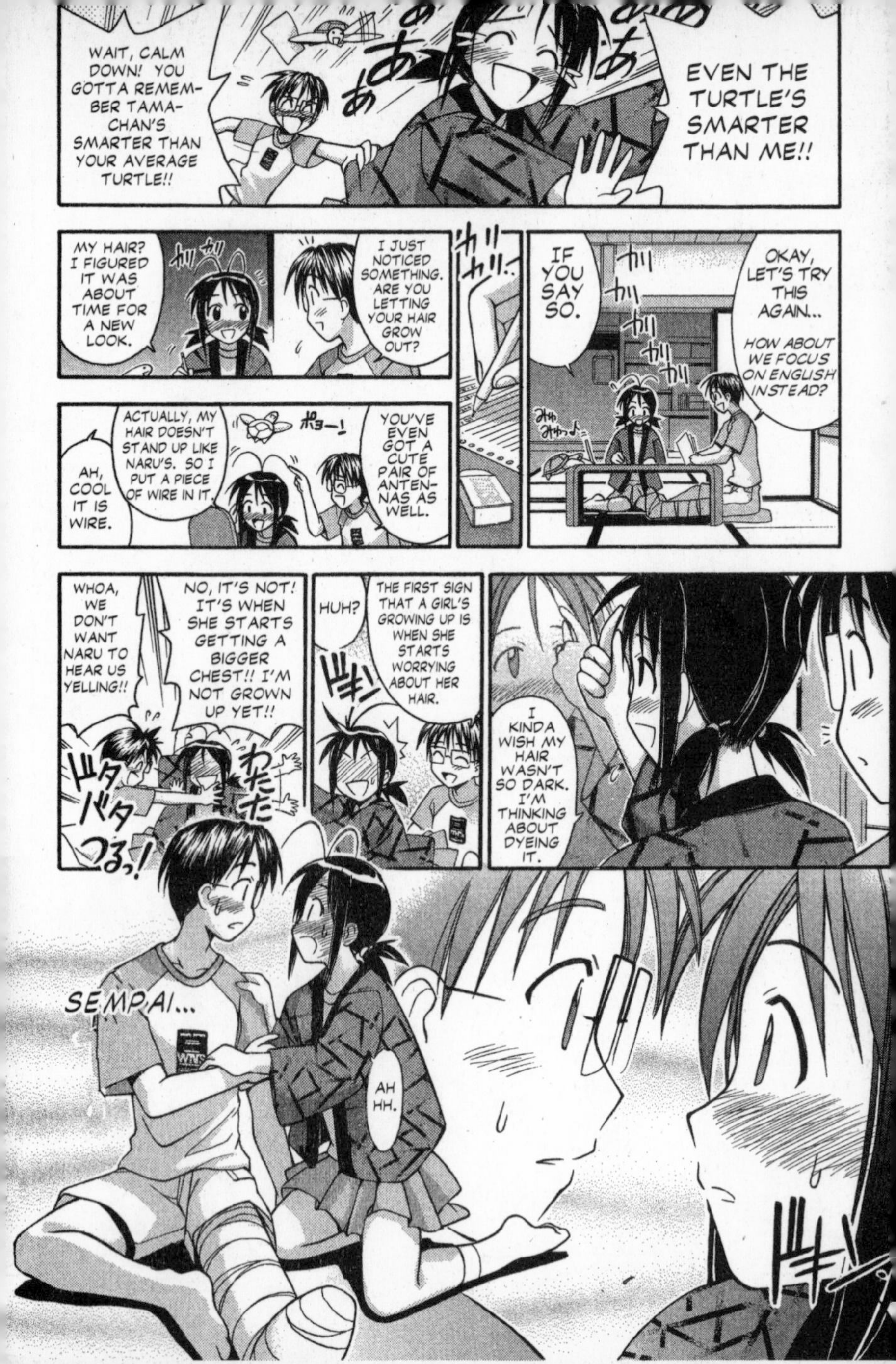

EVEN THE TURTLE'S SMARTER THAN ME!!
WAIT, CALM DOWN! YOU GOTTA REMEMBER TAMA-CHAN'S SMARTER THAN YOUR AVERAGE TURTLE!!
OKAY, LET'S TRY THIS AGAIN...
HOW ABOUT WE FOCUS ON ENGLISH INSTEAD?
IF YOU SAY SO.
I JUST NOTICED SOMETHING. ARE YOU LETTING YOUR HAIR GROW OUT?
MY HAIR? I FIGURED IT WAS ABOUT TIME FOR A NEW LOOK.
YOU'VE EVEN GOT A CUTE PAIR OF ANTENNAS AS WELL.
ACTUALLY, MY HAIR DOESN'T STAND UP LIKE NARU'S. SO I PUT A PIECE OF WIRE IN IT.
AH, COOL IT IS WIRE.
I KINDA WISH MY HAIR WASN'T SO DARK. I'M THINKING ABOUT DYEING IT.
THE FIRST SIGN THAT A GIRL'S GROWING UP IS WHEN SHE STARTS WORRYING ABOUT HER HAIR.
HUH?
NO, IT'S NOT! IT'S WHEN SHE STARTS GETTING A BIGGER CHEST!! I'M NOT GROWN UP YET!!
WHOA, WE DON'T WANT NARU TO HEAR US YELLING!!
SEMPAI...
AH HH.

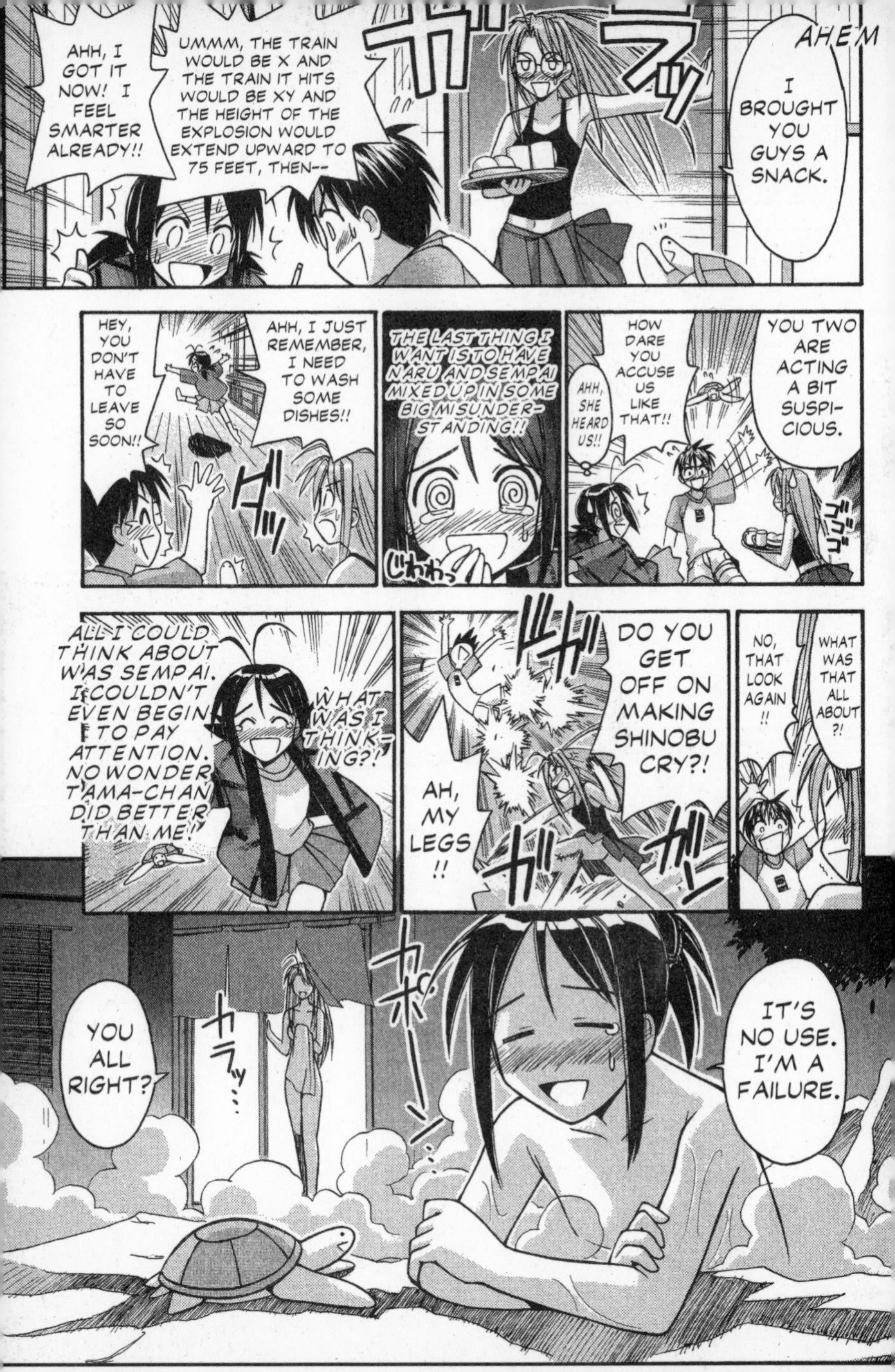
AHEM
I BROUGHT YOU GUYS A SNACK.
UMMM, THE TRAIN WOULD BE X AND THE TRAIN IT HITS WOULD BE XY AND THE HEIGHT OF THE EXPLOSION WOULD EXTEND UPWARD TO 75 FEET, THEN--
AHH, I GOT IT NOW! I FEEL SMARTER ALREADY!!
YOU TWO ARE ACTING A BIT SUSPICIOUS.
HOW DARE YOU ACCUSE US LIKE THAT!!
AHH, SHE HEARD US!!
THE LAST THING I WANT IS TO HAVE NARU AND SEMPAI MIXED UP IN SOME BIG MISUNDERSTANDING!!
AHH, I JUST REMEMBER, I NEED TO WASH SOME DISHES!!
HEY, YOU DON'T HAVE TO LEAVE SO SOON!!
WHAT WAS THAT ALL ABOUT?!
NO, THAT LOOK AGAIN!!
DO YOU GET OFF ON MAKING SHINOBU CRY?!
AH, MY LEGS!!
ALL I COULD THINK ABOUT WAS SEMPAI. I COULDN'T EVEN BEGIN TO PAY ATTENTION. NO WONDER TAMA-CHAN DID BETTER THAN ME!
WHAT WAS I THINKING?!
IT'S NO USE. I'M A FAILURE.
YOU ALL RIGHT?

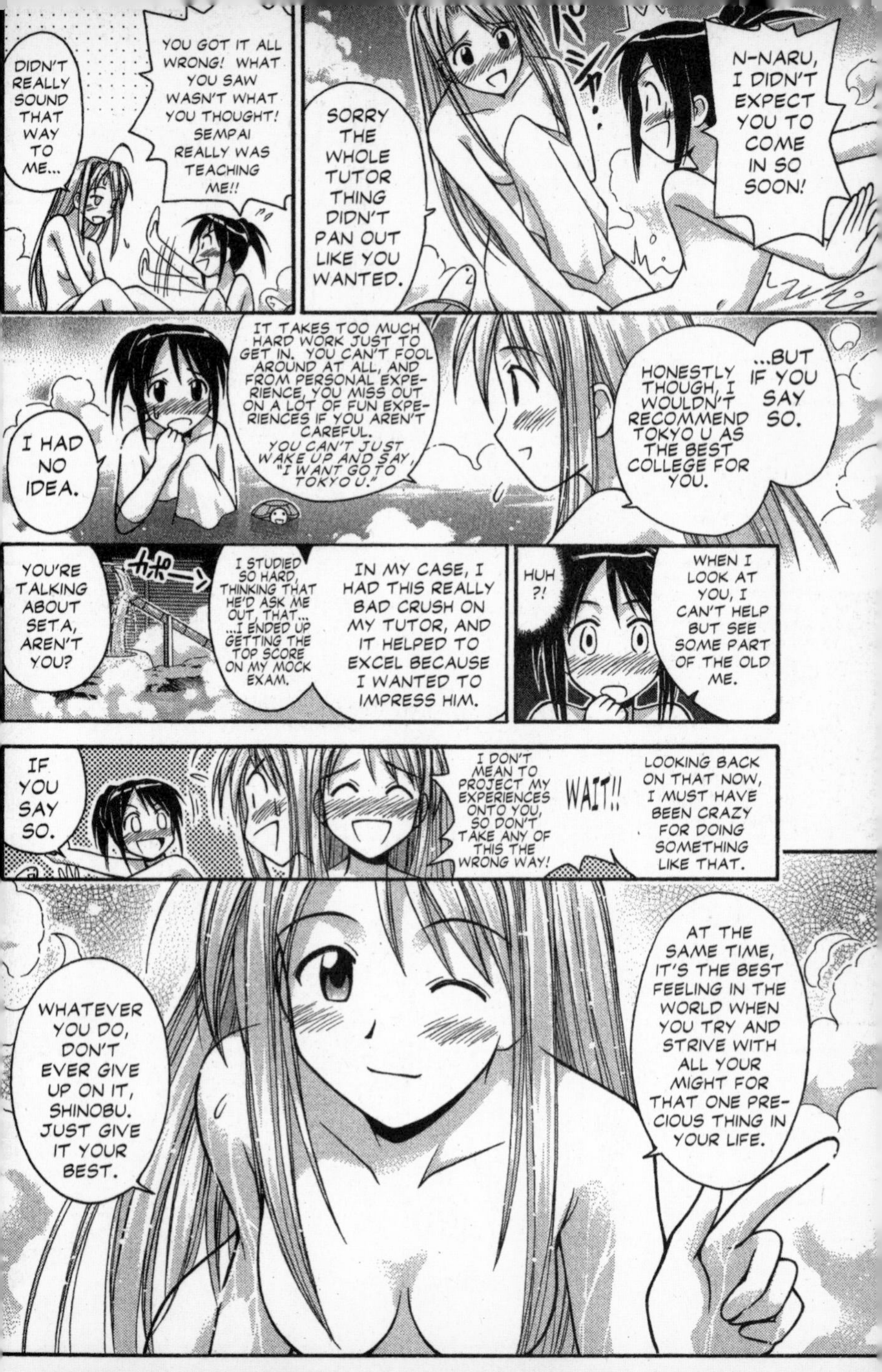
N-NARU, I DIDN'T EXPECT YOU TO COME IN SO SOON!
SORRY THE WHOLE TUTOR THING DIDN'T PAN OUT LIKE YOU WANTED.
YOU GOT IT ALL WRONG! WHAT YOU SAW WASN'T WHAT YOU THOUGHT! SEMPAI REALLY WAS TEACHING ME!!
DIDN'T REALLY SOUND THAT WAY TO ME...
...BUT IF YOU SAY SO.
HONESTLY THOUGH, I WOULDN'T RECOMMEND TOKYO U AS THE BEST COLLEGE FOR YOU.
IT TAKES TOO MUCH HARD WORK JUST TO GET IN. YOU CAN'T FOOL AROUND AT ALL, AND FROM PERSONAL EXPERIENCE, YOU MISS OUT ON A LOT OF FUN EXPERIENCES IF YOU AREN'T CAREFUL. YOU CAN'T JUST WAKE UP AND SAY, "I WANT GO TO TOKYO U."
I HAD NO IDEA.
WHEN I LOOK AT YOU, I CAN'T HELP BUT SEE SOME PART OF THE OLD ME.
HUH ?!
IN MY CASE, I HAD THIS REALLY BAD CRUSH ON MY TUTOR, AND IT HELPED TO EXCEL BECAUSE I WANTED TO IMPRESS HIM.
I STUDIED SO HARD, THINKING THAT HE'D ASK ME OUT, THAT... ...I ENDED UP GETTING THE TOP SCORE ON MY MOCK EXAM.
YOU'RE TALKING ABOUT SETA, AREN'T YOU?
LOOKING BACK ON THAT NOW, I MUST HAVE BEEN CRAZY FOR DOING SOMETHING LIKE THAT.
WAIT!!
I DON'T MEAN TO PROJECT MY EXPERIENCES ONTO YOU, SO DON'T TAKE ANY OF THIS THE WRONG WAY!
IF YOU SAY SO.
AT THE SAME TIME, IT'S THE BEST FEELING IN THE WORLD WHEN YOU TRY AND STRIVE WITH ALL YOUR MIGHT FOR THAT ONE PRECIOUS THING IN YOUR LIFE.
WHATEVER YOU DO, DON'T EVER GIVE UP ON IT, SHINOBU. JUST GIVE IT YOUR BEST.

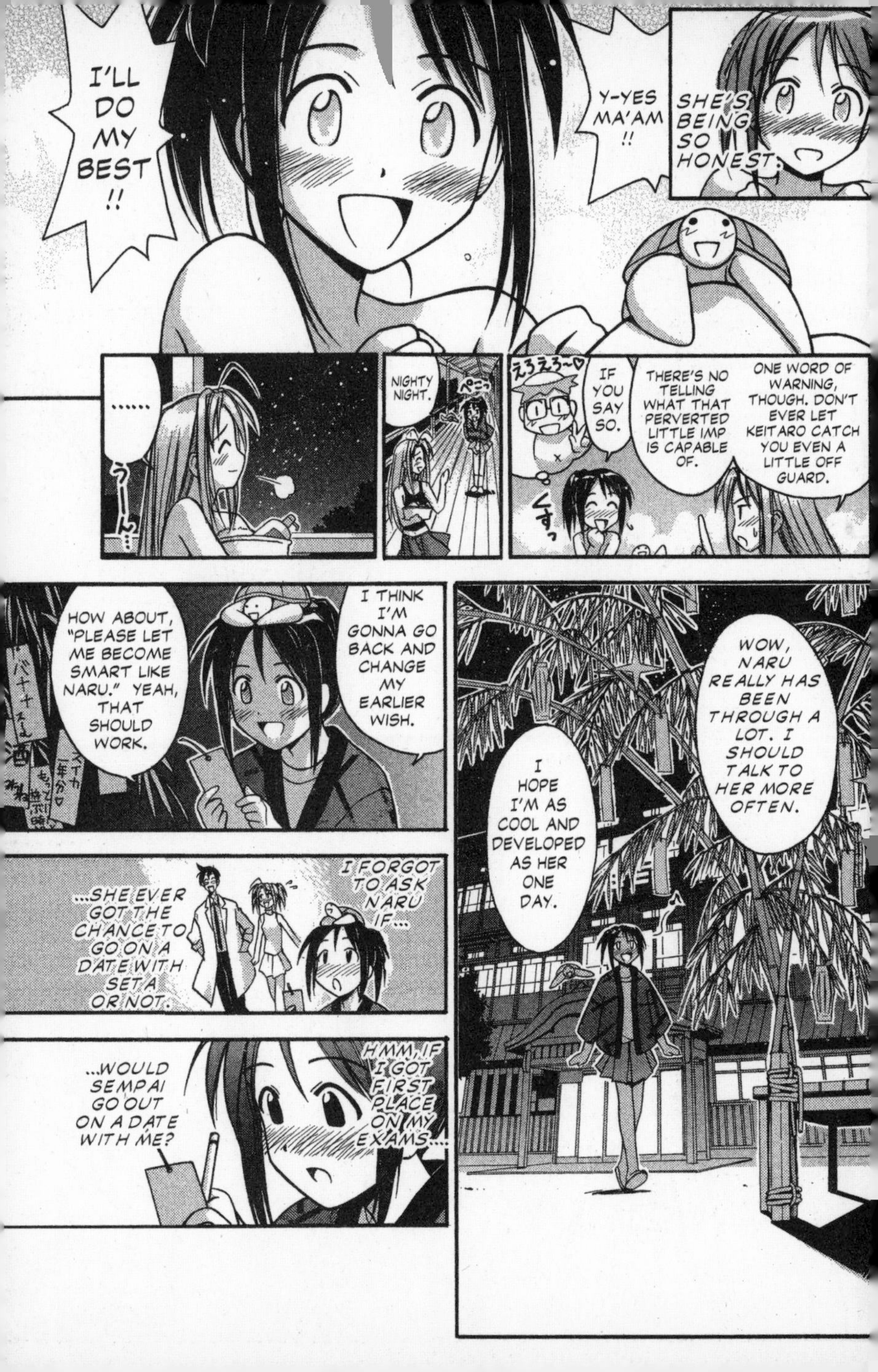
Y-YES MA'AM !!
SHE'S BEING SO HONEST.
I'LL DO MY BEST !!
ONE WORD OF WARNING, THOUGH. DON'T EVER LET KEITARO CATCH YOU EVEN A LITTLE OFF GUARD.
THERE'S NO TELLING WHAT THAT PERVERTED LITTLE IMP IS CAPABLE OF.
IF YOU SAY SO.
えろえろ~♡
くすっ
NIGHTY NIGHT.
ぺこっ
......
うーん...
WOW, NARU REALLY HAS BEEN THROUGH A LOT. I SHOULD TALK TO HER MORE OFTEN.
I HOPE I'M AS COOL AND DEVELOPED AS HER ONE DAY.
I THINK I'M GONNA GO BACK AND CHANGE MY EARLIER WISH.
HOW ABOUT, "PLEASE LET ME BECOME SMART LIKE NARU." YEAH, THAT SHOULD WORK.
I FORGOT TO ASK NARU IF...
...SHE EVER GOT THE CHANCE TO GO ON A DATE WITH SETA OR NOT.
HMM, IF I GOT FIRST PLACE ON MY EXAMS...
...WOULD SEMPAI GO OUT ON A DATE WITH ME?

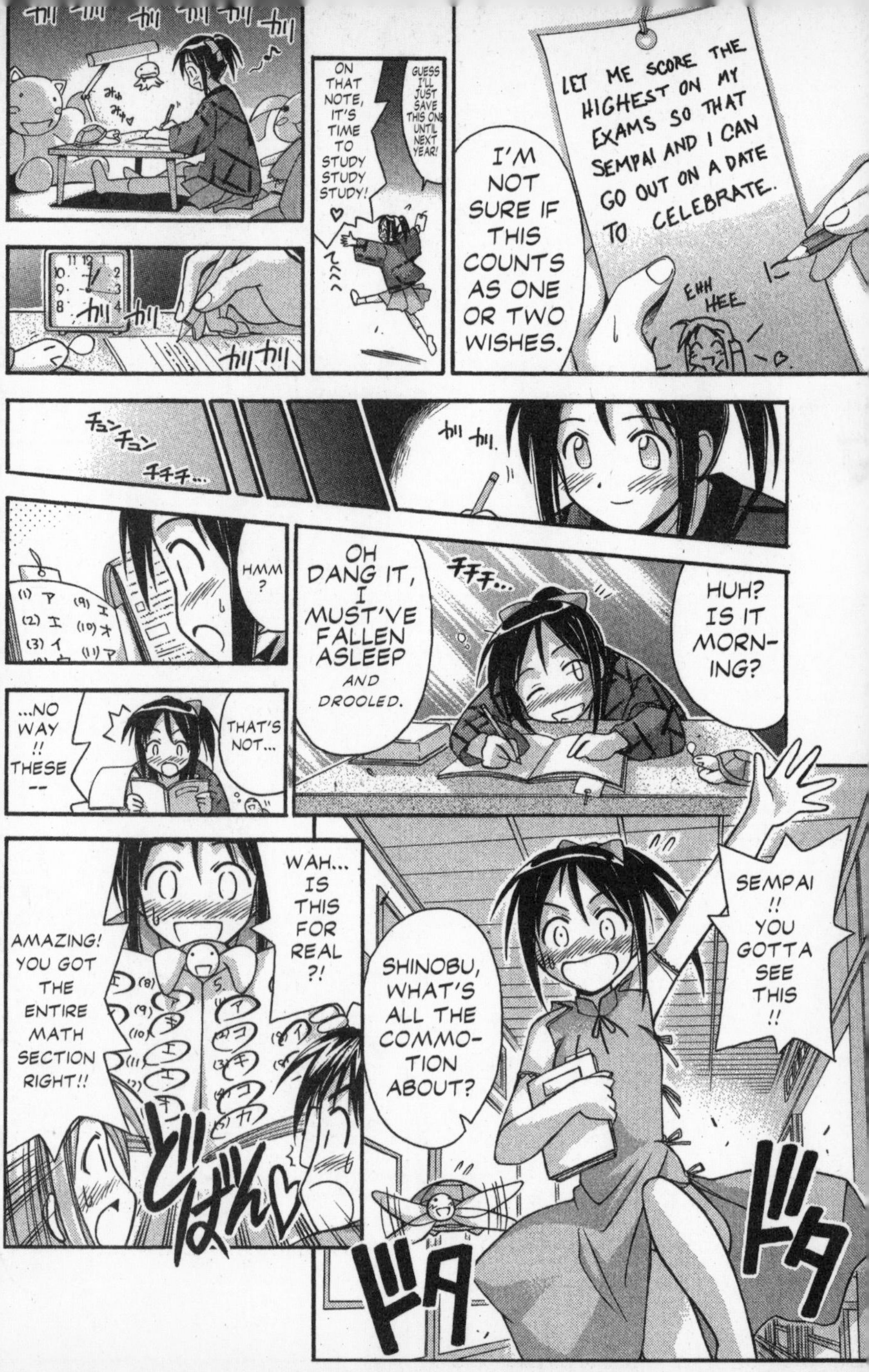
LET ME SCORE THE HIGHEST ON MY EXAMS SO THAT SEMPAI AND I CAN GO OUT ON A DATE TO CELEBRATE.
I'M NOT SURE IF THIS COUNTS AS ONE OR TWO WISHES.
EHH HEE
GUESS I'LL JUST SAVE THIS ONE UNTIL NEXT YEAR!
ON THAT NOTE, IT'S TIME TO STUDY STUDY STUDY! ♡
カリ カリ カリ カリ カリ
カリ カリ
カリカリ
チュン チュン
チチチ...
カリ カリ.
HUH? IS IT MORNING?
チチチ...
OH DANG IT, I MUST'VE FALLEN ASLEEP AND DROOLED.
HMM?
THAT'S NOT...
...NO WAY!! THESE --
SEMPAI!! YOU GOTTA SEE THIS!!
SHINOBU, WHAT'S ALL THE COMMOTION ABOUT?
WAH... IS THIS FOR REAL?!
AMAZING! YOU GOT THE ENTIRE MATH SECTION RIGHT!!
ドタ
ドタ
どばん♡

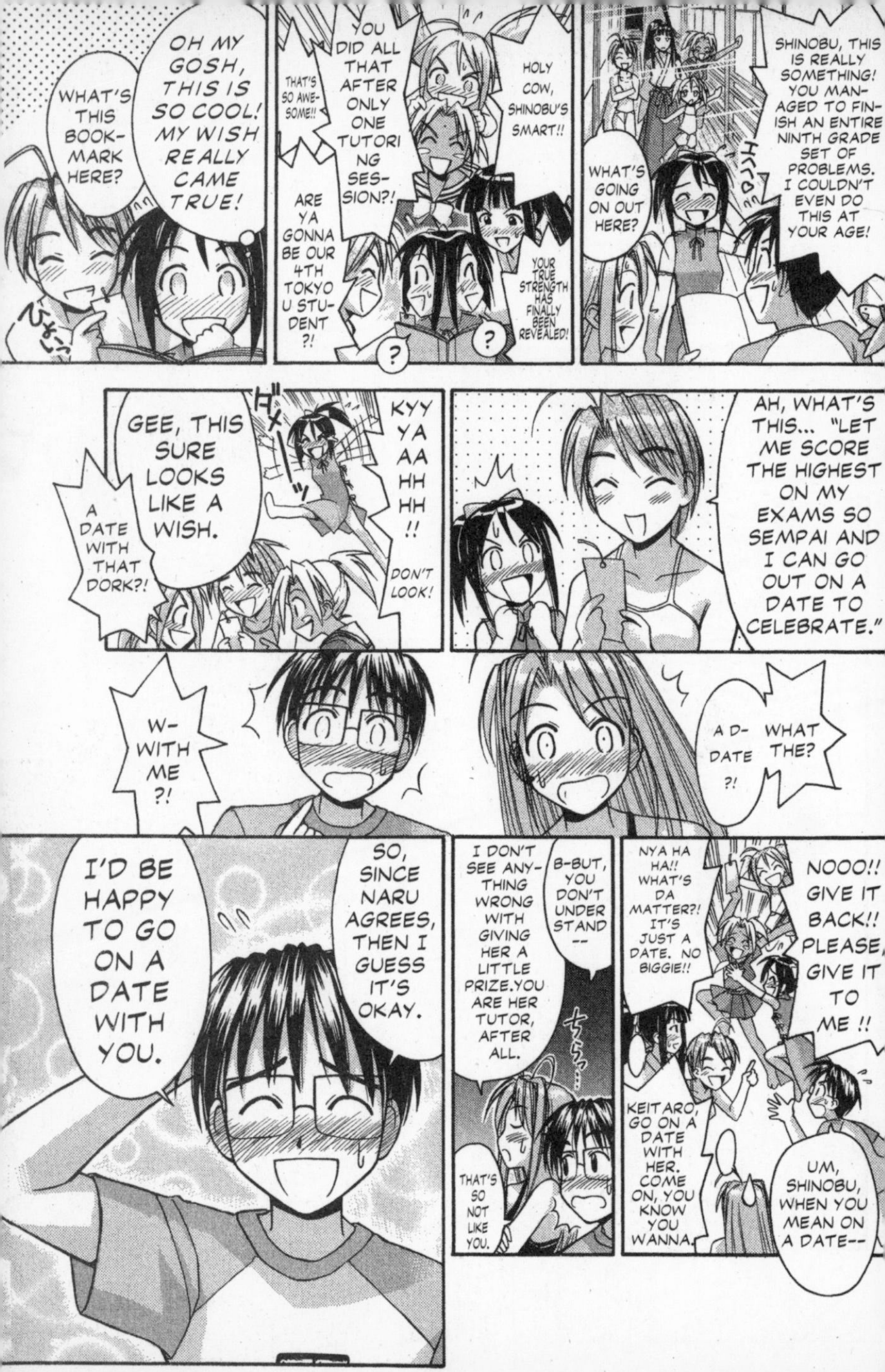
SHINOBU, THIS IS REALLY SOMETHING! YOU MANAGED TO FINISH AN ENTIRE NINTH GRADE SET OF PROBLEMS. I COULDN'T EVEN DO THIS AT YOUR AGE!
WHAT'S GOING ON OUT HERE?
HOLY COW, SHINOBU'S SMART!!
YOU DID ALL THAT AFTER ONLY ONE TUTORING SESSION?!
THAT'S SO AWESOME!!
ARE YA GONNA BE OUR 4TH TOKYO U STUDENT?!
YOUR TRUE STRENGTH HAS FINALLY BEEN REVEALED!
?
?
OH MY GOSH, THIS IS SO COOL! MY WISH REALLY CAME TRUE!
WHAT'S THIS BOOKMARK HERE?
AH, WHAT'S THIS... "LET ME SCORE THE HIGHEST ON MY EXAMS SO SEMPAI AND I CAN GO OUT ON A DATE TO CELEBRATE."
KYYYAAAHHHH!!
DON'T LOOK!
GEE, THIS SURE LOOKS LIKE A WISH.
A DATE WITH THAT DORK?!
WHAT THE?
A D-DATE?!
W-WITH ME?!
NOOO!! GIVE IT BACK!! PLEASE, GIVE IT TO ME!!
NYA HA HA!! WHAT'S DA MATTER?! IT'S JUST A DATE. NO BIGGIE!!
KEITARO, GO ON A DATE WITH HER. COME ON, YOU KNOW YOU WANNA.
UM, SHINOBU, WHEN YOU MEAN ON A DATE--
B-BUT, YOU DON'T UNDERSTAND--
I DON'T SEE ANYTHING WRONG WITH GIVING HER A LITTLE PRIZE. YOU ARE HER TUTOR, AFTER ALL.
THAT'S SO NOT LIKE YOU.
SO, SINCE NARU AGREES, THEN I GUESS IT'S OKAY.
I'D BE HAPPY TO GO ON A DATE WITH YOU.

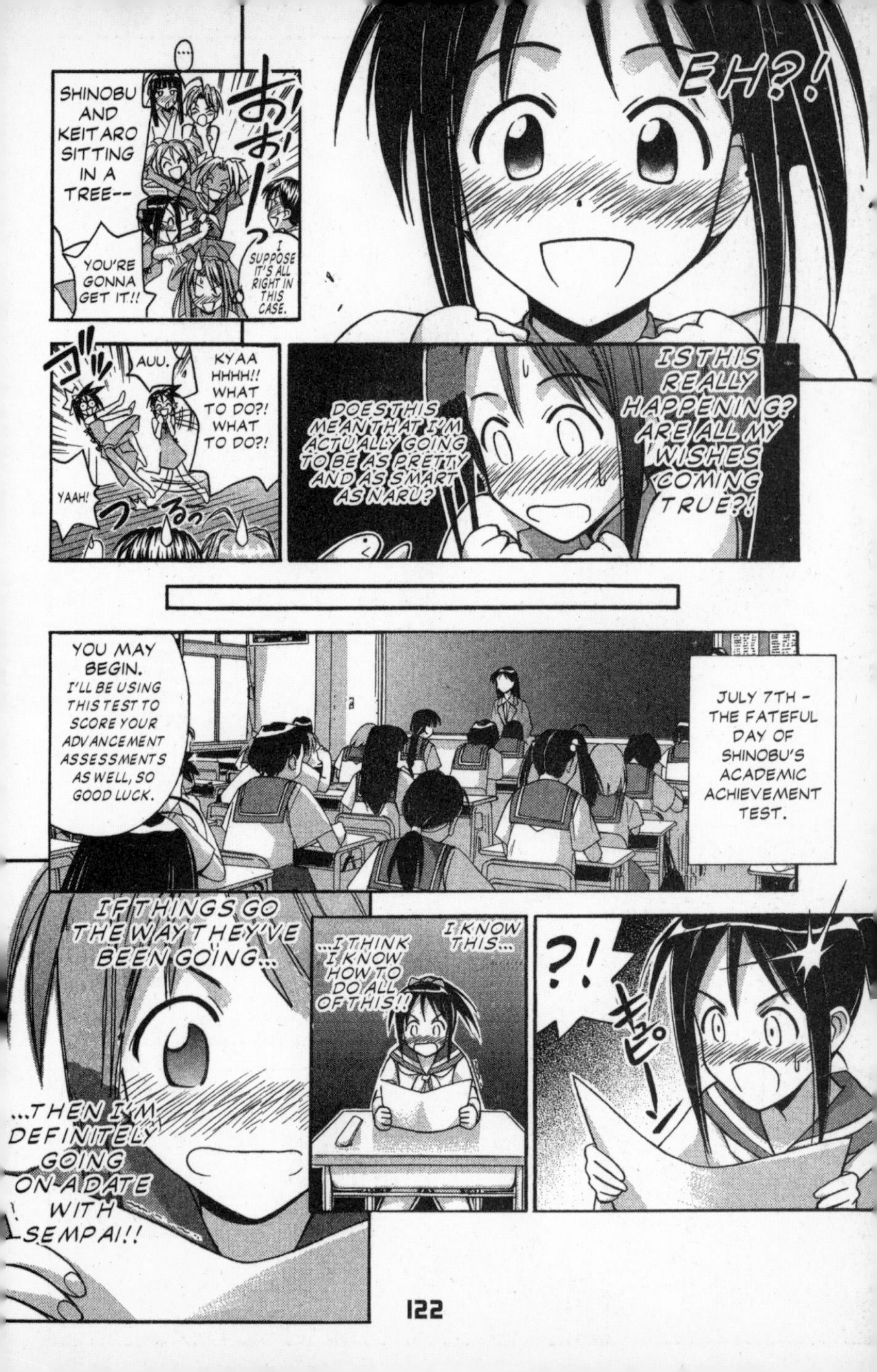
EH?!
...
おぉーっ
SHINOBU AND KEITARO SITTING IN A TREE--
I SUPPOSE IT'S ALL RIGHT IN THIS CASE.
YOU'RE GONNA GET IT!!
IS THIS REALLY HAPPENING? ARE ALL MY WISHES COMING TRUE?!
DOES THIS MEAN THAT I'M ACTUALLY GOING TO BE AS PRETTY AND AS SMART AS NARU?
KYAA HHHH!! WHAT TO DO?! WHAT TO DO?!
AUU.
ゴッ
YAAH!
つるっ
JULY 7TH - THE FATEFUL DAY OF SHINOBU'S ACADEMIC ACHIEVEMENT TEST.
YOU MAY BEGIN. I'LL BE USING THIS TEST TO SCORE YOUR ADVANCEMENT ASSESSMENTS AS WELL, SO GOOD LUCK.
?!
I KNOW THIS...
...I THINK I KNOW HOW TO DO ALL OF THIS!!
IF THINGS GO THE WAY THEY'VE BEEN GOING...
...THEN I'M DEFINITELY GOING ON A DATE WITH SEMPAI!!

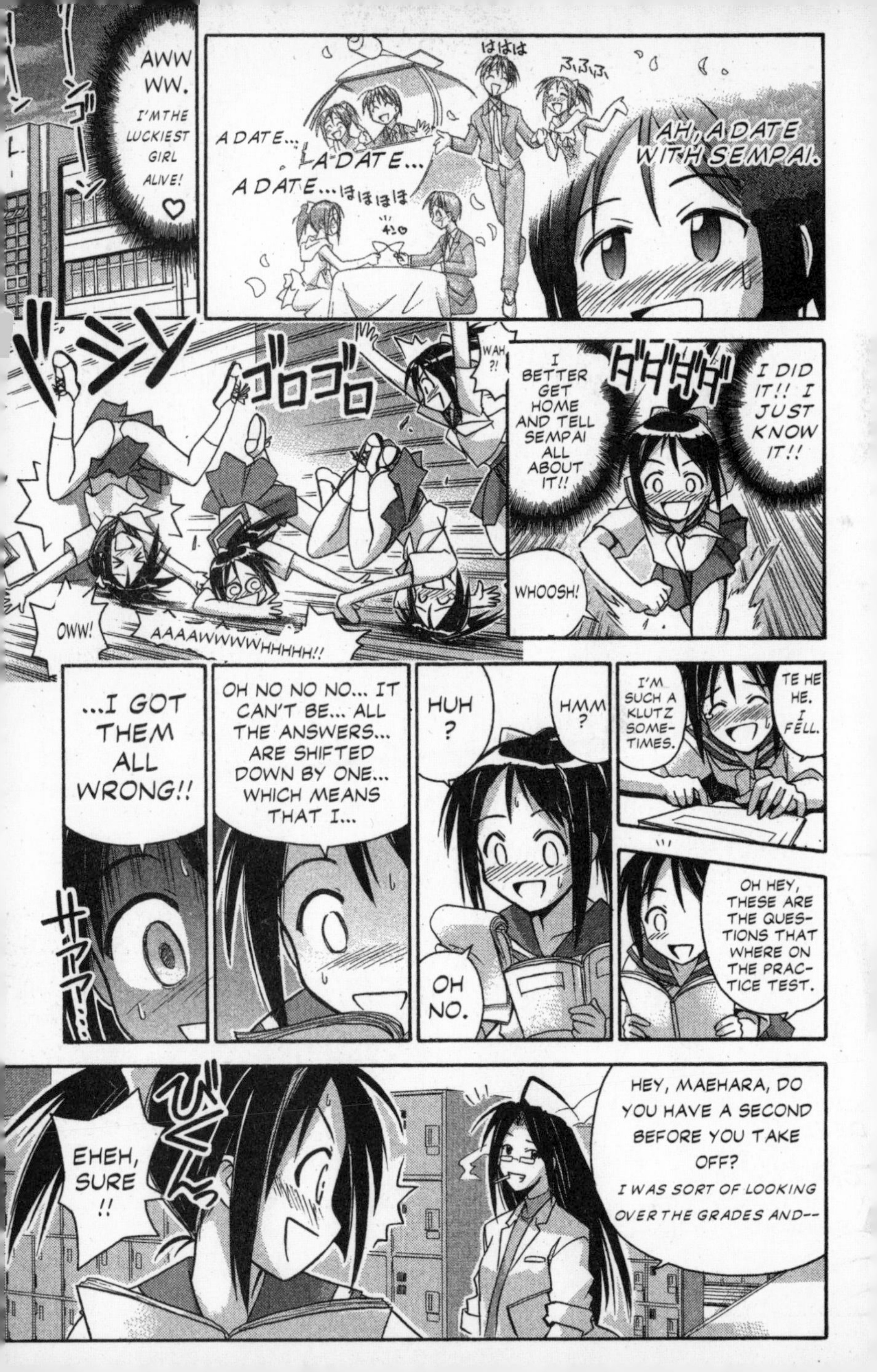
AH, A DATE WITH SEMPAI.
ははは
ふふふ
A DATE... A DATE... A DATE... ほほほほ
AWWWW.
I'M THE LUCKIEST GIRL ALIVE! ♡
ダダダダ
I DID IT!! I JUST KNOW IT!!
I BETTER GET HOME AND TELL SEMPAI ALL ABOUT IT!!
WHOOSH!
WAH ?!
ゴロゴロ
OWW!
AAAAWWWWHHHHH!!
TE HE HE. I FELL.
I'M SUCH A KLUTZ SOMETIMES.
OH HEY, THESE ARE THE QUESTIONS THAT WHERE ON THE PRACTICE TEST.
HMM ?
HUH ?
OH NO.
OH NO NO NO... IT CAN'T BE... ALL THE ANSWERS... ARE SHIFTED DOWN BY ONE... WHICH MEANS THAT I...
...I GOT THEM ALL WRONG!!
HEY, MAEHARA, DO YOU HAVE A SECOND BEFORE YOU TAKE OFF?
I WAS SORT OF LOOKING OVER THE GRADES AND--
EHEH, SURE !!

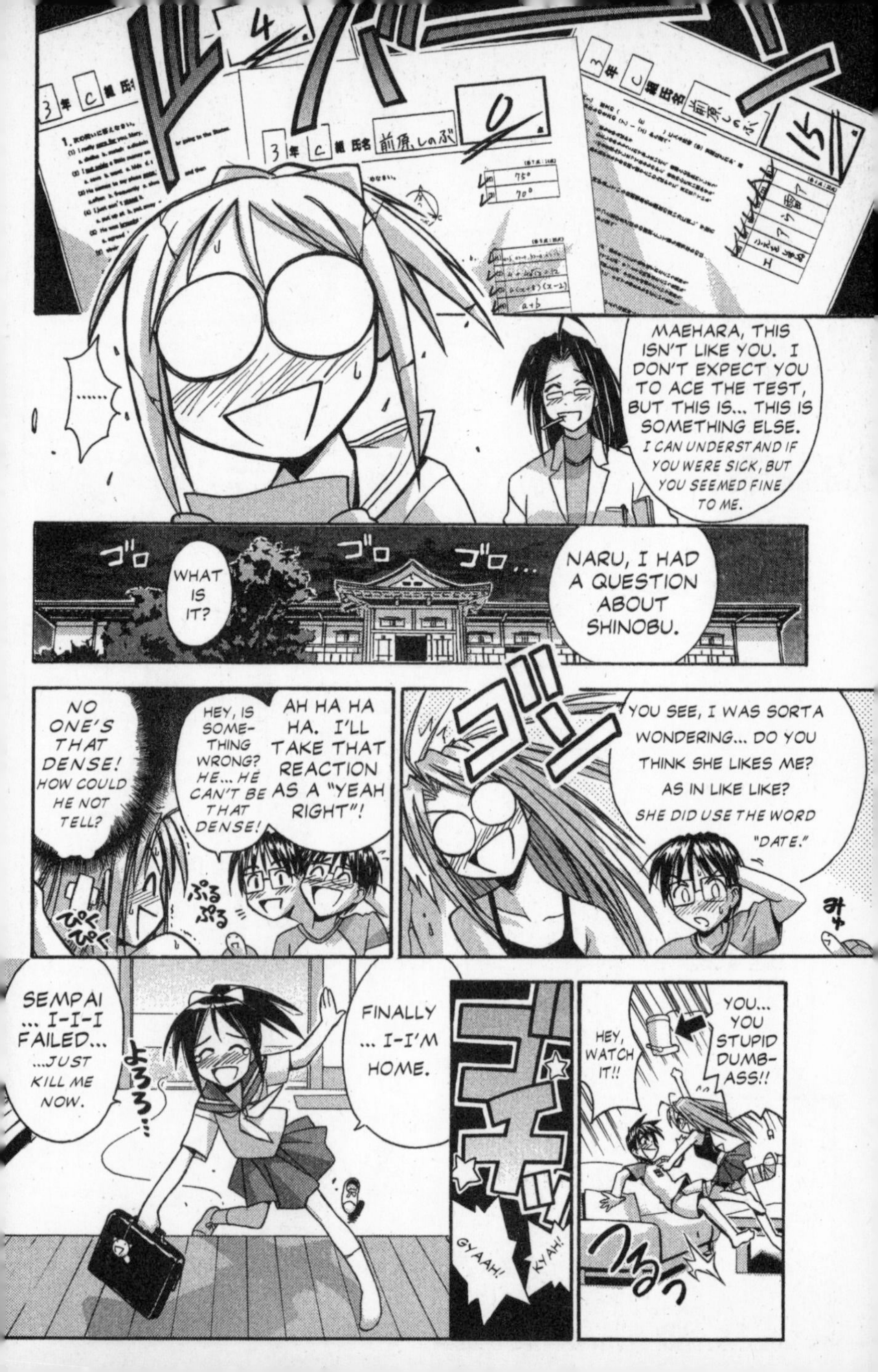
3年 C 組 氏名 前原しのぶ
0
MAEHARA, THIS ISN'T LIKE YOU. I DON'T EXPECT YOU TO ACE THE TEST, BUT THIS IS... THIS IS SOMETHING ELSE. I CAN UNDERSTAND IF YOU WERE SICK, BUT YOU SEEMED FINE TO ME.
......
NARU, I HAD A QUESTION ABOUT SHINOBU.
ゴロ ゴロ ゴロ...
WHAT IS IT?
YOU SEE, I WAS SORTA WONDERING... DO YOU THINK SHE LIKES ME? AS IN LIKE LIKE? SHE DID USE THE WORD "DATE."
AH HA HA HA. I'LL TAKE THAT REACTION AS A "YEAH RIGHT"!
HEY, IS SOMETHING WRONG? HE... HE CAN'T BE THAT DENSE!
NO ONE'S THAT DENSE! HOW COULD HE NOT TELL?
ぷるぷる
ぴくぴく
YOU... YOU STUPID DUMB-ASS!!
HEY, WATCH IT!!
GYAAH!
KYAH!
FINALLY ... I-I'M HOME.
SEMPAI ... I-I-I FAILED... ...JUST KILL ME NOW.
よろろ...

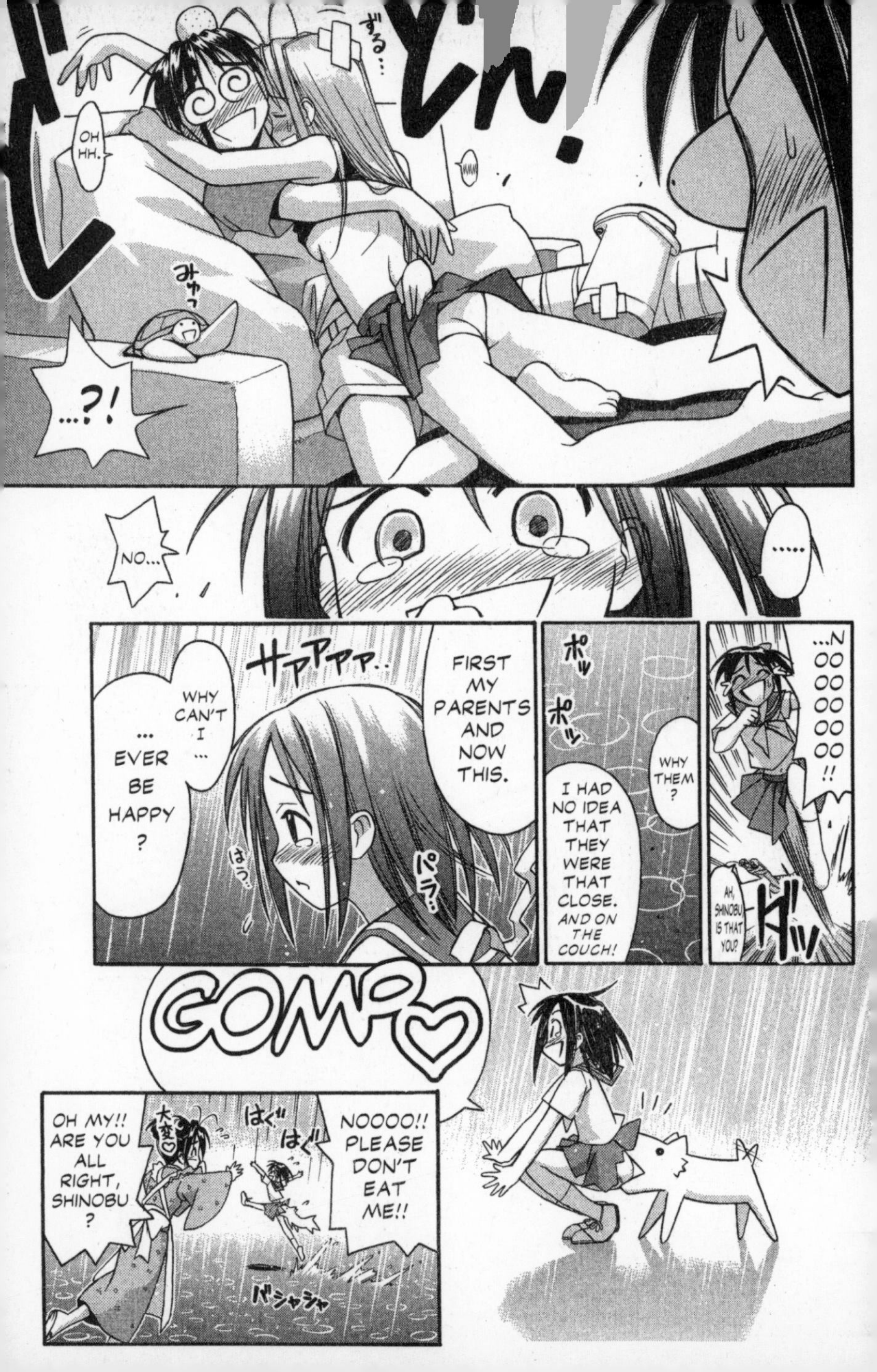
どん!
ずる…
OH HH.
みゃっ
...?!
......
NO...
...NOOOOOOOOOOOOO!!
AH, SHINOBU IS THAT YOU?
ダッ
ポッ
ポッ
WHY THEM?
I HAD NO IDEA THAT THEY WERE THAT CLOSE. AND ON THE COUCH!
FIRST MY PARENTS AND NOW THIS.
サァァァァ..
WHY CAN'T I ...
... EVER BE HAPPY?
はう..
パラ…
GOMP♡
NOOOO!! PLEASE DON'T EAT ME!!
はぐ
はぐ
大変♡
OH MY!! ARE YOU ALL RIGHT, SHINOBU?
バシャシャ

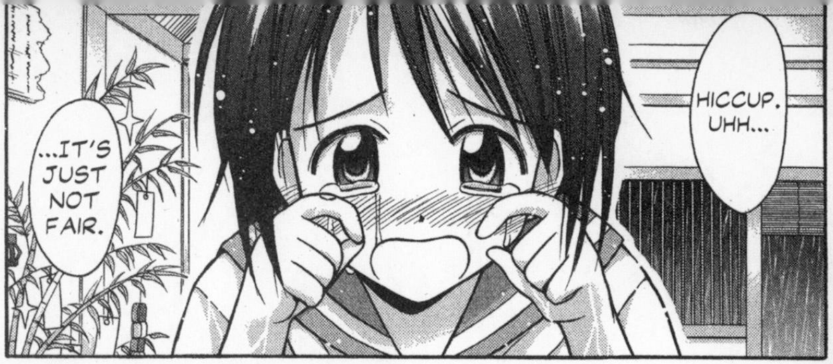
HICCUP. UHH...
...IT'S JUST NOT FAIR.

Love Hina

HINATA.76 I Wanna Grow Up!

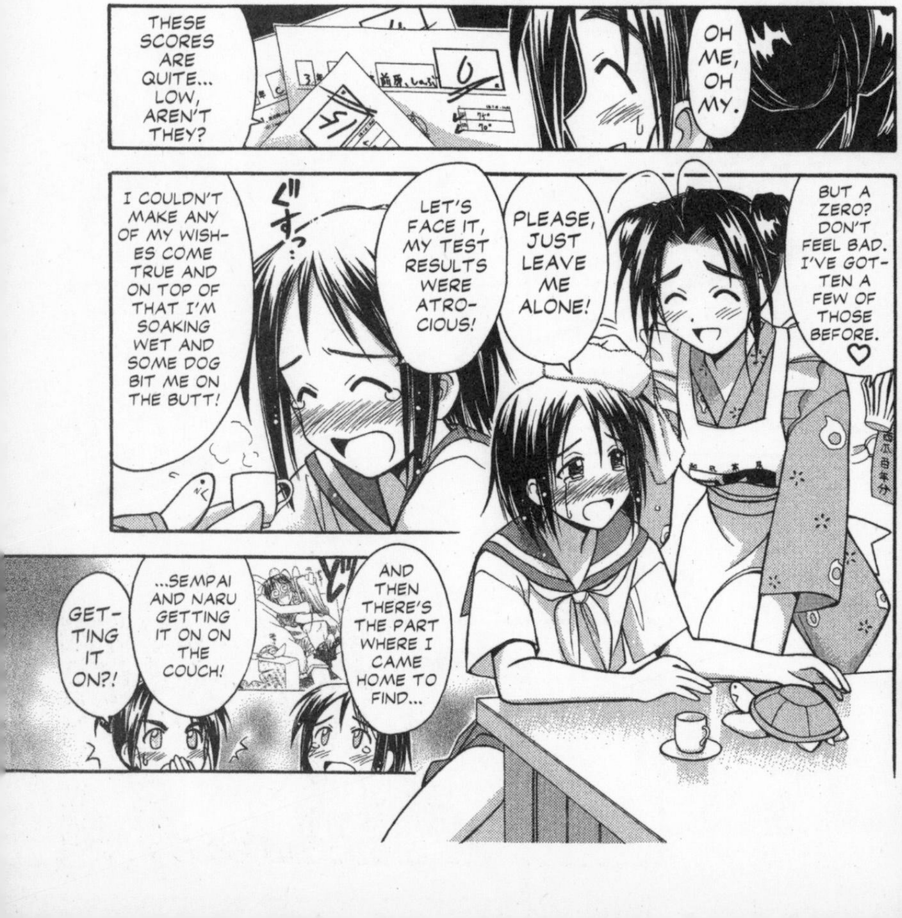
OH ME, OH MY.
THESE SCORES ARE QUITE... LOW, AREN'T THEY?
BUT A ZERO? DON'T FEEL BAD. I'VE GOTTEN A FEW OF THOSE BEFORE. ♡
PLEASE, JUST LEAVE ME ALONE!
LET'S FACE IT, MY TEST RESULTS WERE ATROCIOUS!
I COULDN'T MAKE ANY OF MY WISHES COME TRUE AND ON TOP OF THAT I'M SOAKING WET AND SOME DOG BIT ME ON THE BUTT!
AND THEN THERE'S THE PART WHERE I CAME HOME TO FIND...
...SEMPAI AND NARU GETTING IT ON ON THE COUCH!
GET-TING IT ON?!

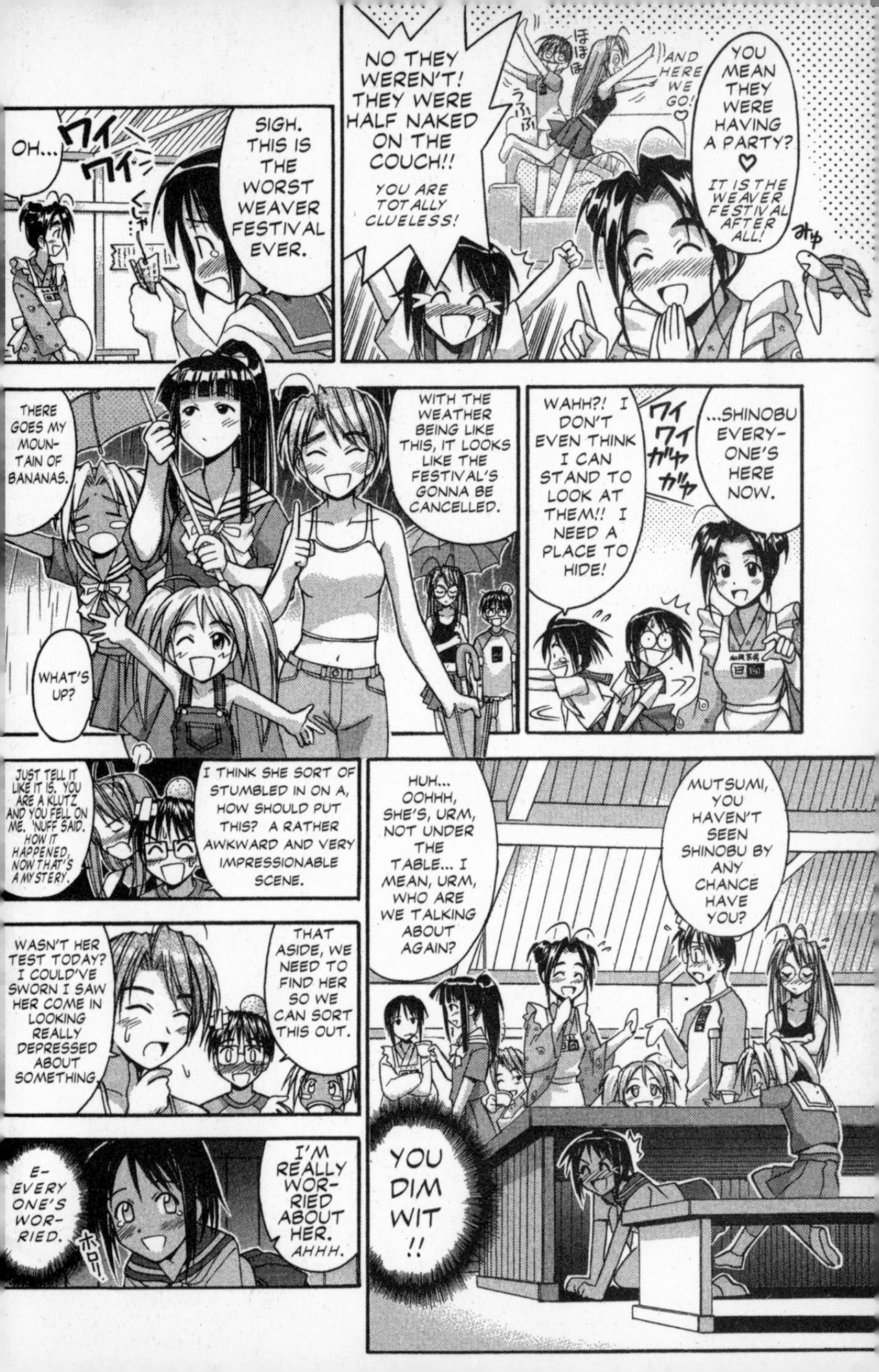
YOU MEAN THEY WERE HAVING A PARTY? ♡
IT IS THE WEAVER FESTIVAL AFTER ALL!
みゅ
AND HERE WE GO! ♡
ほほほ
うふふ
NO THEY WEREN'T! THEY WERE HALF NAKED ON THE COUCH!!
YOU ARE TOTALLY CLUELESS!
SIGH. THIS IS THE WORST WEAVER FESTIVAL EVER.
ワイワイ
くしゃ
OH...
...SHINOBU EVERYONE'S HERE NOW.
ワイワイガヤガヤ
WAHH?! I DON'T EVEN THINK I CAN STAND TO LOOK AT THEM!! I NEED A PLACE TO HIDE!
WITH THE WEATHER BEING LIKE THIS, IT LOOKS LIKE THE FESTIVAL'S GONNA BE CANCELLED.
THERE GOES MY MOUNTAIN OF BANANAS.
WHAT'S UP?
MUTSUMI, YOU HAVEN'T SEEN SHINOBU BY ANY CHANCE HAVE YOU?
HUH... OOHHH, SHE'S, URM, NOT UNDER THE TABLE... I MEAN, URM, WHO ARE WE TALKING ABOUT AGAIN?
YOU DIM WIT!!
I THINK SHE SORT OF STUMBLED IN ON A, HOW SHOULD PUT THIS? A RATHER AWKWARD AND VERY IMPRESSIONABLE SCENE.
JUST TELL IT LIKE IT IS. YOU ARE A KLUTZ AND YOU FELL ON ME. 'NUFF SAID. HOW IT HAPPENED, NOW THAT'S A MYSTERY.
THAT ASIDE, WE NEED TO FIND HER SO WE CAN SORT THIS OUT.
WASN'T HER TEST TODAY? I COULD'VE SWORN I SAW HER COME IN LOOKING REALLY DEPRESSED ABOUT SOMETHING.
I'M REALLY WORRIED ABOUT HER. AHHH.
E-EVERYONE'S WORRIED.
ホロ

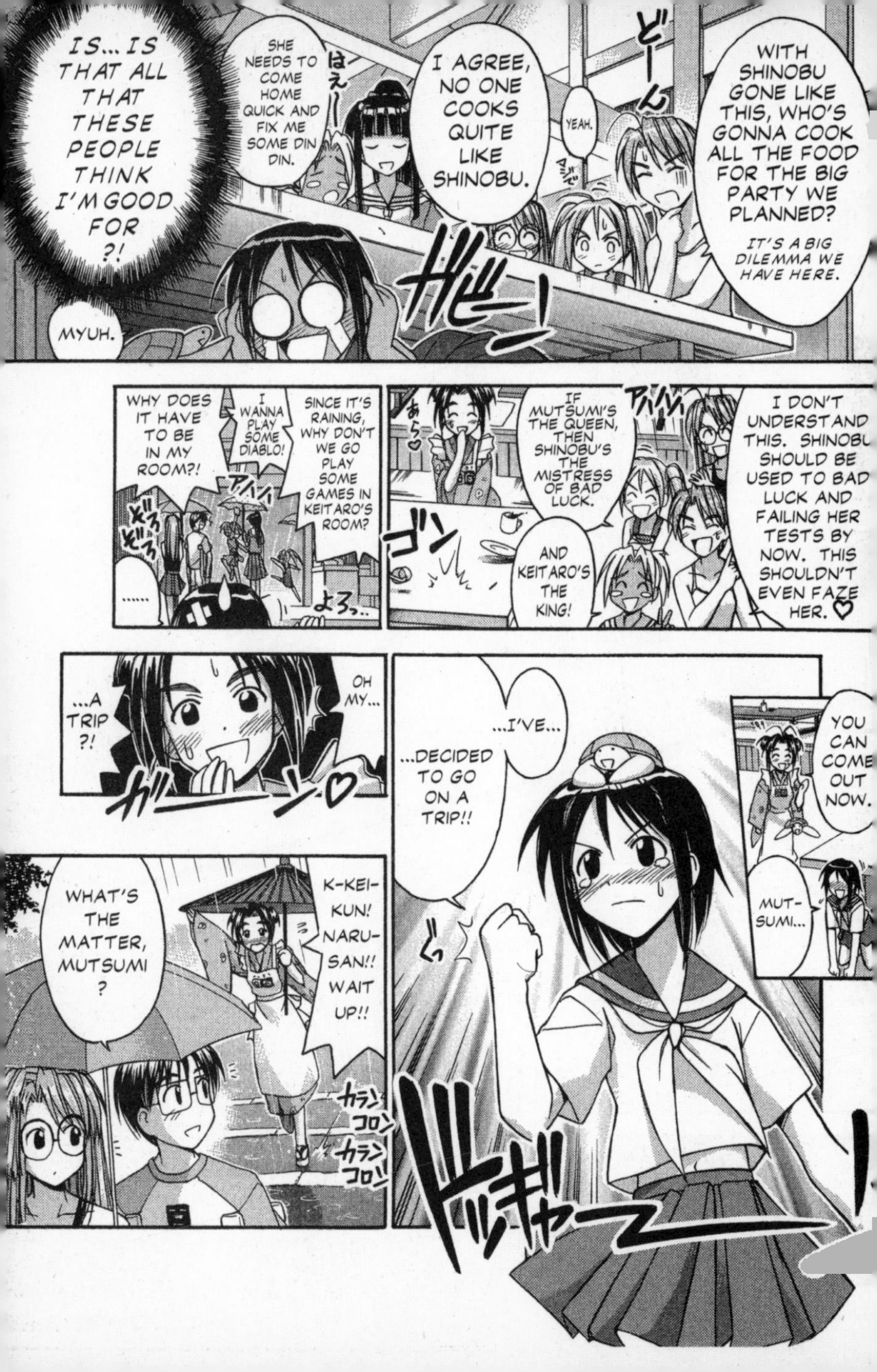

WITH SHINOBU GONE LIKE THIS, WHO'S GONNA COOK ALL THE FOOD FOR THE BIG PARTY WE PLANNED?
IT'S A BIG DILEMMA WE HAVE HERE.
どーん
YEAH.
I AGREE, NO ONE COOKS QUITE LIKE SHINOBU.
SHE NEEDS TO COME HOME QUICK AND FIX ME SOME DIN DIN.
IS... IS THAT ALL THAT THESE PEOPLE THINK I'M GOOD FOR ?!
MYUH.
I DON'T UNDERSTAND THIS. SHINOBU SHOULD BE USED TO BAD LUCK AND FAILING HER TESTS BY NOW. THIS SHOULDN'T EVEN FAZE HER. ♡
IF MUTSUMI'S THE QUEEN, THEN SHINOBU'S THE MISTRESS OF BAD LUCK.
AND KEITARO'S THE KING!
SINCE IT'S RAINING, WHY DON'T WE GO PLAY SOME GAMES IN KEITARO'S ROOM?
I WANNA PLAY SOME DIABLO!
WHY DOES IT HAVE TO BE IN MY ROOM?!
......
YOU CAN COME OUT NOW.
MUT-SUMI...
...I'VE...
...DECIDED TO GO ON A TRIP!!
OH MY...
...A TRIP ?!
K-KEI-KUN! NARU-SAN!! WAIT UP!!
WHAT'S THE MATTER, MUTSUMI ?

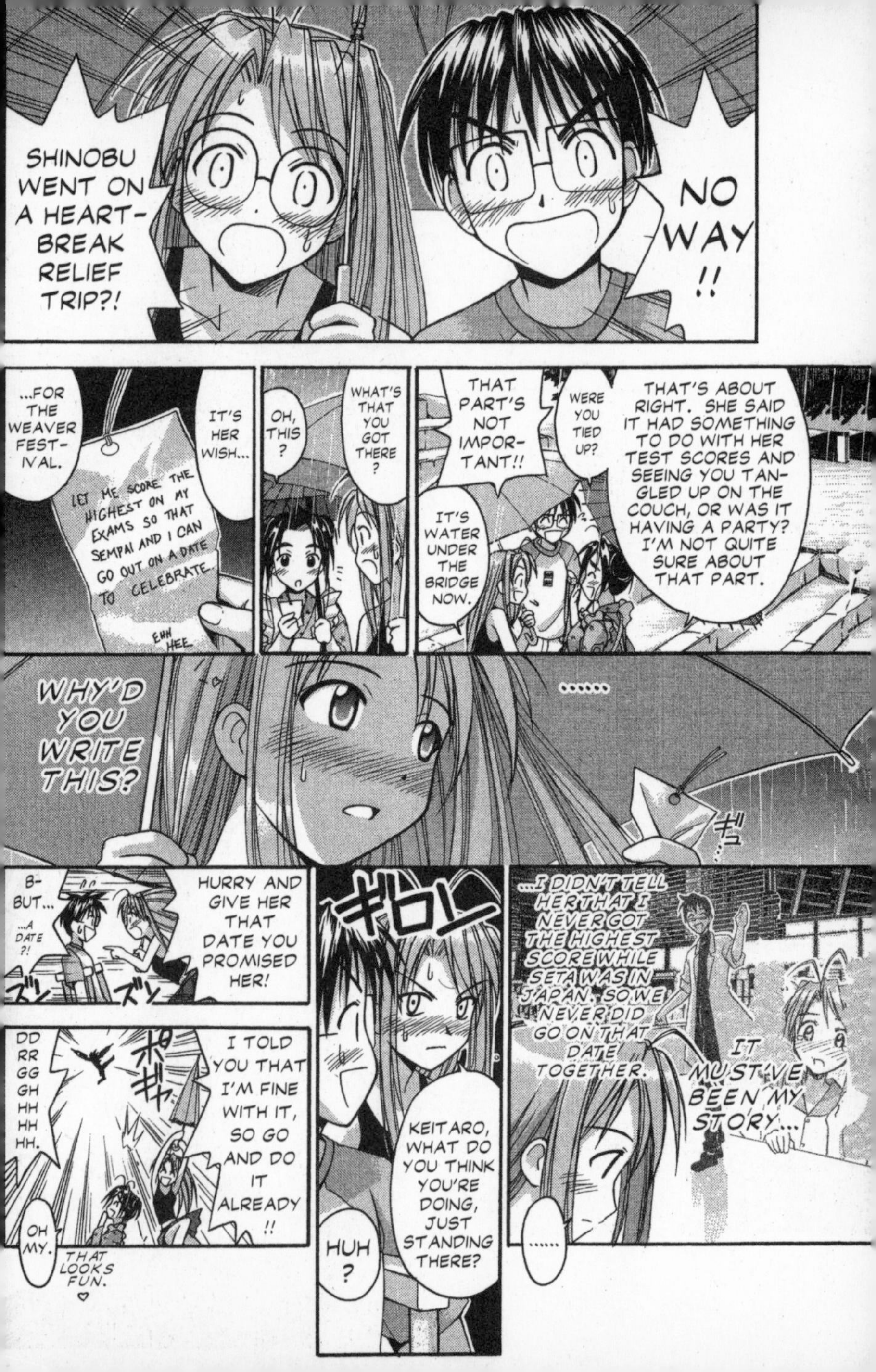
NO WAY !!
SHINOBU WENT ON A HEART-BREAK RELIEF TRIP?!
THAT'S ABOUT RIGHT. SHE SAID IT HAD SOMETHING TO DO WITH HER TEST SCORES AND SEEING YOU TANGLED UP ON THE COUCH, OR WAS IT HAVING A PARTY? I'M NOT QUITE SURE ABOUT THAT PART.
WERE YOU TIED UP?
THAT PART'S NOT IMPORTANT!!
IT'S WATER UNDER THE BRIDGE NOW.
WHAT'S THAT YOU GOT THERE?
OH, THIS?
IT'S HER WISH...
...FOR THE WEAVER FESTIVAL.
LET ME SCORE THE HIGHEST ON MY EXAMS SO THAT SEMPAI AND I CAN GO OUT ON A DATE TO CELEBRATE.
EHH HEE
......
WHY'D YOU WRITE THIS?
ギュ...
...I DIDN'T TELL HER THAT I NEVER GOT THE HIGHEST SCORE WHILE SETA WAS IN JAPAN, SO WE NEVER DID GO ON THAT DATE TOGETHER.
IT MUST'VE BEEN MY STORY...
......
KEITARO, WHAT DO YOU THINK YOU'RE DOING, JUST STANDING THERE?
HUH?
HURRY AND GIVE HER THAT DATE YOU PROMISED HER!
B-BUT...
...A DATE?!
I TOLD YOU THAT I'M FINE WITH IT, SO GO AND DO IT ALREADY!!
DDRRGGGHHHHHHHH.
OH MY.
THAT LOOKS FUN. ♡

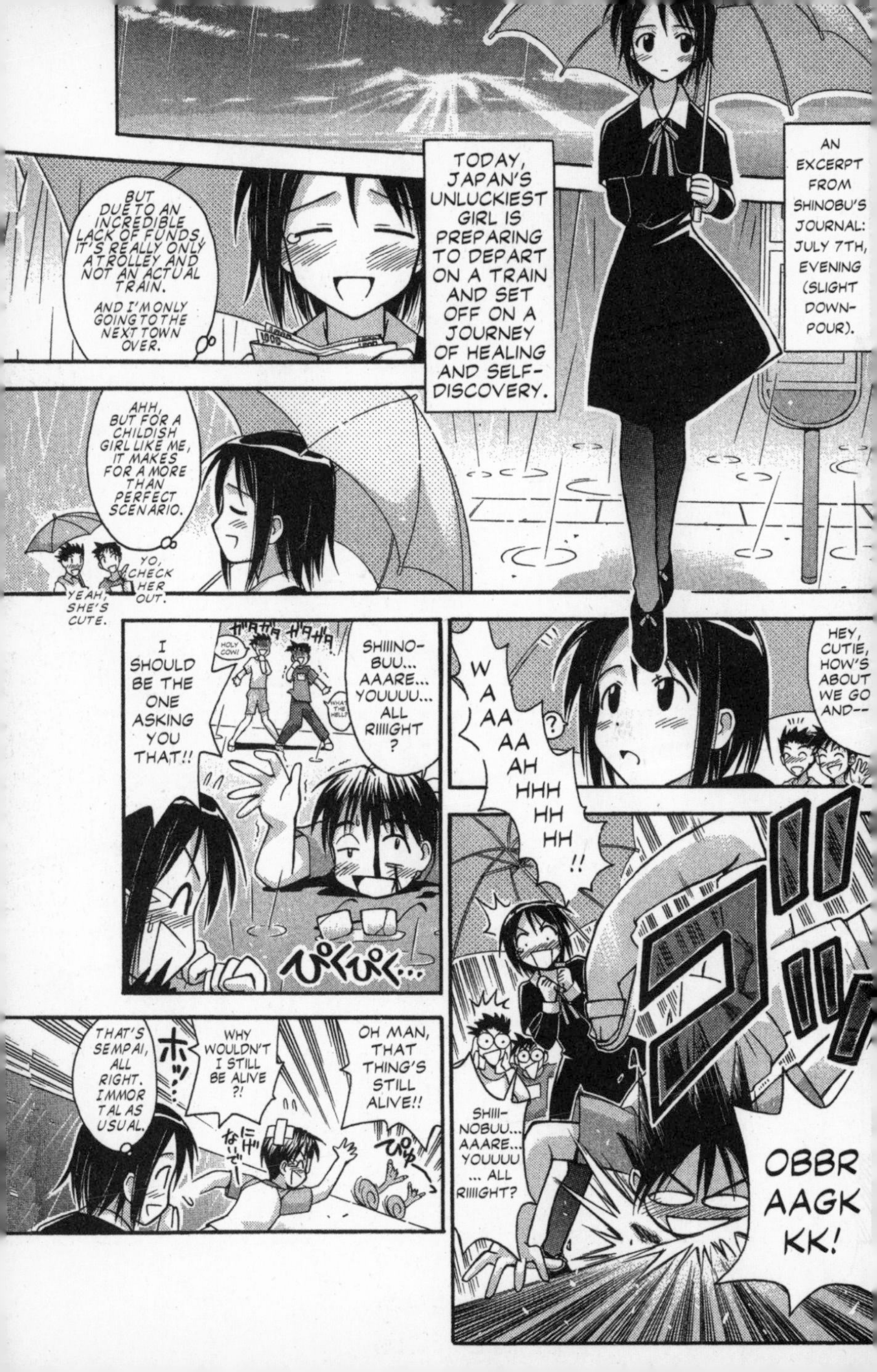

AN EXCERPT FROM SHINOBU'S JOURNAL: JULY 7TH, EVENING (SLIGHT DOWNPOUR).
TODAY, JAPAN'S UNLUCKIEST GIRL IS PREPARING TO DEPART ON A TRAIN AND SET OFF ON A JOURNEY OF HEALING AND SELF-DISCOVERY.
BUT DUE TO AN INCREDIBLE LACK OF FUNDS, IT'S REALLY ONLY A TROLLEY AND NOT AN ACTUAL TRAIN.
AND I'M ONLY GOING TO THE NEXT TOWN OVER.
AHH, BUT FOR A CHILDISH GIRL LIKE ME, IT MAKES FOR A MORE THAN PERFECT SCENARIO.
YO, CHECK HER OUT.
YEAH, SHE'S CUTE.
HEY, CUTIE, HOW'S ABOUT WE GO AND--
?
WAAAAAAAHHHHHHH!!
OBBRAAGKK!
SHIII-NOBUU... AAARE... YOUUUU ... ALL RIIIGHT?
SHIIINO-BUU... AAARE... YOUUUU... ALL RIIIGHT?
HOLY COW!
WHAT THE HELL?
I SHOULD BE THE ONE ASKING YOU THAT!!
ぴくぴく...
OH MAN, THAT THING'S STILL ALIVE!!
WHY WOULDN'T I STILL BE ALIVE?!
ホッ...
THAT'S SEMPAI, ALL RIGHT. IMMORTAL AS USUAL.

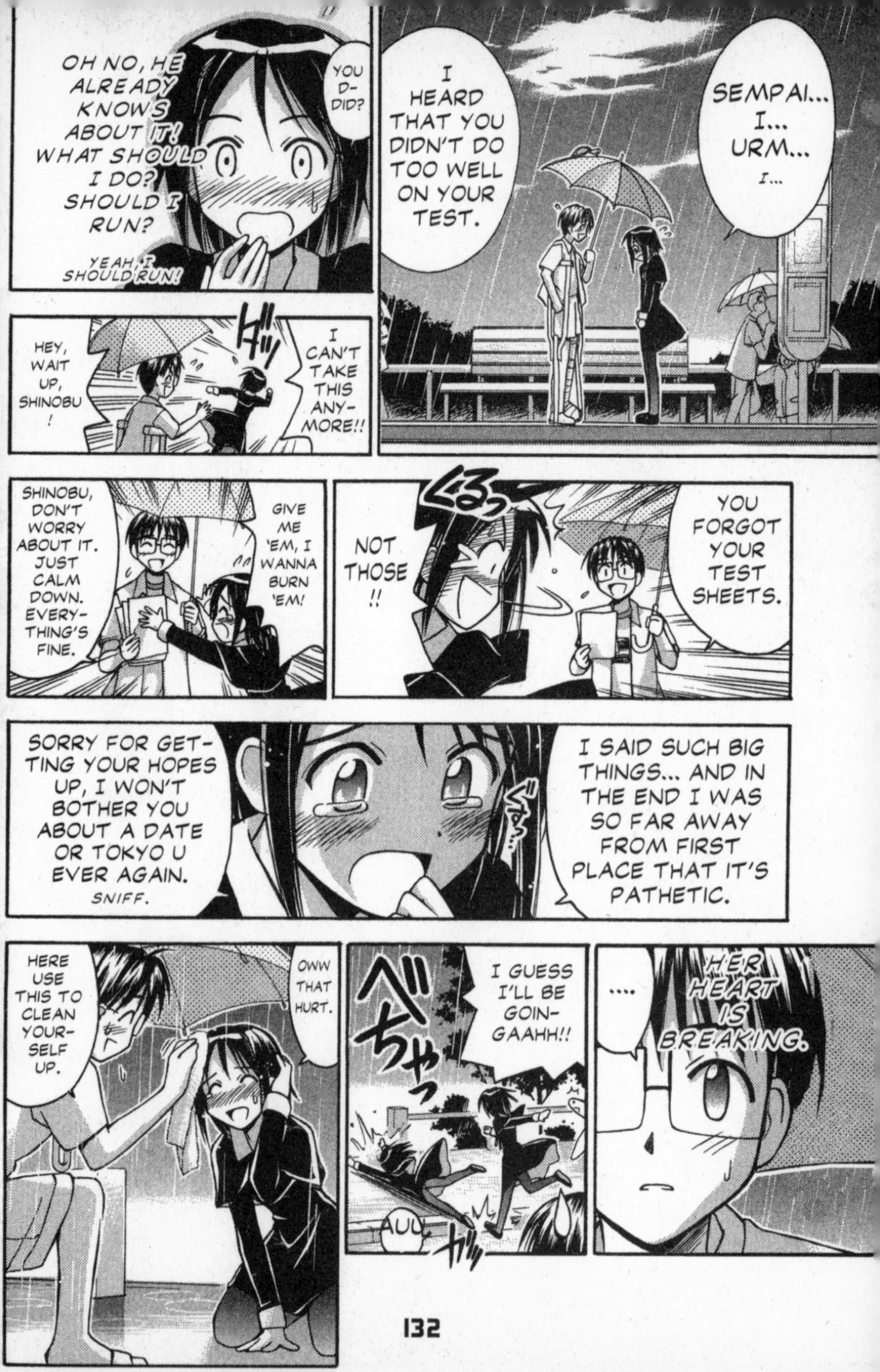
SEMPAI... I... URM... I...
I HEARD THAT YOU DIDN'T DO TOO WELL ON YOUR TEST.
YOU D-DID?
OH NO, HE ALREADY KNOWS ABOUT IT! WHAT SHOULD I DO? SHOULD I RUN?
YEAH, I SHOULD RUN!
I CAN'T TAKE THIS ANY-MORE!!
HEY, WAIT UP, SHINOBU!
YOU FORGOT YOUR TEST SHEETS.
NOT THOSE!!
GIVE ME 'EM, I WANNA BURN 'EM!
SHINOBU, DON'T WORRY ABOUT IT. JUST CALM DOWN. EVERY-THING'S FINE.
I SAID SUCH BIG THINGS... AND IN THE END I WAS SO FAR AWAY FROM FIRST PLACE THAT IT'S PATHETIC.
SORRY FOR GET-TING YOUR HOPES UP, I WON'T BOTHER YOU ABOUT A DATE OR TOKYO U EVER AGAIN.
SNIFF.
HER HEART IS BREAKING.
....
I GUESS I'LL BE GOIN-GAAHH!!
AUU
OWW THAT HURT.
HERE USE THIS TO CLEAN YOUR-SELF UP.

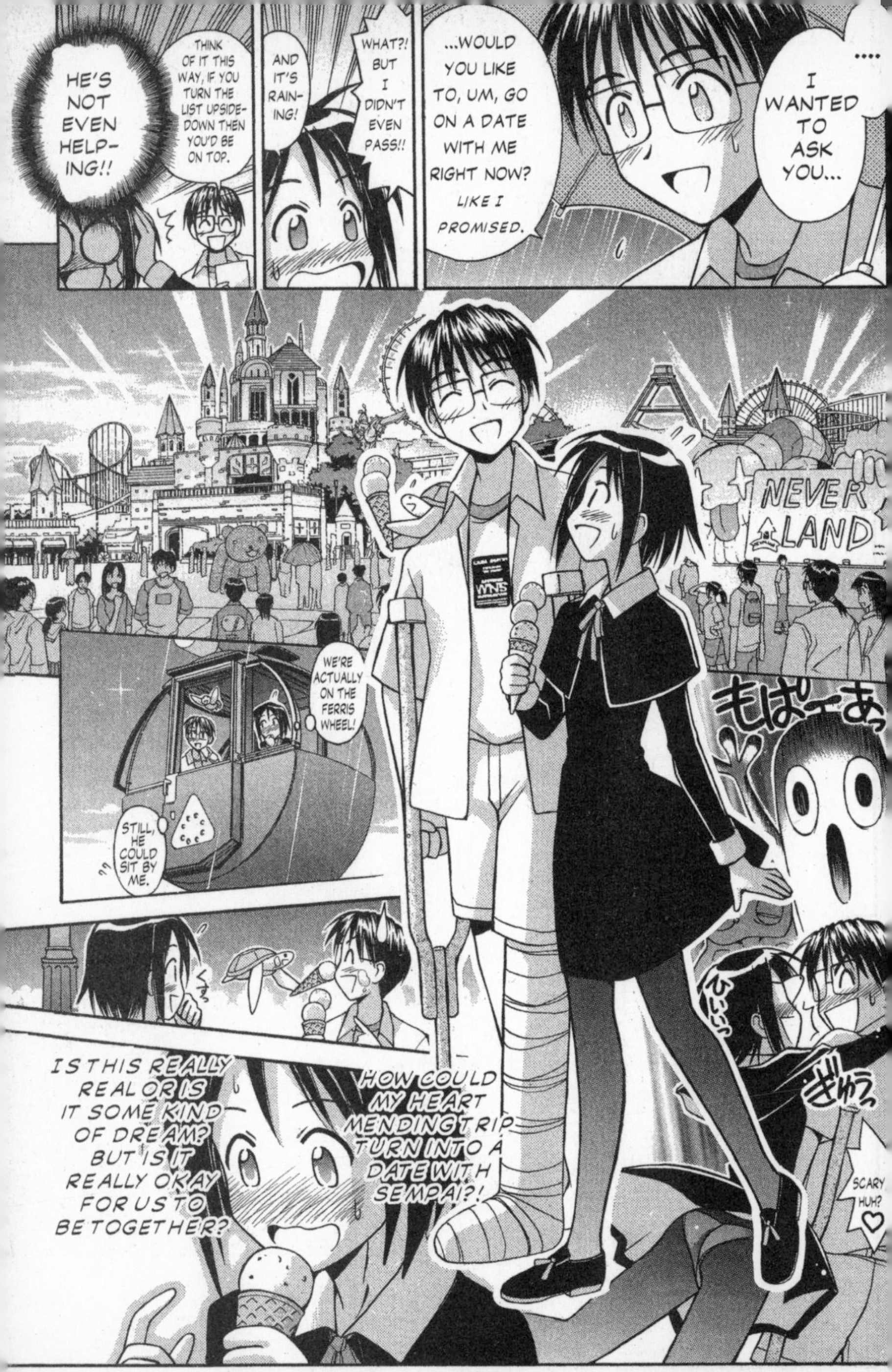
....
I WANTED TO ASK YOU...
...WOULD YOU LIKE TO, UM, GO ON A DATE WITH ME RIGHT NOW? LIKE I PROMISED.
WHAT?! BUT I DIDN'T EVEN PASS!!
AND IT'S RAINING!
THINK OF IT THIS WAY, IF YOU TURN THE LIST UPSIDE-DOWN THEN YOU'D BE ON TOP.
HE'S NOT EVEN HELPING!!
NEVER LAND
WE'RE ACTUALLY ON THE FERRIS WHEEL!
STILL, HE COULD SIT BY ME.
ぎゅうっ
SCARY HUH? ♡
HOW COULD MY HEART MENDING TRIP TURN INTO A DATE WITH SEMPAI?!
IS THIS REALLY REAL OR IS IT SOME KIND OF DREAM? BUT IS IT REALLY OKAY FOR US TO BE TOGETHER?

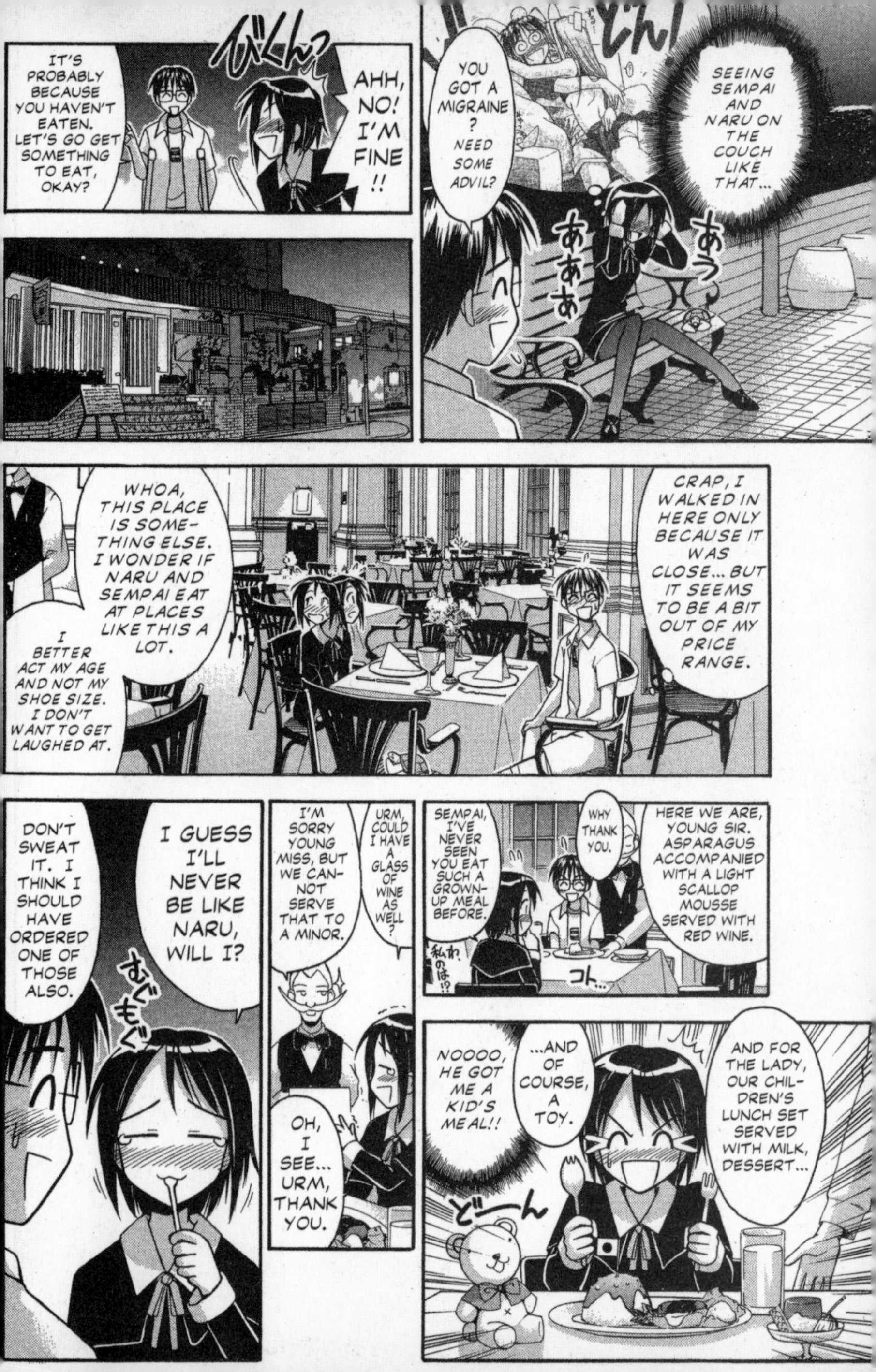
どん!
SEEING SEMPAI AND NARU ON THE COUCH LIKE THAT...
YOU GOT A MIGRAINE? NEED SOME ADVIL?
あう
あああ
びくんっ
AHH, NO! I'M FINE!!
IT'S PROBABLY BECAUSE YOU HAVEN'T EATEN. LET'S GO GET SOMETHING TO EAT, OKAY?
CRAP, I WALKED IN HERE ONLY BECAUSE IT WAS CLOSE... BUT IT SEEMS TO BE A BIT OUT OF MY PRICE RANGE.
WHOA, THIS PLACE IS SOMETHING ELSE. I WONDER IF NARU AND SEMPAI EAT AT PLACES LIKE THIS A LOT.
I BETTER ACT MY AGE AND NOT MY SHOE SIZE. I DON'T WANT TO GET LAUGHED AT.
HERE WE ARE, YOUNG SIR. ASPARAGUS ACCOMPANIED WITH A LIGHT SCALLOP MOUSSE SERVED WITH RED WINE.
WHY THANK YOU.
SEMPAI, I'VE NEVER SEEN YOU EAT SUCH A GROWN-UP MEAL BEFORE.
コト...
AND FOR THE LADY, OUR CHILDREN'S LUNCH SET SERVED WITH MILK, DESSERT...
...AND OF COURSE, A TOY.
NOOOO, HE GOT ME A KID'S MEAL!!
どーん
URM, COULD I HAVE A GLASS OF WINE AS WELL?
I'M SORRY YOUNG MISS, BUT WE CANNOT SERVE THAT TO A MINOR.
OH, I SEE... URM, THANK YOU.
I GUESS I'LL NEVER BE LIKE NARU, WILL I?
DON'T SWEAT IT. I THINK I SHOULD HAVE ORDERED ONE OF THOSE ALSO.
むぐもぐ

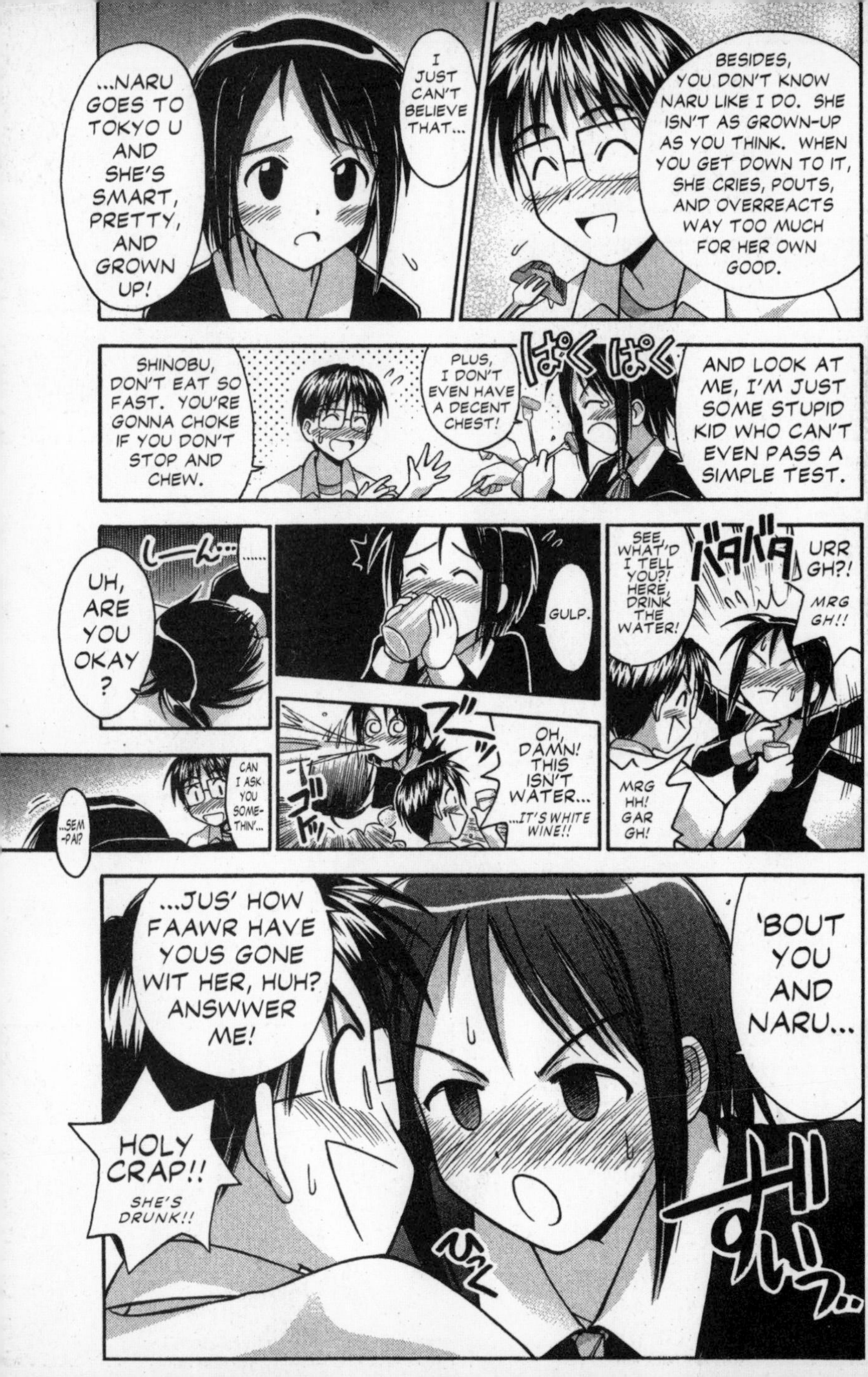
BESIDES, YOU DON'T KNOW NARU LIKE I DO. SHE ISN'T AS GROWN-UP AS YOU THINK. WHEN YOU GET DOWN TO IT, SHE CRIES, POUTS, AND OVERREACTS WAY TOO MUCH FOR HER OWN GOOD.
I JUST CAN'T BELIEVE THAT...
...NARU GOES TO TOKYO U AND SHE'S SMART, PRETTY, AND GROWN UP!
AND LOOK AT ME, I'M JUST SOME STUPID KID WHO CAN'T EVEN PASS A SIMPLE TEST.
ぱくぱく
PLUS, I DON'T EVEN HAVE A DECENT CHEST!
SHINOBU, DON'T EAT SO FAST. YOU'RE GONNA CHOKE IF YOU DON'T STOP AND CHEW.
URRGH?!
MRGGH!!
バタバタ
SEE, WHAT'D I TELL YOU?! HERE, DRINK THE WATER!
MRGHH! GARGH!
GULP.
......
しーん...
UH, ARE YOU OKAY?
OH, DAMN! THIS ISN'T WATER... ...IT'S WHITE WINE!!
CAN I ASK YOU SOME-THIN'...
...SEM-PAI?
'BOUT YOU AND NARU...
...JUS' HOW FAAWR HAVE YOUS GONE WIT HER, HUH? ANSWWER ME!
HOLY CRAP!! SHE'S DRUNK!!

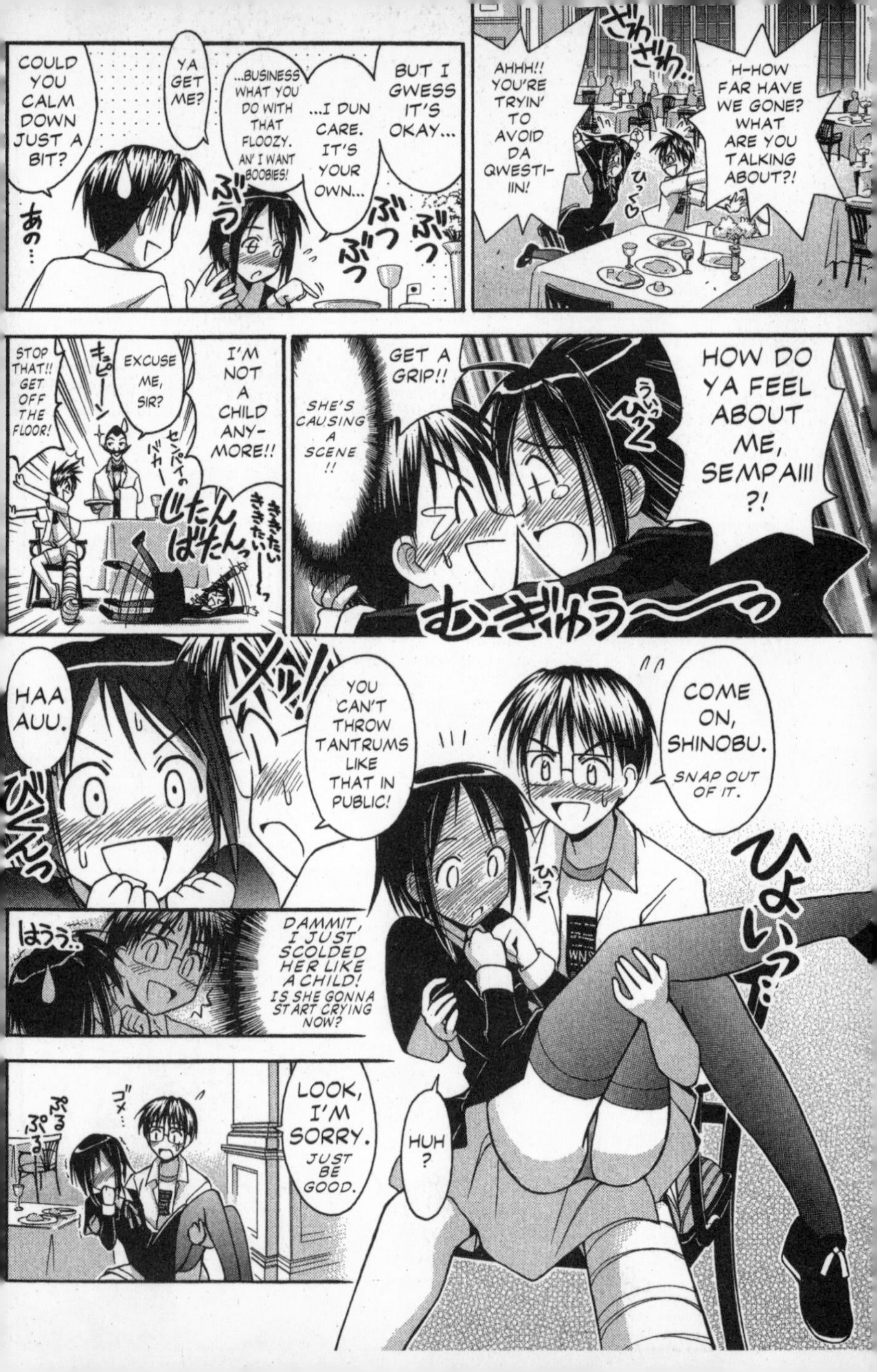
ざわざわ…
H-HOW FAR HAVE WE GONE? WHAT ARE YOU TALKING ABOUT?!
AHHH!! YOU'RE TRYIN' TO AVOID DA QWESTI-IIN!
ひっく
BUT I GWESS IT'S OKAY...
...I DUN CARE. IT'S YOUR OWN...
...BUSINESS WHAT YOU DO WITH THAT FLOOZY. AN' I WANT BOOBIES!
YA GET ME?
ぶつぶつ
COULD YOU CALM DOWN JUST A BIT?
あの…
HOW DO YA FEEL ABOUT ME, SEMPAIII?!
GET A GRIP!!
SHE'S CAUSING A SCENE!!
むぎゅう〜〜っ
I'M NOT A CHILD ANYMORE!!
EXCUSE ME, SIR?
STOP THAT!! GET OFF THE FLOOR!
キュピーン
センパイのバカー
じたんばたんっ
ききききたいーっ
COME ON, SHINOBU.
SNAP OUT OF IT.
ひょいっ
YOU CAN'T THROW TANTRUMS LIKE THAT IN PUBLIC!
HAA AUU.
はうう…
DAMMIT, I JUST SCOLDED HER LIKE A CHILD! IS SHE GONNA START CRYING NOW?
HUH?
LOOK, I'M SORRY.
JUST BE GOOD.
ゴメ…
ぷるぷる

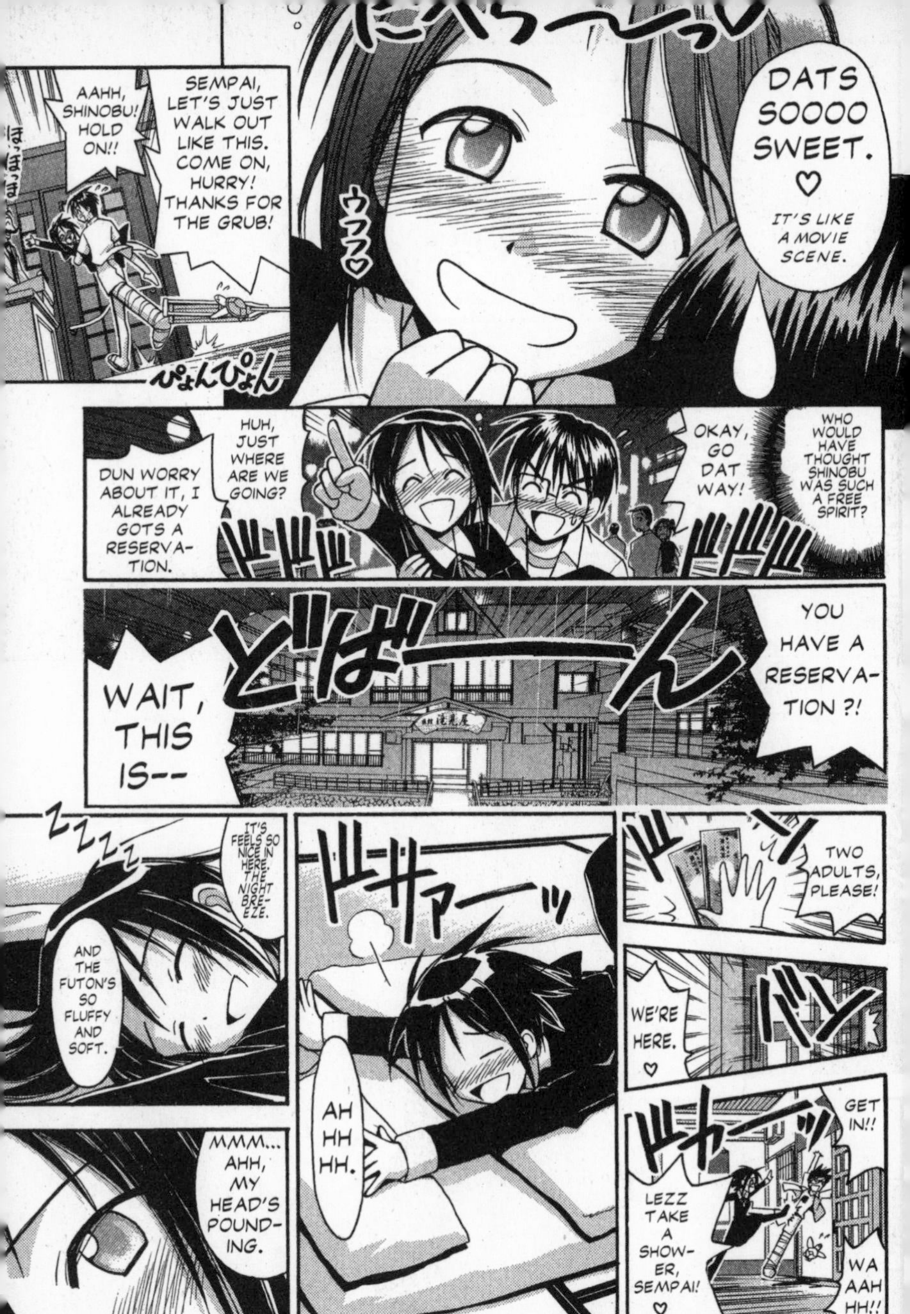

にへら～～っ
DATS SOOOO SWEET. ♡
IT'S LIKE A MOVIE SCENE.
ウフフ♡
SEMPAI, LET'S JUST WALK OUT LIKE THIS. COME ON, HURRY! THANKS FOR THE GRUB!
AAHH, SHINOBU! HOLD ON!!
ぴょんぴょん
WHO WOULD HAVE THOUGHT SHINOBU WAS SUCH A FREE SPIRIT?
OKAY, GO DAT WAY!
HUH, JUST WHERE ARE WE GOING?
DUN WORRY ABOUT IT, I ALREADY GOTS A RESERVATION.
YOU HAVE A RESERVATION ?!
どばーーん
WAIT, THIS IS--
TWO ADULTS, PLEASE!
WE'RE HERE. ♡
GET IN!!
LEZZ TAKE A SHOWER, SEMPAI! ♡
WA AAH HH!!
ドサァーーッ
AH HH HH.
ZZZZ
IT'S FEELS SO NICE IN HERE. THE NIGHT BREEZE.
AND THE FUTON'S SO FLUFFY AND SOFT.
MMM... AHH, MY HEAD'S POUNDING.

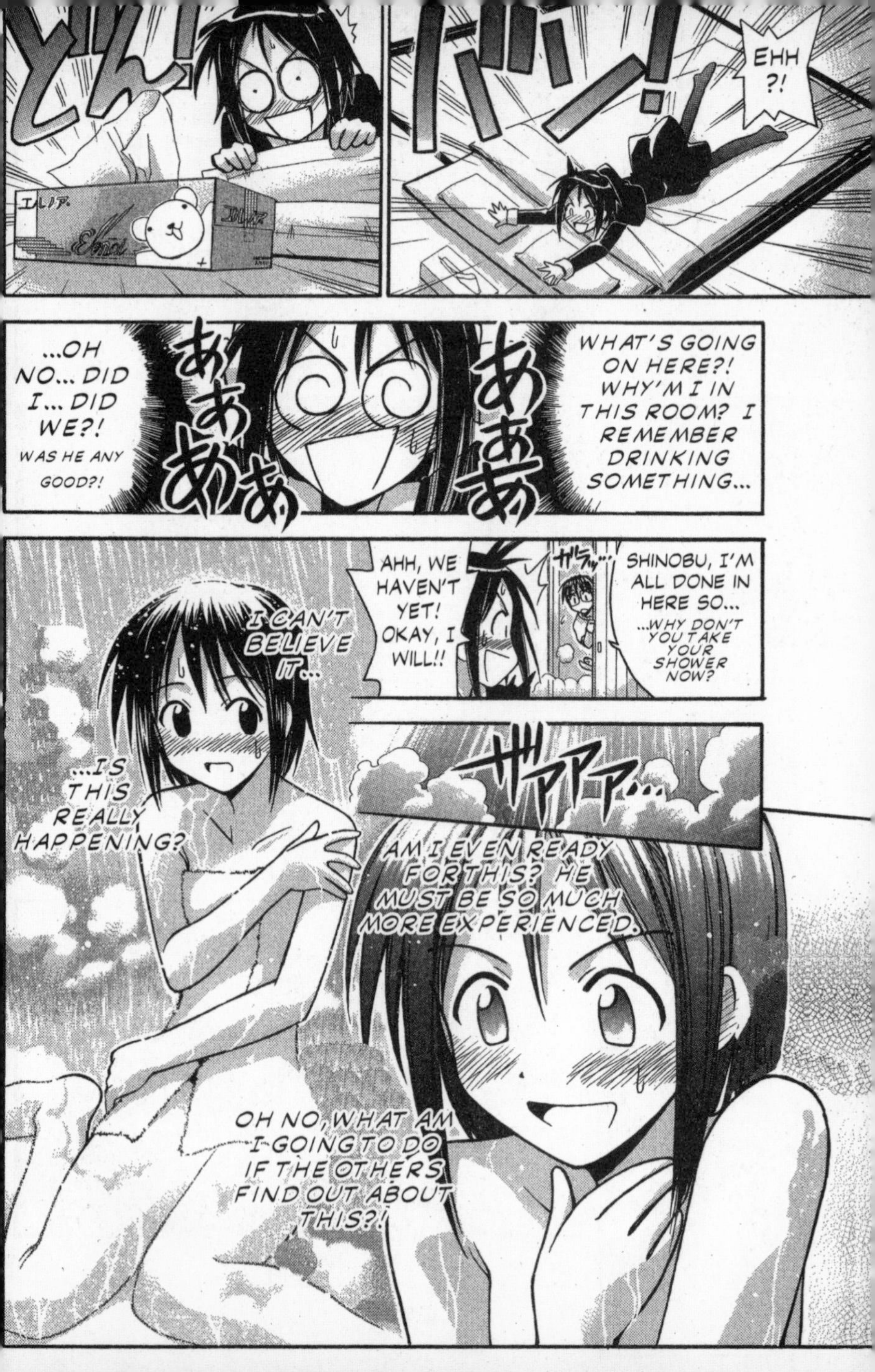

ばっ!
EHH ?!
どん!
WHAT'S GOING ON HERE?! WHY'M I IN THIS ROOM? I REMEMBER DRINKING SOMETHING...
ああああ
ああああ
...OH NO... DID I... DID WE?!
WAS HE ANY GOOD?!
SHINOBU, I'M ALL DONE IN HERE SO...
...WHY DON'T YOU TAKE YOUR SHOWER NOW?
ガラッ
AHH, WE HAVEN'T YET! OKAY, I WILL!!
ザァァァ...
AM I EVEN READY FOR THIS? HE MUST BE SO MUCH MORE EXPERIENCED.
OH NO, WHAT AM I GOING TO DO IF THE OTHERS FIND OUT ABOUT THIS?!
I CAN'T BELIEVE IT...
...IS THIS REALLY HAPPENING?

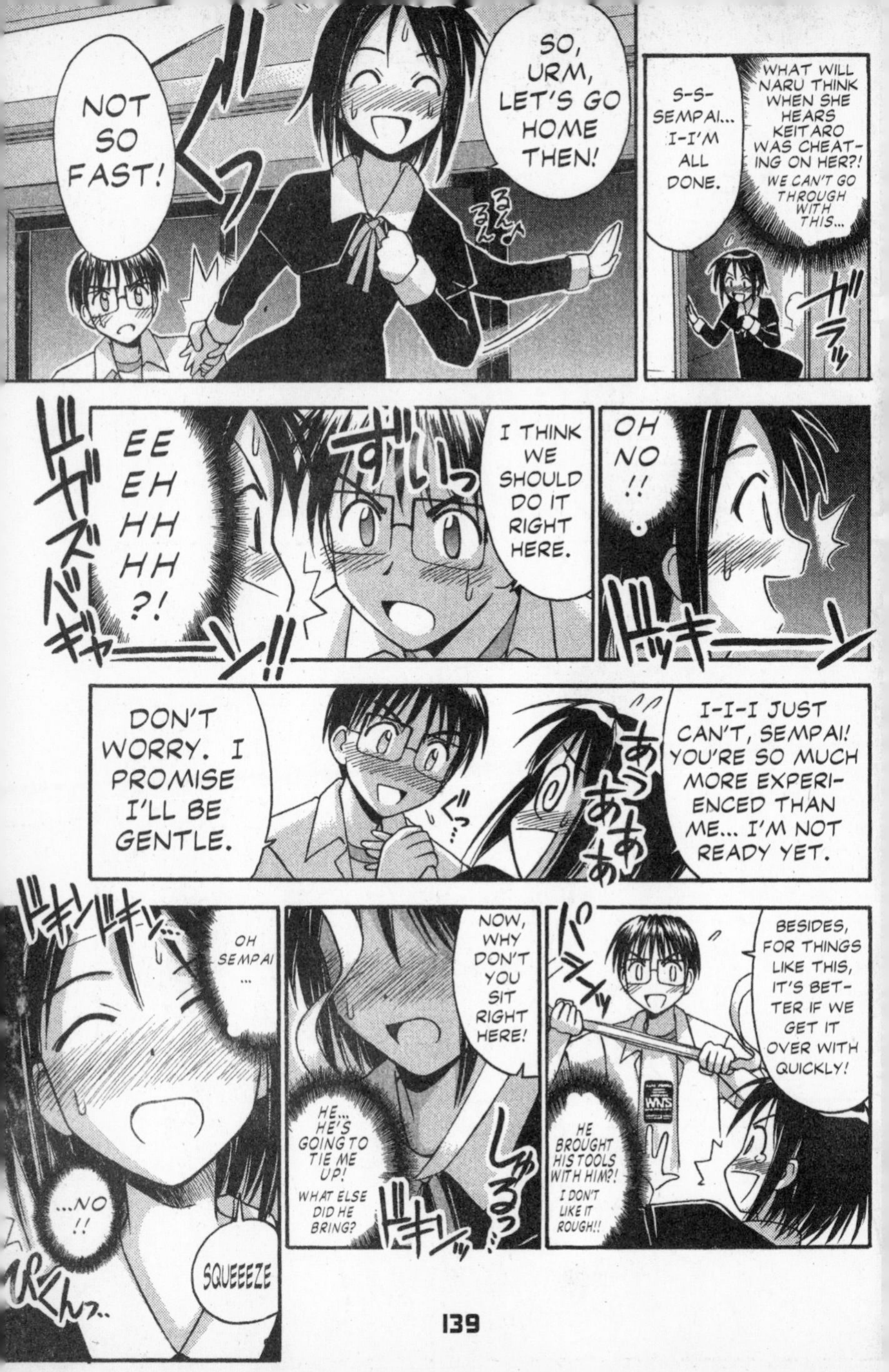
S-S-SEMPAI... I-I'M ALL DONE.
WHAT WILL NARU THINK WHEN SHE HEARS KEITARO WAS CHEATING ON HER?!
WE CAN'T GO THROUGH WITH THIS...
SO, URM, LET'S GO HOME THEN!
NOT SO FAST!
OH NO!!
I THINK WE SHOULD DO IT RIGHT HERE.
EEEHHHHHH?!
I-I-I JUST CAN'T, SEMPAI! YOU'RE SO MUCH MORE EXPERIENCED THAN ME... I'M NOT READY YET.
DON'T WORRY. I PROMISE I'LL BE GENTLE.
BESIDES, FOR THINGS LIKE THIS, IT'S BETTER IF WE GET IT OVER WITH QUICKLY!
HE BROUGHT HIS TOOLS WITH HIM?!
I DON'T LIKE IT ROUGH!!
NOW, WHY DON'T YOU SIT RIGHT HERE!
HE... HE'S GOING TO TIE ME UP!
WHAT ELSE DID HE BRING?
OH SEMPAI...
...NO!!
SQUEEEZE

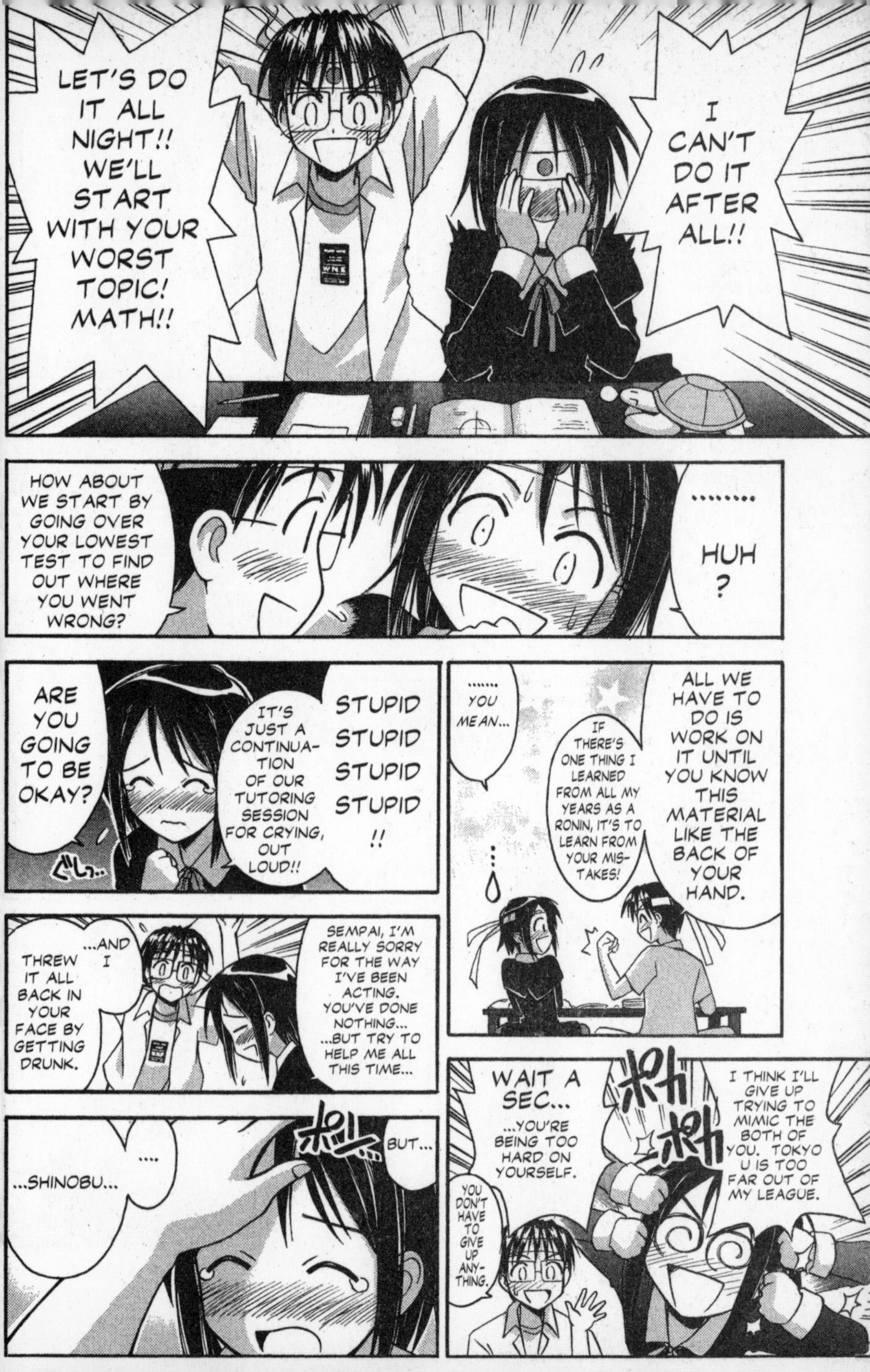
I CAN'T DO IT AFTER ALL!!
LET'S DO IT ALL NIGHT!! WE'LL START WITH YOUR WORST TOPIC! MATH!!
.... HUH ?
HOW ABOUT WE START BY GOING OVER YOUR LOWEST TEST TO FIND OUT WHERE YOU WENT WRONG?
ALL WE HAVE TO DO IS WORK ON IT UNTIL YOU KNOW THIS MATERIAL LIKE THE BACK OF YOUR HAND.
...... YOU MEAN...
IF THERE'S ONE THING I LEARNED FROM ALL MY YEARS AS A RONIN, IT'S TO LEARN FROM YOUR MIS-TAKES!
STUPID STUPID STUPID STUPID !!
IT'S JUST A CONTINUA-TION OF OUR TUTORING SESSION FOR CRYING, OUT LOUD!!
ARE YOU GOING TO BE OKAY?
ぐしっ..
SEMPAI, I'M REALLY SORRY FOR THE WAY I'VE BEEN ACTING. YOU'VE DONE NOTHING... ...BUT TRY TO HELP ME ALL THIS TIME...
...AND I THREW IT ALL BACK IN YOUR FACE BY GETTING DRUNK.
I THINK I'LL GIVE UP TRYING TO MIMIC THE BOTH OF YOU. TOKYO U IS TOO FAR OUT OF MY LEAGUE.
ポカ ポカ
WAIT A SEC... ...YOU'RE BEING TOO HARD ON YOURSELF.
YOU DON'T HAVE TO GIVE UP ANY-THING.
BUT...
ポン...
....
...SHINOBU...

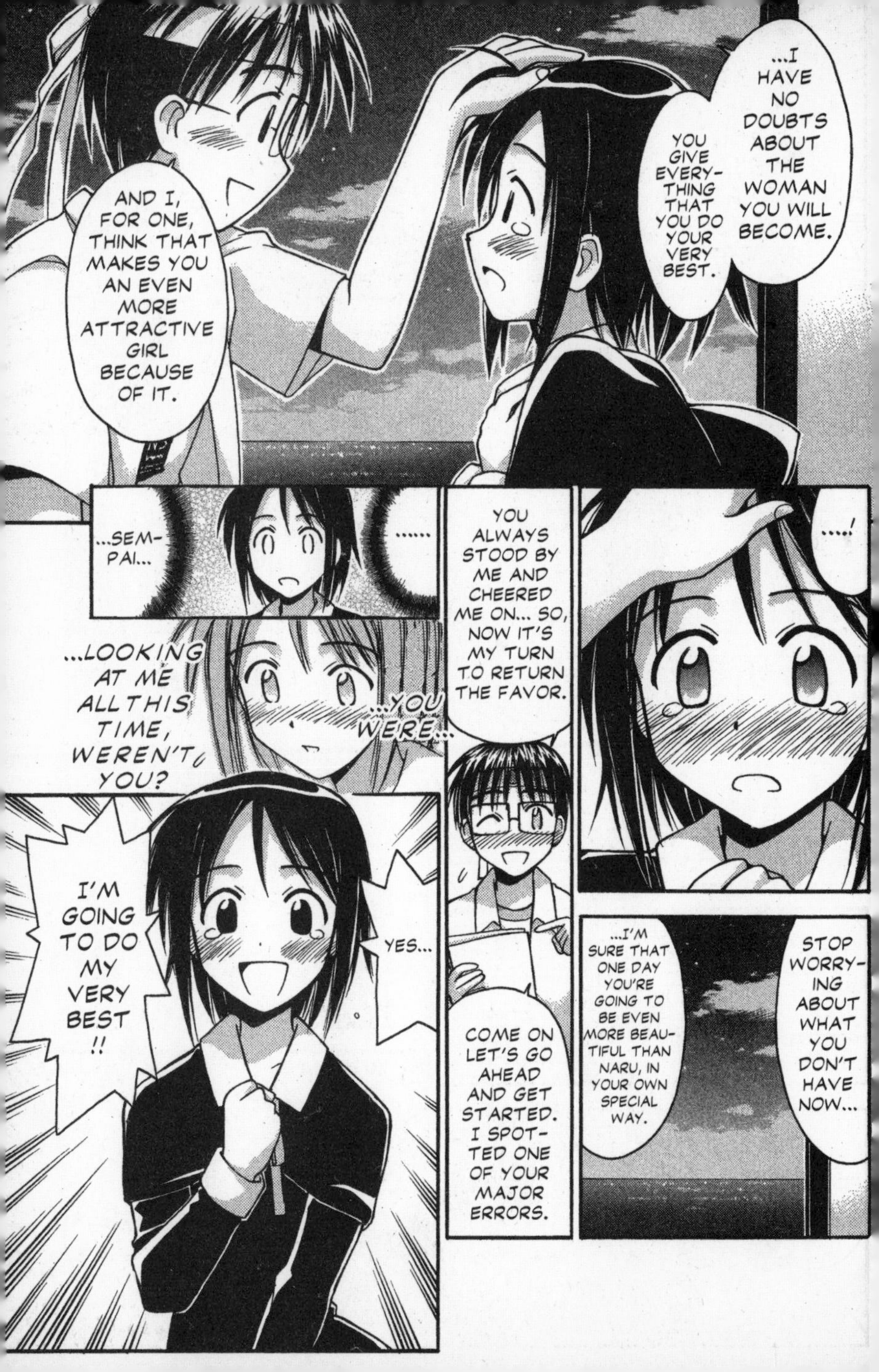
...I HAVE NO DOUBTS ABOUT THE WOMAN YOU WILL BECOME.
YOU GIVE EVERY-THING THAT YOU DO YOUR VERY BEST.
AND I, FOR ONE, THINK THAT MAKES YOU AN EVEN MORE ATTRACTIVE GIRL BECAUSE OF IT.
....!
YOU ALWAYS STOOD BY ME AND CHEERED ME ON... SO, NOW IT'S MY TURN TO RETURN THE FAVOR.
......
...SEM-PAI...
...YOU WERE...
...LOOKING AT ME ALL THIS TIME, WEREN'T YOU?
STOP WORRY-ING ABOUT WHAT YOU DON'T HAVE NOW...
...I'M SURE THAT ONE DAY YOU'RE GOING TO BE EVEN MORE BEAU-TIFUL THAN NARU, IN YOUR OWN SPECIAL WAY.
COME ON LET'S GO AHEAD AND GET STARTED. I SPOT-TED ONE OF YOUR MAJOR ERRORS.
YES...
I'M GOING TO DO MY VERY BEST !!

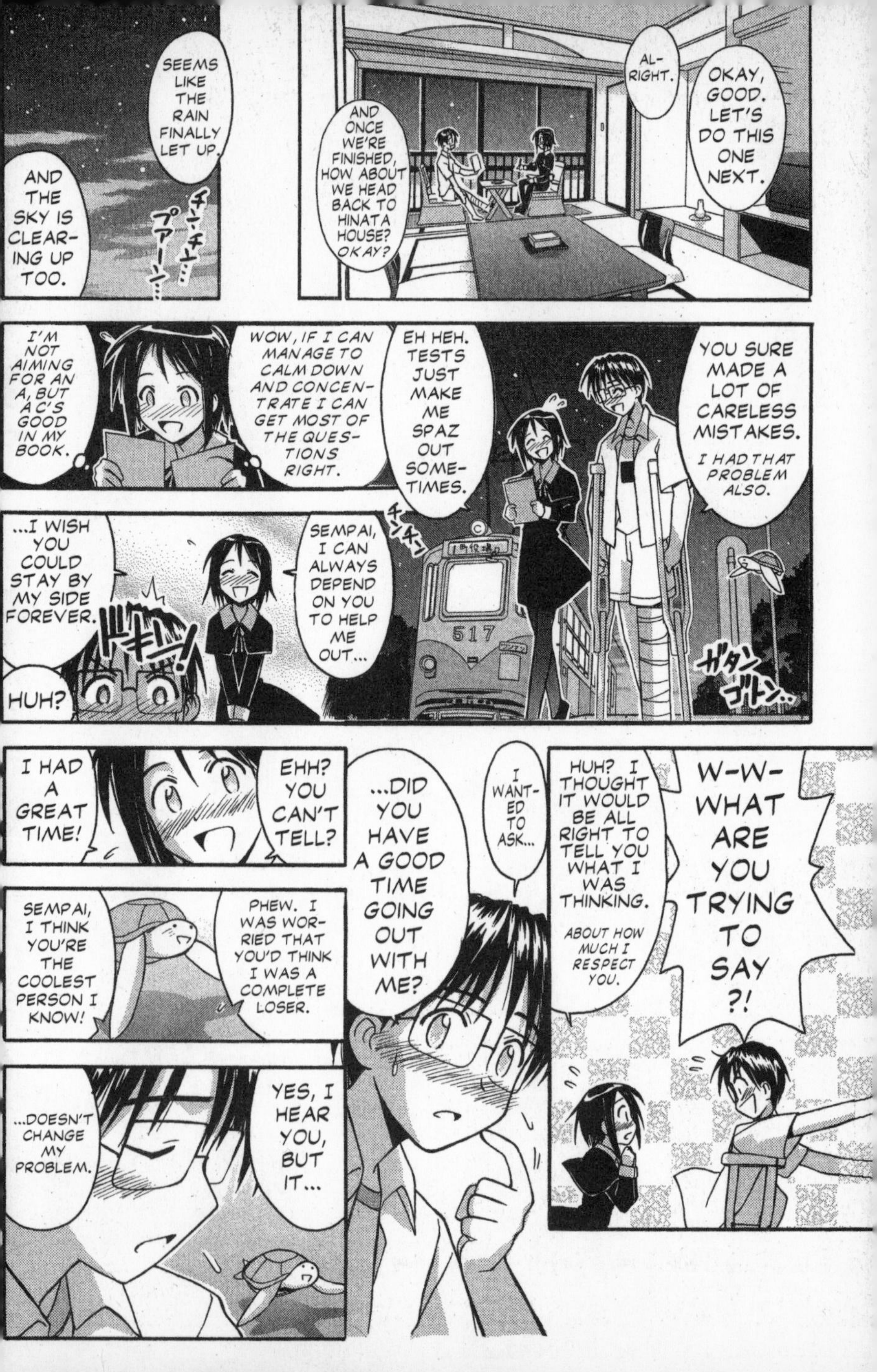
OKAY, GOOD. LET'S DO THIS ONE NEXT.
AL-RIGHT.
AND ONCE WE'RE FINISHED, HOW ABOUT WE HEAD BACK TO HINATA HOUSE? OKAY?
SEEMS LIKE THE RAIN FINALLY LET UP.
AND THE SKY IS CLEARING UP TOO.
YOU SURE MADE A LOT OF CARELESS MISTAKES.
I HAD THAT PROBLEM ALSO.
EH HEH. TESTS JUST MAKE ME SPAZ OUT SOMETIMES.
WOW, IF I CAN MANAGE TO CALM DOWN AND CONCENTRATE I CAN GET MOST OF THE QUESTIONS RIGHT.
I'M NOT AIMING FOR AN A, BUT A C'S GOOD IN MY BOOK.
517
SEMPAI, I CAN ALWAYS DEPEND ON YOU TO HELP ME OUT...
...I WISH YOU COULD STAY BY MY SIDE FOREVER.
HUH?
W-W-WHAT ARE YOU TRYING TO SAY?!
HUH? I THOUGHT IT WOULD BE ALL RIGHT TO TELL YOU WHAT I WAS THINKING.
ABOUT HOW MUCH I RESPECT YOU.
I WANTED TO ASK...
...DID YOU HAVE A GOOD TIME GOING OUT WITH ME?
EHH? YOU CAN'T TELL?
I HAD A GREAT TIME!
PHEW. I WAS WORRIED THAT YOU'D THINK I WAS A COMPLETE LOSER.
SEMPAI, I THINK YOU'RE THE COOLEST PERSON I KNOW!
YES, I HEAR YOU, BUT IT...
...DOESN'T CHANGE MY PROBLEM.

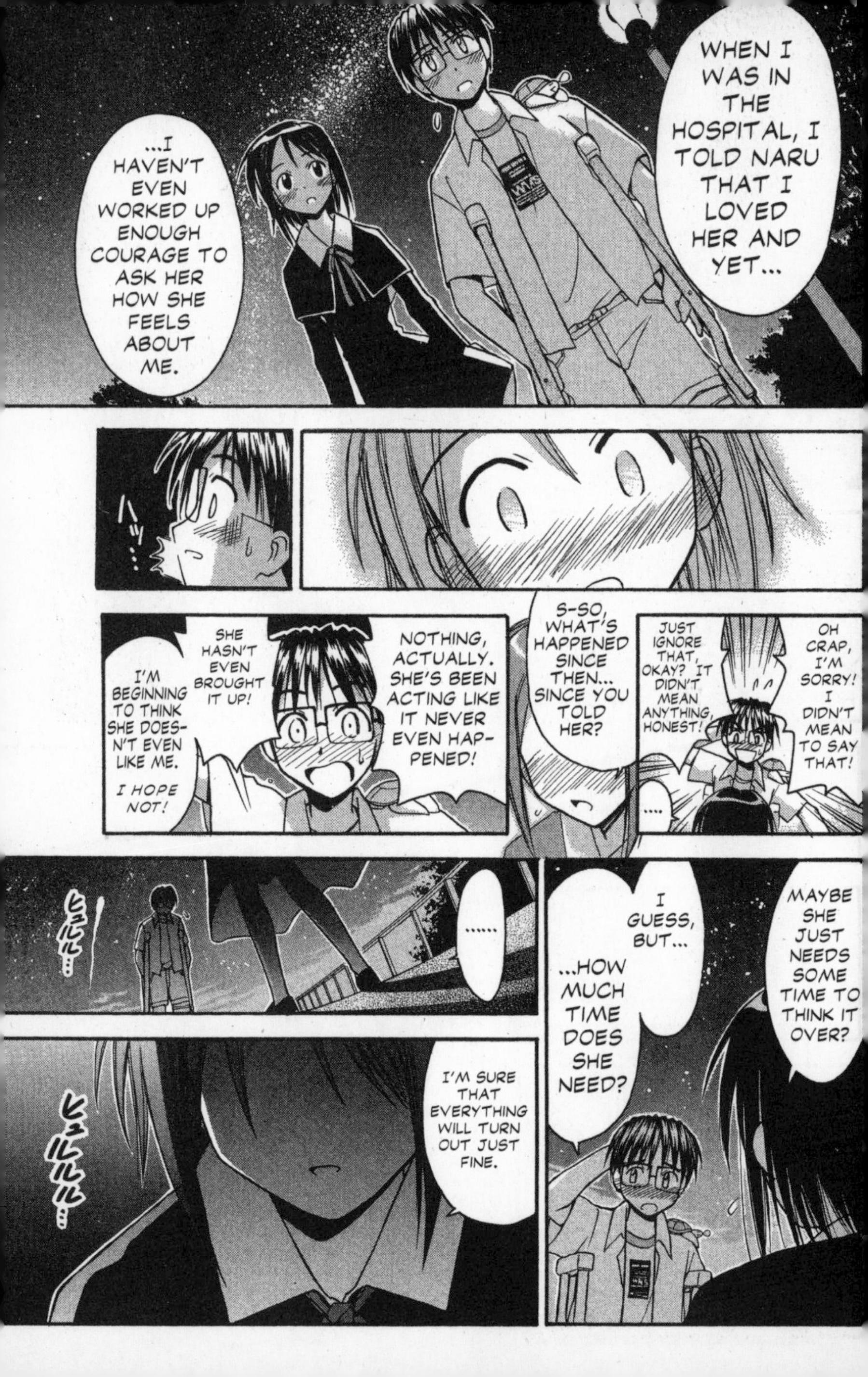
WHEN I WAS IN THE HOSPITAL, I TOLD NARU THAT I LOVED HER AND YET...
...I HAVEN'T EVEN WORKED UP ENOUGH COURAGE TO ASK HER HOW SHE FEELS ABOUT ME.
ハッ…
OH CRAP, I'M SORRY! I DIDN'T MEAN TO SAY THAT!
JUST IGNORE THAT, OKAY? IT DIDN'T MEAN ANYTHING, HONEST!
....
S-SO, WHAT'S HAPPENED SINCE THEN... SINCE YOU TOLD HER?
NOTHING, ACTUALLY. SHE'S BEEN ACTING LIKE IT NEVER EVEN HAP-PENED!
SHE HASN'T EVEN BROUGHT IT UP!
I'M BEGINNING TO THINK SHE DOES-N'T EVEN LIKE ME.
I HOPE NOT!
MAYBE SHE JUST NEEDS SOME TIME TO THINK IT OVER?
I GUESS, BUT...
...HOW MUCH TIME DOES SHE NEED?
......
ヒュルル…
I'M SURE THAT EVERYTHING WILL TURN OUT JUST FINE.
ヒュルルル…

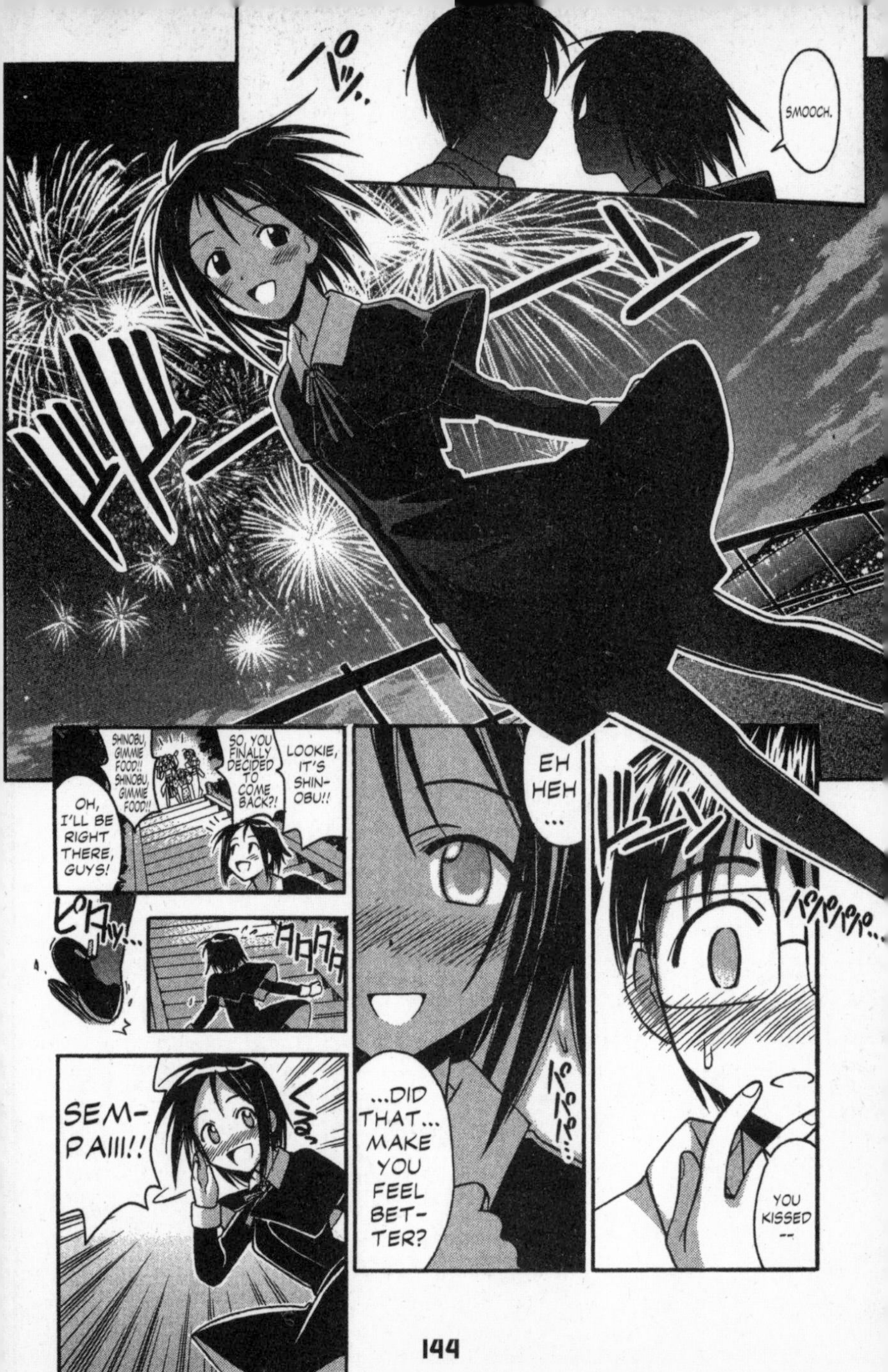
SMOOCH.
YOU KISSED --
EH HEH ...
...DID THAT... MAKE YOU FEEL BET-TER?
LOOKIE, IT'S SHIN-OBU!!
SO, YOU FINALLY DECIDED TO COME BACK?!
SHINOBU, GIMMIE FOOD!! SHINOBU, GIMMIE FOOD!!
OH, I'LL BE RIGHT THERE, GUYS!
SEM-PAIIII!!

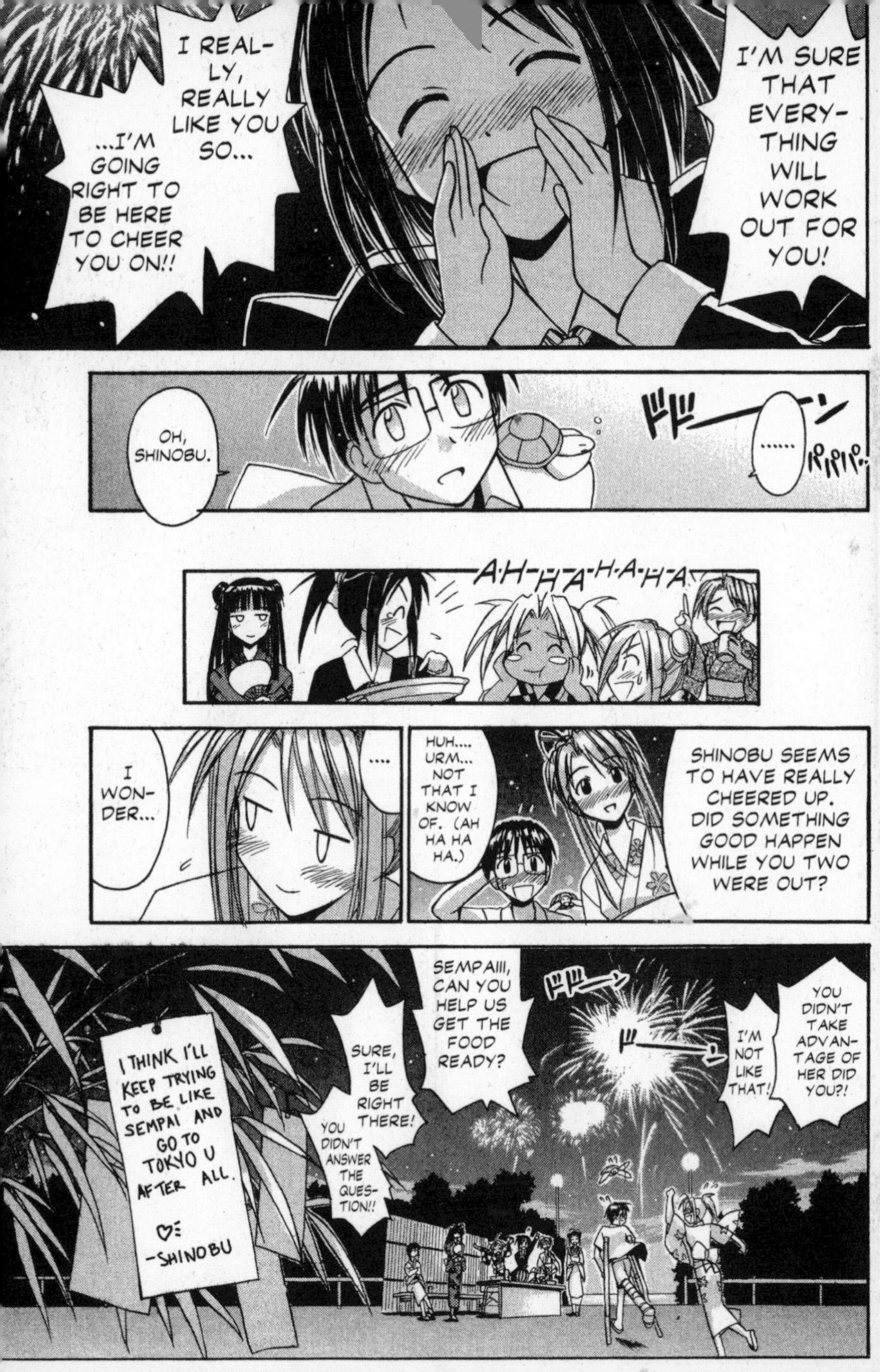
I'M SURE THAT EVERY-THING WILL WORK OUT FOR YOU!
I REAL-LY, REALLY LIKE YOU SO...
...I'M GOING RIGHT TO BE HERE TO CHEER YOU ON!!
ドドーーン
......
パパパ..
OH, SHINOBU.
A-H-HA-H-A-HA
SHINOBU SEEMS TO HAVE REALLY CHEERED UP. DID SOMETHING GOOD HAPPEN WHILE YOU TWO WERE OUT?
HUH.... URM... NOT THAT I KNOW OF. (AH HA HA HA.)
....
I WON-DER...
YOU DIDN'T TAKE ADVAN-TAGE OF HER DID YOU?!
I'M NOT LIKE THAT!
ドドーン
ドーン
SEMPAIII, CAN YOU HELP US GET THE FOOD READY?
SURE, I'LL BE RIGHT THERE!
YOU DIDN'T ANSWER THE QUES-TION!!
I THINK I'LL KEEP TRYING TO BE LIKE SEMPAI AND GO TO TOKYO U AFTER ALL.
♡ -SHINOBU

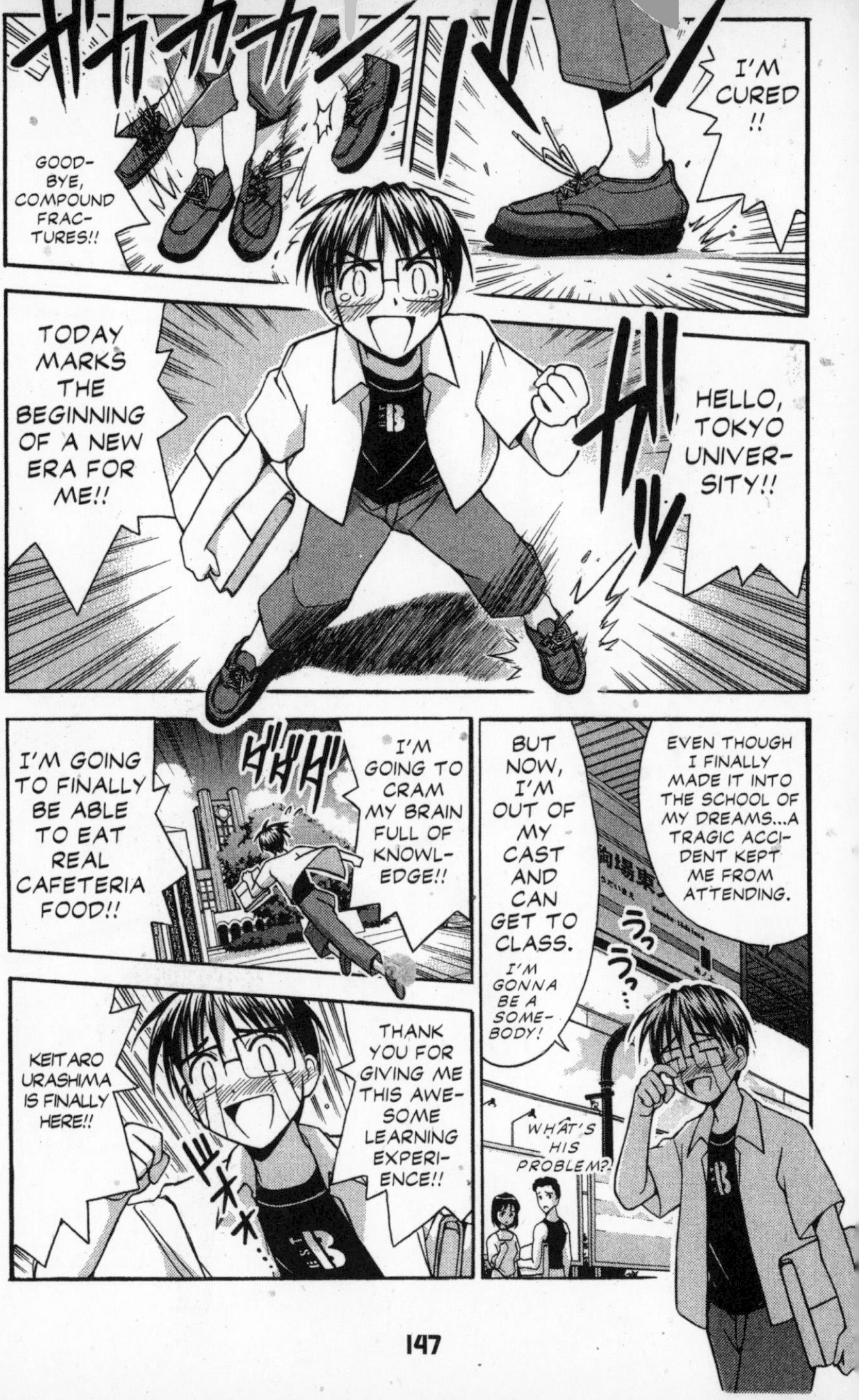
I'M CURED!!
GOOD-BYE, COMPOUND FRACTURES!!
HELLO, TOKYO UNIVERSITY!!
TODAY MARKS THE BEGINNING OF A NEW ERA FOR ME!!
EVEN THOUGH I FINALLY MADE IT INTO THE SCHOOL OF MY DREAMS...A TRAGIC ACCIDENT KEPT ME FROM ATTENDING.
BUT NOW, I'M OUT OF MY CAST AND CAN GET TO CLASS.
I'M GONNA BE A SOMEBODY!
WHAT'S HIS PROBLEM?
I'M GOING TO CRAM MY BRAIN FULL OF KNOWLEDGE!!
I'M GOING TO FINALLY BE ABLE TO EAT REAL CAFETERIA FOOD!!
THANK YOU FOR GIVING ME THIS AWESOME LEARNING EXPERIENCE!!
KEITARO URASHIMA IS FINALLY HERE!!

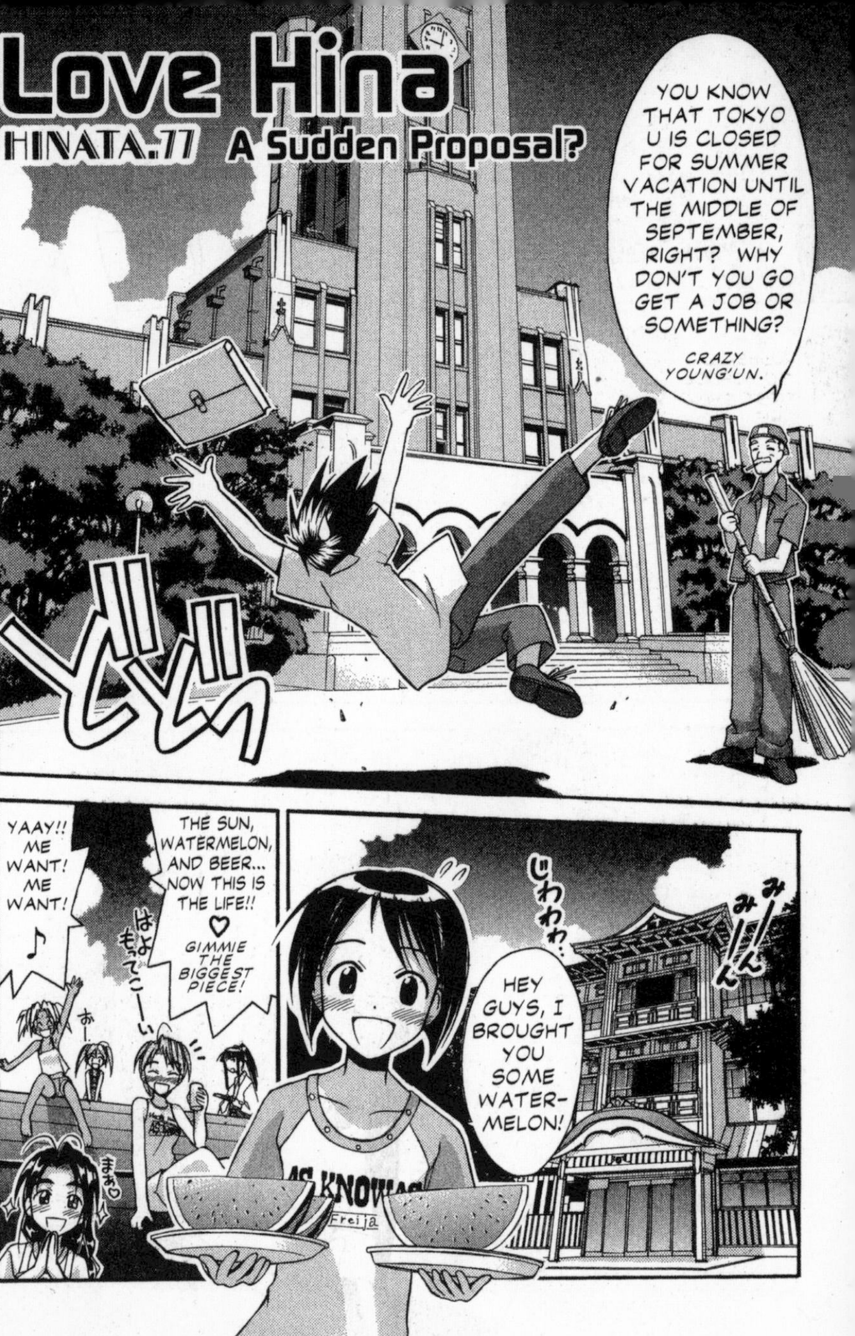
Love Hina
HINATA.77 A Sudden Proposal?
YOU KNOW THAT TOKYO U IS CLOSED FOR SUMMER VACATION UNTIL THE MIDDLE OF SEPTEMBER, RIGHT? WHY DON'T YOU GO GET A JOB OR SOMETHING?
CRAZY YOUNG'UN.
みーんみーん
じわわわ…
HEY GUYS, I BROUGHT YOU SOME WATER-MELON!
Freija
THE SUN, WATERMELON, AND BEER... NOW THIS IS THE LIFE!! ♡
はよもってこーい
GIMMIE THE BIGGEST PIECE!
YAAY!! ME WANT! ME WANT! ♪
あー
まあ♡

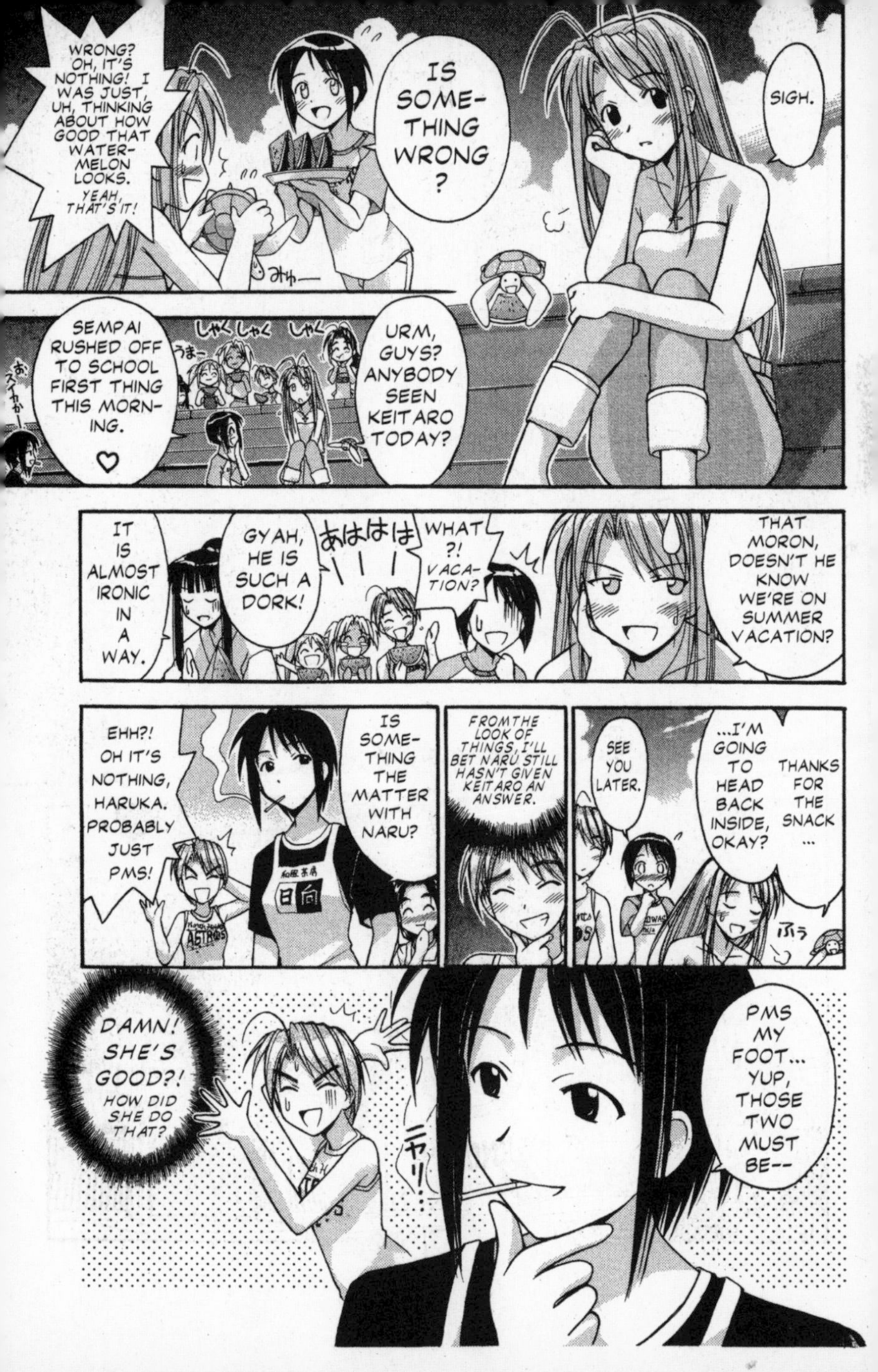
SIGH.
IS SOME-THING WRONG?
WRONG? OH, IT'S NOTHING! I WAS JUST, UH, THINKING ABOUT HOW GOOD THAT WATER-MELON LOOKS. YEAH, THAT'S IT!
みゅー
URM, GUYS? ANYBODY SEEN KEITARO TODAY?
しゃくしゃく しゃく
うまー
SEMPAI RUSHED OFF TO SCHOOL FIRST THING THIS MORN-ING. ♡
お、スイカかー
THAT MORON, DOESN'T HE KNOW WE'RE ON SUMMER VACATION?
WHAT?! VACA-TION?
あははは
GYAH, HE IS SUCH A DORK!
IT IS ALMOST IRONIC IN A WAY.
THANKS FOR THE SNACK ...
...I'M GOING TO HEAD BACK INSIDE, OKAY?
SEE YOU LATER.
ふぅ
FROM THE LOOK OF THINGS, I'LL BET NARU STILL HASN'T GIVEN KEITARO AN ANSWER.
IS SOME-THING THE MATTER WITH NARU?
EHH?! OH IT'S NOTHING, HARUKA. PROBABLY JUST PMS!
PMS MY FOOT... YUP, THOSE TWO MUST BE--
ニヤリ…
DAMN! SHE'S GOOD?! HOW DID SHE DO THAT?

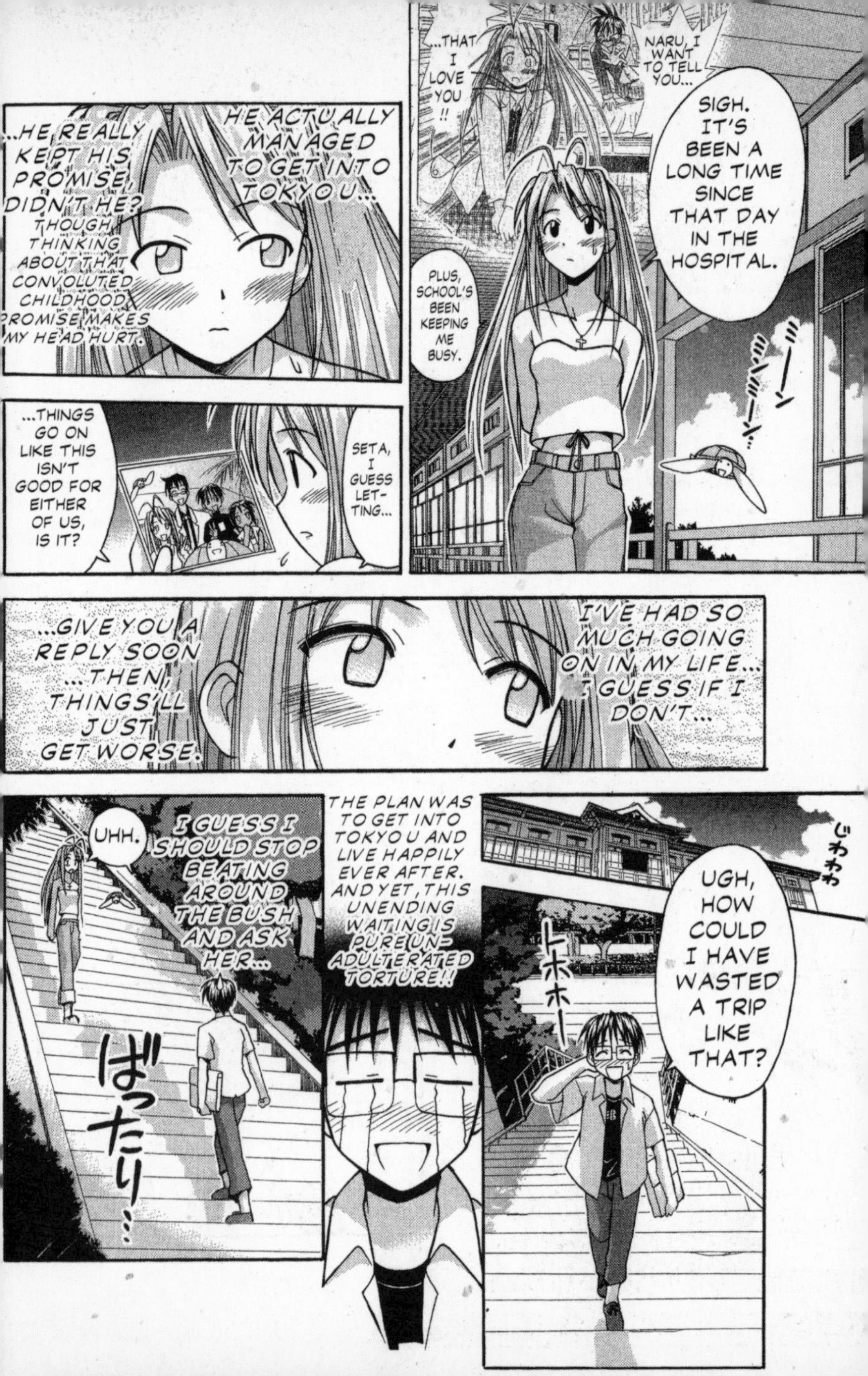
NARU, I WANT TO TELL YOU...
...THAT I LOVE YOU!!
SIGH. IT'S BEEN A LONG TIME SINCE THAT DAY IN THE HOSPITAL.
PLUS, SCHOOL'S BEEN KEEPING ME BUSY.
ミーン ミンミーン
HE ACTUALLY MANAGED TO GET INTO TOKYO U...
...HE REALLY KEPT HIS PROMISE, DIDN'T HE?
THOUGH, THINKING ABOUT THAT CONVOLUTED CHILDHOOD PROMISE MAKES MY HEAD HURT.
SETA, I GUESS LETTING...
...THINGS GO ON LIKE THIS ISN'T GOOD FOR EITHER OF US, IS IT?
I'VE HAD SO MUCH GOING ON IN MY LIFE... I GUESS IF I DON'T...
...GIVE YOU A REPLY SOON ...THEN, THINGS'LL JUST GET WORSE.
じわわわ
UGH, HOW COULD I HAVE WASTED A TRIP LIKE THAT?
トホホー
THE PLAN WAS TO GET INTO TOKYO U AND LIVE HAPPILY EVER AFTER. AND YET, THIS UNENDING WAITING IS PURE UN-ADULTERATED TORTURE!!
I GUESS I SHOULD STOP BEATING AROUND THE BUSH AND ASK HER...
UHH.
ぱったり…

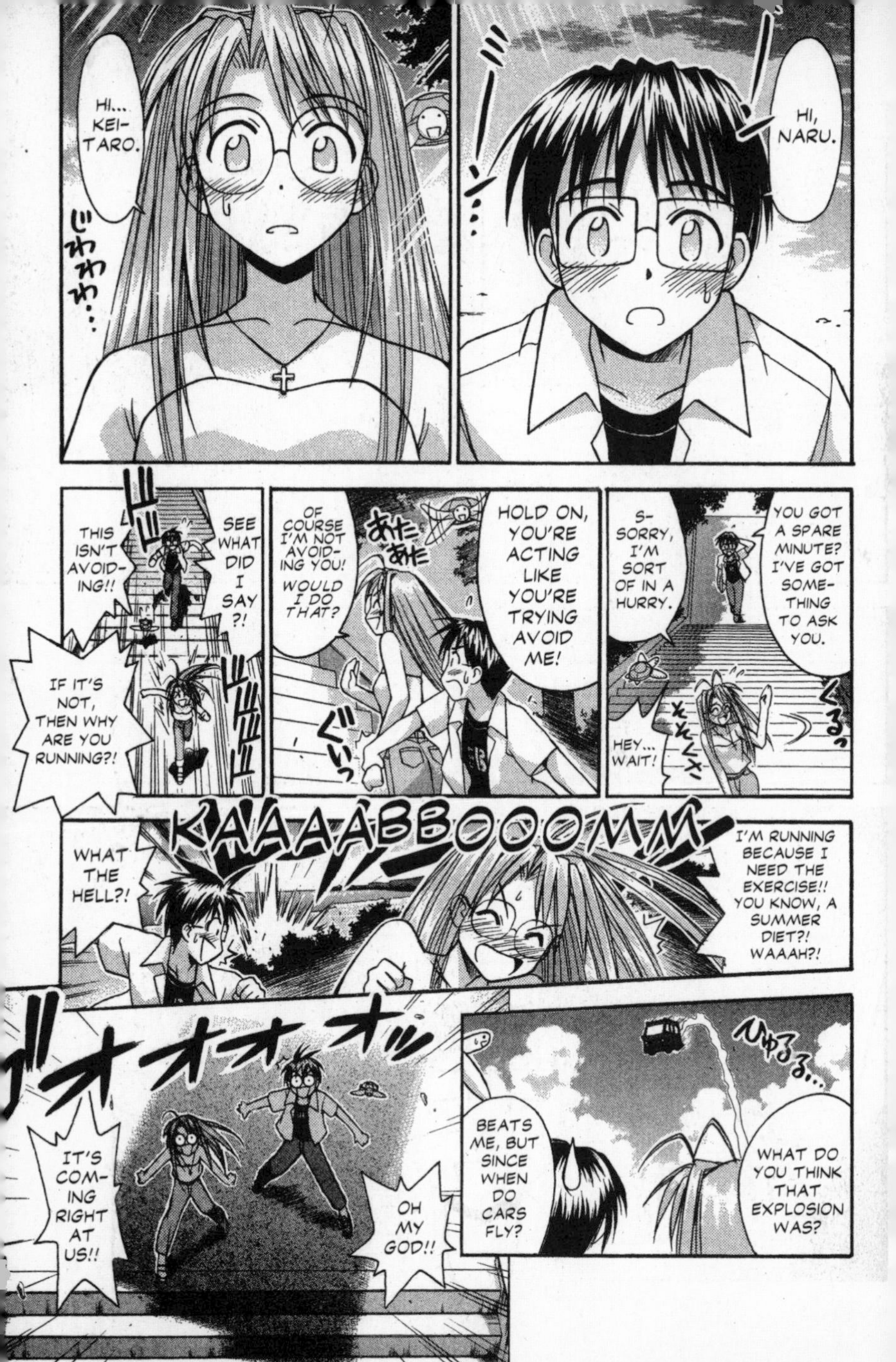
HI, NARU.
HI... KEI-TARO.
YOU GOT A SPARE MINUTE? I'VE GOT SOME-THING TO ASK YOU.
S-SORRY, I'M SORT OF IN A HURRY.
HEY... WAIT!
HOLD ON, YOU'RE ACTING LIKE YOU'RE TRYING AVOID ME!
OF COURSE I'M NOT AVOID-ING YOU!
WOULD I DO THAT?
SEE WHAT DID I SAY?!
THIS ISN'T AVOID-ING!!
IF IT'S NOT, THEN WHY ARE YOU RUNNING?!
I'M RUNNING BECAUSE I NEED THE EXERCISE!! YOU KNOW, A SUMMER DIET?! WAAAH?!
KAAAABBOOOOMM
WHAT THE HELL?!
WHAT DO YOU THINK THAT EXPLOSION WAS?
BEATS ME, BUT SINCE WHEN DO CARS FLY?
OH MY GOD!!
IT'S COMING RIGHT AT US!!

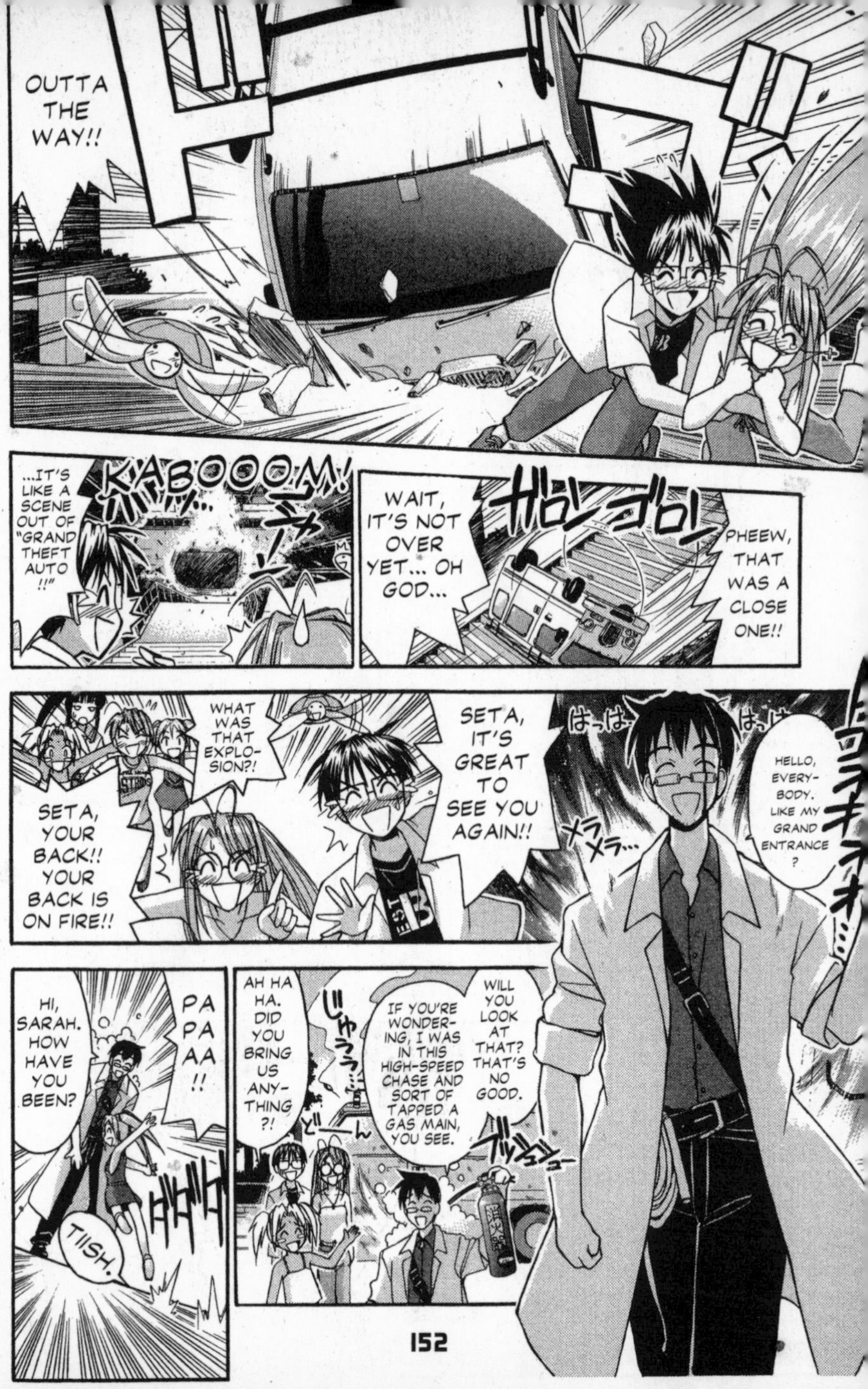
OUTTA THE WAY!!
PHEEW, THAT WAS A CLOSE ONE!!
WAIT, IT'S NOT OVER YET... OH GOD...
...IT'S LIKE A SCENE OUT OF "GRAND THEFT AUTO!!"
KABOOOM!
HELLO, EVERYBODY. LIKE MY GRAND ENTRANCE?
はっは
はっは
メラメラ...
SETA, IT'S GREAT TO SEE YOU AGAIN!!
WHAT WAS THAT EXPLOSION?!
SETA, YOUR BACK!! YOUR BACK IS ON FIRE!!
WILL YOU LOOK AT THAT? THAT'S NO GOOD.
IF YOU'RE WONDERING, I WAS IN THIS HIGH-SPEED CHASE AND SORT OF TAPPED A GAS MAIN, YOU SEE.
AH HA HA. DID YOU BRING US ANYTHING?!
PAPAAA!!
HI, SARAH. HOW HAVE YOU BEEN?
TIISH.

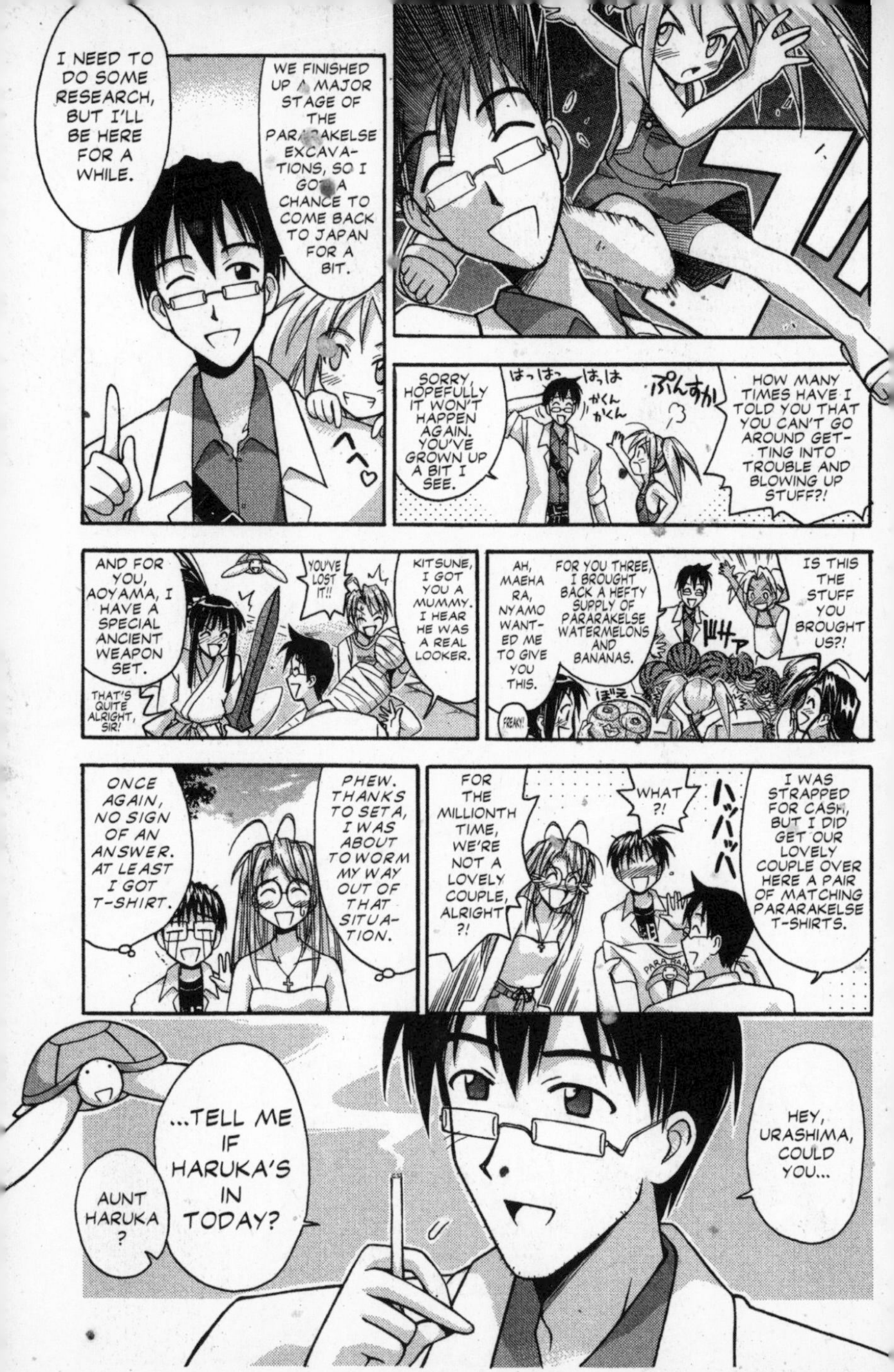
HOW MANY TIMES HAVE I TOLD YOU THAT YOU CAN'T GO AROUND GET-TING INTO TROUBLE AND BLOWING UP STUFF?!
ぷんすか
はっは はっは
かくん かくん
SORRY, HOPEFULLY IT WON'T HAPPEN AGAIN. YOU'VE GROWN UP A BIT I SEE.
WE FINISHED UP A MAJOR STAGE OF THE PARARAKELSE EXCAVA-TIONS, SO I GOT A CHANCE TO COME BACK TO JAPAN FOR A BIT.
I NEED TO DO SOME RESEARCH, BUT I'LL BE HERE FOR A WHILE.
IS THIS THE STUFF YOU BROUGHT US?!
ドサァ
FOR YOU THREE, I BROUGHT BACK A HEFTY SUPPLY OF PARARAKELSE WATERMELONS AND BANANAS.
AH, MAEHARA, NYAMO WANT-ED ME TO GIVE YOU THIS.
ぼえ
FREAKY!
KITSUNE, I GOT YOU A MUMMY. I HEAR HE WAS A REAL LOOKER.
YOU'VE LOST IT!!
AND FOR YOU, AOYAMA, I HAVE A SPECIAL ANCIENT WEAPON SET.
THAT'S QUITE ALRIGHT, SIR!
I WAS STRAPPED FOR CASH, BUT I DID GET OUR LOVELY COUPLE OVER HERE A PAIR OF MATCHING PARARAKELSE T-SHIRTS.
ハッハッハ
WHAT ?!
FOR THE MILLIONTH TIME, WE'RE NOT A LOVELY COUPLE, ALRIGHT ?!
PHEW. THANKS TO SETA, I WAS ABOUT TO WORM MY WAY OUT OF THAT SITUA-TION.
ONCE AGAIN, NO SIGN OF AN ANSWER. AT LEAST I GOT T-SHIRT.
HEY, URASHIMA, COULD YOU...
...TELL ME IF HARUKA'S IN TODAY?
AUNT HARUKA ?

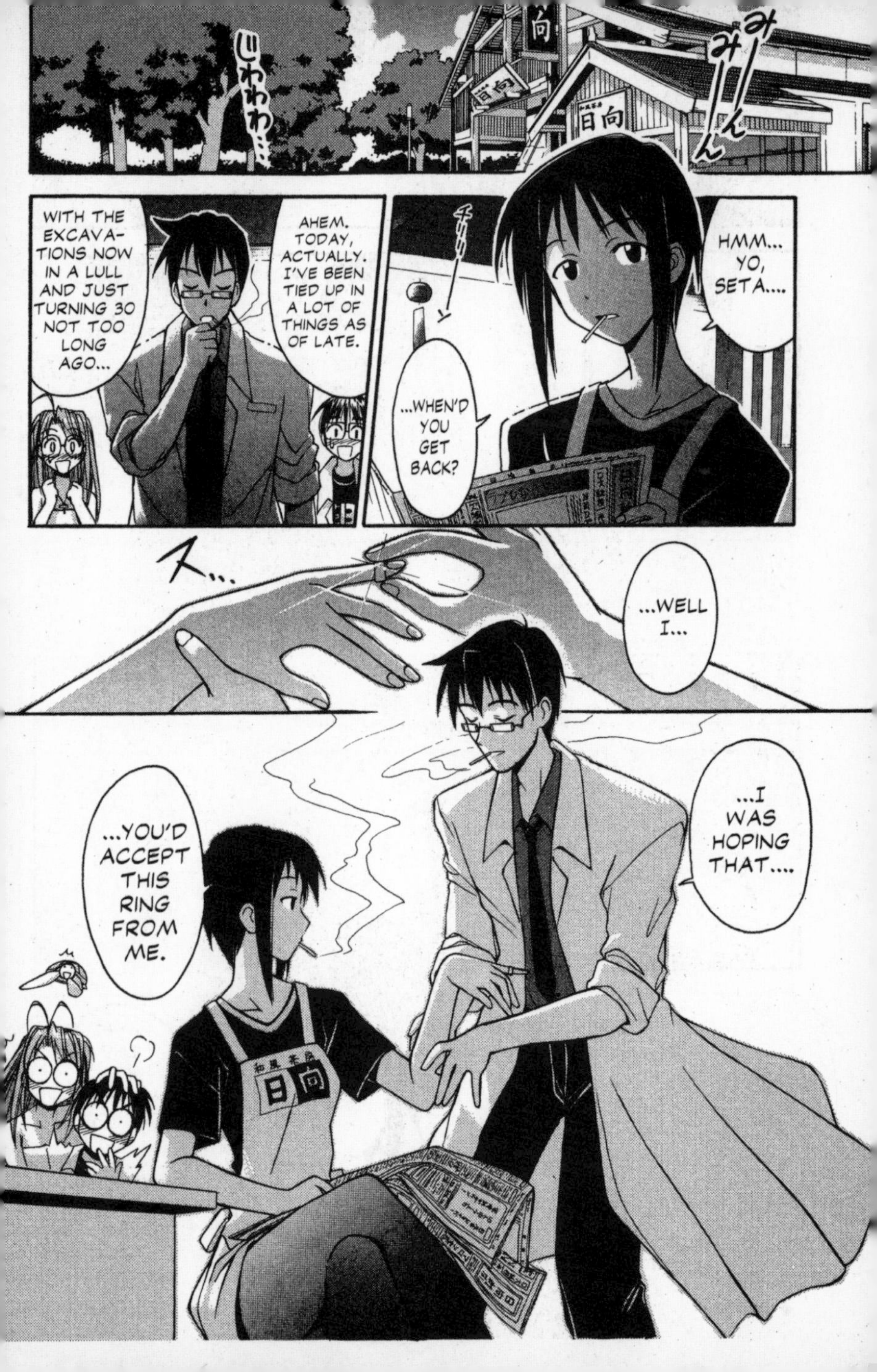
HMM... YO, SETA....
...WHEN'D YOU GET BACK?
AHEM. TODAY, ACTUALLY. I'VE BEEN TIED UP IN A LOT OF THINGS AS OF LATE.
WITH THE EXCAVATIONS NOW IN A LULL AND JUST TURNING 30 NOT TOO LONG AGO...
...WELL I...
ス…
...I WAS HOPING THAT....
...YOU'D ACCEPT THIS RING FROM ME.

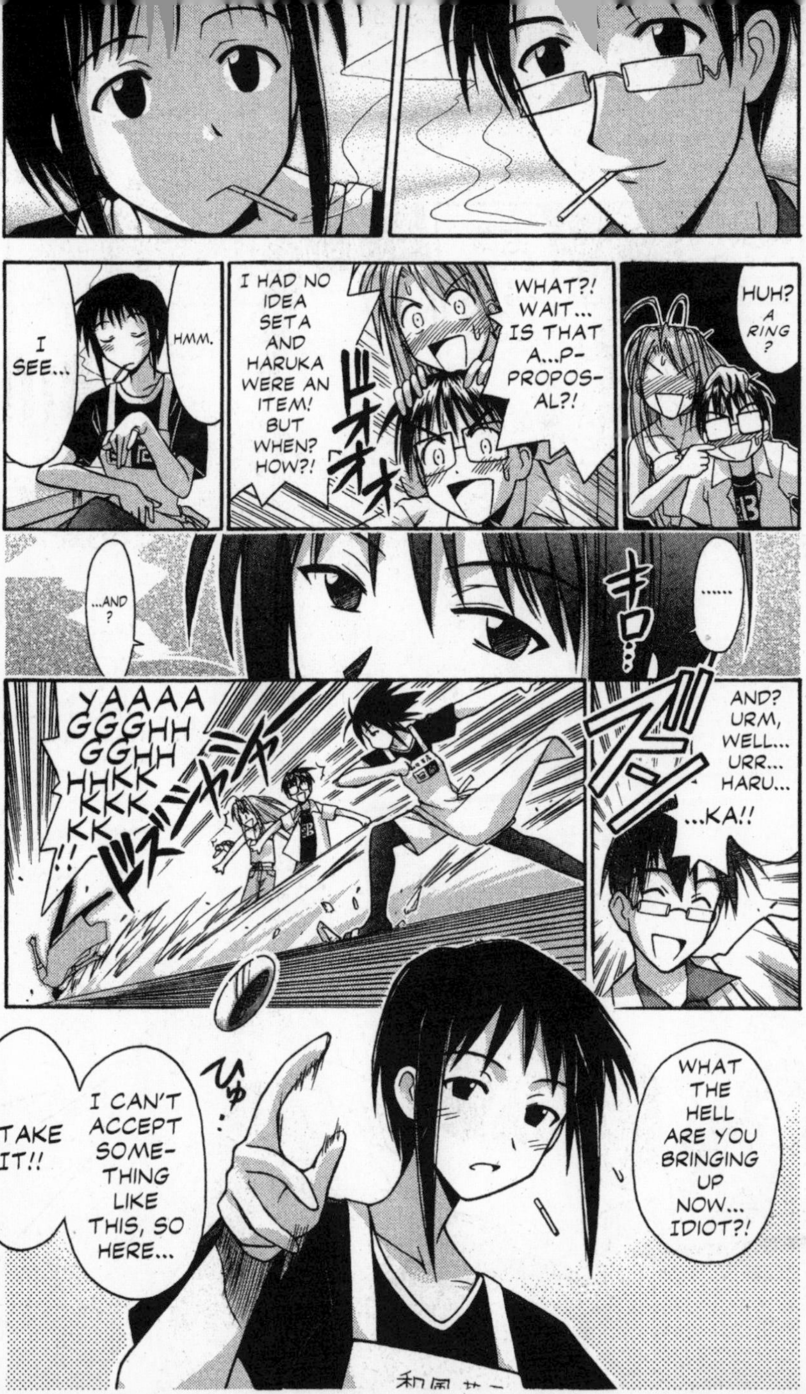
HUH? A RING?
WHAT?! WAIT... IS THAT A...P-PROPOSAL?!
I HAD NO IDEA SETA AND HARUKA WERE AN ITEM! BUT WHEN? HOW?!
HMM.
I SEE...
......
...AND ?
AND? URM, WELL... URR... HARU...
...KA!!
YAAAAGGGHHGGHHHHKKKKKKK!!
WHAT THE HELL ARE YOU BRINGING UP NOW... IDIOT?!
I CAN'T ACCEPT SOMETHING LIKE THIS, SO HERE...
...TAKE IT!!

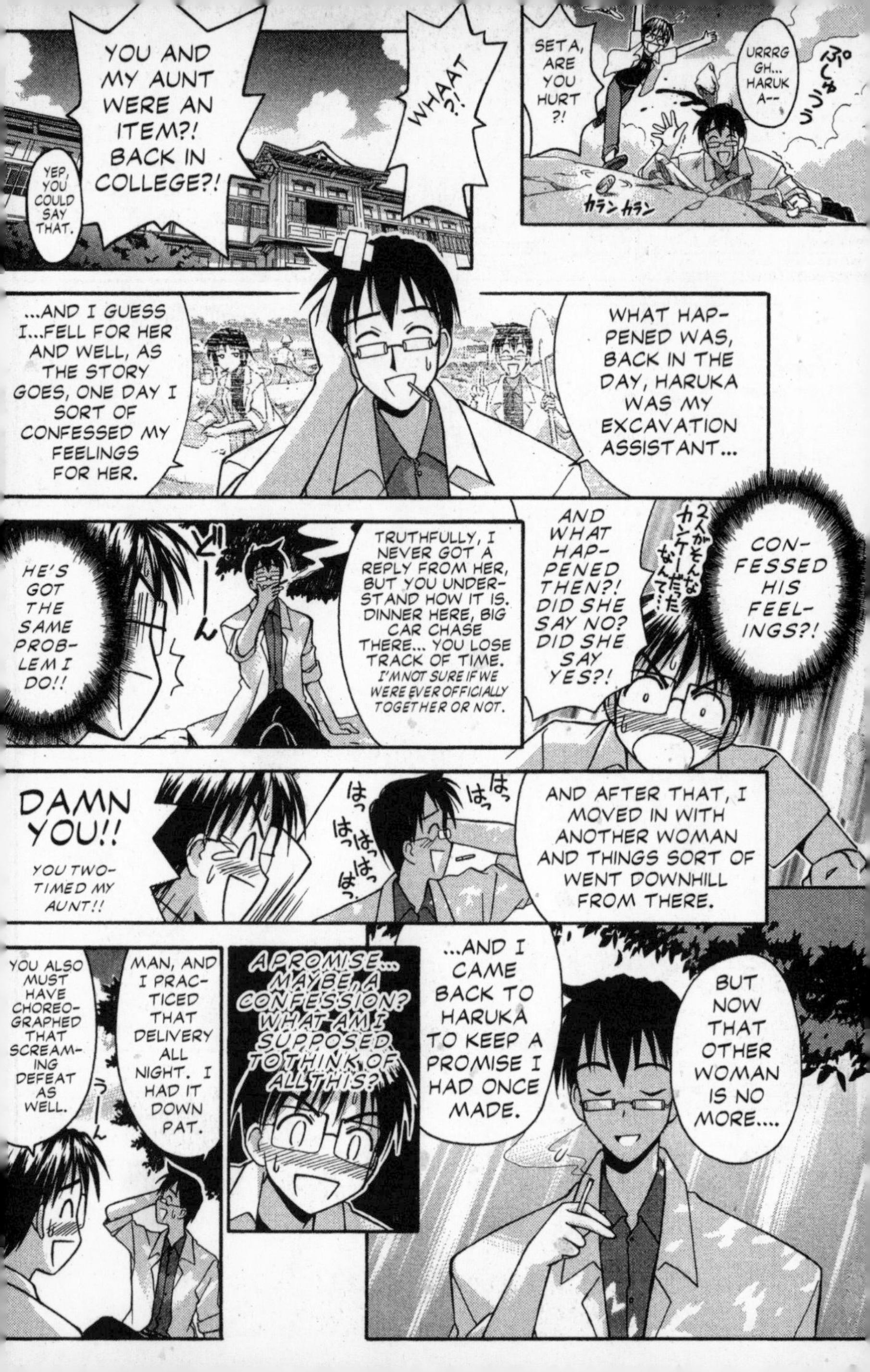
URRRG GH... HARUK A--
ぷしゅう
SETA, ARE YOU HURT?!
カラン カラン
WHAAT?!
YOU AND MY AUNT WERE AN ITEM?! BACK IN COLLEGE?!
YEP, YOU COULD SAY THAT.
WHAT HAP-PENED WAS, BACK IN THE DAY, HARUKA WAS MY EXCAVATION ASSISTANT...
...AND I GUESS I...FELL FOR HER AND WELL, AS THE STORY GOES, ONE DAY I SORT OF CONFESSED MY FEELINGS FOR HER.
CON-FESSED HIS FEEL-INGS?!
2人がそんなカンケーだったなんて…
AND WHAT HAP-PENED THEN?! DID SHE SAY NO? DID SHE SAY YES?!
TRUTHFULLY, I NEVER GOT A REPLY FROM HER, BUT YOU UNDER-STAND HOW IT IS. DINNER HERE, BIG CAR CHASE THERE... YOU LOSE TRACK OF TIME. I'M NOT SURE IF WE WERE EVER OFFICIALLY TOGETHER OR NOT.
どーん
HE'S GOT THE SAME PROB-LEM I DO!!
AND AFTER THAT, I MOVED IN WITH ANOTHER WOMAN AND THINGS SORT OF WENT DOWNHILL FROM THERE.
はっ はっ はっ はっ はっ
DAMN YOU!!
YOU TWO-TIMED MY AUNT!!
BUT NOW THAT OTHER WOMAN IS NO MORE....
...AND I CAME BACK TO HARUKA TO KEEP A PROMISE I HAD ONCE MADE.
A PROMISE... MAYBE, A CONFESSION? WHAT AM I SUPPOSED TO THINK OF ALL THIS?
MAN, AND I PRAC-TICED THAT DELIVERY ALL NIGHT. I HAD IT DOWN PAT.
うーん
YOU ALSO MUST HAVE CHOREO-GRAPHED THAT SCREAM-ING DEFEAT AS WELL.

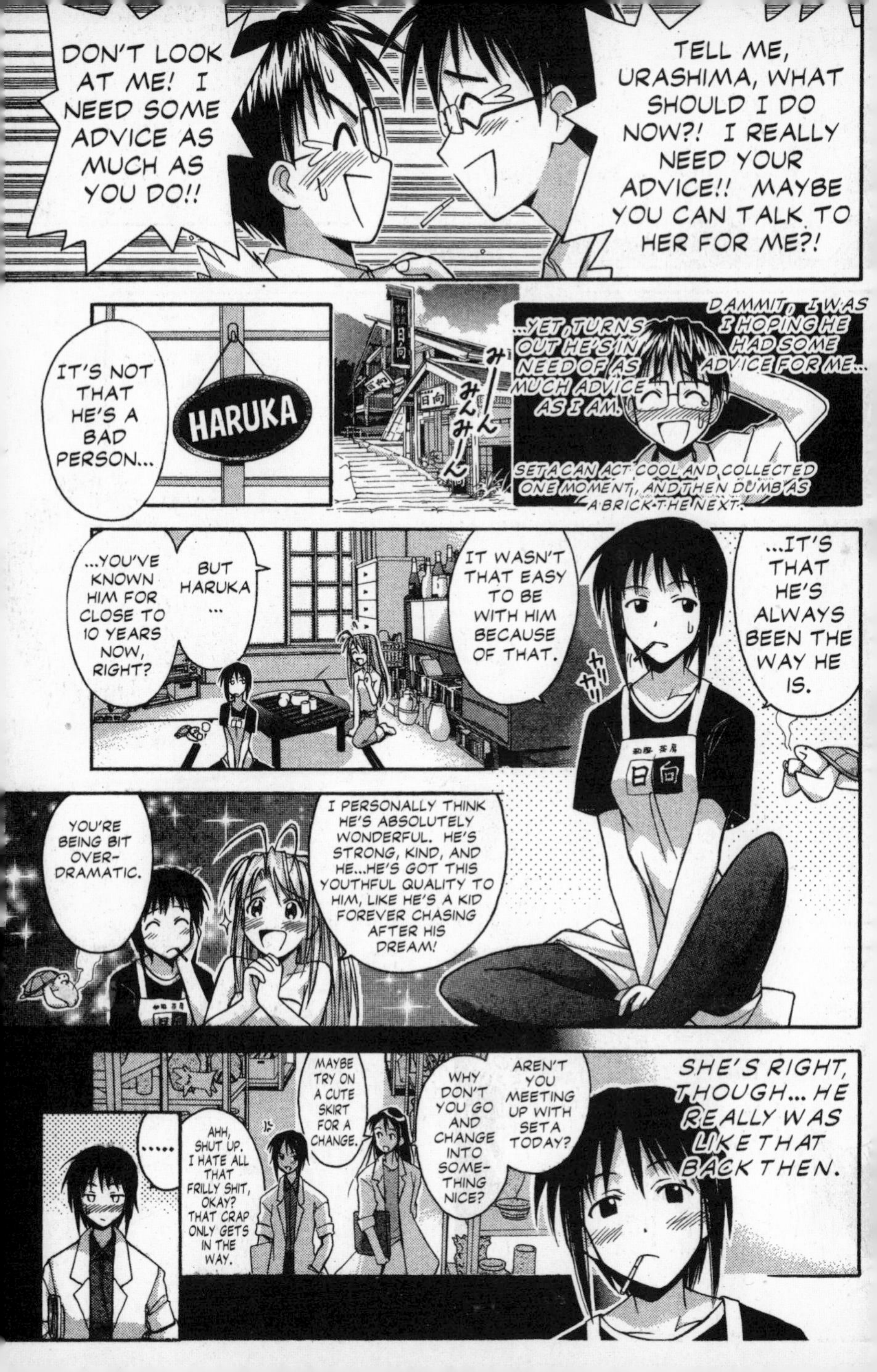
TELL ME, URASHIMA, WHAT SHOULD I DO NOW?! I REALLY NEED YOUR ADVICE!! MAYBE YOU CAN TALK TO HER FOR ME?!
DON'T LOOK AT ME! I NEED SOME ADVICE AS MUCH AS YOU DO!!
DAMMIT, I WAS HOPING HE HAD SOME ADVICE FOR ME...
...YET, TURNS OUT HE'S IN NEED OF AS MUCH ADVICE AS I AM.
SETA CAN ACT COOL AND COLLECTED ONE MOMENT, AND THEN DUMB AS A BRICK THE NEXT.
み～ん みんみ～ん
HARUKA
IT'S NOT THAT HE'S A BAD PERSON...
...IT'S THAT HE'S ALWAYS BEEN THE WAY HE IS.
IT WASN'T THAT EASY TO BE WITH HIM BECAUSE OF THAT.
BUT HARUKA ...
...YOU'VE KNOWN HIM FOR CLOSE TO 10 YEARS NOW, RIGHT?
I PERSONALLY THINK HE'S ABSOLUTELY WONDERFUL. HE'S STRONG, KIND, AND HE...HE'S GOT THIS YOUTHFUL QUALITY TO HIM, LIKE HE'S A KID FOREVER CHASING AFTER HIS DREAM!
YOU'RE BEING BIT OVER-DRAMATIC.
SHE'S RIGHT, THOUGH... HE REALLY WAS LIKE THAT BACK THEN.
AREN'T YOU MEETING UP WITH SETA TODAY?
WHY DON'T YOU GO AND CHANGE INTO SOME-THING NICE?
MAYBE TRY ON A CUTE SKIRT FOR A CHANGE.
AHH, SHUT UP. I HATE ALL THAT FRILLY SHIT, OKAY? THAT CRAP ONLY GETS IN THE WAY.
.....

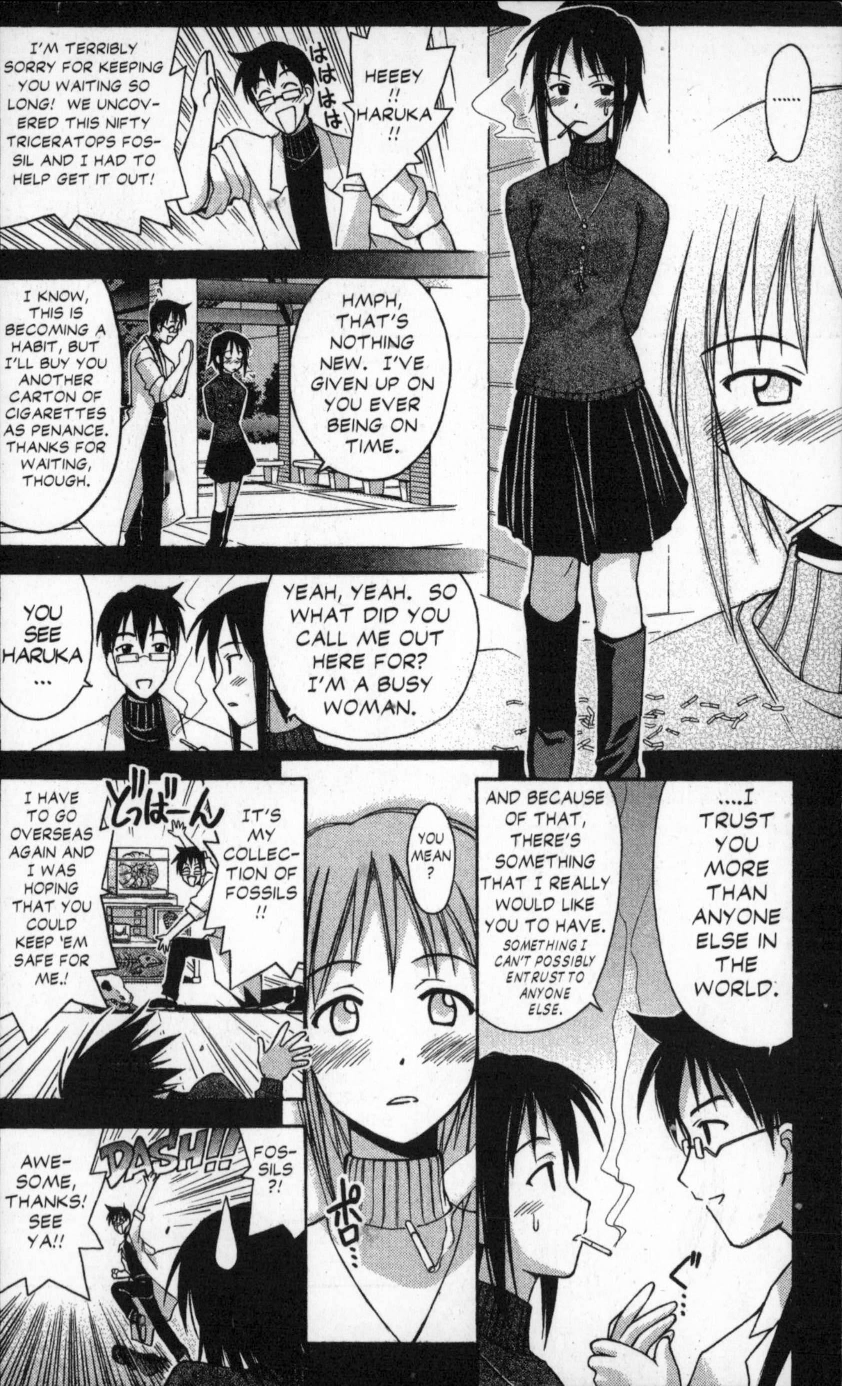
......
HEEEY!! HARUKA!!
ははははは
I'M TERRIBLY SORRY FOR KEEPING YOU WAITING SO LONG! WE UNCOVERED THIS NIFTY TRICERATOPS FOSSIL AND I HAD TO HELP GET IT OUT!
HMPH, THAT'S NOTHING NEW. I'VE GIVEN UP ON YOU EVER BEING ON TIME.
I KNOW, THIS IS BECOMING A HABIT, BUT I'LL BUY YOU ANOTHER CARTON OF CIGARETTES AS PENANCE. THANKS FOR WAITING, THOUGH.
YEAH, YEAH. SO WHAT DID YOU CALL ME OUT HERE FOR? I'M A BUSY WOMAN.
YOU SEE HARUKA...
....I TRUST YOU MORE THAN ANYONE ELSE IN THE WORLD.
AND BECAUSE OF THAT, THERE'S SOMETHING THAT I REALLY WOULD LIKE YOU TO HAVE. SOMETHING I CAN'T POSSIBLY ENTRUST TO ANYONE ELSE.
ぐ...
YOU MEAN?
ポロ...
IT'S MY COLLECTION OF FOSSILS!!
どっばーん
I HAVE TO GO OVERSEAS AGAIN AND I WAS HOPING THAT YOU COULD KEEP 'EM SAFE FOR ME.!
FOSSILS?!
DASH!!
AWESOME, THANKS! SEE YA!!

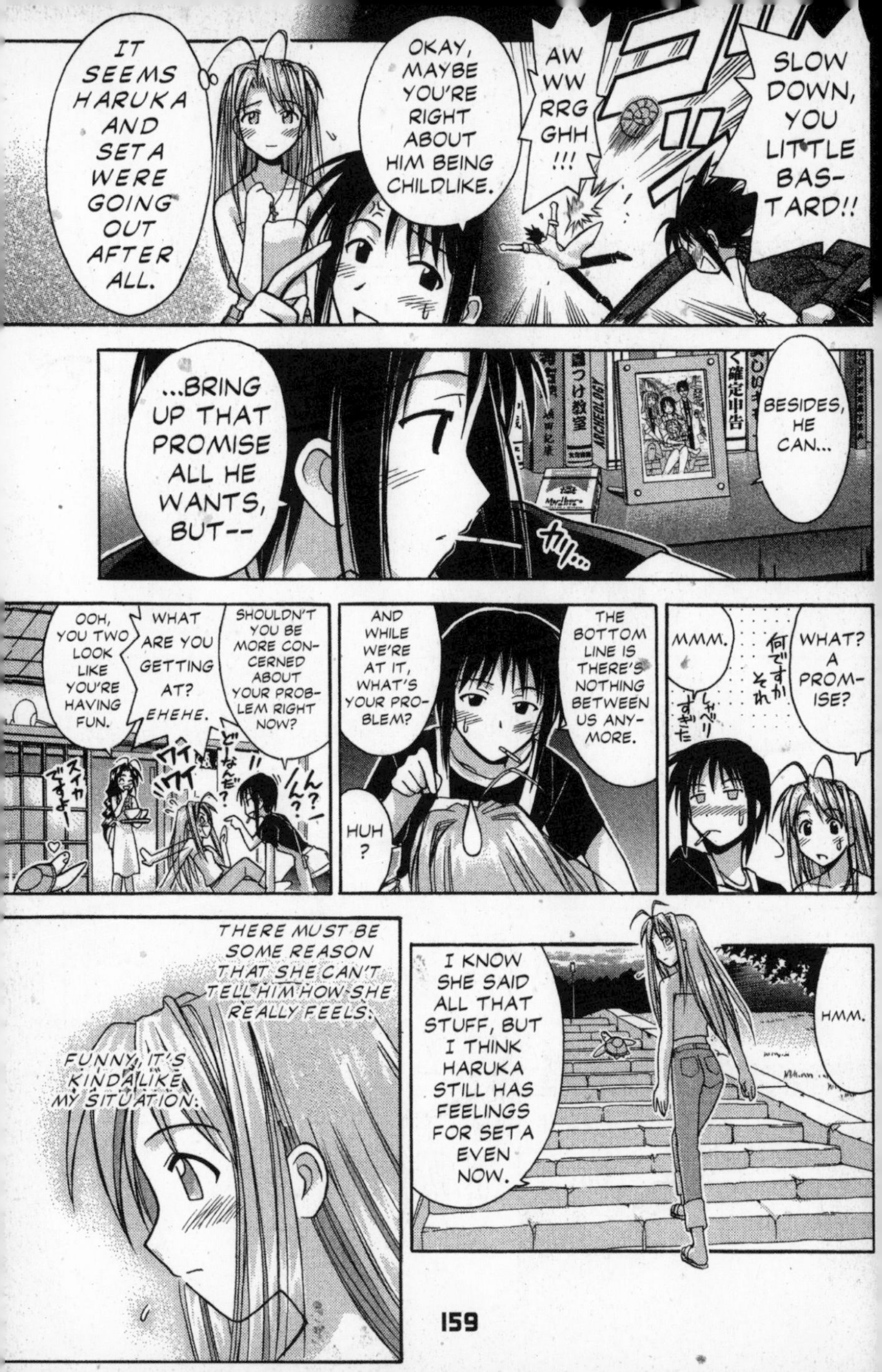
SLOW DOWN, YOU LITTLE BASTARD!!
AWWWRRGGHH!!!
OKAY, MAYBE YOU'RE RIGHT ABOUT HIM BEING CHILDLIKE.
IT SEEMS HARUKA AND SETA WERE GOING OUT AFTER ALL.
BESIDES, HE CAN...
...BRING UP THAT PROMISE ALL HE WANTS, BUT--
WHAT? A PROMISE?
何ですかそれ
MMM.
しゃべりすぎた
THE BOTTOM LINE IS THERE'S NOTHING BETWEEN US ANYMORE.
AND WHILE WE'RE AT IT, WHAT'S YOUR PROBLEM?
HUH?
SHOULDN'T YOU BE MORE CONCERNED ABOUT YOUR PROBLEM RIGHT NOW?
ん?ん?
どーなんだ?
WHAT ARE YOU GETTING AT? EHEHE.
ワイワイ
OOH, YOU TWO LOOK LIKE YOU'RE HAVING FUN.
スイカですよー
HMM.
I KNOW SHE SAID ALL THAT STUFF, BUT I THINK HARUKA STILL HAS FEELINGS FOR SETA EVEN NOW.
THERE MUST BE SOME REASON THAT SHE CAN'T TELL HIM HOW SHE REALLY FEELS.
FUNNY, IT'S KINDA LIKE MY SITUATION.

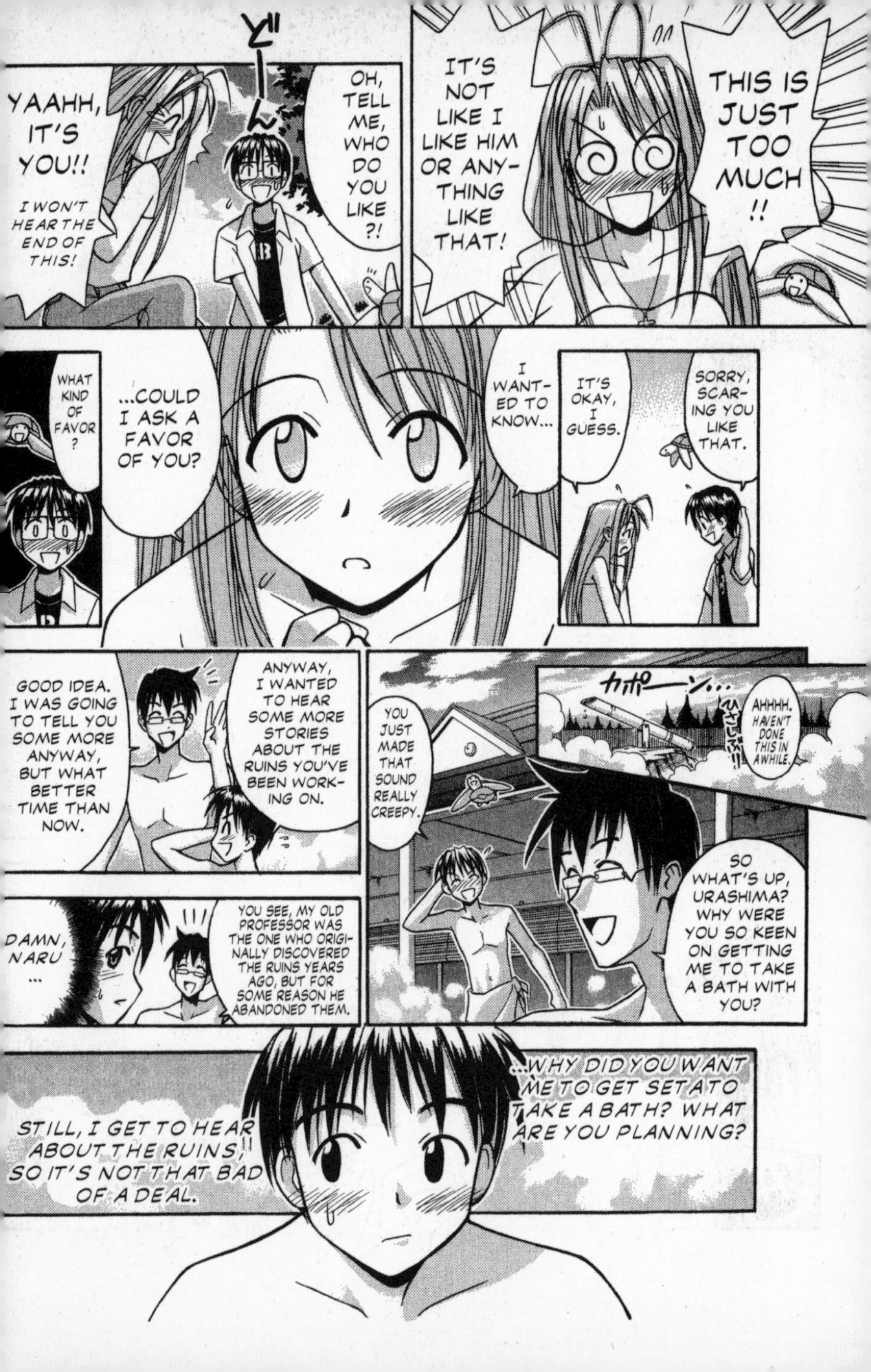
THIS IS JUST TOO MUCH!!
IT'S NOT LIKE I LIKE HIM OR ANYTHING LIKE THAT!
OH, TELL ME, WHO DO YOU LIKE?!
どーん
YAAHH, IT'S YOU!!
I WON'T HEAR THE END OF THIS!
SORRY, SCARING YOU LIKE THAT.
IT'S OKAY, I GUESS.
I WANTED TO KNOW...
...COULD I ASK A FAVOR OF YOU?
WHAT KIND OF FAVOR?
カポーン…
AHHHH. HAVEN'T DONE THIS IN AWHILE.
SO WHAT'S UP, URASHIMA? WHY WERE YOU SO KEEN ON GETTING ME TO TAKE A BATH WITH YOU?
YOU JUST MADE THAT SOUND REALLY CREEPY.
ANYWAY, I WANTED TO HEAR SOME MORE STORIES ABOUT THE RUINS YOU'VE BEEN WORKING ON.
GOOD IDEA. I WAS GOING TO TELL YOU SOME MORE ANYWAY, BUT WHAT BETTER TIME THAN NOW.
YOU SEE, MY OLD PROFESSOR WAS THE ONE WHO ORIGINALLY DISCOVERED THE RUINS YEARS AGO, BUT FOR SOME REASON HE ABANDONED THEM.
DAMN, NARU...
...WHY DID YOU WANT ME TO GET SET A TO TAKE A BATH? WHAT ARE YOU PLANNING?
STILL, I GET TO HEAR ABOUT THE RUINS, SO IT'S NOT THAT BAD OF A DEAL.

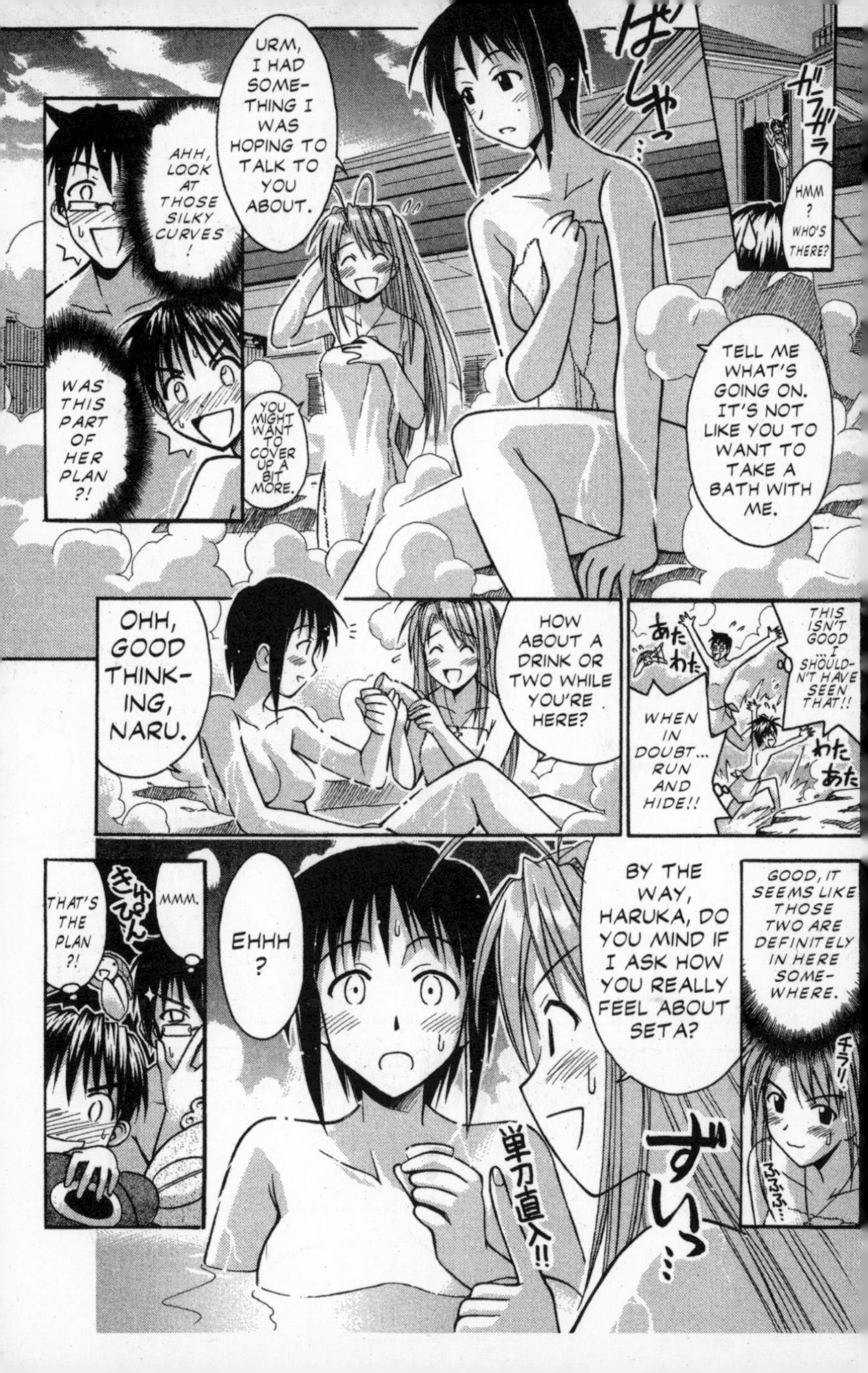

ガラガラ
HMM? WHO'S THERE?
ぱしゃっ…
URM, I HAD SOME-THING I WAS HOPING TO TALK TO YOU ABOUT.
TELL ME WHAT'S GOING ON. IT'S NOT LIKE YOU TO WANT TO TAKE A BATH WITH ME.
YOU MIGHT WANT TO COVER UP A BIT MORE.
AHH, LOOK AT THOSE SILKY CURVES!
WAS THIS PART OF HER PLAN?!
THIS ISN'T GOOD... I SHOULDN'T HAVE SEEN THAT!!
あたわた
WHEN IN DOUBT... RUN AND HIDE!!
わたあた
HOW ABOUT A DRINK OR TWO WHILE YOU'RE HERE?
OHH, GOOD THINKING, NARU.
GOOD, IT SEEMS LIKE THOSE TWO ARE DEFINITELY IN HERE SOME-WHERE.
チラリ
ふふふ…
BY THE WAY, HARUKA, DO YOU MIND IF I ASK HOW YOU REALLY FEEL ABOUT SETA?
ずいっ…
単刀直入!!
EHHH?
MMM.
きゅぴーん
THAT'S THE PLAN?!

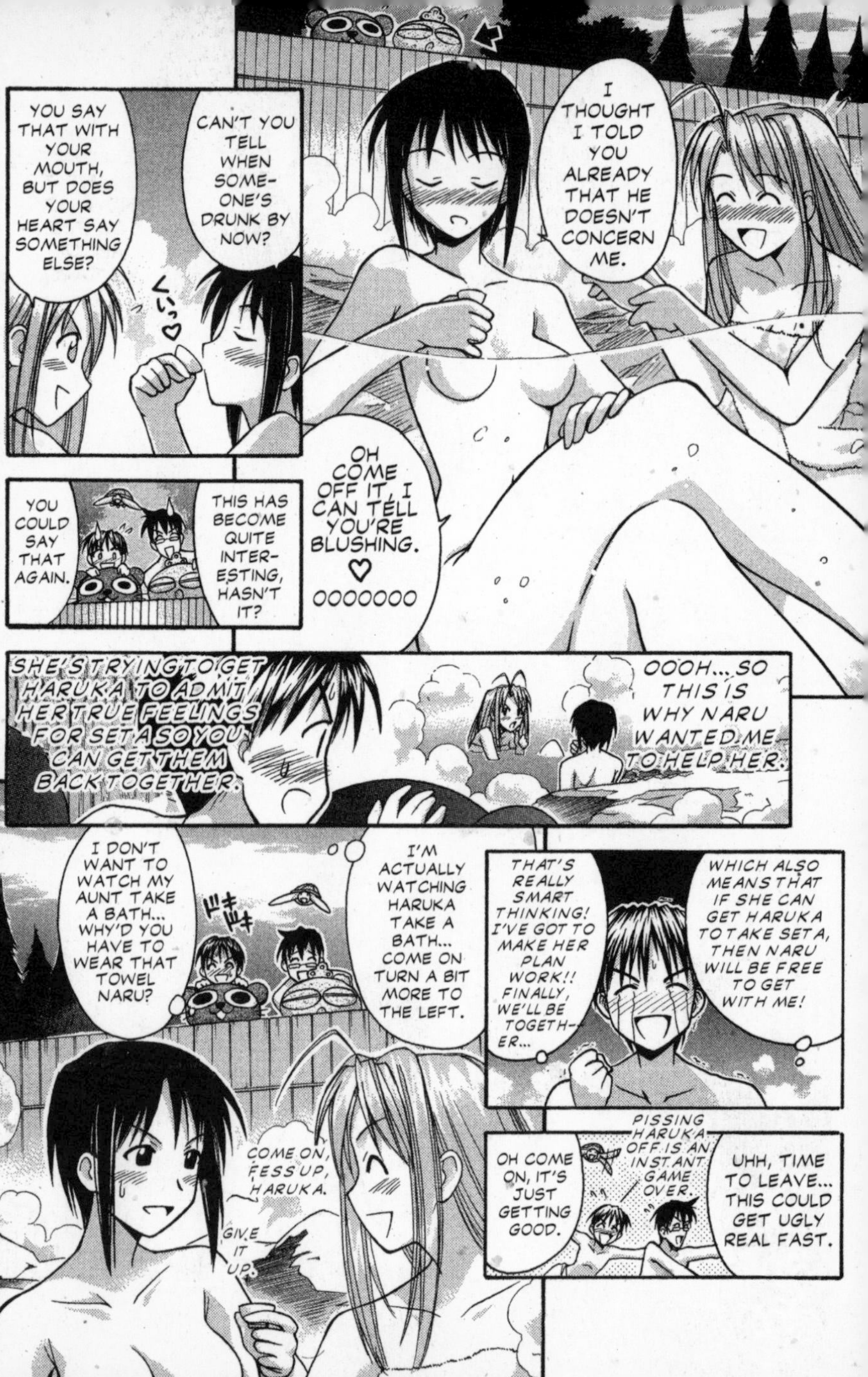
I THOUGHT I TOLD YOU ALREADY THAT HE DOESN'T CONCERN ME.
OH COME OFF IT, I CAN TELL YOU'RE BLUSHING. ♥
OOOOOOO
CAN'T YOU TELL WHEN SOME-ONE'S DRUNK BY NOW?
YOU SAY THAT WITH YOUR MOUTH, BUT DOES YOUR HEART SAY SOMETHING ELSE?
くいっ♥
THIS HAS BECOME QUITE INTER-ESTING, HASN'T IT?
YOU COULD SAY THAT AGAIN.
OOOH... SO THIS IS WHY NARU WANTED ME TO HELP HER.
SHE'S TRYING TO GET HARUKA TO ADMIT HER TRUE FEELINGS FOR SETA SO YOU CAN GET THEM BACK TOGETHER.
WHICH ALSO MEANS THAT IF SHE CAN GET HARUKA TO TAKE SETA, THEN NARU WILL BE FREE TO GET WITH ME!
THAT'S REALLY SMART THINKING! I'VE GOT TO MAKE HER PLAN WORK!! FINALLY, WE'LL BE TOGETH-ER...
UHH, TIME TO LEAVE... THIS COULD GET UGLY REAL FAST.
PISSING HARUKA OFF IS AN INSTANT GAME OVER.
OH COME ON, IT'S JUST GETTING GOOD.
I'M ACTUALLY WATCHING HARUKA TAKE A BATH... COME ON TURN A BIT MORE TO THE LEFT.
I DON'T WANT TO WATCH MY AUNT TAKE A BATH... WHY'D YOU HAVE TO WEAR THAT TOWEL NARU?
ドキドキ
COME ON, FESS UP, HARUKA.
GIVE IT UP.

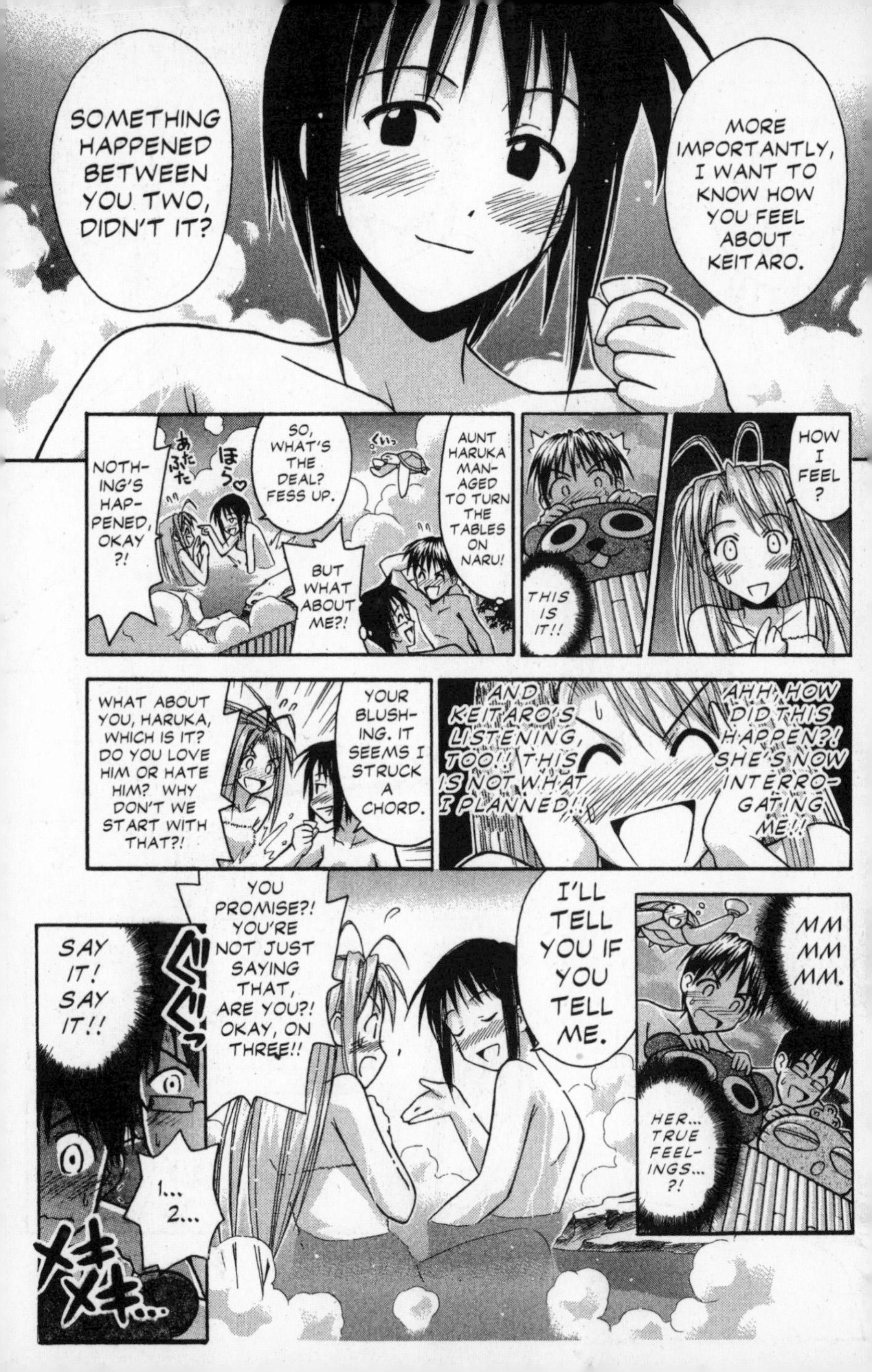
MORE IMPORTANTLY, I WANT TO KNOW HOW YOU FEEL ABOUT KEITARO.
SOMETHING HAPPENED BETWEEN YOU TWO, DIDN'T IT?
HOW I FEEL?
THIS IS IT!!
AUNT HARUKA MAN-AGED TO TURN THE TABLES ON NARU!
SO, WHAT'S THE DEAL? FESS UP.
くいっ
ほら♡
あたふた
NOTH-ING'S HAP-PENED, OKAY?!
BUT WHAT ABOUT ME?!
AHH, HOW DID THIS HAPPEN?! SHE'S NOW INTERRO-GATING ME!!
AND KEITARO'S LISTENING, TOO!! THIS IS NOT WHAT I PLANNED!!
YOUR BLUSH-ING. IT SEEMS I STRUCK A CHORD.
WHAT ABOUT YOU, HARUKA, WHICH IS IT? DO YOU LOVE HIM OR HATE HIM? WHY DON'T WE START WITH THAT?!
MM MM MM.
HER... TRUE FEEL-INGS... ?!
I'LL TELL YOU IF YOU TELL ME.
YOU PROMISE?! YOU'RE NOT JUST SAYING THAT, ARE YOU?! OKAY, ON THREE!!
ぐぐっ
SAY IT! SAY IT!!
1... 2...
メキメキ...

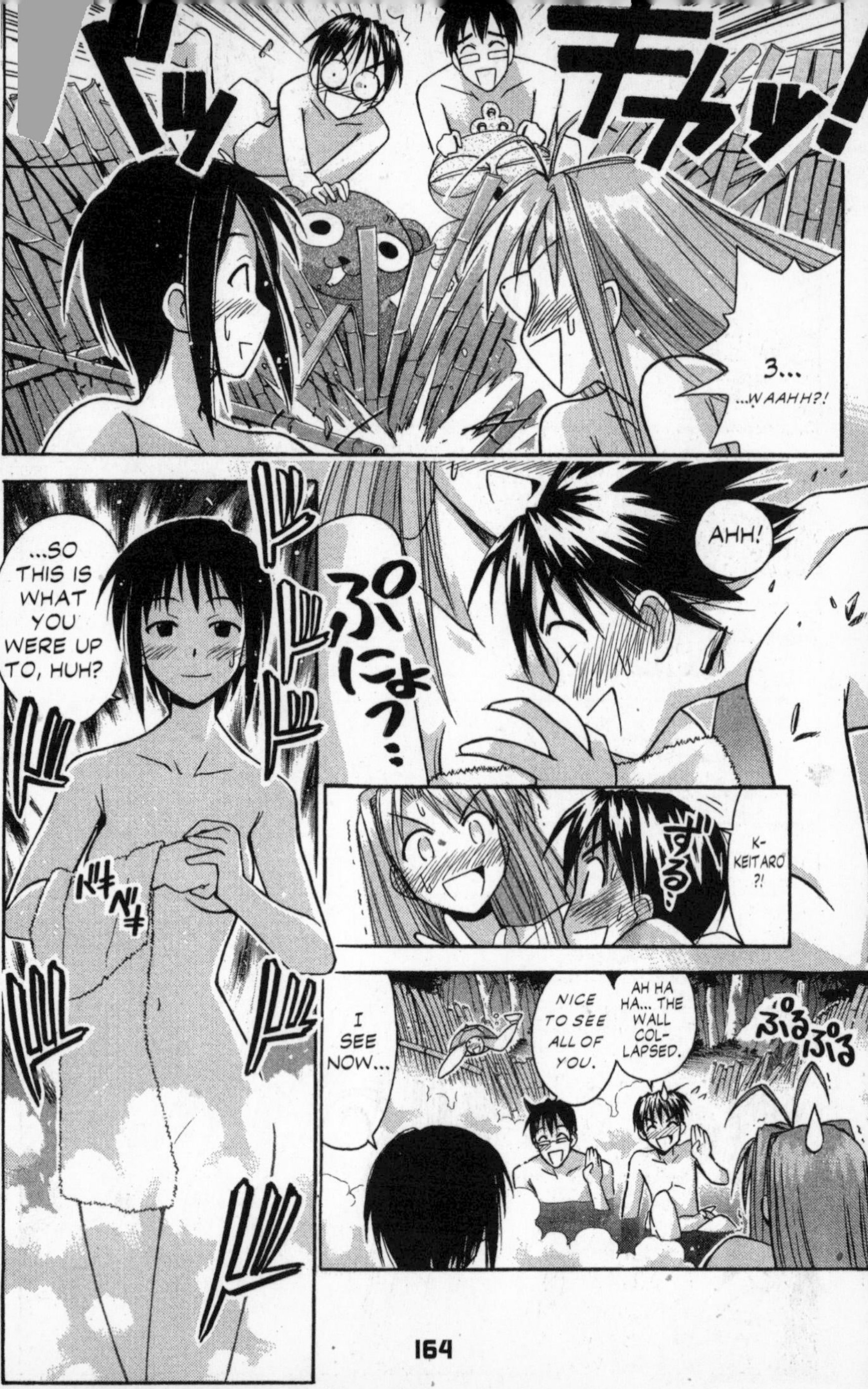
キャッ!
ドッ
3...
...WAAHH?!
AHH!
ぷにょっ
K-KEITARO?!
ずる
ぷるぷる
AH HA HA... THE WALL COL-LAPSED.
NICE TO SEE ALL OF YOU.
I SEE NOW...
...SO THIS IS WHAT YOU WERE UP TO, HUH?

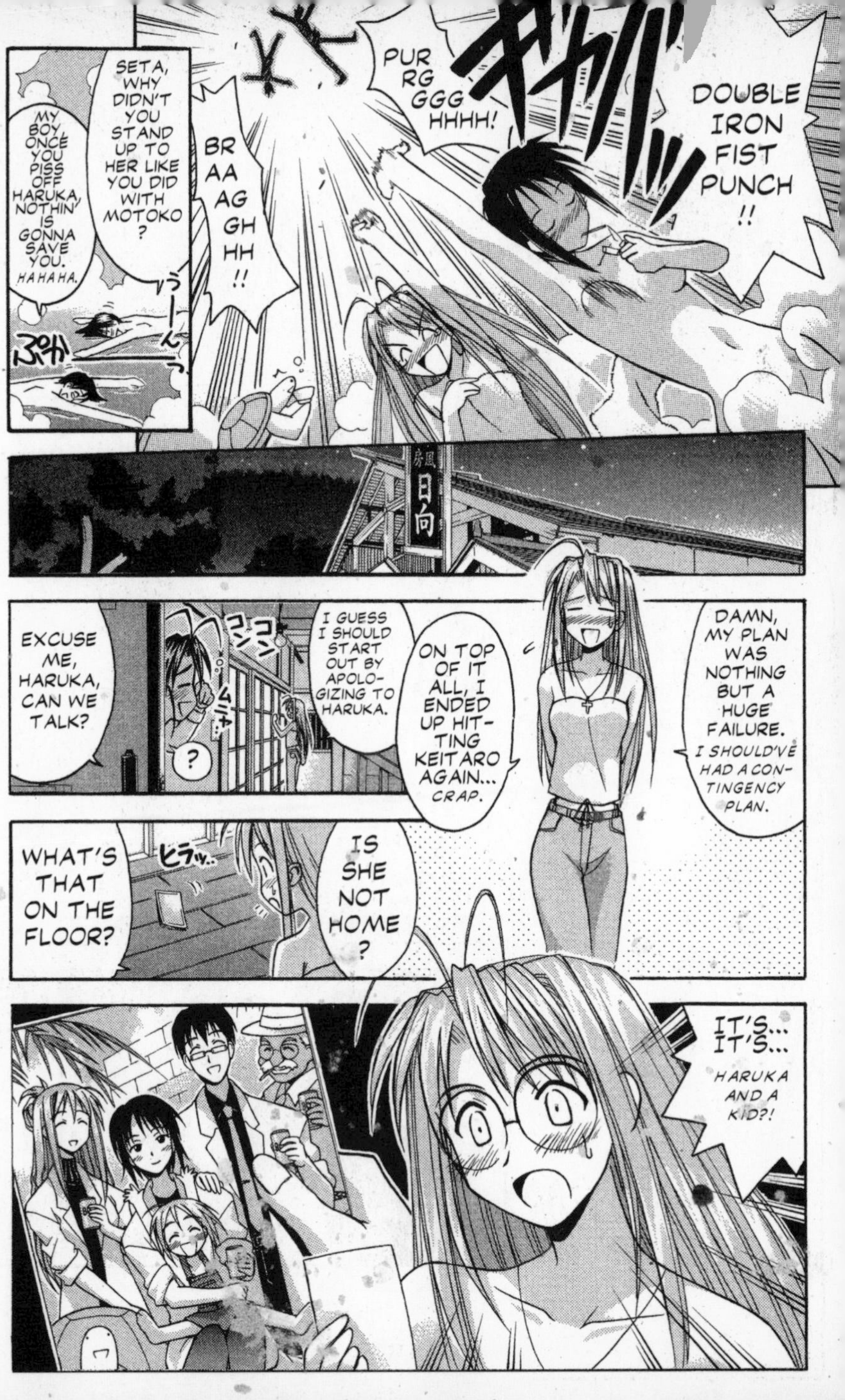
DOUBLE IRON FIST PUNCH !!
PUR RG GGG HHHH!
BR AA AG GH HH !!
SETA, WHY DIDN'T YOU STAND UP TO HER LIKE YOU DID WITH MOTOKO?
MY BOY, ONCE YOU PISS OFF HARUKA, NOTHIN' IS GONNA SAVE YOU. HAHAHA.
うーんっ
ぷかー
日向
DAMN, MY PLAN WAS NOTHING BUT A HUGE FAILURE. I SHOULD'VE HAD A CONTINGENCY PLAN.
ON TOP OF IT ALL, I ENDED UP HITTING KEITARO AGAIN... CRAP.
I GUESS I SHOULD START OUT BY APOLOGIZING TO HARUKA.
コンコン
EXCUSE ME, HARUKA, CAN WE TALK?
?
IS SHE NOT HOME?
WHAT'S THAT ON THE FLOOR?
IT'S... IT'S... HARUKA AND A KID?!

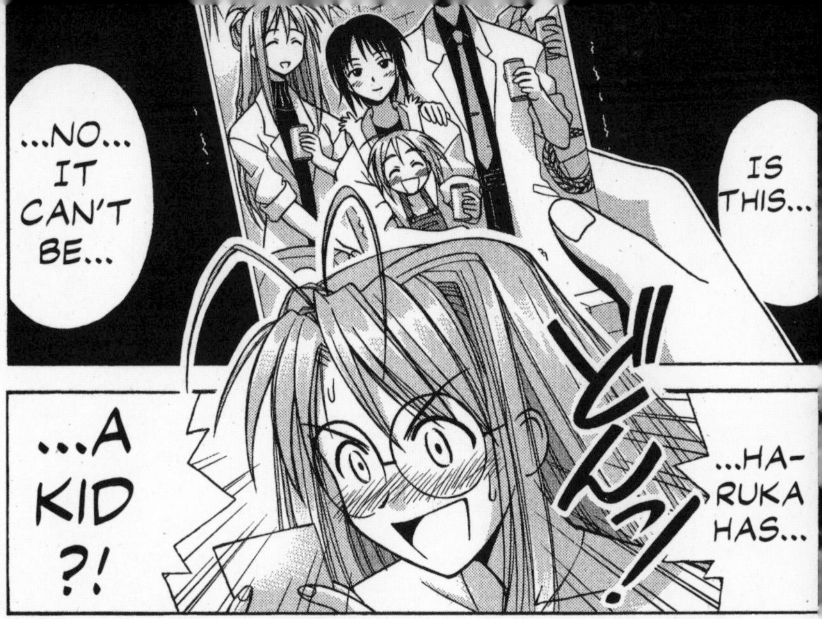
IS THIS...
...NO... IT CAN'T BE...
...HA-RUKA HAS...
...A KID ?!

Love Hina

HINATA.78 An Honest I Love You

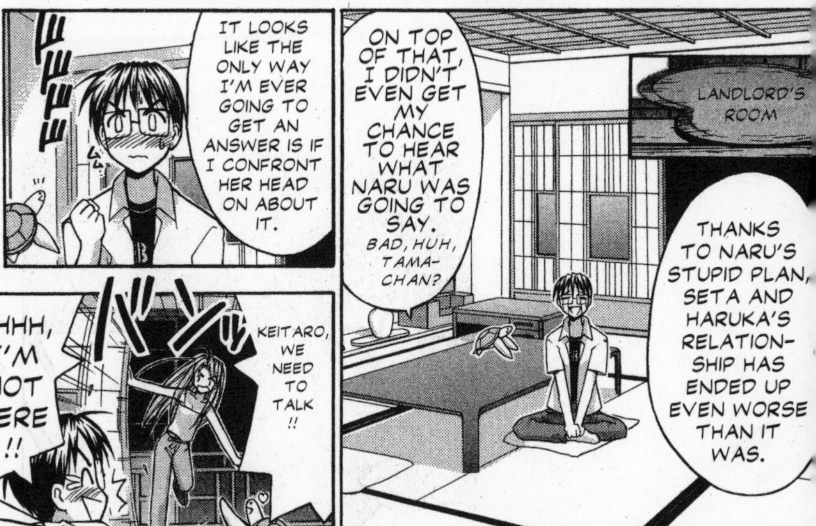
LANDLORD'S ROOM
THANKS TO NARU'S STUPID PLAN, SETA AND HARUKA'S RELATIONSHIP HAS ENDED UP EVEN WORSE THAN IT WAS.
ON TOP OF THAT, I DIDN'T EVEN GET MY CHANCE TO HEAR WHAT NARU WAS GOING TO SAY.
BAD, HUH, TAMA-CHAN?
IT LOOKS LIKE THE ONLY WAY I'M EVER GOING TO GET AN ANSWER IS IF I CONFRONT HER HEAD ON ABOUT IT.
KEITARO, WE NEED TO TALK !!
AHHH, I'M NOT HERE !!

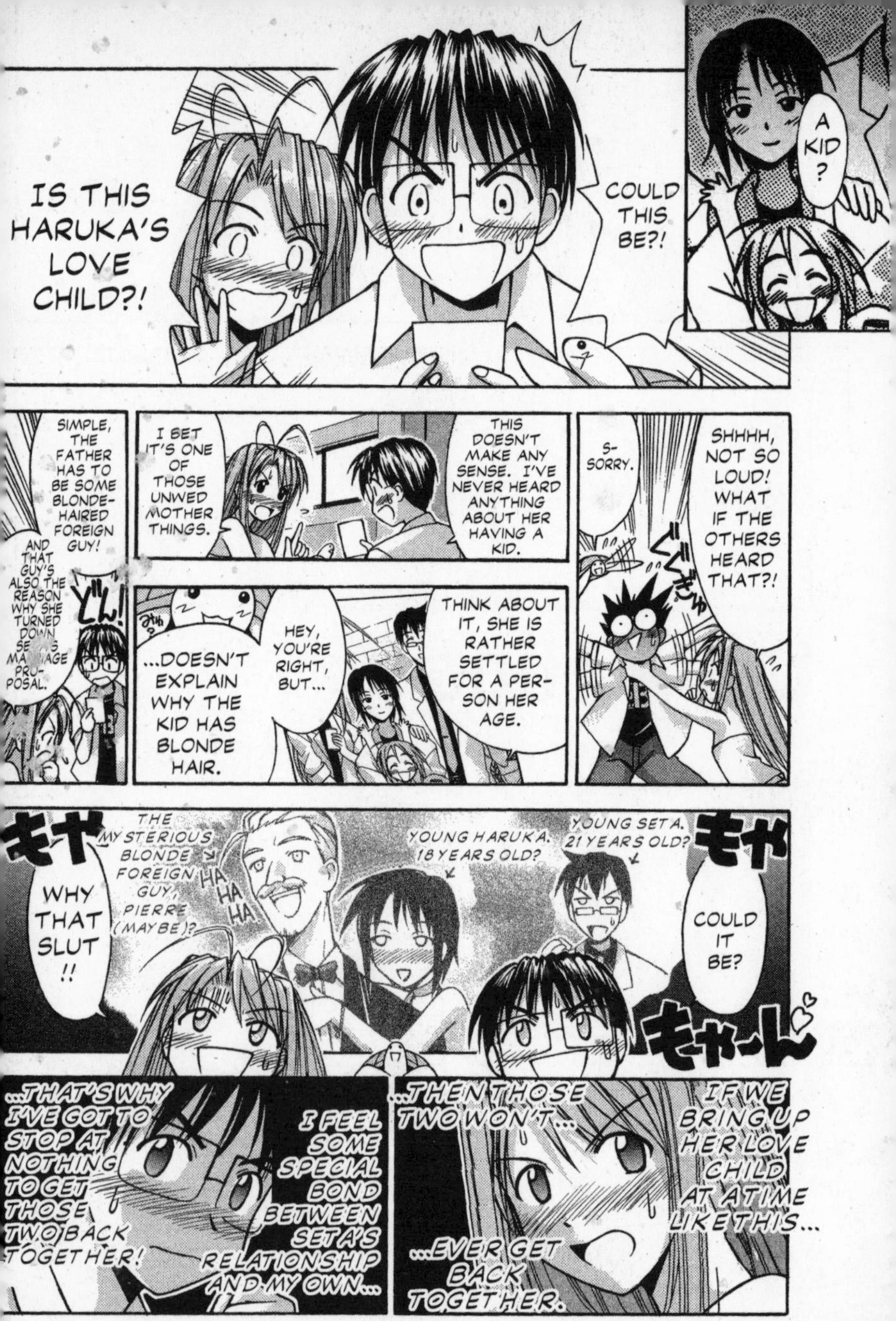
A KID?
COULD THIS BE?!
IS THIS HARUKA'S LOVE CHILD?!
SHHHH, NOT SO LOUD! WHAT IF THE OTHERS HEARD THAT?!
S-SORRY.
THIS DOESN'T MAKE ANY SENSE. I'VE NEVER HEARD ANYTHING ABOUT HER HAVING A KID.
I BET IT'S ONE OF THOSE UNWED MOTHER THINGS.
THINK ABOUT IT, SHE IS RATHER SETTLED FOR A PERSON HER AGE.
HEY, YOU'RE RIGHT, BUT...
...DOESN'T EXPLAIN WHY THE KID HAS BLONDE HAIR.
SIMPLE, THE FATHER HAS TO BE SOME BLONDE-HAIRED FOREIGN GUY!
AND THAT GUY'S ALSO THE REASON WHY SHE TURNED DOWN
どん!
もや
COULD IT BE?
YOUNG SETA. 21 YEARS OLD?
YOUNG HARUKA. 18 YEARS OLD?
THE MYSTERIOUS BLONDE FOREIGN GUY, PIERRE (MAYBE)?
HA HA HA
WHY THAT SLUT!!
もや
IF WE BRING UP HER LOVE CHILD AT A TIME LIKE THIS...
...THEN THOSE TWO WON'T...
...EVER GET BACK TOGETHER.
I FEEL SOME SPECIAL BOND BETWEEN SETA'S RELATIONSHIP AND MY OWN...
...THAT'S WHY I'VE GOT TO STOP AT NOTHING TO GET THOSE TWO BACK TOGETHER!

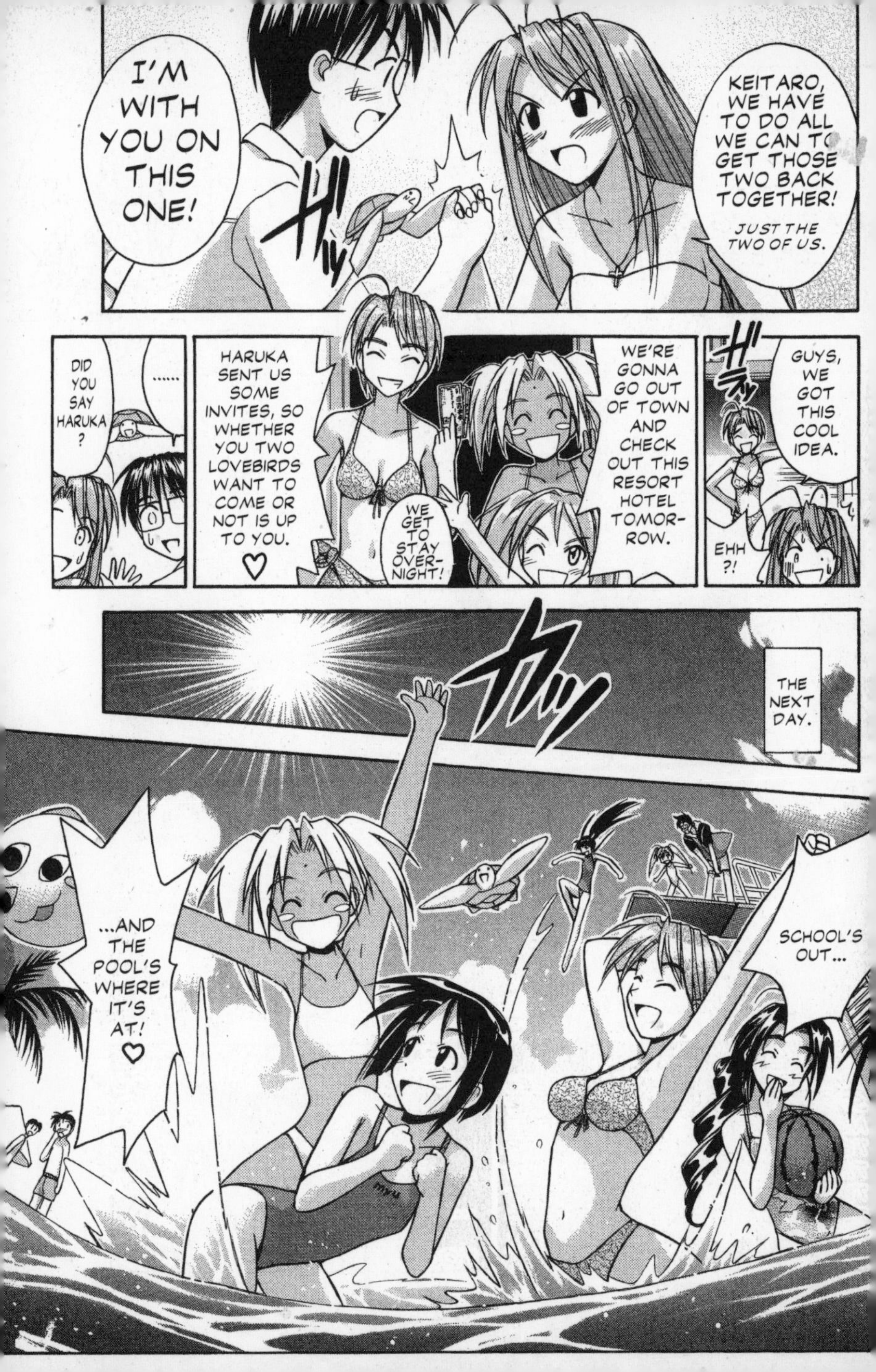
KEITARO, WE HAVE TO DO ALL WE CAN TO GET THOSE TWO BACK TOGETHER!
JUST THE TWO OF US.
I'M WITH YOU ON THIS ONE!
GUYS, WE GOT THIS COOL IDEA.
EHH?!
WE'RE GONNA GO OUT OF TOWN AND CHECK OUT THIS RESORT HOTEL TOMORROW.
HARUKA SENT US SOME INVITES, SO WHETHER YOU TWO LOVEBIRDS WANT TO COME OR NOT IS UP TO YOU. ♥
WE GET TO STAY OVERNIGHT!
......
DID YOU SAY HARUKA?
THE NEXT DAY.
SCHOOL'S OUT...
...AND THE POOL'S WHERE IT'S AT! ♥

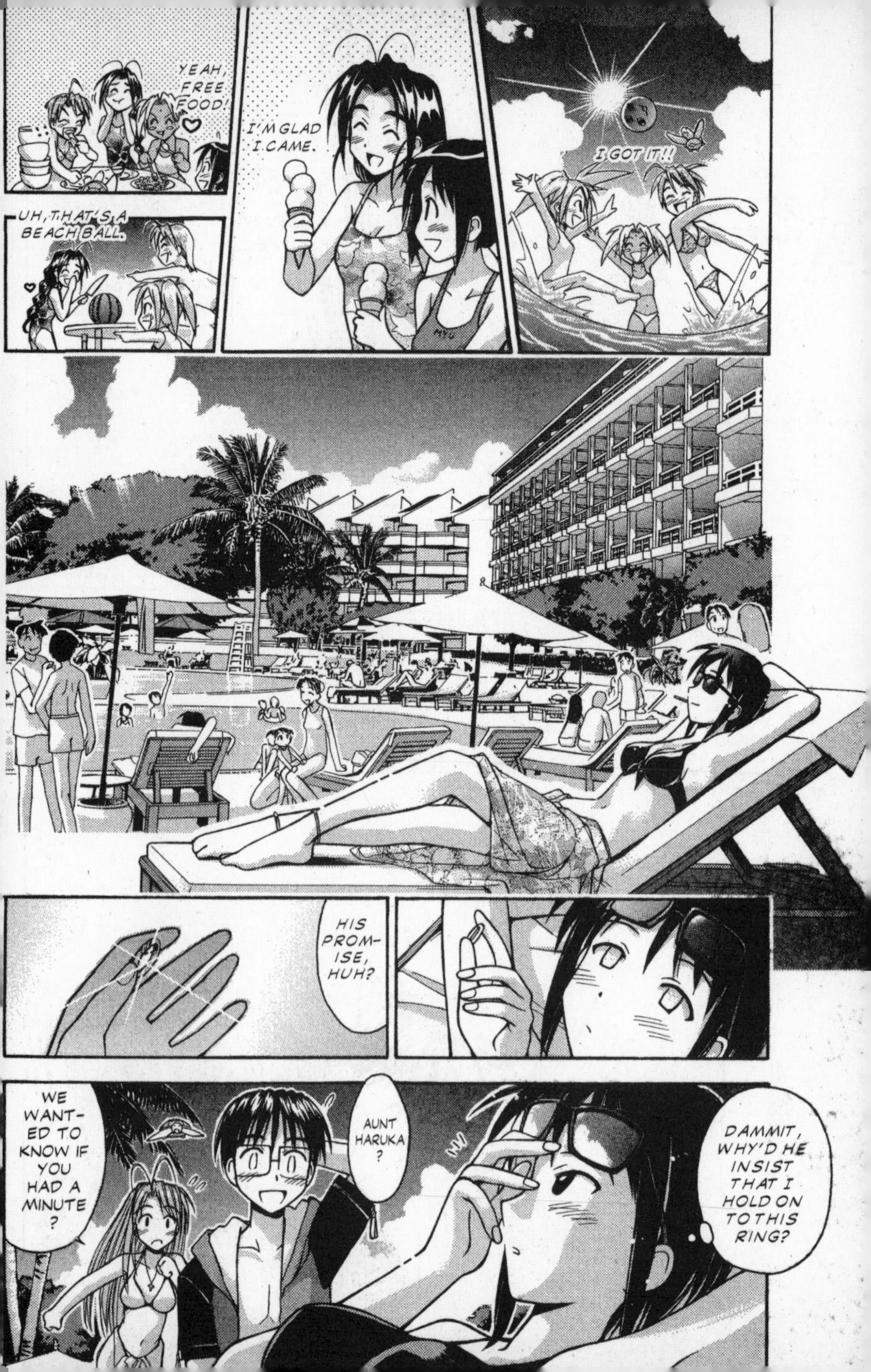
I GOT IT!!
I'M GLAD I CAME.
YEAH, FREE FOOD!
UH, THAT'S A BEACH BALL.
HIS PROMISE, HUH?
DAMMIT, WHY'D HE INSIST THAT I HOLD ON TO THIS RING?
AUNT HARUKA?
WE WANTED TO KNOW IF YOU HAD A MINUTE?

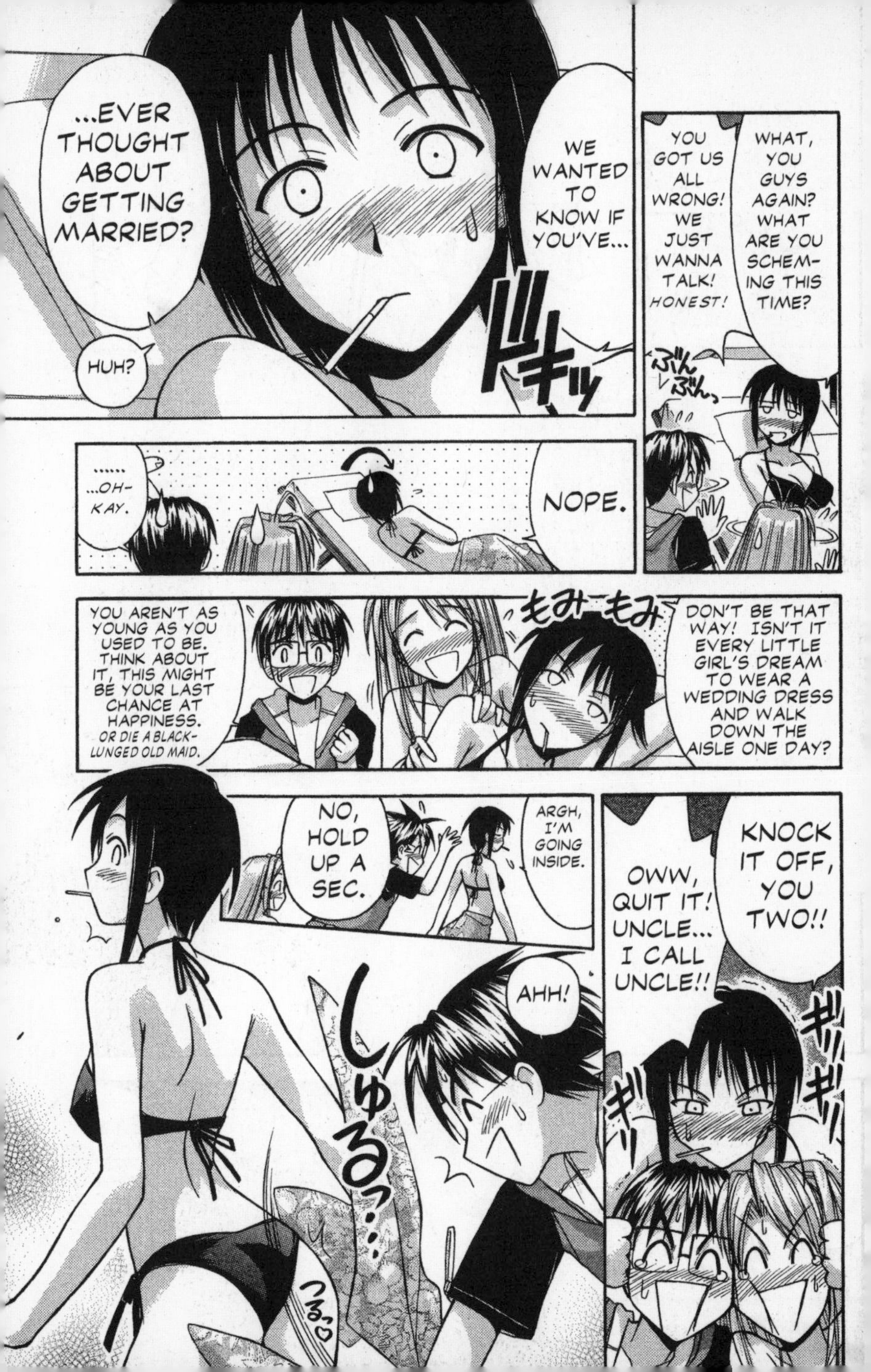
WHAT, YOU GUYS AGAIN? WHAT ARE YOU SCHEMING THIS TIME?
YOU GOT US ALL WRONG! WE JUST WANNA TALK! HONEST!
ぶんぶんっ
WE WANTED TO KNOW IF YOU'VE...
...EVER THOUGHT ABOUT GETTING MARRIED?
ドキッ
HUH?
NOPE.
....OH-KAY.
DON'T BE THAT WAY! ISN'T IT EVERY LITTLE GIRL'S DREAM TO WEAR A WEDDING DRESS AND WALK DOWN THE AISLE ONE DAY?
もみもみ
YOU AREN'T AS YOUNG AS YOU USED TO BE. THINK ABOUT IT, THIS MIGHT BE YOUR LAST CHANCE AT HAPPINESS. OR DIE A BLACK-LUNGED OLD MAID.
KNOCK IT OFF, YOU TWO!!
OWW, QUIT IT! UNCLE... I CALL UNCLE!!
ギリギリ
ARGH, I'M GOING INSIDE.
NO, HOLD UP A SEC.
AHH!
しゅるっ...
つるっ♡

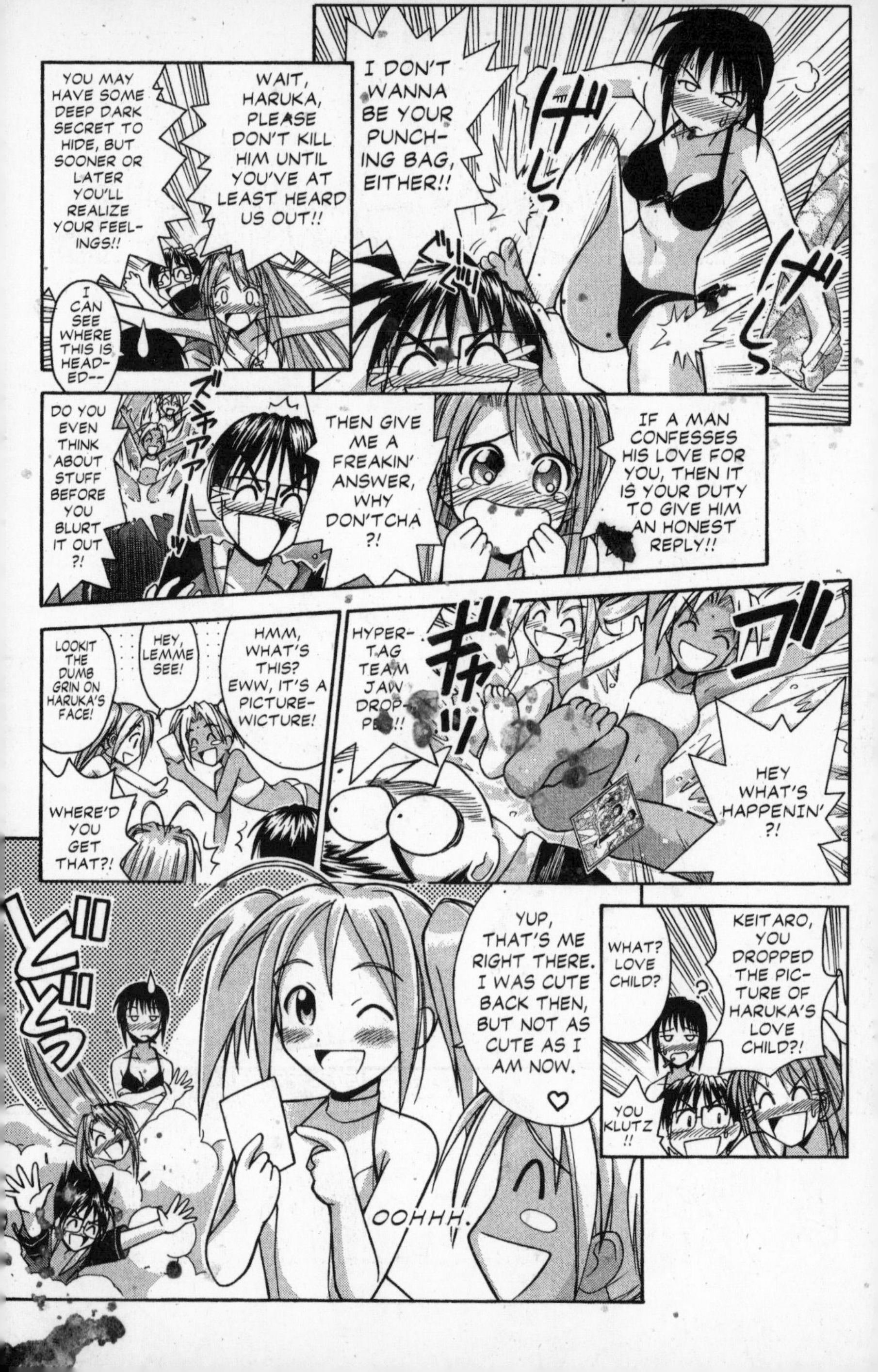
I DON'T WANNA BE YOUR PUNCHING BAG, EITHER!!
WAIT, HARUKA, PLEASE DON'T KILL HIM UNTIL YOU'VE AT LEAST HEARD US OUT!!
YOU MAY HAVE SOME DEEP DARK SECRET TO HIDE, BUT SOONER OR LATER YOU'LL REALIZE YOUR FEELINGS!!
I CAN SEE WHERE THIS IS HEADED--
IF A MAN CONFESSES HIS LOVE FOR YOU, THEN IT IS YOUR DUTY TO GIVE HIM AN HONEST REPLY!!
THEN GIVE ME A FREAKIN' ANSWER, WHY DON'TCHA?!
DO YOU EVEN THINK ABOUT STUFF BEFORE YOU BLURT IT OUT?!
HEY WHAT'S HAPPENIN'?!
HYPER-TAG TEAM JAW DROP-PERS!!
HMM, WHAT'S THIS? EWW, IT'S A PICTURE-WICTURE!
HEY, LEMME SEE!
LOOKIT THE DUMB GRIN ON HARUKA'S FACE!
WHERE'D YOU GET THAT?!
KEITARO, YOU DROPPED THE PICTURE OF HARUKA'S LOVE CHILD?!
WHAT? LOVE CHILD?
YOU KLUTZ!!
YUP, THAT'S ME RIGHT THERE. I WAS CUTE BACK THEN, BUT NOT AS CUTE AS I AM NOW. ♡
OOHHH.

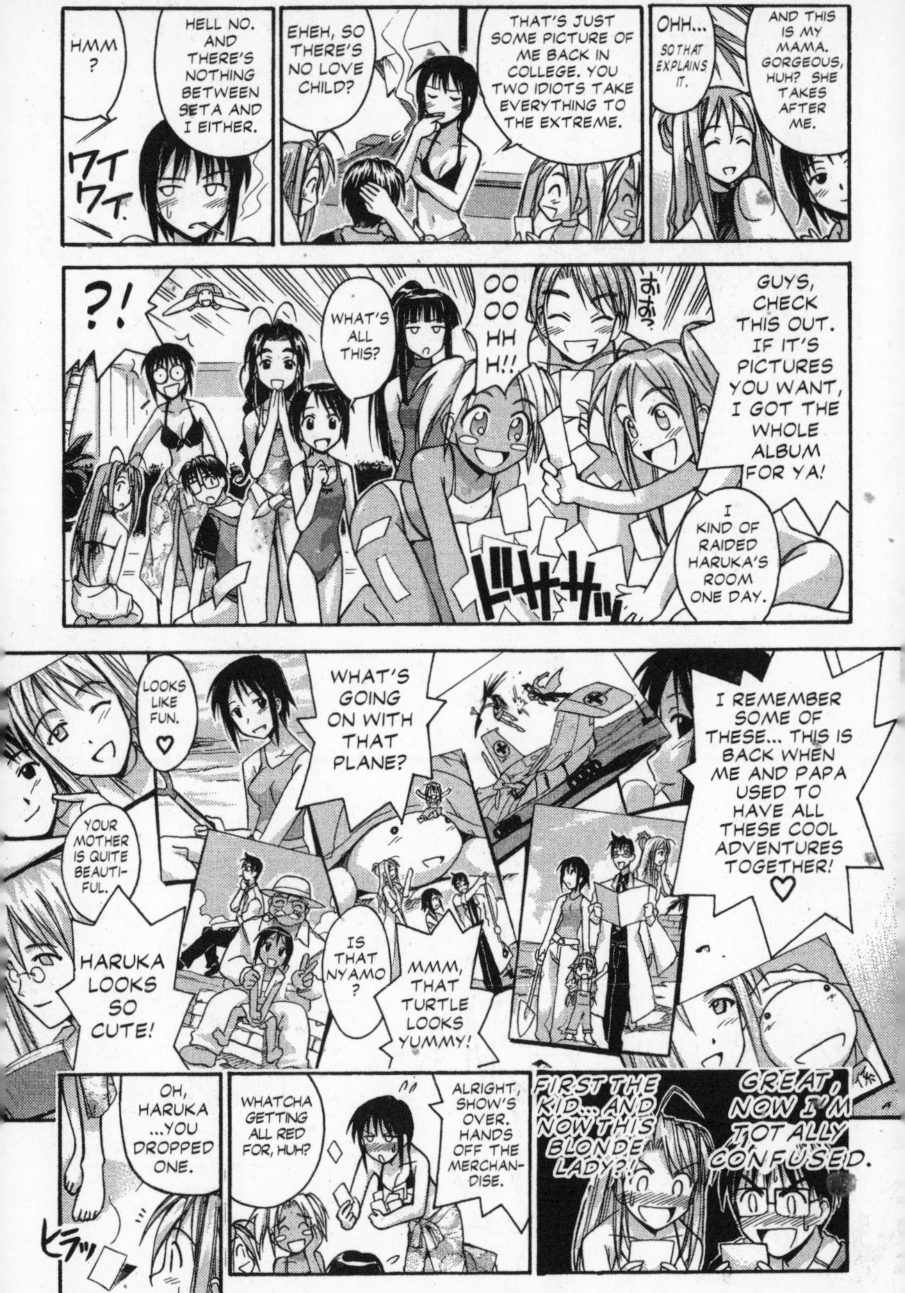
AND THIS IS MY MAMA. GORGEOUS, HUH? SHE TAKES AFTER ME.
OHH... SO THAT EXPLAINS IT.
THAT'S JUST SOME PICTURE OF ME BACK IN COLLEGE. YOU TWO IDIOTS TAKE EVERYTHING TO THE EXTREME.
EHEH, SO THERE'S NO LOVE CHILD?
HELL NO. AND THERE'S NOTHING BETWEEN SETA AND I EITHER.
HMM ?
ワイワイ
GUYS, CHECK THIS OUT. IF IT'S PICTURES YOU WANT, I GOT THE WHOLE ALBUM FOR YA!
I KIND OF RAIDED HARUKA'S ROOM ONE DAY.
おぉっ
OOOOHHH!!
WHAT'S ALL THIS?
?!
ドサササッ
I REMEMBER SOME OF THESE... THIS IS BACK WHEN ME AND PAPA USED TO HAVE ALL THESE COOL ADVENTURES TOGETHER! ♡
WHAT'S GOING ON WITH THAT PLANE?
MMM, THAT TURTLE LOOKS YUMMY!
IS THAT NYAMO?
LOOKS LIKE FUN. ♡
YOUR MOTHER IS QUITE BEAUTIFUL.
HARUKA LOOKS SO CUTE!
GREAT, NOW I'M TOTALLY CONFUSED.
FIRST THE KID... AND NOW THIS BLONDE LADY?!
ALRIGHT, SHOW'S OVER. HANDS OFF THE MERCHANDISE.
WHATCHA GETTING ALL RED FOR, HUH?
OH, HARUKA ...YOU DROPPED ONE.
ヒラッ

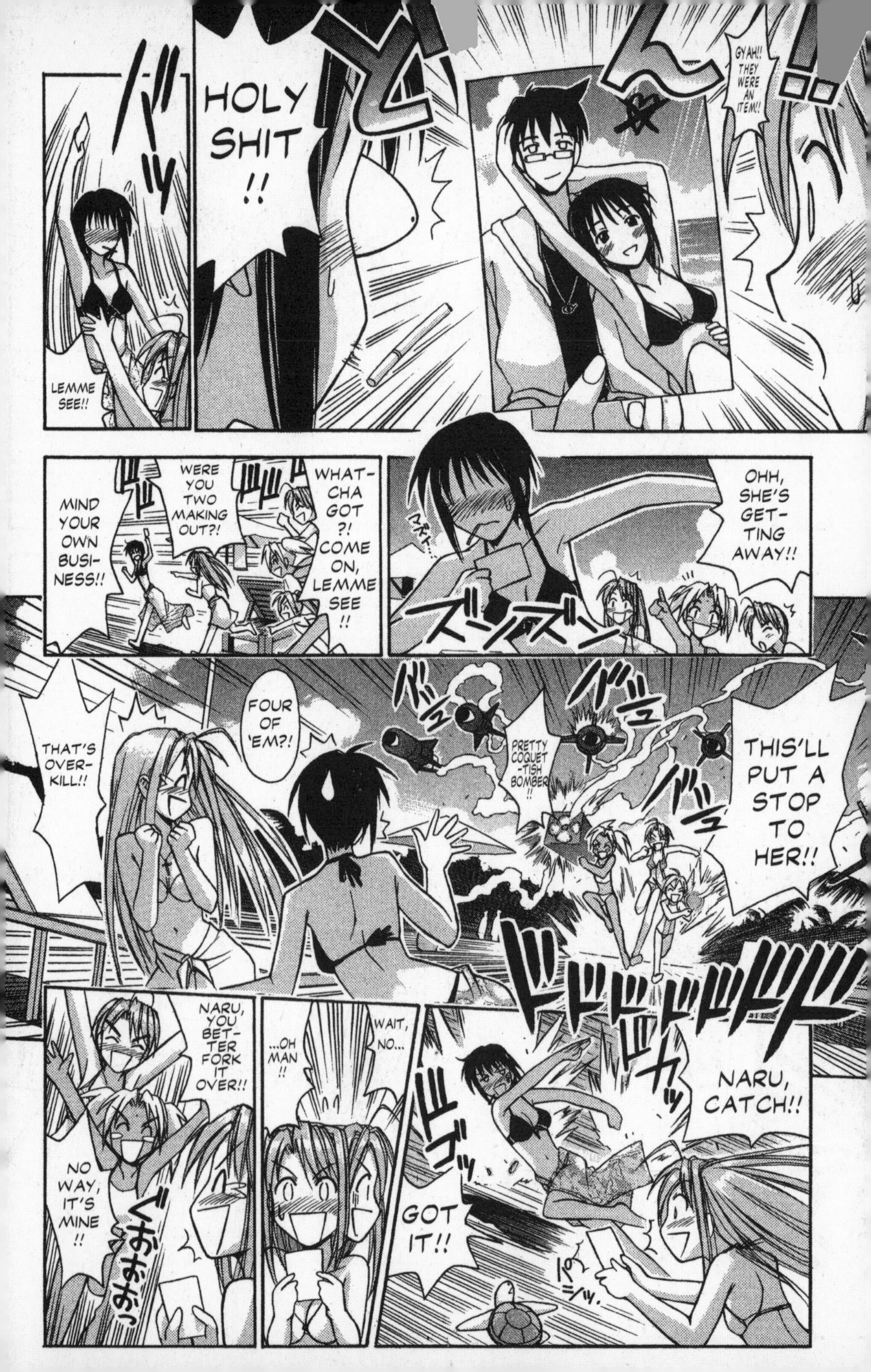
GYAH!! THEY WERE AN ITEM!!
HOLY SHIT !!
LEMME SEE!!
OHH, SHE'S GET-TING AWAY!!
WHAT-CHA GOT ?! COME ON, LEMME SEE !!
WERE YOU TWO MAKING OUT?!
MIND YOUR OWN BUSI-NESS!!
THIS'LL PUT A STOP TO HER!!
PRETTY COQUET -TISH BOMBER !!
FOUR OF 'EM?!
THAT'S OVER-KILL!!
NARU, CATCH!!
GOT IT!!
WAIT, NO...
...OH MAN !!
NARU, YOU BET-TER FORK IT OVER!!
NO WAY, IT'S MINE !!

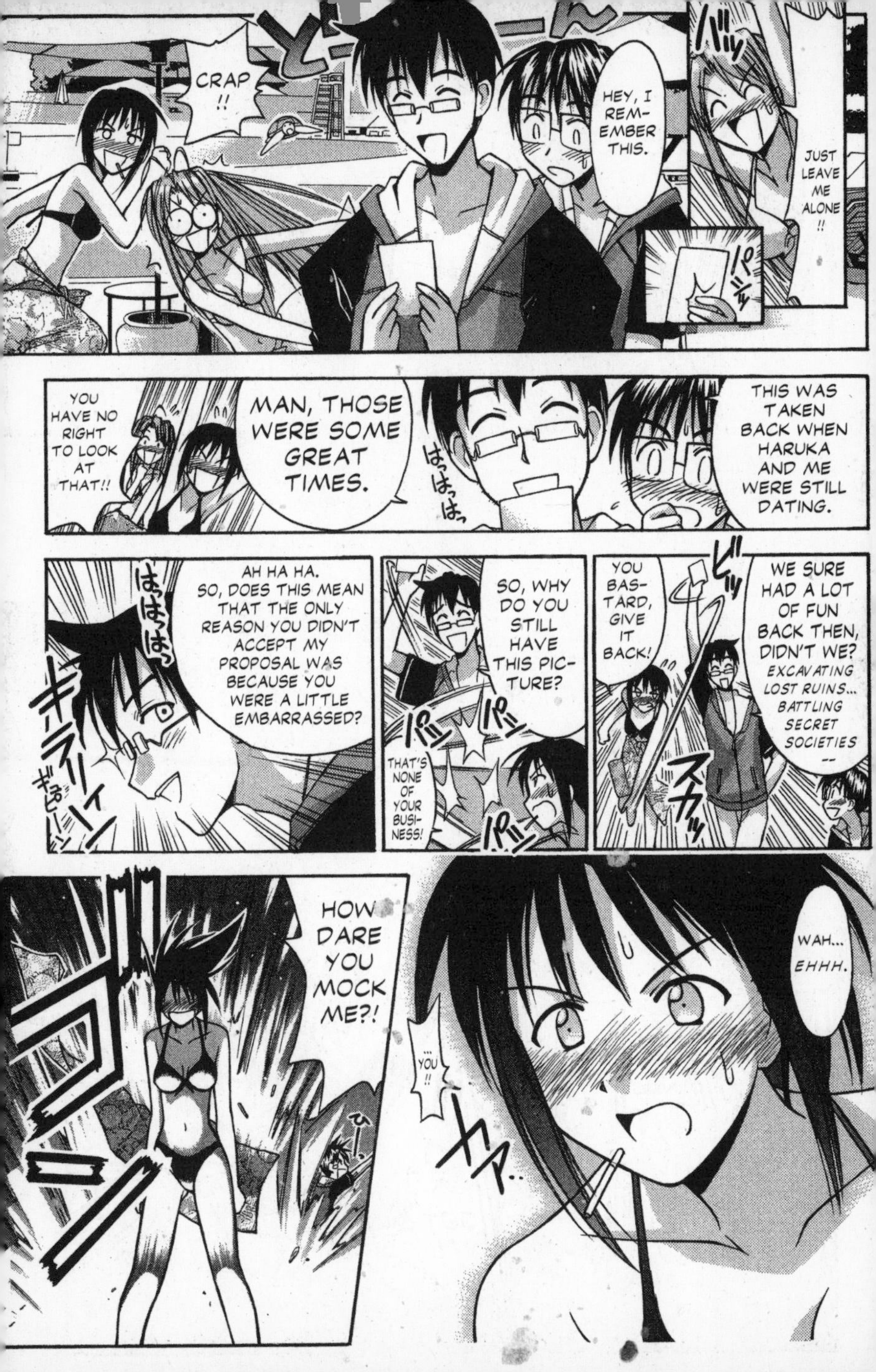
JUST LEAVE ME ALONE !!
HEY, I REMEMBER THIS.
CRAP !!
THIS WAS TAKEN BACK WHEN HARUKA AND ME WERE STILL DATING.
MAN, THOSE WERE SOME GREAT TIMES.
YOU HAVE NO RIGHT TO LOOK AT THAT!!
WE SURE HAD A LOT OF FUN BACK THEN, DIDN'T WE? EXCAVATING LOST RUINS... BATTLING SECRET SOCIETIES --
YOU BASTARD, GIVE IT BACK!
SO, WHY DO YOU STILL HAVE THIS PICTURE?
THAT'S NONE OF YOUR BUSINESS!
AH HA HA. SO, DOES THIS MEAN THAT THE ONLY REASON YOU DIDN'T ACCEPT MY PROPOSAL WAS BECAUSE YOU WERE A LITTLE EMBARRASSED?
WAH... EHHH.
...YOU !!
HOW DARE YOU MOCK ME?!

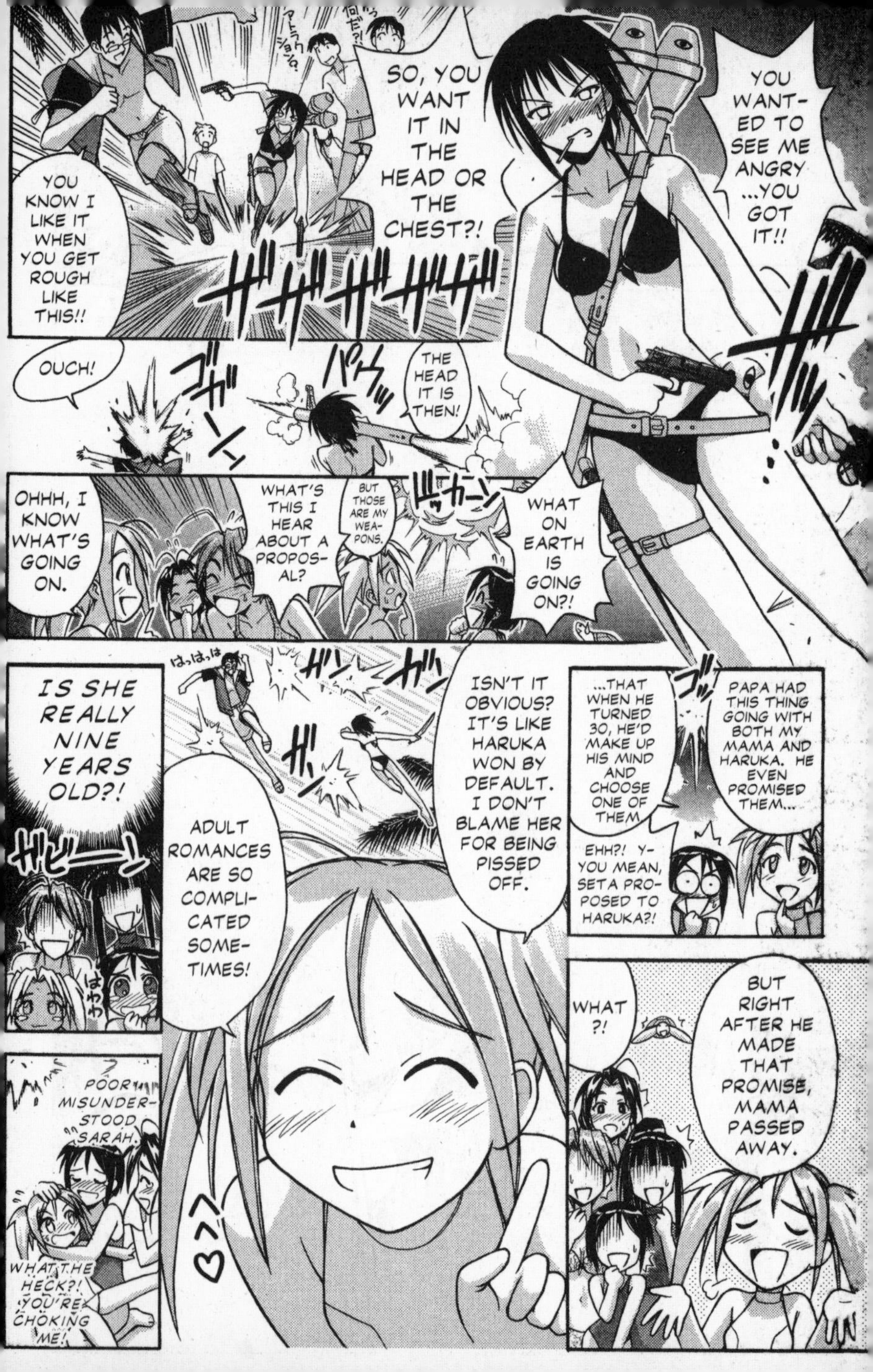
YOU WANTED TO SEE ME ANGRY ...YOU GOT IT!!
SO, YOU WANT IT IN THE HEAD OR THE CHEST?!
YOU KNOW I LIKE IT WHEN YOU GET ROUGH LIKE THIS!!
THE HEAD IT IS THEN!
OUCH!
WHAT ON EARTH IS GOING ON?!
BUT THOSE ARE MY WEAPONS.
WHAT'S THIS I HEAR ABOUT A PROPOSAL?
OHHH, I KNOW WHAT'S GOING ON.
PAPA HAD THIS THING GOING WITH BOTH MY MAMA AND HARUKA. HE EVEN PROMISED THEM...
...THAT WHEN HE TURNED 30, HE'D MAKE UP HIS MIND AND CHOOSE ONE OF THEM
EHH?! Y-YOU MEAN, SETA PROPOSED TO HARUKA?!
BUT RIGHT AFTER HE MADE THAT PROMISE, MAMA PASSED AWAY.
WHAT?!
ISN'T IT OBVIOUS? IT'S LIKE HARUKA WON BY DEFAULT. I DON'T BLAME HER FOR BEING PISSED OFF.
ADULT ROMANCES ARE SO COMPLICATED SOMETIMES!
IS SHE REALLY NINE YEARS OLD?!
POOR MISUNDERSTOOD SARAH.
WHAT THE HECK?! YOU'RE CHOKING ME!

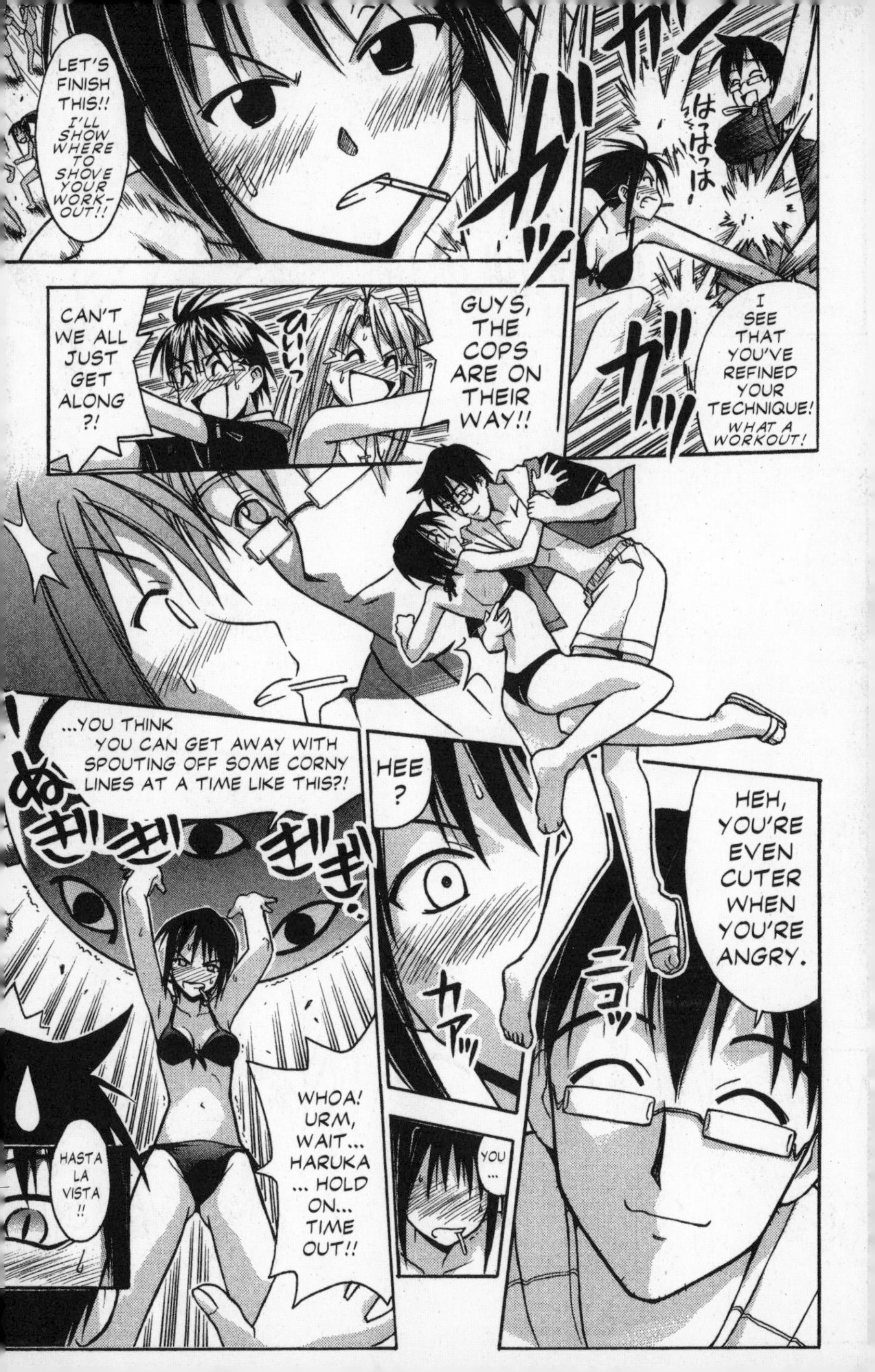

ガッ
はっはっは！
I SEE THAT YOU'VE REFINED YOUR TECHNIQUE! WHAT A WORKOUT!
ガッ
LET'S FINISH THIS!! I'LL SHOW WHERE TO SHOVE YOUR WORK-OUT!!
GUYS, THE COPS ARE ON THEIR WAY!!
ひいいっ
CAN'T WE ALL JUST GET ALONG?!
HEH, YOU'RE EVEN CUTER WHEN YOU'RE ANGRY.
ニコッ
HEE?
カアッ
...YOU THINK YOU CAN GET AWAY WITH SPOUTING OFF SOME CORNY LINES AT A TIME LIKE THIS?!
ぬぎぎぎぎ
YOU...
WHOA! URM, WAIT... HARUKA ... HOLD ON... TIME OUT!!
HASTA LA VISTA!!

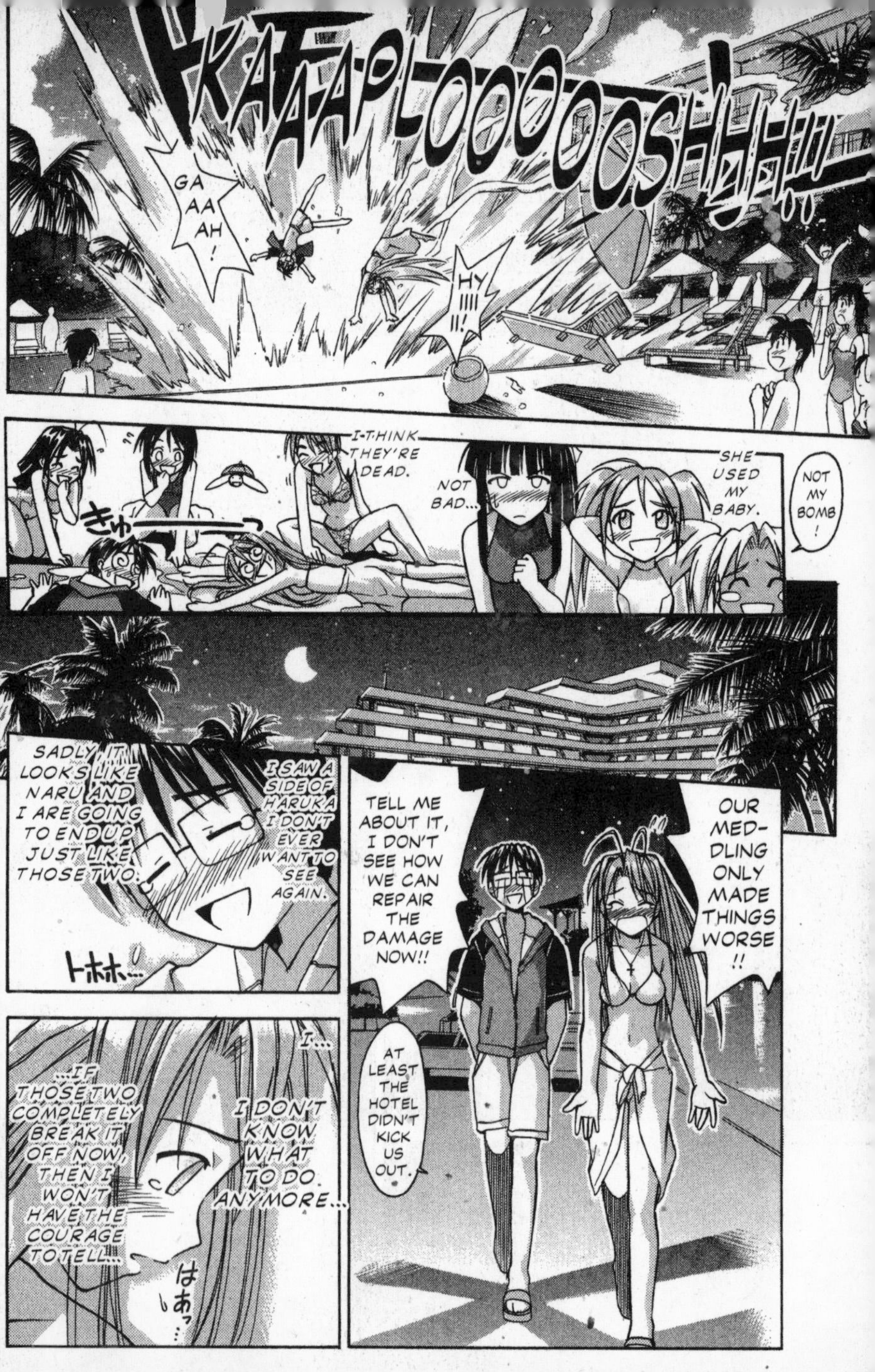
KA-A-PLOOOOOOSHHH!!!
HY!!!!!!!
GA AAA AH!
NOT MY BOMB!
SHE USED MY BABY.
NOT BAD...
I-THINK THEY'RE DEAD.
きゅ〜〜〜
OUR MED-DLING ONLY MADE THINGS WORSE!!
TELL ME ABOUT IT, I DON'T SEE HOW WE CAN REPAIR THE DAMAGE NOW!!
AT LEAST THE HOTEL DIDN'T KICK US OUT.
I SAW A SIDE OF HARUKA I DON'T EVER WANT TO SEE AGAIN.
SADLY, IT LOOKS LIKE NARU AND I ARE GOING TO END UP JUST LIKE THOSE TWO.
トホホ…
I...
I DON'T KNOW WHAT TO DO ANYMORE...
...IF THOSE TWO COMPLETELY BREAK IT OFF NOW, THEN I WON'T HAVE THE COURAGE TO TELL...
はぁっ…

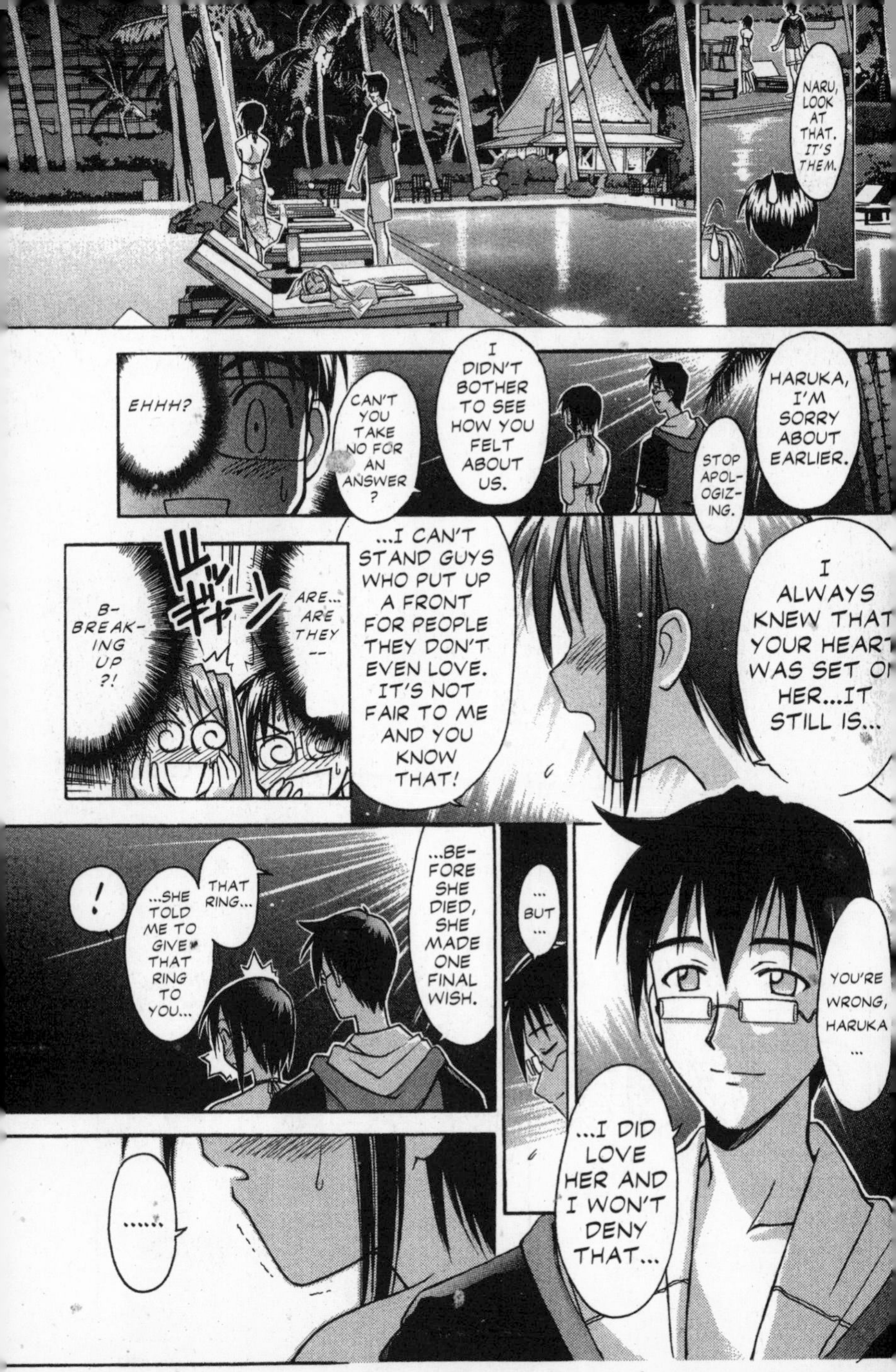
NARU, LOOK AT THAT. IT'S THEM.
HARUKA, I'M SORRY ABOUT EARLIER.
STOP APOLOGIZING.
I DIDN'T BOTHER TO SEE HOW YOU FELT ABOUT US.
CAN'T YOU TAKE NO FOR AN ANSWER?
EHHH?
I ALWAYS KNEW THAT YOUR HEART WAS SET ON HER...IT STILL IS...
...I CAN'T STAND GUYS WHO PUT UP A FRONT FOR PEOPLE THEY DON'T EVEN LOVE. IT'S NOT FAIR TO ME AND YOU KNOW THAT!
ムッギャーン
ARE... ARE THEY --
B-BREAKING UP?!
YOU'RE WRONG, HARUKA...
...I DID LOVE HER AND I WON'T DENY THAT...
...BUT...
...BEFORE SHE DIED, SHE MADE ONE FINAL WISH.
THAT RING...
...SHE TOLD ME TO GIVE THAT RING TO YOU...
!
......

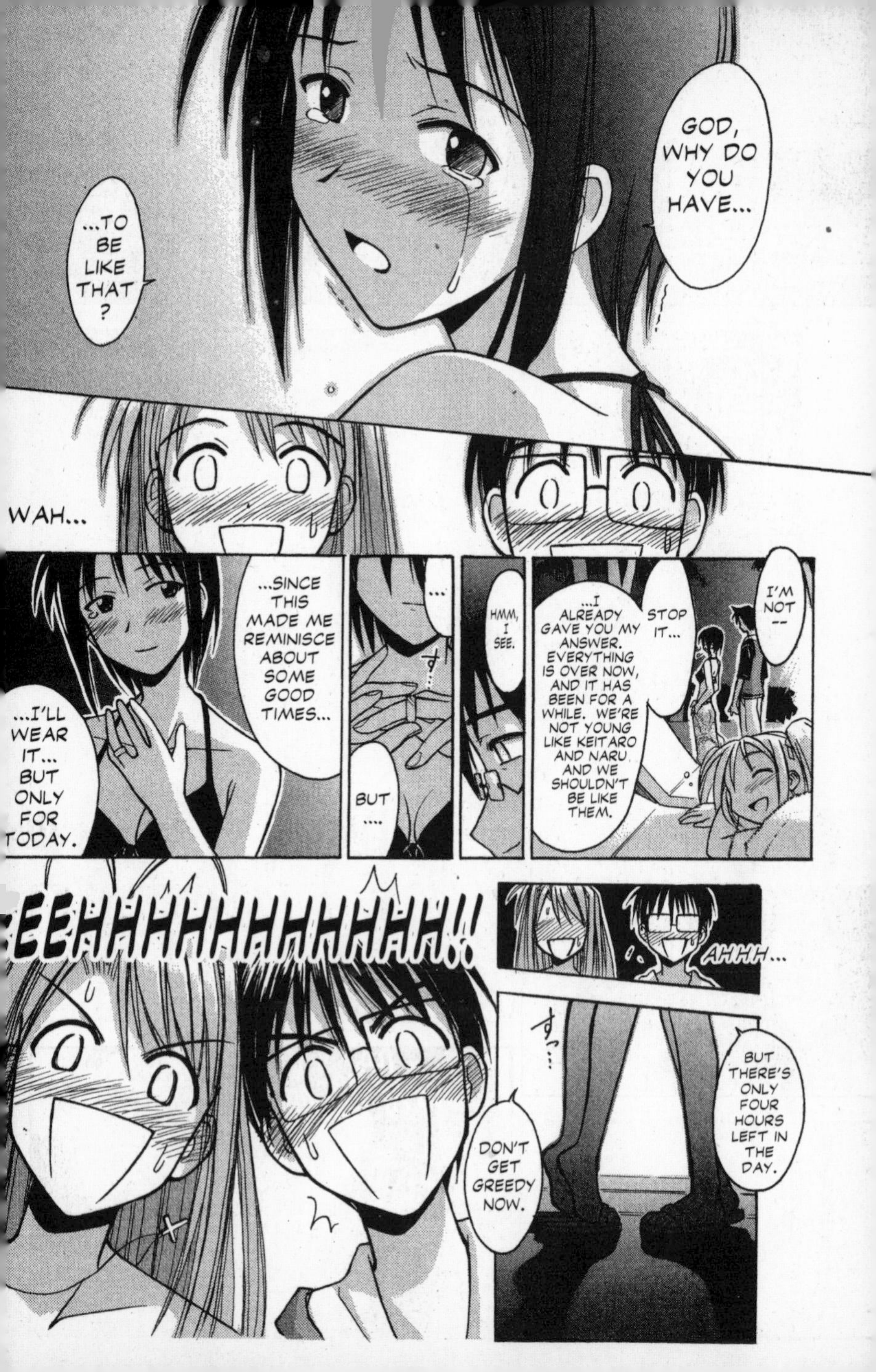
GOD, WHY DO YOU HAVE...
...TO BE LIKE THAT?
WAH...
I'M NOT --
STOP IT...
...I ALREADY GAVE YOU MY ANSWER. EVERYTHING IS OVER NOW, AND IT HAS BEEN FOR A WHILE. WE'RE NOT YOUNG LIKE KEITARO AND NARU, AND WE SHOULDN'T BE LIKE THEM.
HMM, I SEE.
...
BUT ....
...SINCE THIS MADE ME REMINISCE ABOUT SOME GOOD TIMES...
...I'LL WEAR IT... BUT ONLY FOR TODAY.
AHHH...
EEHHHHHHHHHHHHHH!!
BUT THERE'S ONLY FOUR HOURS LEFT IN THE DAY.
DON'T GET GREEDY NOW.

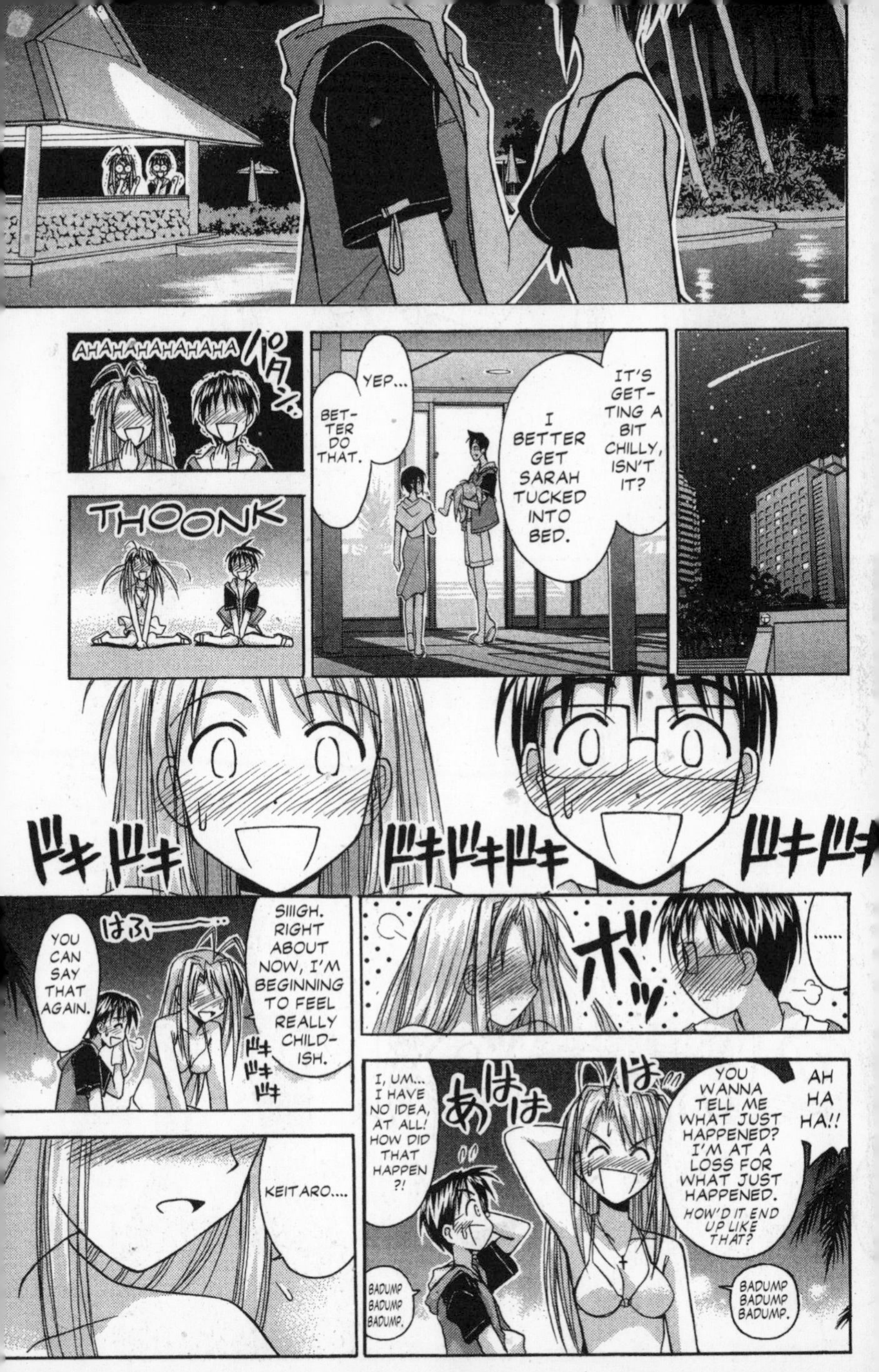
IT'S GETTING A BIT CHILLY, ISN'T IT?
I BETTER GET SARAH TUCKED INTO BED.
YEP... BETTER DO THAT.
AHAHAHAHAHAHA
パタン
THOONK
ドキドキ
ドキドキドキ
ドキドキ
......
ボッ
SIIIGH. RIGHT ABOUT NOW, I'M BEGINNING TO FEEL REALLY CHILDISH.
はふーー
YOU CAN SAY THAT AGAIN.
ドキドキドキ
AH HA HA!!
YOU WANNA TELL ME WHAT JUST HAPPENED? I'M AT A LOSS FOR WHAT JUST HAPPENED. HOW'D IT END UP LIKE THAT?
あはは
I, UM... I HAVE NO IDEA, AT ALL! HOW DID THAT HAPPEN?!
BADUMP BADUMP BADUMP.
BADUMP BADUMP BADUMP.
KEITARO....

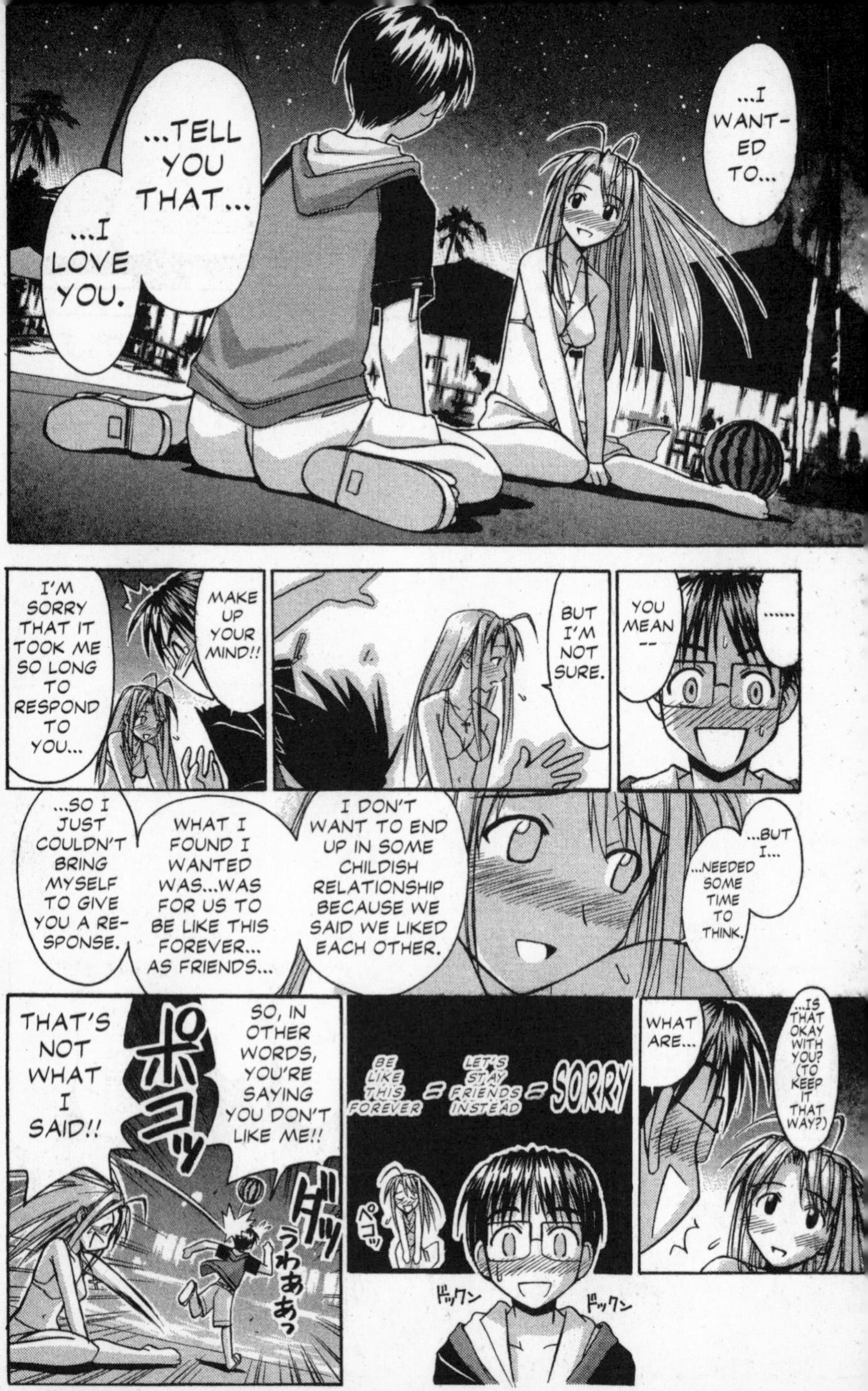
...I WANT-ED TO...
...TELL YOU THAT...
...I LOVE YOU.
......
YOU MEAN --
BUT I'M NOT SURE.
MAKE UP YOUR MIND!!
I'M SORRY THAT IT TOOK ME SO LONG TO RESPOND TO YOU...
...BUT I...
...NEEDED SOME TIME TO THINK.
I DON'T WANT TO END UP IN SOME CHILDISH RELATIONSHIP BECAUSE WE SAID WE LIKED EACH OTHER.
WHAT I FOUND I WANTED WAS...WAS FOR US TO BE LIKE THIS FOREVER... AS FRIENDS...
...SO I JUST COULDN'T BRING MYSELF TO GIVE YOU A RE-SPONSE.
...IS THAT OKAY WITH YOU? (TO KEEP IT THAT WAY?)
WHAT ARE...
BE LIKE THIS FOREVER = LET'S STAY FRIENDS INSTEAD = SORRY
ペコッ
ドックン
ドックン
SO, IN OTHER WORDS, YOU'RE SAYING YOU DON'T LIKE ME!!
THAT'S NOT WHAT I SAID!!
ポコッ
ガッ
うわあぁっ

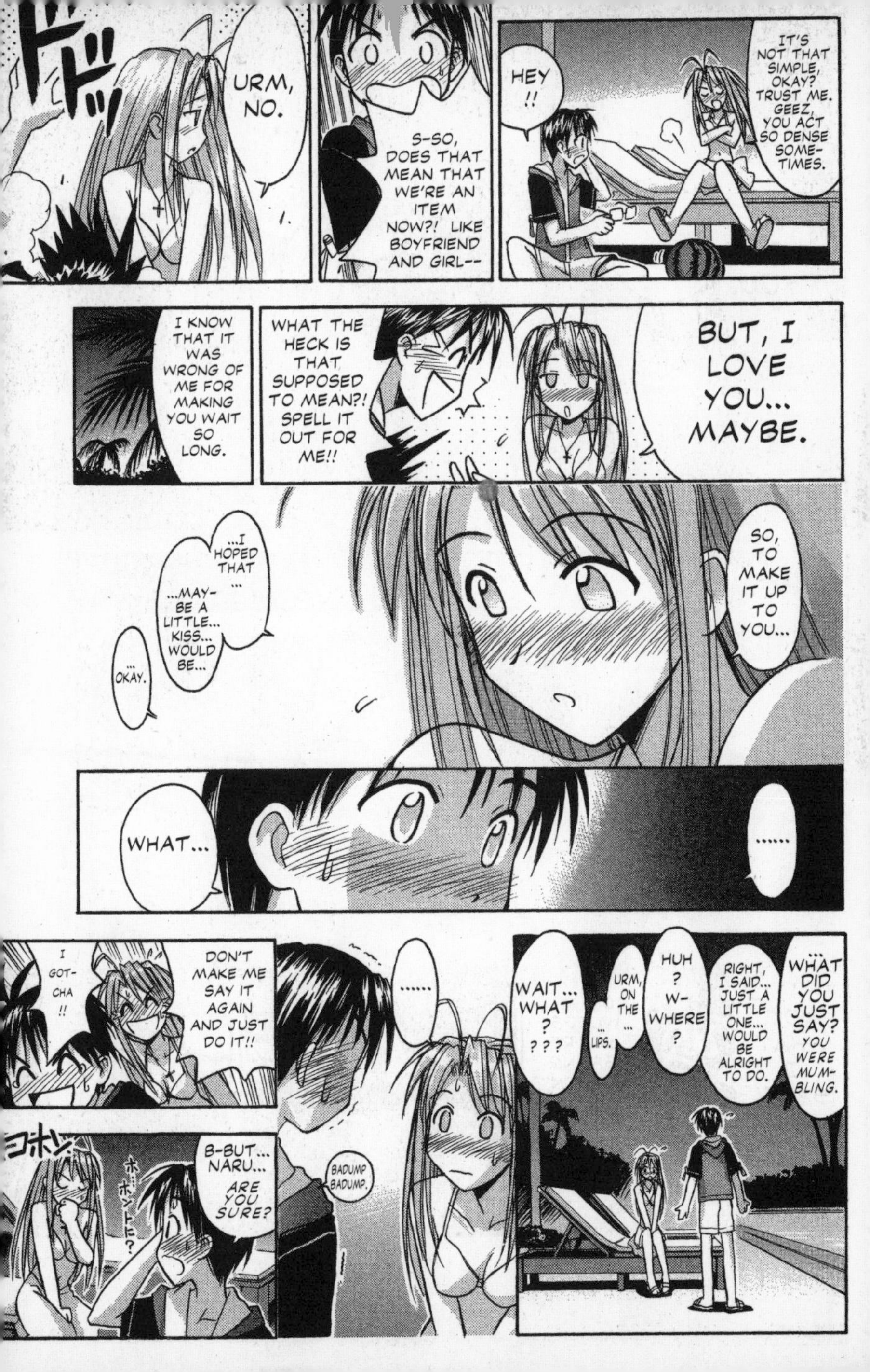
IT'S NOT THAT SIMPLE, OKAY? TRUST ME. GEEZ, YOU ACT SO DENSE SOME-TIMES.
HEY !!
S-SO, DOES THAT MEAN THAT WE'RE AN ITEM NOW?! LIKE BOYFRIEND AND GIRL--
URM, NO.
BUT, I LOVE YOU... MAYBE.
WHAT THE HECK IS THAT SUPPOSED TO MEAN?! SPELL IT OUT FOR ME!!
I KNOW THAT IT WAS WRONG OF ME FOR MAKING YOU WAIT SO LONG.
SO, TO MAKE IT UP TO YOU...
...I HOPED THAT ...
...MAY-BE A LITTLE... KISS... WOULD BE...
...OKAY.
......
WHAT...
...WHAT DID YOU JUST SAY? YOU WERE MUM-BLING.
RIGHT, I SAID... JUST A LITTLE ONE... WOULD BE ALRIGHT TO DO.
HUH ? W-WHERE ?
URM, ON THE ...
...LIPS.
WAIT... WHAT ? ? ? ?
......
BADUMP BADUMP.
DON'T MAKE ME SAY IT AGAIN AND JUST DO IT!!
I GOT-CHA !!
B-BUT... NARU... ARE YOU SURE?
ホ…ホントに?

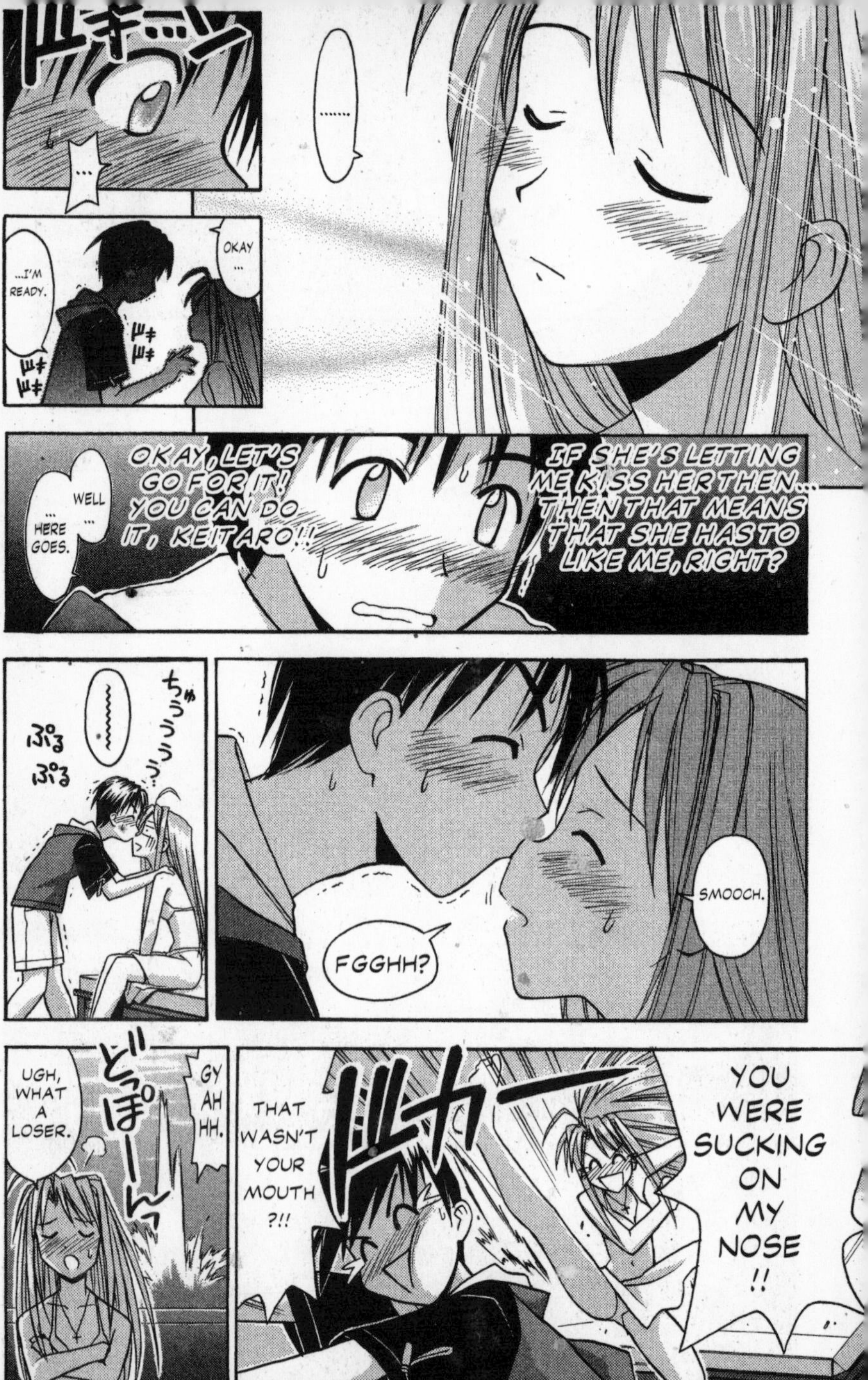
......
....
OKAY ...
...I'M READY.
ドキドキ
ドキドキ
IF SHE'S LETTING ME KISS HER THEN... THEN THAT MEANS THAT SHE HAS TO LIKE ME, RIGHT?
OKAY, LET'S GO FOR IT! YOU CAN DO IT, KEITARO!!
WELL ...
... HERE GOES.
SMOOCH.
FGGHH?
ぷるぷる
YOU WERE SUCKING ON MY NOSE !!
ドカー
THAT WASN'T YOUR MOUTH ?!!
GY AH HH.
どっぽーん
UGH, WHAT A LOSER.

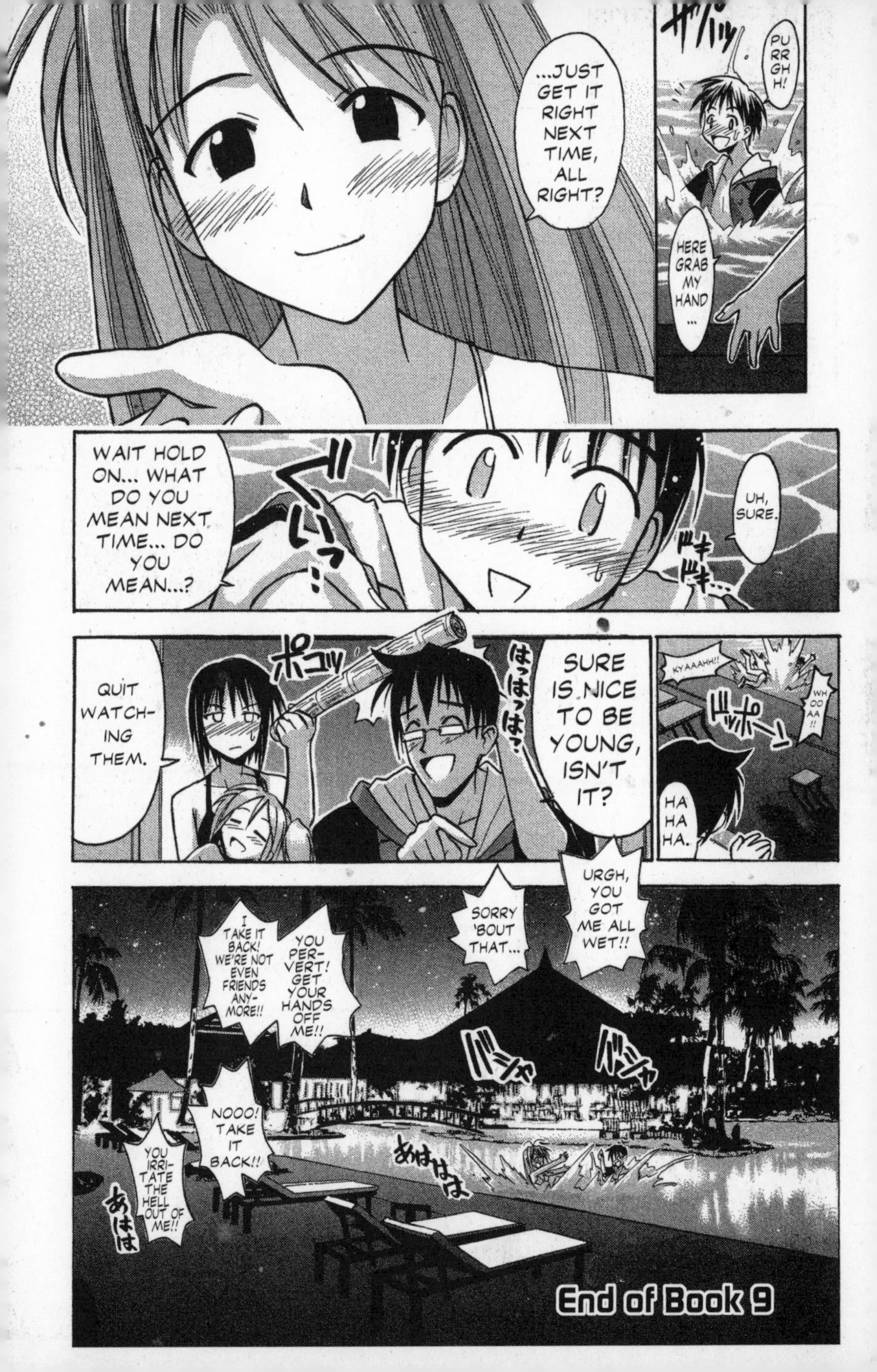
PURRGH!
HERE GRAB MY HAND...
...JUST GET IT RIGHT NEXT TIME, ALL RIGHT?
UH, SURE.
WAIT HOLD ON... WHAT DO YOU MEAN NEXT TIME... DO YOU MEAN...?
KYAAAHH!!
WHOOAA!!
HA HA HA HA.
SURE IS NICE TO BE YOUNG, ISN'T IT?
QUIT WATCHING THEM.
URGH, YOU GOT ME ALL WET!!
SORRY 'BOUT THAT...
YOU PERVERT! GET YOUR HANDS OFF ME!!
I TAKE IT BACK! WE'RE NOT EVEN FRIENDS ANYMORE!!
NOOO! TAKE IT BACK!!
YOU IRRITATE THE HELL OUT OF ME!!
End of Book 9

STAFF

Ken Akamatsu
Takashi Takemoto
Kenichi Nakamura
Takaaki Miyahara
Masaki Ohyama
Yumiko Shinohara

EDITOR

Noboru Ohno
Tomoyuki Shiratsuchi
Yasushi Yamanaka

KC Editor

Shinichiro Yoshihara

Love Hina

Preview for Volume 10

With all the grace and reluctance of a three legged giraffe on a tightrope, Naru and Keitaro take their first steps in the high-tension game of love when a power outage puts Hinata House in the dark. As old memories come to light, Naru realizes that she may be the girl from Keitaro's past after all. However, Keitaro must choose between his blossoming relationship with Naru and his desire study abroad with Seta.

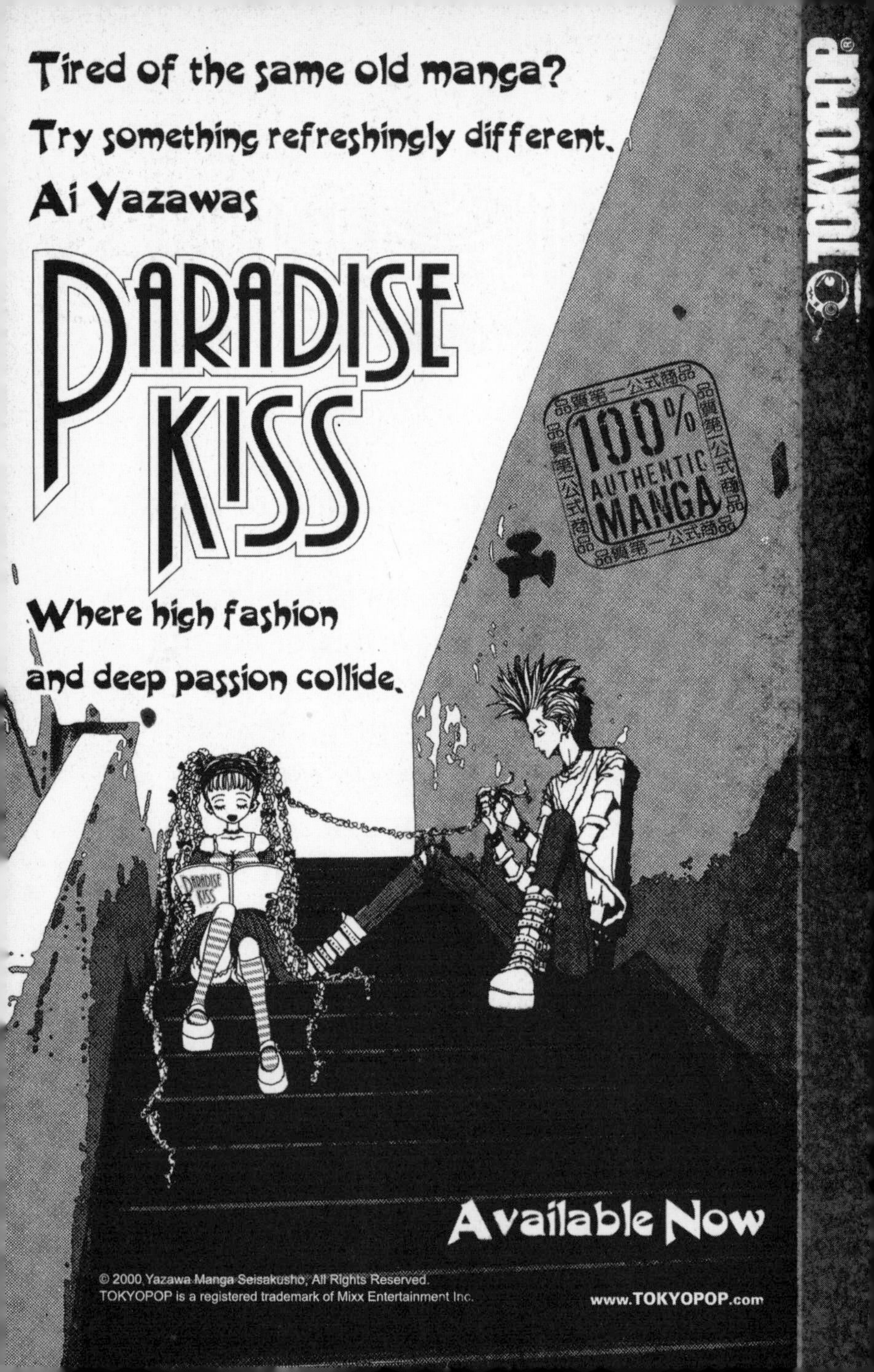

Tired of the same old manga?
Try something refreshingly different.
Ai Yazawas
PARADISE KISS
100% AUTHENTIC MANGA
Where high fashion
and deep passion collide.
Available Now
© 2000 Yazawa Manga Seisakusho, All Rights Reserved.
TOKYOPOP is a registered trademark of Mixx Entertainment Inc.
www.TOKYOPOP.com
TOKYOPOP

STOP!

This is the back of the book.
ou wouldn't want to spoil a great ending!

This book is printed "manga-style," in the authentic Japanese right-to-left format. Since none of the artwork has been flipped or altered, readers get to experience the story just as the creator intended. You've been asking for it, so TOKYOPOP® delivered: authentic, hot-off-the-press, and far more fun!

DIRECTIONS

If this is your first time reading manga-style, here's a quick guide to help you understand how it works.

It's easy... just start in the top right panel and follow the numbers. Have fun, and look for more 100% authentic manga from TOKYOPOP®!